D0770536

# THE LAW OF CORPORATIONS

## IN A NUTSHELL®

### SEVENTH EDITION

**RICHARD D. FREER**
Robert Howell Hall Professor of Law
Emory University School of Law

WEST
ACADEMIC
PUBLISHING

*Nutshell Series, In a Nutshell* and the Nutshell Logo are trademarks registered in the U.S. Patent and Trademark Office.

Printed in the United States of America

**ISBN:** 978-1-63459-701-2

*To Weasie.*

# FOREWORD

Whatever the name of your class—from Business Organizations to Business Associations to Corporations—this book will help you. It provides background on all forms of business organization, including partnerships, limited partnerships, LLPs, LLLPs, and LLCs. In addition it emphasizes the transcendent importance of agency law, in general and as applied in the corporate form.

The centerpiece of any such course, and the centerpiece of this book, is the corporation. We follow the life-cycle of business, from formation through dissolution. We cover the theory of the firm but focus on the nuts-and-bolts of business law, including chapters devoted specifically to particular issues raised by closely-held corporations and by publicly-traded corporations.

This work includes securities law and Sarbanes-Oxley, and addresses business finance as well. Throughout, examples and hypotheticals (with answers) are used to explain the doctrine.

This material intimidated me in law school, in part because I had had no exposure to business. It seemed to me that everyone in the class had majored in business in college—and there I was, a sociology major! The goal of this book is to make business law accessible to everyone—and, hopefully, even fun.

# ACKNOWLEDGMENTS

---

I owe a special debt to David Epstein, who got me interested in teaching in this area, and who recruited me (and has put up with me) as co-author of our casebook BUSINESS STRUCTURES (West Academic 4th ed. 2015). George Shepherd and Mike Roberts fill out the team on that book, and I am proud to be on that team.

I am also grateful to Doug Moll, my co-author on our concise hornbook PRINCIPLES OF BUSINESS ORGANIZATIONS (West Academic 2013).

And I am continually grateful for the friendship and support of the Emory Law faculty and administration. It has been my honor to be a member of that community my entire academic career. DeWitt Perkins and Bunny Sandefur, Emory Law class of 2016, provided terrific research assistance.

RICHARD D. FREER

Atlanta
May 2016

# OUTLINE

# TABLE OF CASES

**References are to Pages**

————————

# THE LAW OF CORPORATIONS

# IN A NUTSHELL®

SEVENTH EDITION

# CHAPTER 1

# MODERN FORMS OF BUSINESS AND THE IMPORTANCE OF AGENCY LAW

## § 1.1 INTRODUCTION: CHARACTERISTICS OF BUSINESSES GENERALLY

Whether you are taking a course on Corporations, Business Associations, or Business Organizations, the centerpiece of your study will be the corporation. It has been the dominant business form in the United States since the early days of independence. But the corporation must be understood in context. It is one of several forms a business may take, including the sole proprietorship, general partnership (usually just called "the partnership"), limited liability partnership (LLP), limited partnership, limited liability limited partnership (LLLP), and limited liability company (LLC).

Do not let this untidy list confuse or intimidate you. The list and the development of each form is explained by history and not by logic. Persons setting up a business will have a choice of structure. More than one form may meet their needs. In determining which form to use, the proprietors of any business—from a front-yard lemonade stand to a multinational hotel chain—should consider eight major issues.

1. How is the business formed and maintained? For example, do we need to file anything with the government or can we just start selling lemonade? Accompanying this question is a legitimate concern about costs, such as

whether we will need an attorney to form the business and keep it in good standing.

2. Is the business considered an entity, separate from the person(s) who run it? The answer to this question may be important in answering the next question.

3. Who is liable to third parties for business debts? By business debts, we mean any liability incurred in operating the business. Suppose you contract with a third party to provide lemon extract with which you will make lemonade. If the business does not pay for it, will you be personally liable? Or if our lemonade is tainted and a customer gets sick, will you be personally liable? This raises the question of "limited liability." Traditionally, only the corporation provided limited liability—meaning that the owners of a corporation are not liable for what the business does.

4. Who owns the business? In the corporation, the shareholders are the owners; the shares of stock are units of ownership.

5. Who makes decisions for the business? For example, do the owners make the business decisions or do they hire somebody to make the decisions? (This is the question of "management.")

6. If one of the owners wants to get out of the business, can she transfer her interest? If so, does the business survive her leaving, or does

it have to be dissolved, and a new business formed? (These questions relate to "continuity of existence.")

7. Does the business pay income tax on its profits? If so, this will result in "double taxation," because the owners also pay income tax on the amounts they receive (such as dividends) from the business.

8. What are the needs for capital? At one level, this is a silly question, because all businesses need money to get started and to grow. We need to note two things, each of which we discuss in detail later.

First, if somebody furnishes money for our business, what does she expect in return? For instance, does she want a guarantee of repayment (plus interest), or does she want a share in profits, or does she want a voice in management of the business, or some combination of these things? The answer to these questions will determine whether we raise capital through "debt" or "equity." If you majored in sociology in college (as I did), these terms may scare you, but they should not. Debt means a loan; the business borrows money and must repay it (with interest as specified in the contract). The person who lends money becomes a *creditor* of the business; she is not an *owner* of the business. Equity, in contrast, means ownership; the person invests in the business and gets an ownership interest (in a corporation, this is stock). The business can raise money either by getting loans or by selling ownership interests (or by using a combination of the two).

Second, if the business gets big enough, can we raise money by selling interests to the public? In other words, will we need (or be able to get) access to the public markets for financing? Registering to sell investments to the public is extremely detailed and expensive.

Many people assume that all corporations are "public" or "publicly-held"—that is, that they are large entities, with their stock traded on the New York Stock Exchange or NASDAQ. This is not true. Most corporations are "close" or "closely-held," with a handful (or even one) shareholder and no public market for the stock. So the lemonade stand business could be formed as a corporation from the outset, even though there was only one owner and even though she did all the work for the business.

The answers to our eight sets of questions will vary depending upon the business form chosen. The business lawyer must explain to her client the ramifications of choosing a particular form, and must help her client weigh the pros and cons of each. The ultimate decision is for the client, and will be influenced by various factors, including her willingness to risk personal liability, ability to share decision-making authority, income tax situation, and access to capital.

Note also that the form of business may change over time. For instance, an individual might start with a sole proprietorship, of which she is the single owner. She may then decide to bring in co-owners and thereby to convert the business to a general partnership. Ultimately, the partners may decide they need access to public markets for money to expand even more. At that point, they may form a corporation and "go public."

## § 1.2  CHARACTERISTICS OF THE CORPORATION—OVERVIEW

We will summarize the corporation by answering each of the eight questions asked in § 1.1 for the corporate form. Along the way, some points about the corporation will be made clearer by contrasting them with the general partnership. Then, in succeeding sections, we will address the partnership and other business forms.

*First*, the corporation can only be formed by satisfying the requirements set forth by state statutes. These invariably require filing a document with the appropriate state officer (usually the secretary of state), appointing a registered agent (on whom process may be served if the corporation is sued), and paying a fee. Maintaining the corporate form will require annual reports to the state and further fees; and, the corporation statutes are rather detailed in requiring meetings of shareholders and of directors and about keeping records. These formalities are a disadvantage over some other business structures, which can be formed simply by selling lemonade (or whatever the business does).

*Second*, the corporation is an entity, separate from the person(s) who own it and run it. As we will see below, this is different from the sole proprietorship and the traditional view of the general partnership.

*Third*, the corporation itself is liable for its contracts and torts, but, generally, its managers and shareholders are not. This fact is termed "limited liability" for the shareholders. That means the most a shareholder might lose is the money she invested in the business; she will not be held liable for debts incurred by the business. Traditionally, limited liability has been seen as the greatest advantage of the corporate form of doing business.

*Fourth*, the corporation is owned by the shareholders (or "stockholders"). Shares of stock are units of ownership, and are issued by the corporation itself. Shareholders have various rights, which are discussed throughout this book. Among other things, shareholders elect the directors, who (acting as a board) manage the business. Thus, shareholders do not directly manage the corporation. They elect those who do. Shareholder power is measured by the number of shares she owns. If you own 50 shares in the corporation and I own 10 shares, you have five times the ownership stake that I do and, unless the appropriate documents say otherwise, you have five times as many votes as I do. (Also, for every dollar I get in dividends, you will get $5.)

Again, the shareholders (as owners) enjoy "limited liability." If the corporation does poorly, the shareholder may lose her investment, but she is not liable for what the business does. There is a narrow exception to this, called "piercing the corporate veil," by which shareholders might be held liable for the corporation's obligations. *See* § 10.4.

*Fifth*, the corporation is managed by the board of directors. Note, then, that the corporation separates ownership from management—the shareholders are the owners and the directors are the managers. (It is possible that the shareholders and the directors will be the same person(s), but their *roles in the corporation* are separate.) This separation is not seen, for example, in the general partnership, in which the law presumes (subject to agreement by the parties to the contrary) that each partner has equal ownership and management rights. One advantage of the corporation, then, is the possibility of *passive investment*—a shareholder can enjoy the fruits of ownership (hopefully, profits) without being burdened with the responsibilities of management.

*Sixth*, a shareholder who tires of that role can simply transfer her stock. She can sell it or give it away (now or in her will). If the stock of the corporation is publicly traded, she can sell with a few clicks of a mouse on her computer (or, if she doesn't mind paying higher commissions, have a broker do it). If the corporation is not publicly traded (a "close" corporation), she may have trouble finding a buyer, but, generally, has the right to sell whenever she can. This transferability flows from the fact that the stockholder is not a manager. In the general partnership, in contrast, because the owners have managerial powers, one cannot simply transfer her entire interest; she does not have a right to force the other partners to accept a new fellow partner.

Transferability also reflects continuity of existence, which is another advantage of the corporation. Because a corporation is an entity separate from those who own and run it, the fact that ownership changes is irrelevant. The corporation goes on, no matter who the owners are. A partnership, in contrast, traditionally has been seen as an aggregate of its individual partners. This means that if a partner withdraws or dies, the partnership ends. Unless the partnership agreement provides differently, the remaining partners must dissolve the business and liquidate the assets. They could then form a new partnership to continue in business. (Modern partnership statutes largely avoid the need to liquidate the business when a partner dissociates from the business. *See* § 1.4.) The corporation avoids these headaches completely.

*Seventh*, the corporation, as a general rule, must pay income tax on its profits. In addition, shareholders must pay personal income tax on dividends they receive. This "double taxation"— taxation of the entity's profits and also of the shareholders' dividends—is a disadvantage of the corporate form of business. Partnerships are not taxed at the business level. The partners pay personal income tax on profits attributed to them. This "flow-through" taxation may be an advantage of the general partnership, depending on the partner's tax bracket (see the last paragraph of this chapter for more on this point).

*Eighth*, every business will need capital (which is a formal word for money). Most businesses are financed, at least initially, by the proprietor herself or her friends and family. The corporation (like any form of business) can raise capital either by getting loans (debt), by selling ownership interests (equity), or by some combination.

The genius of the corporation is that it permits passive investment combined with limited liability. The development of the corporation unlocked an unprecedented economic engine. This engine did far more than create wealth for its investors. It created jobs, spurred innovation, and led to the collection of huge amounts of tax revenue. A century ago, the president of a major university praised the corporation as "the greatest single discovery of modern times."

As we turn now to summaries of the other business structures, keep in mind the importance of limited liability. The main drawback of the sole proprietorship and partnership has been that the business owner is personally liable for what the business does. So if the business breaches a contract or commits a tort, the proprietor of a sole proprietorship or the partners of a partnership were personally liable. The past generation or so has featured the addition of limited liability to business forms that have not traditionally had it, and the development of wholly new business structures that afford limited liability to the owners. The result of this development has not been logical, and has resulted in a sometimes confusing and overlapping set of business structures.[*]

## § 1.3   THE SOLE PROPRIETORSHIP

The sole proprietorship is a business with a single owner. It does not have "entity status"—indeed, it has no legal structure separate from its owner. The proprietor is the business and the business is the proprietor. There are no formalities of formation. A person simply starts doing business, whether it's selling lemonade in the front yard or offering computer programming services. There is nothing to file and there are no magic words to say. The proprietor has the sole right to manage and is solely entitled to the profits. Because the business is not seen as an entity, it does not pay income taxes. Rather, when preparing her personal income tax return, the proprietor prepares a "Schedule C" reflecting the business transactions of the proprietorship. The net profit (or loss) shown on Schedule C is transferred directly to her personal income tax return.

Though the sole proprietorship offers some advantages, the drawback is clear: the proprietor is personally responsible for debts and liabilities of the business. Often, the proprietor herself will be the only person who works for the business. But this is not always the case. A sole proprietorship can have

---

[*]     For detailed discussion of the various business forms, see Freer & Moll, Principles of Business Organizations (2013).

thousands of employees. The defining characteristic is that the business has only one owner.

## § 1.4  THE GENERAL PARTNERSHIP

When we say "partnership," we technically mean "general partnership" (which is different from a limited partnership, which we discuss in § 1.6). A general partnership is universally defined as "an association of two or more persons to carry on as co-owners of a business for profit." The difference between the partnership and the sole proprietorship is the number of owners—the partnership has more than one.

Partnerships are formed by conduct. There is no need to file any document with the state. The proprietors simply agree to start doing business as co-owners. If two people open a lemonade stand with the understanding that they will share control and profits, they have formed a partnership, even if they do not realize or intend it.

Though courts developed partnership law, today the basics are codified in every state. In 1914, the Commission on Uniform State Laws promulgated the Uniform Partnership Act (UPA), intended as a model, which all states except Louisiana ultimately adopted in some form or other. In 1994, the successor to that group, the National Conference of Commissioners on Uniform State Laws (NCCUSL) promulgated the Revised Uniform Limited Partnership Act (RUPA). Of course, states are free to adopt any statutes they wish. The vast majority—

over 35 states—now have adopted some version of RUPA.

It is important to understand, however, that when it comes to relationships (1) among partners and (2) between the partners and the partnership, these statutes provide "default" rules. (These relationships are sometimes called *inter se* or *inter sese*, which is Latin for "between or among themselves.") For these internal operations, the statutes set forth governing principles, which are subject to the partners' agreements to the contrary. Thus, though no particular document is required to *form* a partnership, smart businesspeople will always have a partnership agreement, in which they spell out their understanding on various points. For example, the default provision in all states is that partners have an equal voice in management of the business. But the partners can agree to the contrary, and provide, for example, that a "managing partner" make management decisions. UPA § 18; RUPA § 103. This is quite common in large partnerships, including law firms.

Though the partnership agreement can adjust the *inter se* relationships (1) among the partners and (2) between the partnership and the partners, it cannot affect the rights of third parties. The partnership agreement could not say that Partner A will not be personally liable to third parties for claims by third parties arising from operation of the business.

Traditionally, a partnership has not been considered an entity separate from its owners.

Rather, it has been seen as the aggregate of the partners. As a consequence, partners are personally liable for the debts and obligations of the partnership. So if the business commits a tort or incurs a debt, the partners are personally liable for it.

RUPA § 201 changes the traditional understanding by declaring that the partnership is "an entity distinct from its partners." Despite this declaration, under RUPA, each partner is jointly and severally liable for all obligations of the partnership. (Under UPA, partners are jointly, but not severally, liable; this means that under UPA, a plaintiff must sue all of the partners in a single suit, while under RUPA she can sue one or more partners in a single suit.) RUPA §§ 305, 306, and 307 provide some protection for partners that was not available at common law or under UPA. Specifically, under RUPA, a third party can only enforce a judgment against the assets of a partner if (1) a judgment is entered against that partner personally, (2) a judgment is also entered against the partnership itself, and (3) partnership assets are insufficient to pay that judgment. Under common law and UPA, the plaintiff does not have to win a judgment against the partnership and does not have to attempt to exhaust partnership funds before collecting from an individual partner.

The partners are owners of the business. In the absence of agreement to the contrary, they have equal voice in management and will share profits equally, and will share losses in the same proportion as profits. They also can bind the partnership to agreements entered with third parties in the ordinary course of business. UPA § 9; RUPA § 301. This latter authority derives from the fact that each partner is an *agent* of the partnership. *See* § 1.10.

Partners owe each other fiduciary duties—in other words, they cannot take advantage of one another. The leading case is *Meinhard v. Salmon*, 164 N.E. 545, 546 (N.Y. 1928), in which the managing partner of a real estate business was informed of a new opportunity that would become available after the completion of the partnership's project. *Id.* at 546. The managing partner seized the opportunity without telling his partner about it. This action violated the duty of utmost good faith and fair dealing that each partner owes to the other partners. In oft-quoted language, Chief Judge (later Justice) Cardozo said that partners "owe to one another, while the enterprise continues, the duty of finest loyalty. . . . Not honesty alone, but the punctilio of an honor the most sensitive. . . ."

This broad concept of fiduciary duty seems appropriate for a small partnership with relatively few members. It fits less clearly, though, when there are many partners, among whom relationships are less personal (think of a large law firm with dozens of partners in different offices). Moreover, in recent times there is an increasing sense that businesspeople are grown-ups and ought to be able to tailor their relationships with co-owners. Reflecting these points, RUPA takes a step that would have been anathema to Justice Cardozo and unthinkable a few decades ago. It permits the partners to limit (but not to abolish completely) the fiduciary duties they owe to each other. RUPA §§ 103(b) (partners may agree to limit fiduciary duties of care and loyalty), 404 (listing fiduciary duties).

Financially, it is customary in partnerships to maintain a "capital account" for each partner. The capital account consists of the original contribution of the partner to the partnership (if any), increased by earnings and profits credited to the account, and reduced by losses and distributions (payments made) to the partner. When a partner withdraws from the partnership, or when the partnership is dissolved, she is entitled to receive the amount in her capital account. If the account has a negative balance, she will be required to contribute the shortfall.

A partner may assign to a third party her financial interest in the partnership. She cannot transfer her other interests, such as the interest in managing the partnership. This means that a transferee (or "assignee") does not become a partner; rather, she is entitled only to whatever financial interest the assigning partner transferred (such as the right to receive distributions from the business). Accordingly, the assignee is not personally liable on partnership obligations. The partner who transfers her financial interest remains a partner in the business, with all the rights (except the right to the financial interest she transferred) and liabilities of a partner.

The fact that the transferee does not become a partner reflects the longstanding rule that adding new partners requires the unanimous approval of the existing partners. UPA § 18(g); RUPA § 401(i). Stated another way, each partner has a veto power over the addition of new partners. (This principle is captured in the Latin phrase *delectus personae,* which means "by choice of the person.") This veto power reflects the aggregate nature of the partnership (even in RUPA states); the partnership is a personal relationship, and one partner cannot require the others to accept a new co-owner. (Remember, UPA and RUPA merely give default provisions for *inter se* matters. The partnership agreement can provide a different rule, such as requiring a two-third or majority vote to add new partners.)

We see the same idea in the rules governing expulsion of a partner. Under UPA, partners can expel a partner only in circumstances permitted by the partnership agreement. RUPA retains this provision and also recognizes an inherent power to expel a partner by the unanimous vote of the remaining partners in limited circumstances.

In *Bohatch v. Butler & Binion,* 977 S.W.2d 543, 544, 547 (Tex. 1998), a partner in good faith told the managing partner that she thought another member of the firm was over-billing a client. The managing partner investigated and found that there was no over-billing. The partnership then fired the whistleblower. Even though she had acted in good faith, the court held that the firm had a right to discharge her. The court emphasized the personal relationships among partners: "Partnerships exist by the agreement of the partners; partners have no duty to remain partners." Once the whistleblower made the charge of over-billing, even if it had been true, the court recognized that the "partners may find it impossible to continue to work together to their mutual benefit and the benefit of their clients."

The aggregate nature of the partnership makes it fragile. Under UPA, the partnership is "dissolved" automatically when a partner dies or leaves the partnership or when a partner expressly states that she wishes to withdraw. The word "dissolution" does not mean that the partnership ends immediately. Rather, it is "the change in the relation of the partners caused by any partner ceasing to be associated in the carrying on as distinguished from the winding up of the business." UPA § 29. The partnership continues to exist through "winding up" (or "liquidation"), which is the process by which assets are gathered, creditors paid, and final distribution is made to the partners. At that point, the partnership ceases to exist. This fragility is a disadvantage. Partnership agreements frequently provide that the partnership is not dissolved by the death or withdrawal of a partner, but that the business will continue.

RUPA improves the situation. It introduces a new term, "dissociation," which it defines in RUPA § 601. Some methods by which a partner dissociates will lead to winding up and termination of the partnership. *See* RUPA § 801. Significantly, one of these is when a partner simply expresses her will to leave a partnership at-will (that is, a partnership that was not formed for a specific period or project;

most partnerships are at-will). This fact gives each partner the power to walk away from such a partnership at any time *and force the other partners to dissolve the business and liquidate.* This potential for disruption can be avoided in the partnership agreement by providing that a partner's voluntary dissociation will not require dissolution and liquidation.

Other methods of dissociation (such as the death of a partner) do not result in winding up and termination of the business. *See* RUPA § 701. Instead, the dissociating partner is bought out (she or her estate receives the value of her interest in the business, less any damages caused if she dissociated wrongfully) and the partnership continues in existence.

On the other hand, the aggregate nature of the partnership carries an advantage in income tax law. Because the partnership is not seen as an entity for this purpose, it pays no income tax on its profits. It files an informational tax return, reflecting what share of the profits is allocated to each partner. That share is taxable personally to the partner. This is "flow-through" taxation applies for all partnerships, whether formed under UPA or RUPA.

One abiding drawback of the general partnership is the personal liability of partners for business debts. Might individual proprietors set up a partnership and avoid personal liability? Interestingly, both UPA and RUPA permit partnerships and entities—including corporations— to serve as partners. Though the partners will be liable for partnership debts, if those partners are corporations, no individual should face personal liability for what the business does. But there is a better way to avoid individual liability for partnership debts. We turn to it now.

## § 1.5   THE LIMITED LIABILITY PARTNERSHIP (LLP)

The limited liability partnership (LLP) is a form of general partnership. It developed in the early 1980s in Texas, as a legislative response to the liability faced by partners of law firms and accounting firms for failures of savings and loan associations. *See generally*, Robert Hamilton, *Registered Limited Liability Partnerships: Present at the Birth (Nearly)*, 66 COLO. L. REV. 1065 (1995). The LLP legislation permitted general partnerships to limit the liability of partners who did not participate in wrongdoing. It shielded partners from the liability they would face as partners for the misdeeds of other partners or of the partnership. Like shareholders in a corporation, the most a partner in an LLP can lose is her investment in the firm.

The concept caught on quickly, and now every state recognizes the LLP. Electing LLP status is easy: a general partnership files a statement with the appropriate state officer (usually the secretary of state) electing LLP status.* The business must also

---

\* Every business structure that provides for limited liability (including LLP, LP, LLLP, corporation, and LLC) requires filing an appropriate document with the state. Thus, limited liability is

pay fees to the state, typically a set amount per partner.

In some states, LLPs are called "registered LLPs" because the business must "register" with the state. In addition, the business choosing LLP status must change its name to contain a phrase of abbreviation prescribed in the state statute. Common examples are "Limited Liability Partnership," "LLP," "Registered Limited Liability Partnership," and "RLLP." Though any general partnership can elect LLP status, the device is predominantly used by partnerships practicing a profession, such as law or accounting. Several states also require that LLPs maintain certain minimum levels of assets or insurance. Violation of those levels results in loss of limited liability protection.

LLP statutes vary dramatically on the level of protection afforded the partners. Some states provide a "partial shield" from liability; for example, it might limit liability only for claims arising from malpractice and negligence, and not for contract claims that exceed the assets of the partnership. Other states provide "full shield" protection for all claims. A good example of this is § 306 of RUPA, which provides: "[a]n obligation of a partnership while the partnership is a limited liability partnership, whether arising in contract, tort, or otherwise, is solely the obligation of the partnership. A partner is not personally liable, directly or indirectly, by way of contribution or otherwise, for

---

never a secret; it is proclaimed in a document available to the public.

such an obligation solely by reason of being or so acting as a partner." Counsel must be careful to assess the level of protection accorded in her state.

Limited liability under LLP statutes is not available to partners who commit acts of malpractice or negligence. In some states the protection is also not available to partners who have responsibility for overseeing or monitoring those partners, or to partners who are aware of the malpractice or negligence and fail to take steps to stop it.

Whatever level of protection, note the extraordinary change wrought by LLP statutes: partners in a general partnership electing LLP status enjoy (at least to some degree) limited liability. Such partners start to look like shareholders of a corporation; they are owners of the business but are not liable for its debts. Unlike shareholders, though, partners have full rights (and responsibilities) of management.

## § 1.6   THE LIMITED PARTNERSHIP (LP)

A limited partnership (LP) is a hybrid business structure. It consists of two types of partners: there must be at least one *general partner*, who is liable for the debts and other obligations of the business, and there must be at least one *limited partner*, who is not liable for what the business does. Just like the LLP, the limited partnership cannot be formed simply by conduct. The proprietors must file an appropriate document with the state officer (again, usually the secretary of state) and pay a fee to the state.

The general partner has management power; she runs the business. The role of the limited partner, in contrast, looks a great deal like that of a shareholder in a corporation: she invests passively (that is, she is not burdened with managerial responsibility) and can, at worst, lose her investment (but is not liable for business debts).

A limited partnership has entity status, separate from those who own and run it. This business form developed in Europe during the Middle Ages to allow nobles and churches to participate anonymously (as limited partners) in ordinary commerce. In this country, it is a creature of statute. The original Uniform Limited Partnership Act (ULPA) was promulgated in 1916, and was eventually adopted in every state except Louisiana. The Revised Uniform Limited Partnership Act (RULPA) was promulgated in 1976 and amended significantly in 1985. In 2001, yet another version of ULPA was introduced (ULPA 2001 or "Re-RULPA"). Every state now has a limited partnership statute, but they vary considerably.

All this legislative activity belies the fact that the limited partnership has never been widely used. And it has been lost in the rush in recent years to the limited liability company (*see* § 1.8). To the extent the limited partnership is used, it tends to be focused in fairly discreet areas: (1) the "family limited partnership," which is an estate planning device that allows the transfer of wealth from one generation to another while maintaining control and avoiding estate and gift taxes; (2) real estate syndications, particularly for large commercial shopping center and office projects; (3) oil and gas businesses; and (4) by venture capital firms.*

For a while in the 1960s and 1970s, limited partnerships with publicly traded limited partnership interests (called "master limited partnerships") were widely used as tax shelters. This flurry largely ended in 1987, though, when Congress amended the Internal Revenue Code to provide that all businesses with publicly traded ownership interests must be taxed as a corporation. Today, there are some publicly-traded limited partnerships, such as Kinder Morgan Partners, which owns or manages pipelines for the transportation of natural gas, petroleum, and other products.

ULPA and RULPA are not free-standing legislation. That is, they make specific provisions for limited partnerships, and rely on general partnership law (UPA or RUPA) to fill gaps. For example, RULPA § 1105 provides that in any situation not addressed by that Act, the relevant provision of the underlying general partnership law (UPA or RUPA) will apply. This "linkage" between the statutes addressing general partnerships and those dealing with limited partnerships has created some anomalies and practical problems. One of the goals of ULPA 2001 was to "de-link" the legislation, and to provide a complete and free-standing body of

---

* Venture capital (called "VC") is a form of equity financing often turned to when other sources of financing are not available. The VC firm buys a large portion of the company's stock and, because of the risk involved (only about one-third of VC-funded businesses succeed), insists on preferred status for dividends and at liquidation and a voice in management.

statutes for limited partnerships. Again, however, limited partnership legislation varies greatly from state to state, and there is still a widespread sense that general partnership law is an important "gap-filler" in limited partnerships.

One drawback of the limited partnership is that there must be a general partner, who is liable for what the business does. Here we see the genius of combining various business forms. The general partner need not be a human being. It can be (and usually is) a corporation. Because the individual owners of a corporation generally are not liable for corporate debts and obligations, the corporate general partner's liability is not borne by an individual; it is borne by the corporate entity. Thus, a limited partnership with a corporate general partner should expose no individual to personal liability for business debts.

As noted, the general partner is liable for business debts because it makes the business decisions. Limited partners have limited liability because they are passive, and are not engaged in management of the firm. But if a limited partner starts acting like a general partner—by exercising "control" over the business—she may risk becoming liable for the business debts. By taking control, she has de facto become a general partner; she will have to pay the concomitant price of liability for the business debts.

Legislation in most states, however, has eliminated most of the risk in this regard. RULPA § 303(a) provides that even if a limited partner takes "control" of the business, she will not be liable unless she acted in a way that led a third party reasonably to believe that she was a general partner. Moreover, § 303(b) sets forth a list of activities that do not constitute "control" over the business. These "safe harbors" are very broad, and include, for example, serving as a shareholder, officer, or director of a corporate general partner. Thus, the fact that the corporate general partner is actually run by one person does not constitute that person's taking "control" over the business; she is not personally liable for business debts. Likewise, a limited partner's instructing the general partner regarding what to do does not constitute "control." ULPA 2001 goes even farther by abandoning the "control rule" entirely. It provides complete freedom from liability for all limited partners.

Modern law of limited partnerships, like that of general partnerships (*see* § 1.4), permits the parties to the business to tailor the *inter se* relationships (1) among the partners and (2) between the partners and the business. This includes tailoring the fiduciary duties they owe to each other. For example, in *Kahn v. Icahn*, 1998 WL 832629 at *1–2 (Del. Ch. 1998), limited partners sued the general partner for usurping a business opportunity that should have gone, according to the plaintiffs, to the limited partnership. Because the partnership agreement expressly allowed the parties to pursue opportunities for their own benefit, however, the court entered judgment for the defendant. As the court explained, under modern statutes, "the traditional fiduciary duties among and between partners are defaults that may be modified by partnership agreements."

Indeed, there appears to be greater freedom in the limited partnership to eschew fiduciary duties than there is in the general partnership. Specifically, RULPA appears to countenance the complete contractual abolition of fiduciary duties among the partners. *Compare* RULPA § 403(b) (general partner has same liabilities to other partners as partner in general partnership, subject to terms of the partnership agreement) *with* RUPA § 103(b) (permitting parties to limit, but not abolish, fiduciary duties of care and loyalty).

A limited partner—like a partner in a general partnership—can transfer to a third party only her financial interest, and not any other right she may have. Moreover, though a general partner can withdraw from a limited partnership at will, a limited partner generally must give six months' written notice before withdrawing. The difference makes sense when one remembers the roles played by the two. The general partner is the manager; if she leaves, the limited partners can find a new manager. The limited partners, however, are the source of capital for the limited partnership. Accordingly, the theory goes, it should be more difficult for them to walk away from the business.

Though the limited partnership is seen as an entity for general purposes, it is not taxed as one. Accordingly, one advantage of this structure is that the business pays no income tax. Instead, taxation is "flow-through"—it is levied on the profits that accrue to the partners.

## § 1.7   THE LIMITED LIABILITY
## LIMITED PARTNERSHIP (LLLP)

The limited liability limited partnership (LLLP) is the limited partnership analog to the limited liability partnership, which we saw in § 1.5. Here, a firm that has qualified for limited partnership status elects LLLP status by filing the required document with the appropriate state officer and paying a fee to the state. This step affords limited liability to the general partner of the limited partnership. (The limited partners already have limited liability.) In an LLLP, then, no partner is personally liable for the business debts. The entity (and only the entity) is liable for its debts and obligations.

In practice, the LLLP does not appear to be widely used. The more common practice in limited partnerships, as noted in § 1.6, is to have a single general partner that is itself a corporation.

## § 1.8   THE LIMITED LIABILITY
## COMPANY (LLC)

In 1978, Wyoming pioneered a new business form, the limited liability company (LLC). Florida followed suit shortly thereafter. Once it became clear that LLCs would be treated as partnerships for purposes of income tax, the move was on—all states passed LLC statutes. The LLC has become strikingly popular, because it combines so many positive features.

In 1995, the NCCUSL approved the Uniform Limited Liability Company Act ("ULLCA"). By then, though, most states had developed their own statutes. Consequently, ULLCA has not played a central role in developing the law. The following is a general description of the LLC. It is worth keeping in mind, however, that state statutes vary on specifics.

The owners of an LLC are called "members." Though many statutes initially required at least two members, that has changed, and nearly every state now permits LLCs with a single member. The LLC is universally considered an entity, separate from the members. Forming an LLC requires filing a document (often called the "articles of organization") with the appropriate state officer and paying the required fee. The document is usually a short, bare-bones affair. The specifics of operating the LLC are usually set out in the "operating agreement" (sometimes called "regulations") among the members, which is often very detailed.

Though the requirement of filing with the state is similar to that for forming a corporation, there is at least a theoretical difference. Historically, forming a corporation has been seen as receiving a charter or franchise from the state. The same is not true with the LLC. The only practical difference of consequence, however, is that in some states an LLC—because it does not receive a franchise from the state—is not subject to state franchise taxes; a corporation always is. Beyond that, some courts have been sloppy in equating LLCs and corporations, referring, for instance to the state in which an LLC was "incorporated." And there has been some confusion about whether certain aspects of corporate law should apply to the LLC. The best example of that is with the corporate doctrine of "piercing the corporate veil" (*see* § 10.4).

All members of the LLC have limited liability; none is personally liable for the debts of the business. (Of course, a tortfeasor is always liable for her torts; but no member of the LLC is liable for the debts or torts of the business or of her fellow members). Thus, an LLC may be roughly analogized to a limited partnership, but composed only of limited partners. All of the members may freely participate in management of the business without becoming liable for the business's obligations.

Internal management of the LLC is quite flexible. In most states, the proprietors have a choice of how to structure the management. One is for the business to be "member-managed," which means that the owners make the business decisions; this looks a bit like a general partnership, with the usual default position (subject to agreement to the contrary) being that each member has one vote. The other choice is for the business to be "manager-managed," in which the members select persons to make the business decisions; this looks more like a corporation, in which shareholders elect directors to run the show. Beyond this, LLC statutes are remarkably devoid of the formal requirements imposed upon corporations— such as required meetings, record dates, maintenance of minutes and records, and the like.

Membership interests generally are made readily transferable like shares of stock and may be reflected by certificates. As in the closely-held corporation, however, the parties may restrict the ability to transfer in the articles or operating agreement. Duration of the LLC may be perpetual, or for a term, or at will. The LLC does not pay income taxes as an entity. The LLC is, in short, a genuinely novel business form of great flexibility that features limited liability for all members and flow-through taxation. Though most LLCs are small businesses, a few are large entities, the equity interests in which are publicly-traded.

## § 1.9  THE UBIQUITOUS IMPORTANCE OF AGENCY LAW

No matter what business structure we use, agency law will be important. Agency law is the glue that allows all businesses to contract with third parties. It is the law of delegation: the business needs to get something done, and may use an agent to do it. There are always three players: the principal (P), the agent (A), and the third party (TP). Agency arises when P wants A to do something, and A agrees to do it—all under the control of P. By "control" here, we just mean that P is in charge; P does not have to control every last detail of how the job gets done. Every business, no matter how structured—from sole proprietorships through huge publicly-traded corporations—uses agents to get things done. Indeed, people commonly use agents in their personal lives. Agency "works" because it permits A to act for P in a way that binds P to a deal with TP.

For example, suppose you (P) call a travel agent (A) and ask her to make a reservation on a train (TP) from Los Angeles to San Diego. She does so. Can you now refuse to pay for the ticket because you did not personally enter the contract with TP? No. You are bound because A had *authority* to bind you to the deal with the train company. This authority to bind P will usually be "actual" or "apparent."

*Actual authority* is created in one way: by a manifestation from P to A. The simplest example is if P tells A to do something on her behalf; this is what happened with the travel agent. You (P) told the travel agent (A) to book a ticket for you on Amtrak (TP) from Los Angeles to San Diego.

Technically, this fact pattern is an example of "express actual authority." You (P) told A expressly what A was to do. There is also "implied actual authority." This means that when you assign a task to an agent, the agent has authority to take action in furtherance of completing the task.

For example, assume you (P) tell your assistant (A) to "make arrangements" so you can attend a three-day convention in San Diego. This creates express actual authority, but carries with it the implied authority to take the steps necessary to get the job done. Thus, your assistant has implied actual authority to buy the convention tickets, transportation tickets, and reserve a hotel on your behalf. When you granted your assistant the express actual authority to "make arrangements" for the trip, you granted implied actual authority to make travel reservations. You are bound by the various reservations made by your assistant. Without such implied authority, the agent could not get the assigned job done.

*Apparent authority*, in contrast, is created by manifestations from P to TP. So if P tells TP that A has authority to bind her to a contract, A has apparent authority.

- P wants to buy an antique car from TP. P and A meet with TP. At the meeting, P says "A has the authority to negotiate the deal for me to buy this car, and will meet with you tomorrow." Now P and A walk out, and P tells A "you have no authority to do anything on my behalf; do not enter a deal with TP." The next day, A meets with TP and negotiates a deal that requires P to buy the antique car. Is P bound by the contract? Yes. Why? Because though A did not have *actual* authority to bind P to the deal, A did have *apparent* authority to do so; it was based upon P's manifestations to TP. P can sue A for violating her instructions, but agency law dictates that P is bound by the deal with TP.

The manifestation need not be verbal. Suppose P runs a restaurant and tells A to order supplies from TP. Each week A does so and each week P pays TP for the supplies. After several weeks, P tells A that she no longer has authority to order supplies from TP. But A does so. Is P bound to pay for them? Yes. A has apparent authority because P's history of paying for A's orders is a manifestation to TP that A has the authority to bind P. If P wants to cut off that authority, she should inform TP that A can no longer bind her.

Traditionally, courts have also recognized "inherent" authority. As we will see in § 8.4, officers of a corporation are agents and may have authority to bind the business to contracts. Particularly, the president may have inherent authority to bind the company to contracts in the ordinary course of business. This authority (or "power" as the Restatement (Second) of Agency § 8(a) calls it) is integral to the position—it "goes with the territory" of being the corporate president. Some courts cause unnecessary confusion by using "implied" for what should properly be called "inherent" authority.

There has been considerable academic debate about whether the law should recognize inherent authority or power. The common law, reflected in the Restatement (Second) of Agency, which was promulgated in 1958, recognized inherent agency power, as noted above, in § 8A. The Restatement (Third) of Agency, however, promulgated in 2006, rejects it. This rejection is not a matter of great importance in the real world, though. Why? The Restatement (Third) expands the notion of what constitutes a manifestation by P to TP and thus expands the applicability of apparent authority. For instance, by representing (essentially to the world) that someone is the "president" of a corporation, the corporation is manifesting to third parties that this person has apparent authority to bind the corporation to deals in the ordinary course of business. So the Restatement (Third) would reach by apparent authority the same result the common law would reach through inherent authority.

An agent cannot create her own authority. So A cannot go to TP and say "I represent P and have authority to bind her to a deal to buy your antique car." If P did not create actual authority (by making a manifestation to A) or apparent authority (by making a manifestation to TP), A cannot bind P here. Indeed, there is no principal at all, and A will be personally liable as a party to the contract.

Can P be liable to TP for a *tort* committed by A? This question raises the issue of vicarious liability, or *respondeat superior*. P can be liable vicariously *only* if two things are true. First, the relationship between P and A must be that of employer and employee. Traditionally, this was called (and in many states still is called) "master and servant." Employer/employee is a subset of principal/agent. Another way to say this: all employers (or masters) are principals, but not all principals are employers (or masters). And all employees (or servants) are agents, but not all agents are employees (or servants).

The dividing line for the subset is this: an employer (or master) has the right to control the *details* of the way the employee (or servant) does the job. If someone hires you to be a server in her restaurant, she is an employer and you are an employee. Why? She has the right to control the way in which you do your job; she can require you to wear a uniform and to serve and remove dishes in a particular way. The notion of control here goes beyond that inherent in the general agency relationship (which only required that we know who is the principal and the agent). Here, the employer has the right to control how the day-to-day details of the job get done.

An employee is to be contrasted with an independent contractor. Suppose you want a garage added to your house. You hire someone to do it. You have no idea how the garage is to be built and do not care how she does it—just so it gets done. That person is an independent contractor, and you are not vicariously liable for any torts she commits.

The second requirement for vicarious liability is that the tort occur in the scope of the employment. So if P hires A as a server in a restaurant, and A negligently spills scalding food on a Customer, can Customer sue P? Yes. P is liable vicariously liable for the tort under *respondeat superior* because (1) the relationship between P and A is employee/employer and (2) the tort occurred within the "scope of employment."

The latter requirement reflects the fact that the employer should be held liable only for those things fairly considered a risk of the business. Thus, if the employee commits the tort during business hours but while doing something only for her own benefit, courts may conclude that the employee was on a "frolic," which means that the employer will not be vicariously liable. On the other hand, if the employee commits the tort during a minor deviation from the job at hand, courts may conclude that the employee was merely on a "detour," which means that the employer will be vicariously liable. The line between a "frolic" and a "detour" is often hazy.

For example, suppose P is a business (of any structure—even a corporation) and hires A to drive its delivery truck. This is an employer/employee relationship because P has the right to control the details of how A does her job. If A drives negligently and injures Pedestrian, Pedestrian can sue P for vicarious liability. Suppose instead that when A drove negligently, A was 30 miles from where she was supposed to be, having gone there to engage in gambling. Here, a court might conclude that P is not vicariously liable because A was on a "frolic." On the other hand, if A had deviated from the appointed route in only a minor way, perhaps to get lunch, a court might find P vicariously liable. In that case, A may not have been on a "frolic", but merely on a "detour."

Finally, *ratification* is P's *ex post facto* approval of an act by A for which A had no authority. So if A went beyond her authority in entering a deal with TP, P may *ratify* the transaction and thus become liable on it.

## § 1.10   RELEVANCE OF FEDERAL INCOME TAX LAW

In determining the business form that best suits a client's needs, the business lawyer must consider income tax ramifications of the choice. Federal income tax law has three basic regimes for taxation of businesses, routinely referred to by the subchapter of the Internal Revenue Code dealing with that regime.

First, Subchapter C applies to corporations generally. It considers the corporation to be a separate entity independent of its shareholders. I.R.C. § 11(a) thus imposes a tax on the income of the corporation. In addition, § 301 imposes income tax on the distributions (such as dividends) paid by the corporation to its shareholders. This results in "double taxation": there is federal income taxation at the corporate level and a second time at the shareholders' level. Every public corporation is subject to Subchapter C.

In § 1.6, we saw that during the 1960s and 1970s, "master limited partnerships" were publicly traded. The proprietors claimed that because the businesses were not corporations, they should not be taxed under Subchapter C. The argument worked until 1987. Since then, Congress has treated all publicly-traded businesses (even limited partnerships) as Subchapter C corporations for tax purposes.

Second, "Subchapter K" applies to partnerships and "associations taxable as partnerships." It provides that these businesses are not separate taxable units. Instead, any tax consequences of their activities are passed through to the owners of the enterprise (hence the phrase "pass-through" taxation). The partnership files an informational tax return, on which it shows its business income (or loss) and allocates gains, losses, income, deductions, etc. to each partner. Each partner then includes those items in her individual income tax return. "K taxation" is an advantage over "C taxation." The partners pay income tax at their level, but the business does not pay a separate tax.

Third is "Subchapter S," which Congress passed after years of hearing complaints from proprietors of closely-held corporations. These people complained that double taxation was unfair on such small businesses. Subchapter S allows qualifying corporations to elect "S status," which offers flow-through taxation. Thus, there is income tax at the individual level (on dividends paid to the shareholders) but the business does not pay income tax on its profits. Though this looks a lot like "K taxation," technically there are significant distinctions between "K" and "S" businesses. Fortunately, those distinctions are addressed in the course on Corporate Tax, and not in this class!

Subchapter S status is available only to corporations that (1) are formed in the United States, (2) have no more than 100 shareholders, (3) the shareholders of which are not corporations, but are individuals, decedent's estates, or certain types of trusts, (4) have no shareholders who are nonresident aliens, and (5) have only be one class of stock. An S corporation is a true corporation with all attributes of a corporation other than advantageous tax treatment.

So where do the newer forms of business—the LLP, limited partnership, LLLP, and LLC—fit into these regimes? For years, the IRS took the position that pass-through taxation was only available for businesses in which owners were liable for business obligations. The theory seemed to be that because the economic benefits and burdens of the partnership passed directly through to the partners, it was reasonable to impose income taxation on the same basis. By this logic, LLPs, limited partnerships, LLLPs, and LLCs should not be able to take advantage of Subchapter S. After all, owners of those businesses do not face personal liability for the business debts.

Over time, however, the IRS changed its tune. In 1997, the IRS adopted "check the box" regulations. These require that corporations choose either Subchapter C or Subchapter S. "Check the box" gives great flexibility to business forms other than the corporation, including the LLC. Such a business that has at least two members can elect to be classified for tax purposes either as a corporation (Subchapter C or S) or as a partnership (Subchapter K) simply by making an election at the time it files its first tax return. If the entity does not formally elect to be taxed as a corporation, it will be taxed as a partnership. A non-corporate business with only one owner (a sole proprietorship) may elect to be taxed as a corporation or it will be taxed as a "nothing"—that is, as though it had no existence separate from its owner.

Finally, note the impact of income tax rates. Tax minimization strategies will change if tax rates change. For example, for many years after World War II individual marginal tax rates for wealthy individuals were as high as 80 percent, while the maximum corporate tax rate was capped at 52 percent. In such a world, Subchapter K taxation for a profitable business with high-income taxpayers was to be avoided at all costs, since it subjected the business income to the very high individual tax rates. The point is simple: lawyers must provide their clients with advice on the pros and cons of the various business forms, including the income tax regime best aimed at minimizing taxes in the current tax climate.

# CHAPTER 2

# THE CORPORATION IN THEORY AND IN HISTORY

## § 2.1 INTRODUCTION

In Chapter 3, we will see how we form a *de jure* corporation—that is, a legal corporation, one recognized in the eyes of the law. In this Chapter, we discuss what that means as a theoretical matter. At different times, and for different purposes, scholars have viewed the corporation in various theoretical ways. Throughout the discussion in §§ 2.2–2.4, keep in mind that these theories are simply attempts to explain what a corporation "really" is. You might see them as metaphors for the corporation. None is totally correct, none is totally wrong, and each has its place in defining the concept of the corporation. In § 2.5, we turn to the question of whether businesses—particularly public corporations—have any role beyond making money. Specifically, do they have social responsibility? The answer to that question may be affected by the theoretical view one takes of what a corporation is. In §§ 2.6–2.8, we trace the development of American corporate law, including the primacy of state law and the leading role of Delaware law. Finally, in § 2.9, we address whether a corporation can be a "person" for various legal purposes.

## § 2.2  THE CORPORATION
## AS ARTIFICIAL PERSON

The traditional theoretical view is that a corporation is an *artificial person* (to be contrasted with a *natural person*, which is a human being). The corporation is an entity, independent of the people who form it, own it, and run it. It does business, acquires assets, incurs debts, enters contracts—does everything it does—in its own name, rather than in the name of any individual. This artificial person has most of the legal rights of a natural person: it can sue or be sued, apply for business licenses, hire employees, invest in securities, buy and sell property, and it must also pay taxes and fees.

One consequence of this traditional view is that since the corporation is an entity in its own right, it is liable for its own debts. Indeed, the separate entity concept is so deeply ingrained that many corporation statutes (unlike limited partnership and limited liability company statutes) never expressly state that shareholders are not liable for corporate obligations. We considered other characteristics that flow from the corporation's entity status (things like continuity of existence) in § 1.2.

Though well-ingrained, the artificial person theory is formalistic. The corporation has no will of its own and cannot do anything by itself. A corporation is a device by which people conduct a business. In famous terms, Professor Hohfeld summarized: "[I]t has not always been perceived * * * that transacting business under the forms, methods, and procedure pertaining to so-called corporations is simply another mode by which individuals or natural persons can enjoy their property and engage in business. Just as several individuals may transact business collectively as partners, so they may as members of a corporation— the corporation being nothing more than an association of such individuals * * * ." Wesley N. Hohfeld, FUNDAMENTAL LEGAL CONCEPTIONS 197 (1923).

Hohfeld's analysis illustrates the fallacy of accepting the artificial person theory uncritically. A corporation may be treated as an entity for many purposes but not for all. At some point a court may rely on the reality Hohfeld described to trump formalistic arguments. Accordingly, arguments grounded solely on the artificial entity theory and not supported by considerations of fairness, justice, or policy sometimes have not prevailed. An example is the doctrine of piercing the corporate veil, by which shareholders may be held liable for corporate obligations. *See* § 10.4.

## § 2.3 THE CORPORATION AS PRIVILEGE OR CONTRACT

Another metaphorical view is that the corporation is a privilege from the state that permits the owners and investors to conduct business in the corporate form. Sometimes, people use the terms "concession," "grant," or "franchise" to refer to this privilege. This theory may have been more important in earlier times, when states made it relatively difficult to incorporate. Now, as we see in Chapter 3, incorporating is so easy that the privilege theory seems less relevant. On the other hand, the theory still has some impact in the ongoing debate over the social role of corporations. *See* § 2.5. Moreover, the notion that a corporation receives a "franchise" from the state is the theory on which states apply their franchise taxes to corporations but not to other business forms.

Another view is that the document forming the corporation—usually called the articles, but sometimes the certificate or charter—may be seen as a contract or a compact. In *Dartmouth College v. Woodward*, 17 U.S. 518, 590–92 (1819), the Supreme Court held that the document creating Dartmouth College was a contract between the corporation and the state. Under the Contracts Clause of the Constitution, the state could not unilaterally change it. In reaction to this decision, every state has adopted provisions empowering them to amend their corporate law and declaring that corporations are subject to the amendments. Depending on the circumstances, the court may see the corporate articles as a contract among shareholders or between the shareholders and the state. For example, courts sometimes use the contract theory in disputes between holders of different classes of stock. Because the articles are a "contract," they spell out the rights of the holders.

## § 2.4  IMPACT OF LAW AND ECONOMICS SCHOLARSHIP: THE "NEXUS OF CONTRACTS"

Law and economics analysis has challenged many of the traditional beliefs about business. This analysis has come to be associated with scholars at the University of Chicago and is often called "the Chicago School." Key among the academic leaders at the University of Chicago were the late Milton Friedman, who won the Nobel Prize for Economics in 1976 and the late Ronald Coase, who won the same prize in 1991.

Law and economics scholars talk about the "firm" rather than the corporation, to indicate that their theories apply to businesses generally, no matter what their legal structure. One contribution of law and economics scholarship is the "nexus of contracts" theory, which derives from the path-breaking economic analysis by Professor Coase in the 1930s. One of his insights was that every firm is, in essence, a long term relational contract by which each factor of production is affiliated with the other factors contributing to the enterprise. From this, law and economics scholars see a business not as an entity but as a bundle of contracts entered by the managers with persons who provide different things, or "inputs." Thus, shareholders agree to furnish capital, while employees provide labor, and suppliers provide materials, etc. The managers are the glue that hold together all the various contributors in the most efficient way.

Managers should, according to the model, have broad discretion to structure and run the enterprise. The result is a hierarchical structure of control over employees and agents, perhaps softened by principles of participatory management or team production. The principal problem is control over "agency costs," which are the sum of the "monitoring" and "bonding" costs, plus any residual loss, incurred to prevent shirking by agents. Monitoring costs are the expenses of oversight, while bonding costs are devices to assure the fidelity of employees and agents where oversight is impractical or too costly. Shirking is conduct of an individual that diverges from the interests of the enterprise as a whole—including cheating, negligence, incompetence, and culpable mistakes.

In this view of the corporation, shareholders are not the owners. Instead, they are suppliers of capital, the group whose "contract" entitles them to the residual profits of the business and requires them to risk losing their investment. The goal of the corporation is viewed as the maximization of shareholder wealth in the enterprise. A corporation is thus viewed as a set of consensual relationships established by the managers with the goal of maximizing the wealth of those who supplied the capital.

One problem with this model is its use of the term "contract." It is difficult to say that a person who buys 100 shares of Consolidated Edison through a broker on the New York Stock Exchange has entered into a "contract" with the corporation. It is true, of course, that a purchaser of Con Ed stock obtains certain rights, such as the right to receive a declared dividend. But the shareholder who buys her stock on the open market has not given any money to Con Ed or agreed to do anything for the corporation. The corporation will receive money paid for stock only when it "issues" the stock. Issuance, which we study in § 12.3 of this book, is when the corporation sells its own stock; it is at this point the corporation receives the proceeds of the sale. After that, when the stock is bought and sold on a stock exchange, the money goes back and forth between the buyer and the seller, and not to the corporation.

The Con Ed shareholder is certainly bound to accept the judgment of a majority of the shareholders when they vote to elect directors or to approve fundamental corporate changes. But did the shareholder enter into a "contract" agreeing to this? To a lawyer, probably not, because "contract" means an agreement the legal system will enforce. But "to an economist, an implied contract is one that is enforced through marketplace mechanisms such as reputation effects rather than in a court, a means of enforcement that may not bring relief to the aggrieved party but will over time penalize parties who welsh." Jeffrey Gordon, *The Mandatory Structure of Corporate Law*, 89 COLUM. L.REV. 1549, 1550 (1989).

So "contract" may mean something quite different to an economist than to a lawyer. The economist sees the word as encompassing voluntary arrangements generally, even without consensual exchanges. Some of these arrangements "may be implied by courts or legislatures trying to supply the terms that would have been negotiated had people addressed the problem explicitly. Even terms that are invariant— such as the requirement that the board of directors act only by a majority of a quorum—are contractual to the extent that they produce offsetting voluntary arrangements. The result of all of these voluntary arrangements will be contractual." Frank Easterbrook and Daniel Fischel, *The Corporate Contract*, 89 COLUM. L.REV. 1416, 1428 (1989).

To law and economics scholars, corporate law should provide standard default rules which the parties should be free to modify. In other words, the law should not impose mandatory rules so much as enable businesspeople to structure the business as they see fit. There is no denying the impact of this thinking on modern business law. As discussed in §§ 1.6 and 1.8, contemporary statutes on limited partnerships and LLCs permit the proprietors even to contract around fiduciary duties. On the other hand, modern corporation law, while clearly permitting more contractual choice than in previous generations, still includes mandatory requirements that the proprietors are not free to waive or modify. And federal law—for example the Securities Act of 1933—concerning access to public markets is full of mandatory prescriptions that cannot be avoided. *See* Chapter 11.

## § 2.5 THE DEBATE OVER SOCIAL RESPONSIBILITY: PHILANTHROPY, OTHER CONSTITUENCIES, AND THE "BENEFIT CORPORATION"

What is the role of business? Most people who start a business do so to make money. Business is economic activity aimed at the creation of wealth. (We are not dealing in this course with non-profit organizations.) Does the fact that businesses are formed to make money mean, however, that they can have no other purpose? We will focus on large, publicly-traded corporations, because that is where the debate centers. On the one hand, many argue that public corporations—because of their economic power— should be subject to social control, to be required to address the social impact of decisions. This argument is often based upon the view of the corporation as privilege or charter, discussed in § 2.3. Thus, if the state bestows the privilege of a corporate charter, through which the corporation generates great wealth, the state ought to be able to impose social responsibilities—to require that the corporation "give back" in some way for societal good.

The contrary argument is that the goal of business is to make money, period. If you want to use the money you make through business to "do good," great—but do it with your money, not the corporation's. This view is essentially *laissez faire*— that the government should leave corporations alone and let them tend to business and the bottom line.

Many casebooks raise the issue with the famous case of *A.P. Smith Manufacturing Co. v. Barlow*, 98

A.2d 581, 582, 584, 590 (N.J. 1953). There, the corporation (through a decision by its board of directors) made a charitable contribution to Princeton University. Some shareholders objected, and argued that such philanthropy was not an appropriate corporate goal. The court upheld the gift. It noted that in the early days of the Republic, incorporation was permitted only for the social good. Over time, the court said, the goal of private business became focused on profit. When the corporation became the dominant economic force in the country, however, "calls upon the corporations for reasonable philanthropic donations have come to be made with increased public support."

Many, including Milton Friedman, argue that "social responsibility" is for individuals, not for the business. The corporation, Dr. Friedman would assert, should make its money and let the individual shareholders decide whether to make charitable contributions with their own money (and, BTW, perhaps to make contributions to institutions that need the money more than Princeton). But the *A.P. Smith* view has prevailed; the corporation law of every state permits (but does not compel) such charitable giving, and the income tax law permits the corporation to take a deduction for such gifts.

Modern statutes list specific "powers" that corporations automatically have. The list includes the power to make charitable contributions. *See, e.g.*, MBCA § 3.02(13). That does not mean there is no limit on its largesse. These are for-profit enterprises and accordingly cannot give away everything. Charitable contributions must be reasonable.

Corporate philanthropy consists of managers giving away money that otherwise might go to shareholders. Legendary investor Warren Buffett relates a telling tale about a friend who asked corporations for significant charitable contributions. Buffett said: "[I]n the process of raising * * * eight million dollars from 60 corporations from people who nod and say that's a marvelous idea, it's pro-social, etc., not one [executive] reached in[to] his pocket and pulled out ten bucks of his own to give to this marvelous charity." KNIGHTS, RAIDERS AND TARGETS: THE IMPACT OF HOSTILE TAKEOVERS 14 (1988).

Fifty years ago, most people who owned stock in public corporations were relatively wealthy; stock ownership was for the rich. The idea that wealthy people could forego a dividend so the corporation could give money to Princeton did not cause much concern. Today, however, the majority of Americans are invested in the stock market. If you have money in a pension plan or in a savings-and-loan association, it is invested in stocks. Today, then, corporate philanthropy may consist of a millionaire executive's decision to give to a well-endowed private college money that otherwise might go into a blue-collar worker's pension.

The social responsibility discussion, however, is much broader than corporate gifts to charity. The discussion implicates the social ramifications of corporate decisions. Decisions about where to locate manufacturing facilities, how many people to hire, what wages to pay, etc. can carry dramatic consequences for communities and entire geographic regions. Suppose we have a corporation with an obsolete manufacturing plant in a small one-plant town in a northern state. The board of directors is considering closing the plant and moving manufacturing to a different region of the country (or to another country altogether), where labor costs and taxes will be lower. The board would like to build a modern, efficient, environmentally-friendly plant in this other place. In making this decision, should the board of directors take into account the adverse effects on the community it will be leaving? On the persons who will be unemployed? On their families, the local stores currently in the town, the community itself, and the state?

These interests are often described as "other constituencies" of the corporation. Does the corporation "owe" something to these constituencies, who, after all, have supported the business in this community for years? If the company should consider the effect on these other constituencies, how does it balance the possibility that keeping the present plant may result in reduced dividends to shareholders and higher prices to the public? How does it balance that the present plant may not be as efficient or as "green" as a new plant would be?

If the role of the corporation is solely to create wealth for its owners, these considerations would seem irrelevant. Yet, many will argue, corporations benefit from society's laws and ought to benefit that society broadly. The corporation codes in some states reflect this notion by providing, for example, that the managers, when taking corporate acts, are not required "to regard . . . the interests of any particular group affected by such action as a dominant or controlling interest or factor." PA. CONS. STAT. § 1715. Such statutes permit the board of directors to consider broad societal issues (and not just the bottom line for shareholders) when making corporate decisions. These provisions may shield directors from liability if shareholders sue for "waste" of corporate assets on social considerations.

More recently, some states have passed statutes allowing formation of "benefit corporations" or "B Corporations." Such entities are for-profit businesses, but are also committed to benefit some broader constituency or cause. The articles of incorporation of a B Corporation will set forth a social goal, such as paying foreign workers on a scale comparable to American workers or promoting environmentally-friendly acts. Managers of such companies are shielded from liability if their decisions (like paying higher wages) hurt the shareholders' bottom line. (In fact, they might be sued for failing to satisfy the company's social-policy objectives.) Maryland pioneered the B Corporation in 2010. Since then, more than half the states (and the District of Columbia) have enacted B Corporation legislation.

## § 2.6  HISTORICAL DEVELOPMENT
## OF CORPORATE LAW

In the pre-revolutionary period, colonial legislatures granted corporate charters on the authority of the British Crown. After independence and the ratification of the Constitution, state legislatures took up the role. They continued to grant corporate charters. After the War of 1812, the number of corporate charters increased rapidly. In addition to banks, many corporations were formed to construct canals and turnpikes. These early incorporations were franchises from the state, some of them monopolies.

In 1791, the federal government passed a statute incorporating the Bank of the United States for 20 years. There was considerable doubt about whether the federal government had the power to create corporations for general economic purposes. This debate was put to rest by the Supreme Court in *McCulloch v. Maryland*, 17 U.S. 316, 383 (1819). The Court found that although the authority to create corporations was not explicitly given to Congress, it was "a necessary means of accomplishing the ends of all governments," and therefore it was "an authority inherent in * * * all sovereignty." Though it is clear from this decision that the federal government can create corporations, it rarely does so, and even then only for essentially public purposes. For example, the American Red Cross is a federally-chartered corporation.

That means that incorporation has been the purview of the states. In this course, we will deal with some federal law. Specifically, in Chapters 11 and 14, we will study the Securities Act of 1933 and Securities Exchange Act of 1934. But when it comes to the law forming and governing corporations and the various players in the corporate world, we will be dealing with state law.

Originally, each corporation was formed by a legislative act. People wanting to incorporate a business had to convince the state legislature to pass an act creating the corporation. Approval of a charter was a political act, involving lobbying, political influence, campaign contributions (all the hallmarks of legislation). It was not until 1836 that Pennsylvania approved a "general" incorporation statute, by which people could form a corporation by action of an administrative agency rather than requiring a specific statute. Connecticut followed suit in 1840. By 1859 more than half the states had general incorporation laws, and by 1890 it was unanimous.

The populist movement that developed primarily in the agricultural states in the Midwest viewed corporations in general (and railroads in particular) with suspicion and mistrust. In many of these states, legislatures restricted the size, duration, purposes, and capital investment of corporations. These restrictions were ineffective. Because a corporation formed in one state can qualify to do business in any state (*see* § 3.7), companies simply incorporated in states that did not have such restrictions. Over time, states have removed most such limitation.

## § 2.7  STATE COMPETITION FOR INCORPORATION AND THE HEGEMONY OF DELAWARE

Beginning in the late nineteenth century, several states tried to attract businesses to incorporate or reincorporate even though the corporations planned to do no business there. They amended their statutes to simplify procedures, relax restrictions and limitations, reduce fees, and generally make things more attractive, particularly for large corporations doing business in New York. Why would states compete for the incorporation business? Money. States charge fees to incorporate and to maintain corporate status. They also impose franchise taxes on corporations, often based upon the company's assets. And there may be state income taxes as well. Today, between 15 and 20 percent of Delaware's total budget comes from franchise taxes paid by corporations. From a financial standpoint, the Delaware corporation business is the envy of other states.

In the late nineteenth century, leaders in New Jersey estimated that that state could retire its entire Civil War debt by attracting incorporations and charging franchise fees. It liberalized its statutes to allow corporations to do things they generally could not do elsewhere—including invest in the securities of other companies. The effort bore fruit. New Jersey became the dominant state for incorporation and generated an enormous amount of money in this way. But the effort ended in 1911, when Governor Woodrow Wilson led a charge to repeal the changes in New Jersey law.

The beneficiary was Delaware, which became and remains the dominant incorporation state for public corporations. More than half of the Fortune 500 corporations (the 500 largest corporations based upon revenue) are Delaware companies.

Some observers saw the competition among states for the incorporation business of public corporations as unseemly, even inappropriate. Justice Brandeis said it was a "race not of diligence but of laxity." *Liggett Co. v. Lee*, 288 U.S. 517 (1933) (dissenting opinion). One observer called it a "race for the bottom." William Cary, *Federalism and Corporate Law: Reflections Upon Delaware*, 83 YALE L.J. 663, 670 (1974). Such commentators saw the "race" as leading to the systematic elimination of regulatory controls on the corporation, the adoption of a "pro-management" stance whenever conflicts arose between managers and shareholders, and the elimination of preemptive rights and cumulative voting, which were widely viewed as pro-shareholder.

Those complaining about the "race for the bottom" assumed that corporate managers can freely impose their will and that the disorganized shareholders can do nothing about it. Scholars have questioned this assumption. Professor Winter (later appointed to the Second Circuit), argued that the assumption overlooks the existence of an efficient market for corporate securities. If Delaware actually permits management to profit at the expense of shareholders (and other states do not, or do not as much), we would expect earnings of Delaware corporations that are allocable to shareholders to be less than earnings of comparable corporations that are subject to more rigorous control in other states. Thus, if the "race to the bottom" theory is correct, Delaware corporations will be at an economic disadvantage, and ultimately this disadvantage should cause shareholders to invest in non-Delaware corporations. Ralph Winter, GOVERNMENT AND THE CORPORATION (1978).

Several statistical studies tend to show, however, that reincorporation in Delaware more often leads to an *increase* in share prices than to a decrease. Generally, then, they support Winter's thesis and tend to disprove the "race for the bottom" notion. Unfortunately, share prices may be affected by many factors, and it is not possible to say with certainty that Delaware law is the sole, or even the principal, cause of the favorable price movement. Nonetheless, some concluded that the competition for incorporations had actually been a "race to the top," since shareholders benefited from incorporation in Delaware. Roberta Romano, *Law As a Product: Some Pieces of the Incorporation Puzzle*, 1 J. L., ECON. & ORGANIZATION 225 (1985).

Why has the Delaware General Corporation Law been so attractive? The answer seems not to be substantive. Indeed, in many ways Delaware law is more cumbersome than more modern codes. But Delaware is successful in attracting incorporation business because it has created an entire system—with legislation, the bench and bar—that understands business and business law. Lawyers know that they will deal with sophisticated state officials. The bench and bar are generally thought well versed in corporate law. Undeniably, there is also inertia—lawyers have their clients incorporate in Delaware because they always have done it that way.

Recent scholarship questions the continuing loyalty to Delaware. In the past generation, the Delaware Supreme Court has decided several high-profile cases that make the law of that state more indeterminate. In addition, there is a high reversal rate of trial court decisions, which also leads to indeterminacy. Two scholars, noting this and the relative certainty of the Modern Business Corporation Act, find the continuing hegemony of Delaware vexing. William Carney & George Shepherd, *The Mystery of Delaware Law's Continuing Success,* 2009 U. ILL. L. REV. 1.

Trying to capture more business, several states have modernized their statutes. The New York legislature—which must be frustrated at having all those corporate headquarters in Manhattan for businesses incorporated in Delaware—substantially amended its Business Corporation Act in 1998. Massachusetts scrapped its century-old corporation code in 2004 in favor of a modern law, in the process sweeping away some bizarre and arcane requirements. Texas completely overhauled its business organization laws in 2010. It is not clear, however, that these efforts are cutting into Delaware's primacy as the state of incorporation for publicly-traded entities.

## § 2.8   MODERN CORPORATION STATUTES, INCLUDING THE MBCA

Each state, the District of Columbia, and Puerto Rico has its own corporation statute. There is a considerable degree of commonality among these statutes, but there is great divergence on specific provisions. The Model Business Corporation Act (MBCA) has been quite influential. Over half the states have used some version of it as their legislation. There have been three editions of the MBCA—one promulgated in 1969, another in 1984, and the current version, which is known as the third edition or Revised MBCA. Throughout this book, our primary statute will be the most recent version—the Revised MBCA—which we will simply call MBCA.

As a general matter, the trend in corporation statutes—reflected in the MBCA—is toward simplification and the elimination of formalities that have little substantive effect. In particular, modern law routinely permits the shareholders of a closely-held corporation to customize management procedures to their needs. *See* § 10.3. Modern statutes show a trend toward "enabling" rather than "regulating." This movement reflects the influence of the law and economics scholars, as discussed in § 2.4.

## § 2.9   CONSTITUTIONAL STATUS AND POLITICAL ACTIVITY OF CORPORATIONS

One topic of contemporary debate is the proper role of corporations in the political sphere. Some people, fearing that corporate money could swamp political discourse, assert that corporations should have no

First Amendment right of freedom of speech. This debate raises interesting questions: what is the constitutional status of corporations? And are corporations "persons" for various purposes?

Corporations are entitled to some constitutional protections but not others. It is clear, for example, that the Privileges and Immunities Clause, U.S. CONST. art. IV, § 2, does not apply to corporations. *Paul v. Virginia*, 75 U.S. 168, 177 (1869). Accordingly, a state is free to exclude a corporation from entering its territory. On the other hand, the Commerce Clause permits corporations to enter states to engage in interstate commerce. *International Textbook Co. v. Prigg*, 217 U.S. 91, 108–12 (1910).

In recent years, the Supreme Court has extended both the constitutional protection of corporations and their status as "persons" under the law. In *Citizens United v. Federal Election Commission*, 558 U.S. 310, 343 (2010), the Supreme Court held that corporations do have free-speech rights under the First Amendment. In that case, the Court struck down a federal ban on corporate "electioneering communications." The ban meant that corporations could not spend money to advocate the election or defeat of a candidate in a federal election.

Because *Citizens United* struck down a total ban on corporate spending for political advocacy, it may not affect state statutes that impose a cap on political contributions by corporations. New York law provides that corporations (other than those formed for political purposes) cannot contribute more than

$5000 per year to any candidate or political organization. N.Y. ELEC. LAW § 14–116.

In *Burwell v. Hobby Lobby Stores, Inc.*, 134 S. Ct. 2751, 2768, 2770 (2014), the Court held that a closely-held for-profit corporation could challenge federal regulations that required it to provide health-care coverage for certain contraceptives, in violation of the company's religious beliefs. (The company agreed to provide health-care coverage for a broad array of contraceptives, but objected to specific such drugs). The holding rested on statutory, and not on constitutional, grounds. Specifically, the Court held, a small, closely-held corporation is a "person" under the Religious Freedom Restoration Act of 1993 (RFRA) (signed by President Bill Clinton), and the contraceptive mandate burdened the company's exercise of religion. (The holding in *Hobby Lobby* is limited to small, closely-held corporations.)

One argument was that a corporation could not be a "person" under RFRA because the corporation exists only to "make money." The majority opinion rejected the argument as "fl[ying] in the face of modern corporate law," which recognizes that corporations need not "pursue profit at the expense of everything else." If, for example, corporations can pursue pro-environment policies, they ought to be able to "further religious objectives as well."

# CHAPTER 3
# FORMATION OF CORPORATIONS

## § 3.1  INTRODUCTION

In this Chapter we cover how one forms a *de jure* corporation—that is, a corporation recognized by law. Today, it is a very simple process, undertaken by an *incorporator*. For starters, she will need to choose the state in which to incorporate; this decision will determine the law that will govern the corporation's internal affairs (§ 3.2). A corporation formed in one state can do business in others—but it will have to satisfy the requirements for "foreign" corporations in each of those other states (§ 3.7). Though there is some variation from state to state, the basics of formation are similar, and consist of filing a document usually called articles of incorporation (§ 3.4) and taking various organizational acts (§ 3.5). If a corporation engages in activity beyond that stated in its articles, it acts *ultra vires*. Because corporations today generally may state that they will engage in all lawful business, however, this doctrine is of waning importance (§ 3.6).

## § 3.2  CHOOSING THE STATE OF INCORPORATION (AND APPLICATION OF THE INTERNAL AFFAIRS DOCTRINE)

Any corporation may be incorporated in any state. As we saw in § 2.7, most public corporations are formed in Delaware (even if they do little or no business in that state). As a practical matter, smaller corporations will rarely find it worthwhile to incorporate in Delaware. It will be more economical for them to incorporate in the state in which they will operate.

In the corporate world, "domestic" refers to the state in which the corporation is formed, and "foreign" refers to every other state. A corporation formed in New York is a "domestic" corporation in New York and is "foreign" in every other state. We will see in § 3.7 that a corporation can transact business in a state in which it is not incorporated; to do so, however, it must qualify to transact business as a "foreign" corporation.

The choice of state of incorporation determines the substantive law that will govern the business's internal affairs. Each state has adopted the "internal affairs doctrine," which means, for example, that Delaware law will govern the workings of a corporation formed in that state, even if the company does no business in that state.

The Supreme Court explained the policy for the doctrine by saying: "the internal affairs doctrine is a conflict of laws principle which recognizes that only one state should have the authority to regulate a corporation's internal affairs—matters peculiar to the relationships among or between the corporation and its current officers, directors, and shareholders—because otherwise a corporation could be faced with conflicting demands." *Edgar v. MITE Corp.*, 457 U.S. 624, 645 (1982).

The internal affairs doctrine does not encompass every intra-corporate dispute. In *Lidow v. Superior Court*, 206 Cal. App.4th 351, 355, 363–64 (2012), an officer of a Delaware corporation (the headquarters of which was in California) was forced out of his position, allegedly in retaliation for his complaints about possible illegal or harmful activities by the general counsel and others. Under Delaware law, his removal was not actionable. Under California law, however, it was. The California Court of Appeal concluded that though removing an officer ordinarily would be considered an "internal affair," the internal affairs doctrine did not apply. California law is very protective of employees fired allegedly in violation of "public policy" (such as complaining about harmful behavior). Because "claims for wrongful termination in violation of public policy serve vital interests" of California, Delaware law did not apply.

In § 3.7, we will discuss California's legislative effort to avoid the internal affairs doctrine.

### § 3.3  MECHANICS OF FORMATION—OVERVIEW

The mechanics of creating a corporation vary somewhat from state to state. What we discuss here will be a general overview. Every state requires that a document be delivered to the appropriate state official (usually the secretary of state) for filing, and every state imposes a filing fee. Depending on the state, the document may be called the "articles of incorporation," or "articles of organization" (Texas), or "certificate of incorporation" (Delaware and New

York), or the "charter" (Maryland). The most commonly used name is "articles of incorporation," or just the "articles." Every state also requires the corporation to appoint a registered agent (sometimes called statutory agent), who may receive service of process for the company. (In New York, this required agent is the Secretary of State; in most states, it is any person or entity designated by the incorporators.)

An "incorporator" has an easy job; she must execute the articles and will undertake to deliver that document to the appropriate state office for filing. Historically, the law required that three incorporators execute the articles. Today, states require only one. Historically, states imposed residency requirements for incorporators. Today, most states permit anyone of legal age to act as an incorporator, regardless of residence. Most states permit entities (such as a corporation) to serve as an incorporator, though some states (including New York) do not.

The articles may be delivered to the appropriate state official in a variety of ways: by mail, overnight delivery service, courier, facsimile, or, increasingly, by electronic delivery. The document is time-stamped when it arrives at the office. If the articles are approved, corporate existence relates back to the time the document was received. *See, e.g.*, MBCA § 1.23; Del. § 103(c)(3).

A staff member in the office of the state official reviews the articles. If the document fails to meet the statutory requirements, the officer refuses to file them. If the document meets the statutory requirements (and the filing fee is paid), the officer accepts the articles for filing. At that point, the *de jure* corporation is formed. This is true even if there were errors in the articles. In other words, acceptance for filing by the secretary of state's office is conclusive proof of valid formation (except in an action by the state to dissolve the corporation). *See* MBCA § 2.03(b).

After acceptance for filing, the incorporator, depending on the state, may call the first meeting of directors; or, if the initial directors are not named in the articles, may complete the organization of the corporation. *See* § 3.5.

Some states impose additional requirements before acceptance of the articles. Some (including Arizona and Maryland) require evidence that the registered agent has agreed to serve as such. In some states (including Georgia), there must be publication in a local newspaper of the intent to form a corporation. Historically, states required recording in every county in which the corporation would transact business, but this (wasteful) requirement is on the wane. Also, historically, nearly all states required that a minimum of capital investment (usually $1,000) be paid into the corporation before it could do business. This requirement has largely disappeared.

## § 3.4  ARTICLES OF INCORPORATION

A.  <u>*Mandatory Provisions.*</u>  Every state distinguishes between information that *must* be included in the articles and that which *may* be included. The strong trend is to require very little information in the articles. The sparest mandatory provisions are found in MBCA § 2.02(a), which requires only four items:

- The articles must give the corporate name, which must satisfy the requirements of MBCA § 4.01. That statute requires that the name not be misleading about what business the corporation will engage in (for instance, should not say "bank" if it will not be engaged in banking). It also requires that the corporate name contain one of the recognized "magic words" or an abbreviation thereof. The MBCA allows only four such words: company, corporation, incorporated, or limited. Delaware is more creative, saying that the name must include one of 12 listed words (or their abbreviation) "or words . . . of like import." Del. § 102(a)(1). The point is simple—there must be a prescribed word in the corporate name that shows the world that this is a corporation (and, therefore, that the proprietors have limited liability).

- The articles must state the number of shares the corporation will be authorized to issue. *See* § 12.3.

- The articles must give the street address of the registered office and name of the initial registered agent. Thus there will always be someone available at a specific place (during business hours) who can receive legal notices (including service of process and tax documents) on behalf of the corporation. The registered office may be an actual business office, but need not be. In fact, if the corporation does not do business in the state (this happens a lot with Delaware corporations), corporation service companies provide registered offices and registered agents for a fee. The corporation must inform the secretary of state of any change in the registered agent or registered office address.

- The articles must set forth the name and address of each incorporator.

It turns out that *every* state requires these four items. The MBCA, unlike many states, requires nothing else! Regarding corporate name, for example, many states require that it not be "deceptively similar" to the name of another business authorized to act in the state. The secretary of state usually maintains a list of corporate names, available online. Because corporate names are handled on a first-come, first-served basis, many states permit the reservation of a proposed corporate name for a limited time for a nominal fee.

A corporation may do business under an assumed name, so long as it does not engage in unfair competition by using a name confusingly similar with that of another business. Many states have "assumed name statutes," under which a business may operate under a name other than its "official" name. These statutes generally require the business to file a statement disclosing who is actually conducting the business. So ABC Corp. may do business as XYZ

Corp. upon complying with such an assumed name statute.

Regarding stock, in addition to the statement of authorized stock, many states require details about different classes of stock, including the characteristic of each class and the number of shares of each. *See* § 13.4.

Some states require a statement of *corporate duration*. In such states, this usually consists of a single phrase: that the business will have perpetual existence. One of the advantages of the corporate form is continuity of existence; the corporation exists until dissolved or combined with another entity. The MBCA *presumes* perpetual existence, and thus does not require a statement of duration. The articles may provide for a term of years or other lesser term.

Many states also require a statement of *purpose*. In the nineteenth century, articles had to state the specific purposes for which the corporation was formed. In a few states, corporations could only list one purpose. These requirements reflected the mistrust with which the corporation was seen; permission to do business was given grudgingly and only for a limited purpose. If the corporation acted beyond the stated purpose, it acted *ultra vires*, which is discussed in § 3.6.

Today, in almost all states, the articles can provide a general statement of purpose such as: "this corporation may engage in all lawful business." The MBCA requires no statement of purpose because it presumes that the corporation can engage in all lawful business. If the parties wish to limit the business to specific activities, they may do so in the articles. A few states appear not to allow a general statement of purpose. In Arizona, the articles must include "a brief statement of the character of the business that the corporation initially intends to actually conduct in this state." Az. Rev. Stats. § 10–202(A)(3).

B.    *Permissive Provisions.* Lawyers should discuss with their clients whether and how the articles should address other topics. One possibility is whether to name the initial directors in the articles (as opposed to having the incorporators elect them after the company is formed). Another is cumulative voting, which helps smaller shareholders gain some representation on the board. *See* § 6.5. In some states, cumulative voting exists unless the articles take it away. In others, as reflected by MBCA § 7.28(a), cumulative voting exists only if the articles provide for it.

Another topic for discussion between lawyer and client is pre-emptive rights, which allow an existing shareholder to maintain her percentage of ownership by buying new stock when the corporation issues stock. *See* § 12.4. This right is relevant only in close corporations. In some states, pre-emptive rights exist in such corporations unless the articles take them away. In other states, as reflected by § 6.30(a) of the MBCA, pre-emptive rights exist only if the articles say so.

The vast majority of states permit the articles to limit director liability to the corporation or its shareholders for damages in certain circumstances; essentially, these exculpation statutes will apply only to breaches of the "duty of care." We will discuss this duty in § 9.3 and these statutes in § 9.10.

In addition, statutes allow the articles to change quorum and voting requirements for directors and shareholders. For example, MBCA § 7.25(a) provides that a quorum for shareholder meetings will be a majority of the shares entitled and § 7.25(c) provides that the general rule for shareholder voting requires a majority of the votes actually cast on the matter. Both of these can be changed, however, in the articles—to make it easier or harder to establish a quorum or to approve an action. The articles may also provide for staggered terms for directors. See § 7.3.

In the close corporation, counsel and client should discuss the management model to be adopted. Such a business might choose to vest management power in a board of directors (the traditional model) or may elect in the articles to provide for management by shareholders or by others. See § 10.3.

Finally, every statute lists "powers" that every corporation automatically has. (One, which we saw in § 2.5, is to make charitable contributions.) This list of powers should be distinguished from the statement of corporate *purpose*, which we saw in subpart A of this section. A corporation formed for a narrow purpose will have broad powers to effect that purpose. These powers need not be stated in the articles; the corporation has them automatically, simply by being formed in that state. MBCA § 3.02 is typical, and includes the power to sue and be sued, to buy and sell property, to convey and mortgage its property, to serve as a partner in a partnership, and to invest its funds, among many others.

## § 3.5  COMPLETING THE FORMATION— MEETINGS, BYLAWS, ETC.

When the secretary of state's office accepts the articles for filing, a *de jure* corporation is formed. But it is not yet "up and running." There are additional steps for organizing the business. Typically the lawyer for the business takes care of these things. For example, she will obtain a corporate minute book and blank stock certificates, open the corporate bank account, and obtain taxpayer and employer identification numbers from the IRS and state agencies. Though a formal seal may not be required, most corporations use them. The seal is affixed to stock certificates, bonds, evidences of indebtedness, corporate conveyances of land, certified excerpts from minutes of meetings, and important contracts. It serves the useful function of delineating corporate from individual transactions.

The lawyer can also help with calling the *organizational meeting*. If the initial directors were named in the articles, they will hold the organizational meeting. If the initial directors were not named in the articles, the incorporators will hold the organizational meeting. *See* § 3.5. Either way, in lieu of an actual meeting, the acts may be taken by unanimous written consent. (This is handy when there is only one director or one incorporator in the corporation; the formality of a meeting of one person is rather silly.)

Under MBCA § 2.05(a)(1), if the meeting is held by directors, that body will "complete the organization of the corporation." This focuses on two things: adopting bylaws and appointing officers. The board may conduct other appropriate business there as well, such as approve the issuance of stock, and approve payment of the costs of incorporation. Under MBCA § 2.05(a)(2), if the incorporators hold the organizational meeting, they will elect the initial directors. Then there is a choice: either the incorporators then "complete the organization of the corporation" by adopting bylaws and appointing officers or they let the board of directors do those things.

Articles and bylaws are quite different. The articles are filed with the state; it is a public document. The articles form the corporation. In contrast, the bylaws are internal, and are not filed with the state. They are not available to the public. While amending the articles is a fundamental corporate change, which requires approval by the board of directors and the shareholders (*see* § 16.4), amending the bylaws is much easier (*see* § 5.3).

The articles generally contain only very basic information about the business. The bylaws, on the other hand, are more detailed. They comprise what amounts to an operating manual of basic rules for ordinary transactions, sufficiently complete to be relied upon by the directors and officers as a checklist in administering the business affairs. For example, they might lay out the responsibilities of various officers and their authority to bind the corporation. They will routinely set the record dates for meetings and prescribe methods for giving notice of meetings.

Importantly, the board of directors and the shareholders act *as groups*. Individual directors and individual shareholders have no power to take any corporate act. Consequently, the corporate law model calls for these groups to take action at meetings, and set out detailed requirements about notice, quorum and voting. *See* §§ 7.5 (directors) & 6.4 (shareholders). And there must be a record of the acts taken, kept in the minutes book. The lawyer for the business must ride herd on the managers of the corporation to ensure that they do things "by the book."

As a practical matter, the lawyer prepares not only the articles of incorporation and bylaws, but also the minutes or written consents needed to complete the formation of the corporation. These documents are usually prepared in advance of the actual formation. The minutes then can serve as a script for the meeting. In lieu of a meeting, action can be taken by unanimous written consent of the body. Such consents, signed by each (e-mail is increasingly accepted), should be filed in the corporate records.

## § 3.6  ULTRA VIRES

An act is *ultra vires* (literally meaning "beyond the powers") if it is beyond the authority of the corporation—specifically, beyond the corporate purposes state in the articles of incorporation.

Conversely, an act is *intra vires* if it is within the authority of the corporation. Ultra vires acts were a significant problem when statutes required the articles to set forth specific purposes for which the business was formed. Any act beyond the stated purposes was *ultra vires*. Today, there is less of a problem, because most states permit a general statement of corporate purpose; there is no need to list specific business activities. Indeed, in many states, there is a presumption that the corporation can undertake all lawful activity. *See* § 3.4.

Still, this modern view is not universal. A few states require specific statements of initial purpose. The corporation may undertake additional activities, but they may be *ultra vires*. Even in states that do allow a general statement of purpose, there may be businesses in which some of the proprietors think it a good idea to restrict what activities can be pursued. Whenever a corporation acts beyond its stated purpose, it should amend its articles to ensure those activities are intra vires.

Suppose the articles say the corporation will engage in oil and gas exploration, and then the company starts operating organic-food restaurants. The restaurant activity is *ultra vires*. Now assume the corporation enters contracts in the restaurant business. Are those contracts enforceable?

The early common law would say no. It treated *ultra vires* contracts as void. Over time, the common law moderated, and came to consider *ultra vires* acts as voidable, not void. So, under some circumstances, the contract might be enforceable. Today, the issue is addressed by statute. MBCA § 3.04(a) reflects what is likely the universal view: *ultra vires* contracts are valid. So, in our hypo, the contracts entered in pursuance of the organic-food restaurant business are enforceable.

There are two caveats, though. First, a shareholder may sue to enjoin the *ultra vires* activity. So, if a shareholder hears about the proposed *ultra vires* act before it happens, she may try to stop it by getting an injunction against the corporation. Second, if the company undertakes the *ultra vires* activity and loses money, the managers who caused the company to take the act are liable to the corporation for losses sustained. Thus, if the oil and gas company goes into the organic-food restaurant business and loses money, the responsible managers are liable to the corporation for those losses. This is an exception to the general presumption that individuals are not liable for business debts. *See* § 1.2.

We saw at the end of § 3.4 that modern statutes list "powers" that each corporation has, simply by virtue of being formed in a particular state. MBCA § 3.02. Because the corporation has a statutory right to undertake these things, they cannot be *ultra vires*. One abiding question has been whether a corporation can make a loan to one of its own directors or officers. Most modern statutes permit it if the board concludes that the loan is reasonably expected to benefit the corporation. *See* § 9.7, subpart E.

## § 3.7   FOREIGN CORPORATIONS

A corporation formed in one state may operate in another state only if it qualifies to do business there as a "foreign corporation." (Remember from § 3.2 that "foreign" refers to a state other than the one in which the business is incorporated.) So a Delaware corporation can do business in any other state, but must qualify to transact business there. Statutes vary from state to state, but there are general characteristics.

Usually, a foreign corporation is required to qualify only if it is "transacting business" in the state. Under the commerce clause of the Constitution, states can only require qualification from foreign corporations engaged in *intrastate* activities. States have no authority to exclude corporations engaged in *interstate* business and therefore have no authority to force such companies to qualify to do business within their borders. Intrastate business requires more activity in the state than interstate business. How do we draw that line? Most states have statutes that list activities that do *not* constitute intrastate business. MBCA § 15.01(b) provides that litigating, holding meetings, maintaining bank accounts, owning property, and selling through independent contractors in the state do not constitute "transacting business."

If the company is "transacting business," it should seek authority from the appropriate state agency. This usually requires getting what MBCA § 15.03 calls a "certificate of authority." To get this, the corporation must provide information similar to that required in its articles and must prove that it is in good standing in the state in which it is incorporated (for example, that it has paid its taxes and filed its annual reports; the secretary of state of the home state provides this certification). In addition, the foreign corporation usually must appoint a registered agent and have a registered office instate. It must also pay filing fees, file annual reports, and may be subject to state taxation. *See* MBCA §§ 15.01–15.05.

What happens if a foreign corporation transacts business without qualifying? Under the modern view, reflected in MBCA § 15.02(e), the failure to qualify does not affect the validity of corporate acts, so its contracts are valid. But in most states, the foreign corporation will be subject to a civil penalty, and is barred from asserting a claim instate until it qualifies and pays the penalty and fees. MBCA § 15.02(a), (d).

As we saw in § 3.2, the internal affairs doctrine provides that the internal relationships of a corporation are governed by the law of the state of incorporation. Thus, if a Delaware corporation qualifies to do business in California, and is sued there, the California court will apply Delaware law on issues of internal affairs.

Or will it? (We've seen this issue before in California, at § 3.2). Section 2115 of the California Corporation Code provides that the articles of foreign corporations are deemed amended to comply with California law if, *inter alia*, more than half the company's stock is held by California residents and if at least half of its business is done in the Golden

State. In *Wilson v. Louisiana-Pacific Resources, Inc.*, 138 Cal.App.3d 216, 229–32 (Cal.App.1982), the California Court of Appeal used this provision to override the internal affairs rule and require a Utah corporation to provide cumulative voting to all shareholders (even non-Californians).

In *VantagePoint Venture Partners 1996 v. Examen, Inc.*, 871 A.2d 1108, 1109–10, 1113 (Del.2005), the Delaware Supreme Court refused to apply the California statute. In that case, California law would have permitted stockholders to block a proposed merger, but Delaware law would not. The Delaware court applied the internal affairs doctrine and thus held that Delaware law governed. The court concluded that the internal affairs doctrine is more than a choice-of-law rule. It is rooted in constitutional guarantees of due process, because officers, directors, and shareholders have a "significant right . . . to know what law will be applied to their actions." Moreover, the court concluded, the commerce clause of the Constitution forbade California from applying its law to the internal affairs of a Delaware corporation.

# CHAPTER 4

# PRE-INCORPORATION TRANSACTIONS AND PROBLEMS OF DEFECTIVE INCORPORATION

## § 4.1  INTRODUCTION

In Chapter 3, we saw how a *de jure* corporation is formed. In a perfect world, proprietors would form a corporation on Monday and have the corporation commence business on Tuesday. In the real world, however, things are often not that smooth. People (called "promoters," *see* § 4.2) often take steps on behalf of the business before the corporation is formed. This chapter deals with the legal problems raised by such efforts. Sometimes the efforts are undertaken when everyone knows that no corporation has been formed. Examples are when a promoter gets a third party to offer to buy stock after the corporation is formed (*see* § 4.3), or enters an agreement to form a corporation (*see* § 4.4), or enters a pre-incorporation contract (*see* § 4.5), or enters a deal with the corporation itself (*see* § 4.6). Other times, however, the third parties to a transaction are *not* aware that there is no *de jure* corporation. These cases of "defective incorporation" make proprietors nervous because they may be open to personal liability as partners. The doctrines of *de facto* corporation and corporation by estoppel have permitted such proprietors to escape liability in some circumstances (*see* §§ 4.7 & 4.8).

## § 4.2 PROMOTERS

A promoter is someone who takes the initiative in developing and organizing a new business venture. Promoters are often imaginative entrepreneurs who take an idea and create a profitable business to capitalize on it. The role of a promoter is different from the role of an incorporator, who, as we saw in § 3.3, executes the document that forms the corporation. The promoter's role is broader: she is responsible for assuring that the corporation is an economic success. (Remember throughout the materials that one person can play multiple roles, so a promoter may also be an incorporator (*see* § 3.3) and may, after the company is formed, be a shareholder, officer, and director. It is important for us to understand the different *roles* of each position.)

A promoter usually focuses on two things. First, she arranges procurement of the start-up capital. She may invest her own money, obtain money from family members, get a bank loan, or arrange for outside investors. With outside investors, the promoter will negotiate to determine their stake in the corporation and arrange either by contract or subscription to ensure that the capital will be forthcoming when needed. Second, the promoter must set things up so the corporation can "hit the ground running" once it is formed. This means she arranges for office space, personnel, supplies, and other things necessary for the business to function.

If the promoter does these things after the corporation is formed, the contracts (for example, to lease office space or buy supplies) should be entered into by the corporation itself. The promoter will not be a party to such contracts and will not risk being liable for them. Sometimes, though, the promoter will jump the gun and enter into a contract before the corporation is formed. For example, a great lease is available, but will be lost if the promoter waits for formation to be completed. When she enters a contract on behalf of the entity not-yet-formed, it is a *pre-incorporation contract,* which raises interesting questions of liability.

## § 4.3  PRE-INCORPORATION CONTRACTS

- Patti, a promoter for XYZ Corp., finds a perfect office location for the business, available to lease from Third Party (TP), at a great price. If she doesn't act quickly, though, the price will go up. On April 7, she signs the lease "Patti." On April 10, XYZ Corp. is formed.

Patti is a party to the lease, and is liable on it. If the corporation is never formed, she will remain liable for the lease payments. If the corporation is formed, Patti will remain liable for payments on the lease until there is a *novation*: an agreement among TP, the corporation, and Patti that the corporation will replace Patti under the contract.

Mere formation of the corporation does not make the entity liable on the deal. The corporation is liable only if it *adopts* the lease. Even then, Patti remains liable on the lease until novation. In other words, the corporation's adoption of the contract will not relieve Patti of liability; only a novation will do that.

- Same facts, but Patti signs the lease "XYZ Corp., a corporation not yet formed."

Here, the lack of a corporate entity is clear. Whether Patti is liable on the lease is determined by the intent of the parties. Good lawyers will avoid litigation by stating the intention clearly in the lease. For example, the lease could say that TP may enforce the contract only against the corporation after it is formed. If the lease is silent on intention, courts generally will hold Patti liable as a party to the contract, especially if the corporation is never formed. Some cases go the other way, however, so the result is not always clear.

Assume Patti is liable on the contract. Now the corporation is formed. As noted, its formation does not make it liable. The result is dictated by agency law. Patti acted as agent for a principal (the corporation) that did not exist at the time she entered the deal. The corporation becomes liable only if it adopts the contract.

It may adopt the contract *expressly* (by an act of the board of directors) or *impliedly*. Implied adoption arises from the corporation's conduct. For example, if the company is formed and moves its operation into the leased office space, it has accepted a benefit of the contract and has thereby adopted it. (Technically, though the corporation can adopt the contract, it cannot *ratify* the deal. Ratification (*see* § 1.9) applies only if the party ratifying the act existed when the original deal was made; the corporation did not.)

- Same facts but Patti signs the lease "XYZ Corp.," without indicating that it has not yet been formed.

Absent clear statement of intention, most courts will treat this case the same as the preceding one. Patti acted for a non-existent principal, and thus is liable on the contract regardless of whether the corporation is formed. If formed, the corporation will be liable only if it adopts the contract. Even if it adopts the contract, Patti is still liable on it until there is a novation.

## § 4.4  SUBSCRIPTIONS FOR STOCK

A subscription is an offer to buy stock from the corporation. Promoters use subscriptions to raise capital for the business. The subscriber agrees to buy a particular number of shares at a set consideration.

One legal issue is whether the subscriber may revoke her offer. The rules depend upon when the offer was made. If the offer is made after the corporation was formed, the subscriber may revoke the subscription anytime before the corporation accepts it. Once the corporation accepts the subscription, the parties have entered a "subscription agreement." *See* MBCA § 6.20(e). Then, the subscriber is required to pay the subscription price and the corporation is required to sell to the subscriber.

On the other hand, what happens if the offer was made before the corporation was formed? Such "pre-incorporation subscriptions" are common; they permit the founders of a new venture to ensure that there will be adequate capitalization once the business is incorporated. By statute, pre-incorporation subscriptions are irrevocable for a set period, usually six months. *See* MBCA 6.20(a). This rule allows the proprietors to rely on the subscribers to provide capital for the new corporation.

These statutes give a default rule. Thus, the subscriber and the proprietors can agree that a pre-incorporation offer will be revocable for a different period, or even that it will be freely revocable. And, under the statutes, even an irrevocable subscription can be revoked if all the other subscribers agree to allow revocation.

After the corporation is formed, its board of directors will call upon the subscribers to pay for the stock and, after payment, it will issue the stock. Generally, calls for payment must be uniform among subscribers to a class of stock. *See, e.g.*, MBCA § 6.20(b). So if there were two subscribers to a class of stock, the board could not decide to sell to one and not to the other. A subscriber does not become a shareholder until she pays the stock.

Subscriptions are used in small, closely-held corporations. Publicly-traded corporations would find it impracticable to use them because the subscriptions themselves constitute securities under federal and state securities acts and must be "registered." Because the underlying securities themselves also must be registered, the use of subscriptions would result double the considerable expense of registration (*see* § 11.2).

## § 4.5  AGREEMENT TO FORM
## A CORPORATION

An agreement to form a corporation (sometimes called a "pre-incorporation agreement") is a contract among proposed shareholders to incorporate a business. The contribution of each participant and the number of shares each is to receive are specified in this contract. Because it is a contract among the proprietors (and not between the proprietors and an entity (because no entity has yet been formed)), it is enforceable as any other contract.

Pre-incorporation agreements may be simple, reciting only the main points of agreement, or they may be quite formal, setting forth all aspects of the agreement, including understandings as to employment, capitalization, voting power, and membership of the initial board of directors. Such an agreement may include as exhibits copies of proposed articles and bylaws. Pre-incorporation agreements frequently impose restrictions upon the subsequent transfer of shares. *See* § 6.8.

One potential question is whether the terms of the pre-incorporation agreement survive the formation of the corporation. Parties to an agreement to form a corporation are joint venturers. The object of their venture is to establish the business as a corporation. Once the entity is formed, perhaps the joint venture ends. The question is one of the parties' intent. If they desire that some provisions of their contract survive the creation of the corporation, they should make this clear.

## § 4.6  THE SECRET PROFIT RULE

In § 4.3, we saw contracts between a promoter and a third party. In this section, we deal with a contract between a promoter and the corporation itself. Specifically, the corporation has been formed and now a promoter sells something to it. We are nervous that the promoter might get a sweetheart deal because she had served as a promoter. Courts in such cases often use overly broad language about "fiduciary duty" and "promoter's fraud."

Some (not all) states follow the "Massachusetts rule" and find that the promoter has a "fiduciary duty" here. *Old Dominion Copper Mining & Smelting Co. v. Bigelow*, 89 N.E. 193, 201 (Mass. 1909). The duty, however, is rather limited. It boils down to this: a promoter may not make a secret profit on her dealings with the corporation. It is usually called the "secret profit rule." (Thus this is not one of the broad fiduciary duties of the type we discuss in Chapter 9.)

- Pam is a promoter for XYZ Corp. After XYZ Corp. is formed, she sells land to the corporation. Pam makes a profit of $8,000 on the sale of the land. If Pam did not disclose this profit when the transaction was approved by the corporation, the $8,000 can be disgorged under the secret profit rule. The corporation will recover that profit. But if Pam did disclose to the corporation that she would make a profit of $8,000 on the transaction, there is no liability.

Thus, even where the rule applies, it does not say that a promoter cannot make a profit on her dealings with the corporation. It merely says that she cannot make a *secret* profit on those dealings.

## § 4.7 DEFECTIVE INCORPORATION—
## *DE FACTO* CORPORATION

Here and in the next section we deal with transactions that take place while the parties are under the mistaken belief that a *de jure* corporation existed. Without a *de jure* corporation, the proprietors will be nervous. Why? Because they are operating a partnership, and all partners are liable for partnership debts. *See* § 1.4. The doctrines of *de facto* corporation (here) and corporation by estoppel (*see* § 4.8) allow the proprietors to avoid personal liability. It bears emphasis at the outset that these are equitable doctrines and are only available to those who were unaware of the failure to form a *de jure* corporation.

- Louise and Leslie execute all the papers required to form a corporation. Their lawyer assures them that she will file the documents and pay the required fee on May 10, and that they may start doing business as a corporation the next day. On May 12, believing that the corporation had been formed, Louise, as president of the corporation, enters a contract ordering $5,000 worth of supplies from Third Party (TP). It turns out that Louise and Leslie's lawyer never filed the papers to form the corporation. Are Louise and Leslie liable on the contract with TP?

Because there is no *de jure* corporation, Louise and Leslie are acting as partners in a partnership. As such, they are personally liable on the contract. But under the *de facto* corporation doctrine, they may escape liability. This common law doctrine provides that a court may treat the situation as though there was a corporation. Doing so saves the proprietors from personal liability. To invoke the doctrine, Louise and Leslie must show three things.

First there must be a statute under which incorporation was permitted. This is not a problem, because every state has a general incorporation law.

Second, Louise and Leslie must have made a good faith, colorable attempt to comply with that statute. This means that they came very close to complying with the requirements for forming a *de jure* corporation, and are unaware of their failure to comply. This is clearly true here: they did everything required to form the corporation, had a right to rely on the lawyer to get the documents filed, and had no reason to know of the lawyer's failure.

Third, they must "use the corporate privilege" in the meantime. This means that the proprietors are acting as though a corporation existed. This is met, because Louise entered the contract "as president."

*De facto* corporation is a broad doctrine—it is applied in contract and tort. Indeed, it can apply in any case except one brought by the state. The state could file a "quo warranto" action to demand "by what right" the proprietors purport to act in the name of a corporation. Outside of that, though, from the proprietors' standpoint, *de facto* is just as good as *de jure*.

Though the doctrine was well established in common law, legislation may abolish it. Most states provide, in substance, that corporate existence begins either upon the filing of the articles of incorporation or their acceptance by the state. *See, e.g.*, MBCA § 2.03(a). Most statutes add that acceptance of the articles by the state is "conclusive proof" that all conditions precedent to incorporation have been complied with except in suits brought by the State. *See, e.g.*, MBCA § 2.03(b).

These statutes arguably create a negative inference that the corporate existence has *not* begun before the articles are accepted for filing. If courts accept this inference, there would be personal liability for all pre-incorporation transactions. In other words, it is arguable that modern statutes have abolished the concept of *de facto* corporation. On the other hand, MBCA § 2.04 provides that "all persons purporting to act as or on behalf of a corporation, *knowing there was no incorporation under this Act*, are jointly and severally liable for all liabilities created while so acting" (emphasis added). This provision seems consistent with the *de facto* corporation doctrine, which required, *inter alia*, that the persons relying upon it be unaware of the failure to form a *de jure* corporation.

The uncertainty is exacerbated by the fact that in many states there is no definitive case law on whether *de facto* corporation survives the negative inference in the legislation. Today, then, states are all over the lot: in some states *de facto* corporation has been abolished, in others it has been recognized, and in many (perhaps most), the status is not clear.

## § 4.8  CORPORATION BY ESTOPPEL

Corporation by estoppel, like *de facto* corporation (*see* § 4.7), was created by courts, is relevant when there is no *de jure* corporation, and is available only for those who act in the good faith belief that a corporation had been formed. Further, like *de facto* corporation, it will allow proprietors to avoid personal liability. Corporation by estoppel is narrower than *de facto* corporation, however, in that it generally applies only in contract (not tort) cases.

- Third party (TP) enters a contract with what she believes to be a *de jure* corporation. The proprietors also think they are operating a *de jure* corporation. The business then fails to pay TP. TP investigates and finds that there never was a *de jure* corporation. Are the proprietors of the business personally liable on the contract?

Because there is no *de jure* corporation, the proprietors are operating a partnership (*see* § 1.4). As partners, they are personally liable for the business debts. Under corporation by estoppel, however, TP may be "estopped" from denying that the business was a corporation. That means that TP cannot seek to impose personal liability on the proprietors, but must satisfy her claim from the assets of the business. The idea is that, in entering the deal, TP relied on the existence of a corporation and, presumably, its assets. To allow her to recover from the personal assets of the proprietors would give TP a windfall. The doctrine thus puts a burden on TP: before entering the contract, she could have insisted on looking at the business's financial records. If it had no assets, TP could have insisted that the proprietors provide personal guarantees for payment as a condition to the contract. Having done none of this, TP should be limited to recovering only from business assets.

Where the doctrine is recognized, it may also work the other way around to "estop" the business from denying its own lack of valid formation. Suppose a "corporation" enters a contract with TP. The proprietors then discover that the corporation had not been formed. Then they form a *de jure* corporation to operate the business. If TP sues the corporation, it should not be able to avoid liability to TP by claiming that the "deal" was with a non-existent entity. *See, e.g., Southern-Gulf Marine Co. No. 9, Inc. v. Camcraft, Inc.*, 410 So.2d 1181, 1183–84 (La.App. 1982).

It is important to re-emphasize two points. First, corporation by estoppel applies in contract cases, because only in such cases can TP investigate the business's assets before entering the deal and, if necessary, demand a personal guarantee. Second, the doctrine only applies if the proprietors were acting in good faith, meaning that they were not aware of the failure to form a *de jure* corporation.

Corporation by estoppel is followed in some states and not in others. Section 2.04 of MBCA (quoted in § 4.7) is consistent with application of the doctrine.

*De facto* corporation and corporation by estoppel appear to be alternative theories. The first relates to the extent to which incorporators complied with the incorporation statute. The second relates to the extent to which plaintiffs have treated the business as a corporation. Professor McChesney has argued that the two doctrines are actually one. Fred McChesney, *Doctrinal Analysis and the Statistical Modeling in Law: The Case of Defective Incorporation*, 71 WASH.U.L.Q. 493, 530–31 (1993) ("[C]ourts will more likely accord defendants limited liability when they have tried to comply and plaintiffs have treated the firm as a corporation. * * * Evaluated by what they do, not by what they say, judges apply one unitary doctrine—that of defective incorporation. * * * The apparent confusion shown by many judges in distinguishing the two doctrines reflects the fact that they are really not two doctrines at all.").

# CHAPTER 5

# THE DISTRIBUTION OF POWERS IN A CORPORATION

## § 5.1 INTRODUCTION

We have formed a corporation. The question in this chapter is "who does what?" Corporation statutes embrace a traditional model of management and control, typically called the "statutory scheme" or "statutory norm." It envisions certain roles for shareholders (*see* § 5.3), the board of directors (*see* § 5.4), and officers (*see* § 5.5). In this chapter we discuss the basic roles of each of these groups, but will not exhaust our discussion of these groups. Chapter 6 will address shareholders, Chapter 7 directors, and Chapter 8 officers in considerably more detail. The point here is to set up the big picture.

Historically, corporation statutes have been "cookie-cutter" efforts that seem based on an assumption that every corporation has the same characteristics—that one size fits all. In the real world, though, corporations distribute authority quite differently. The main distinction is between "close" and "public" corporations. We will define these in § 5.6, and discuss the tension between the traditional model and how things work in the real world. This tension has led to legislative change, and statutes governing corporations in the twenty-first century recognize far greater flexibility than the traditional model. To appreciate these developments,

however, we first need to understand that traditional
model.

## § 5.2  THE TRADITIONAL
## "STATUTORY SCHEME"

There are three groups with responsibility in the
corporation: shareholders, the board of directors, and
officers. The first two can perform acts only as
groups. That is, individual shareholders have no
power to do anything on behalf of the corporation. So
whatever shareholders do on behalf of the business,
they do as a group. The same is true of directors.
Individual directors have no power to decide
anything for the corporation or to bind it to
agreements. Whatever directors do, they do as a
group, as a board. That is why there are rules in
every state's corporation law for determining
whether there is a quorum at meetings of these
groups and concerning what vote is required. We will
discuss these voting requirements in detail in the
later sections on shareholder voting (*see* § 6.4) and
director voting (*see* § 7.5). When a group (of
shareholders or directors) approves an act, it usually
does so by passing a "resolution."

By providing detailed rules for meetings, the
statutory model assumes there will be multiple
shareholders and directors. Requirements for a
quorum and majority vote and for advance notice of
meetings only make sense if there are multiple
decision-makers in the group. In reality, however,
there are many corporations with one shareholder
and one director. As we will see, there are ways to

adapt the traditional model in small, closely-held corporations.

Officers, in contrast, do not operate in groups. Individual officers—like the president, secretary, and treasurer—are agents of the corporation. Agency law (*see* § 1.9) governs the relationship between the principal (the corporation) and the agent (the officer). As agents, officers may have authority to bind the corporation to contracts or to speak for the corporation in various ways.

The traditional model envisions shareholders as the owners of the corporation. They elect (and can remove) the members of the board of directors. The board of directors "manages" the corporation; it makes the business decisions. The board hires and fires and monitors the officers, who carry out the board's directions.

One person can wear more than one hat at a time. Thus, one person might be a shareholder, a director, and an officer at the same time. Do not confuse her roles. When she acts as a director, apply the rules applicable to directors; the rules applicable to shareholders are irrelevant at that point. When she acts as a shareholder, apply those rules. In other words, the fact that the traditional model envisions three distinct groups of actors does not mean they are necessarily different human beings.

## § 5.3  ROLE OF SHAREHOLDERS

The shareholders in the traditional statutory scheme are the owners of the corporation, but have limited power to participate in management and control. One of the advantages of the corporation is separation of ownership from control. Those who own the business need not be burdened with management responsibilities; they can be passive investors. The model contemplates that shareholders have decision-making authority only in discrete areas.

A. _Electing    and    Removing    Directors._ Shareholders elect directors and can remove them before their terms expire. So though shareholders do not make management decisions, they hire those who (in theory) do. At common law, a director could be removed only "for cause," and only after a complicated procedure known as "amotion." This protection of directors was consistent with the principle that directors are hired to be independent and that shareholders should not interfere with the directors' discretionary business judgments.

Today, every state allows shareholders to remove directors for cause, and most states allow removal without cause. Typical of the modern view is MBCA § 8.08(a), which provides that "[t]he shareholders may remove one or more directors with or without cause unless the articles . . . provide that directors may be removed only for cause." Some states (including New York) permit removal without cause only if the articles (which New York calls the "certificate") allows.

Modern statutes permitting removal without cause fundamentally change the historic relation between shareholders and directors. It is now possible to remove a director either for policy or personal reasons. This can be important when one has recently acquired a majority of the outstanding shares (or at least working control) and desires to put "her own people" in control. To avoid such threats, some corporations provide in their articles that directors can be removed only for cause. This obviously enhances directors' job security, and makes it difficult for new ownership to obtain immediate control over the board.

B. *Amending Bylaws.* Shareholders usually have a role in amending the bylaws. In most states, the initial bylaws are adopted by the directors or incorporators, whichever group completes the organization of the corporation (*see* § 3.5). Thereafter, states vary on who has the power to amend or repeal bylaws. In some states the shareholders have the authority, and in some states the board does. Often, state law permits either group to change the bylaws. In some of these states, the board may not repeal or amend bylaws that were adopted by the shareholders; in others, the shareholders may designate bylaws that may not be amended by the board. MBCA § 10.20(a) provides that the shareholders have the power to amend or repeal bylaws, and § 10.20(b) provides that the board also has that authority, subject to specified exceptions.

C. *Approving Fundamental Corporate Changes.* Shareholders generally must approve certain fundamental changes to the corporation. These changes—including amendment of the articles, mergers, disposition of substantially all corporate assets, and voluntary dissolution—are so important that the board cannot do them alone. Note that the shareholders' role here is reactive. In other words, the shareholders only get a voice because the board asks them to approve a fundamental change that the board has already approved. We will discuss fundamental changes in Chapter 16.

D.    *Approval of Other Matters.* Occasionally, shareholders are requested to approve various other matters. A good example is the interested director transaction—that is, a deal between the corporation and one of its directors (or some other business owned by that director). Such transactions may be approved by the shareholders (*see* § 9.7). In some states, shareholders must approve various less substantial transactions, such as distributions from of capital surplus or a loan of corporate assets to a director. The modern trend is to reduce the number of things that require shareholder approval.

Independent of statute, shareholders may make recommendations to the board on various corporate matters. Though these resolutions have no legal effect, they express the views of the owners and may be influential. In *Auer v. Dressel*, 118 N.E.2d 590, 597–98 (N.Y. 1954), the court held it proper for shareholders to adopt a resolution that approved of the administration of an ousted president and demanded his reinstatement. The court said there was "nothing invalid in their so expressing themselves and thus putting on notice the directors who will stand for election at the annual meeting."

E.    *Other Shareholder Powers.* What we have listed so far are shareholders' powers over decision-making in the corporation. Shareholders have other statutory powers that do not relate directly to decision-making. Two of their powers are especially significant, and will be discussed in later chapters: the right to inspect books and records of the corporation (*see* § 6.9) and the right to bring "derivative suits" (which are brought to vindicate a right that belongs to the corporation). Because managers owe fiduciary duties to the corporation, any breach of those duties potentially could be the basis of a derivative suit. We will discuss the shareholders' power to bring this type of litigation in Chapter 15.

## § 5.4  ROLE OF BOARD OF DIRECTORS

Over the past generation, statutory language concerning the role of the board of directors has changed. Traditionally, legislation required that the business and affairs "shall be managed" by the board. Now, statutes are broader, and provide that the business and affairs of the corporation "be exercised by *or under the direction, and subject to the oversight*" of the board. MBCA § 8.01(b) (emphasis added). *See also* Del. § 141(a) (business and affairs "shall be managed by or under the direction" of the board).

The italicized language recognizes the business reality that the board of directors in big companies does not really "manage" the day-to-day affairs. Its role is less management than oversight. Modern statutes authorize corporations to vest management authority in the executive officers, with the board monitoring them. In smaller businesses, the board usually formulates corporate policy and authorizes important contracts. Even here, the board may delegate details of the actual daily operation to officers and other agents. In a public corporation, most management decisions are delegated to corporate officers subject only to general oversight by the board of directors.

The power of directors flows from statute and is not delegated from the shareholders. As a result, directors may disregard the desires of shareholders and act as they think best. This freedom is always subject, however, to the shareholders' ultimate power to elect different directors at the next opportunity (or to remove directors without cause (*see* § 5.3)). Directors have specific statutory authority in several areas, such as issuance of stock, declaration of distributions, and initiation of fundamental corporate changes.

Responsibility accompanies power. The directors owe fiduciary duties of *care* and *loyalty* to the corporation. Chapter 9 addresses these duties. Violation of a duty not only constitutes cause for removal, but can open directors to civil liability. In addition, there are potential criminal sanctions for violating some laws, notably some federal securities provisions, such as Rule 10b–5, which we discuss in Chapter 14.

## § 5.5  ROLE OF OFFICERS

Statutes generally do not define the authority of officers. A typical statutory provision states that each officer "has the authority and shall perform the functions set forth in the bylaws or, to the extent consistent with the bylaws, the functions prescribed by the board of directors or by direction of an officer authorized by the board of directors to prescribe the duties of other officers." MBCA § 8.41. In theory, officers administer the day-to-day affairs of the corporation subject to the direction and control of the board. In fact, their authority is often considerably greater, at least in public corporations. Officers are not required to operate in groups, and are individual agents of the corporation (*see* § 5.2). Thus, agency law will govern the relationship between the principal (the corporation) and the agent (the officer) and determine whether the officers can bind the corporation to any act (*see* § 1.9).

## § 5.6  THE TRADITIONAL MODEL AND CLOSE AND PUBLIC CORPORATIONS

We said above that the corporation statutes are basically one-size-fits all. The model they embrace best fits the mid-sized corporation. In the real world, most corporations are not mid-sized. The overwhelming majority of corporations are close (or closely-held) companies. These have few shareholders and the stock is not publicly traded. Many close corporations are modest family businesses, but many have considerable assets and sizable economic clout. There are millions of close corporations in the United States. We discuss issues relating to close corporations in Chapter 10. These are juxtaposed with public corporations, which are corporations whose stock is registered for public trading. There are fewer than 20,000 such companies. We discuss issues relating to public corporations in Chapter 11. The present purpose is to sketch how these corporations actually operate, and how that operation differs from the traditional model.

The small close corporation resembles a partnership. Shareholders, like partners, usually anticipate that they will be employed by the business. Therefore, shareholders of close corporations often look to the business not only as an investment, but as a source of salary. In the partnership, proprietors are largely free to structure management as they see fit. They can appoint a managing partner and delegate authority to her. In contrast, the traditional corporation model imposes rigid requirements: the board of directors and shareholders must hold meetings, for which proper notice is mandated. This formality does not fit a corporation that has only a handful of participants. Yet, according to the model, failure to abide by formalities was dangerous, since it is a factor that may influence a court to "pierce the corporate veil" and hold shareholders liable for business debts (*see* § 10.4).

In Chapter 10, we will see that this tension led to change. Today, statutes permit flexibility to structure management in the close corporation. Indeed, it is possible to abolish the board of directors altogether and to provide for direct management by the shareholders or others. This would have been unthinkable a generation or so ago. The law has moved away from the rigidity of the traditional model to a more pragmatic approach, one that recognizes (within limits) that the businesspeople should be able to structure their relationship. It has moved from an emphasis on strict prescription to one of freedom of contract.

The public corporation also does not mesh perfectly with the traditional model. Modern boards of large companies are less about managing and more about overseeing. The actual management is done by officers who are professionally trained to manage. The officers receive the bulk of their compensation from services, and not from stock ownership. They are encouraged to own stock in the company, and may be given options to purchase stock, but typically own only a tiny fraction of the corporation's voting stock. The management structure is highly bureaucratic, with great discretion lodged in the folks at "the top."

At the top, a management team of officers actually directs the enterprise. They usually have responsibility for specific functional areas. Familiar examples are the chief financial officer (CFO), chief operations officer (COO), chief accounting officer (CAO), and chief legal officer (CLO or, more commonly, general counsel). At the apex of managerial control is the chief executive officer (CEO). She is responsible for the management team and ultimately for the success of the enterprise. If the CEO loses confidence in the CFO, she may fire the

CFO. In theory, the CEO has power to call the shots in the bureaucracy on narrow and broad issues. As a practical matter, though, the CEO cannot unilaterally run all details of the business operations. To be effective, she must delegate authority over operations, including personnel, financing, advertising, and production. The CEO generally concentrates on the broadest issues relating to the business.

"Inside" directors are those who serve on the board while also having their principal employment within the corporation, usually as an officer. "Affiliated outside directors" are those who, while not otherwise employed by the company, have a significant professional or family relationship with it. An example is the lawyer who is partner in a firm, but also retained by the corporation as principal outside counsel. Such people are the functional equivalents of inside directors. "Outside" or "independent" directors are not otherwise employed by or beholden to the corporation. Typical independent directors are present or retired CEOs of other public corporations, university presidents, former public officials, and independent investors.

Historically, the CEO had great influence over the board, which was dominated by inside directors. In many cases, the board provided a rubber stamp for the CEO. Those days are over. The clear trend in public corporations is toward independent directors. And in many corporations, these outside directors meet separately from the CEO and inside directors at least once a year to review the performance of management. In some corporations, the chair of the board of directors is an outside director and not the CEO—something that would have been unthinkable a generation ago. The move toward independence has had an undeniable impact. Starting in the 1990s, it became clear that underperforming CEOs' "heads can roll." More Fortune 500 CEOs have been fired in the past 20 years than at any other similar period. The 2015 firing of the McDonald's CEO was an example.

Modern boards in public companies are composed primarily of outside directors who are busy and successful people, often with their own businesses to run. So the typical board is a part-time board. It may meet six or eight times a year, for perhaps an average of three hours. Much of that time is devoted to routine matters dealing with the board's activities, discussion of financial results, and reports from committees. Director involvement is not limited to formal meetings. There may be communications to and among board members, informal discussions, and committee meetings. Nevertheless, no one can expect the board of a large public corporation to have hands-on involvement in corporate affairs. These boards do not "manage." The management team, led by the CEO, "manages." The board oversees and monitors.

In theory, shareholders elect directors at the annual meeting. Each director must be nominated and must receive the required vote. But the meeting is rarely a scene of political drama; the die is cast before the meeting. Why? Virtually all shareholders in publicly held corporations vote by proxy (*see* § 6.6). Only a handful actually attend shareholder meetings in person. The decision as to who is to be elected is not made by the vote taken at the shareholders' meeting; it is made earlier, when shareholders fill out proxy forms. These proxies are mailed in and tabulated, and the *result* is announced at the meeting. Shareholders voting by proxy generally cannot select from a list of candidates; proxy solicitations usually list only candidates selected by corporate management. The shareholder either votes for these candidates or withholds her vote. (It is possible for an outside group of shareholders to organize and solicit proxies in competition with management—a proxy fight, which is a form of hostile takeover (*see* § 11.5).)

In light of the nominal role that most shareholders play in managing the corporate enterprise, it is questionable whether small investors—those with 100 shares of Procter & Gamble, for example—should be viewed as the "owners" at all. They are passive investors with no real voice. If they are dissatisfied with the investment, they can sell the stock.

In the early 1930s, Professors Berle and Means, in a famous book called THE MODERN CORPORATION AND PRIVATE PROPERTY, noted that the fragmented ownership of public corporations ensures management of virtually dictatorial power. They were right, but there has been a revolutionary change in the pattern of ownership of public corporations in recent decades. Today, "institutional investors"—an unimportant group two generations ago—dominate transactions on stock markets. These include pension funds, banks, university endowments, and insurance companies. Millions of Americans do not think they are invested in the stock market. In fact, most Americans are invested in the stock market, because their pensions, insurance, or banks are invested in the market.

Institutional investors also include "investment companies," which are formed for the specific purpose of investing in other companies. They do not do so to gain control of those companies, but to make money by trading their securities. The commonest type is the *mutual fund,* which pools the assets of many investors into a common fund for investment. Mutual funds may be specialized—as in growth stocks, or income stocks, or stocks in a particular field, such precious metals or petroleum. Mutual fund managers are professionals and usually are compensated by a percentage of the investments. The manager usually diversifies by picking a "basket" of investments for each fund. Each day, the net asset value (NAV) of the fund is calculated per share. Shareholders can redeem their shares at will (the investment is thus "open ended") at the present NAV. Mutual funds provide great advantages for the small investor: they are liquid (can be converted into cash), diversified, and managed by a professional fund manager that most small investors could never afford to hire for individual advice.

A *hedge fund* is another pooled investment vehicle, but with a limited clientele, who are exempt from many regulations that govern investment funds.

Hedge funds invest in more diverse ways than mutual funds. Instead of the traditional long-term holdings in stocks, bonds, and cash, these go into a wide array of investments to "hedge" against the risks of traditional markets. Despite this, hedge funds are often quite volatile because they engage in investing that can be quite risky.

For instance, hedge funds often engage in arbitrage (*see* § 10.2) and in "selling short." Selling short is a gamble that the price of a stock will go down. A short seller borrows stock from her broker—say, 1,000 shares when the stock is selling at $70. She now owes her broker 1,000 shares of that company. She sells the borrowed shares now, in this case for $70,000. Then, when the price goes down over the next few days, she buys 1,000 shares—say, at $62, which costs her $62,000. She returns the 1,000 shares to her broker and has pocketed $8,000 for a couple of days work. She must pay the broker for the right to borrow the stock for those days, and pays commissions on the trades, but (hopefully) comes out ahead. Clearly, this is risky stuff. If the price goes up instead of down, the short seller will have to pay more for the stock than the $70 per share she made when she sold the borrowed stock.

Institutional investors have enormous clout because they represent the pooled investments of many. Depending on the corporation, institutional investors—as a group—may own, say, 80 percent of the voting stock. We emphasize "as a group" because there are legal impediments to one investor's owning more than five percent of the voting stock of a

corporation. Moreover, institutional investors—
investing other people's money—usually diversify
and do not roll the dice with the stock of only one
company.

The market power of institutional investors is so
great that their decisions to buy or sell can have
dramatic (and traumatic) effects on stock prices.
Institutional investors do not hesitate to evaluate
corporate stock performance and management; they
frequently communicate directly with outside
directors about problematic performance. Huge
investors like TIAA/CREF (which probably holds
your professor's retirement accounts) screen the
performance of hundreds of corporations each year
and make governance recommendations for
companies viewed to be underperforming. Implicit is
the threat that the institutional investor will sell
stock in companies that refuse make the suggested
changes.

# CHAPTER 6
# SHAREHOLDERS

## § 6.1  INTRODUCTION

In Chapter 5, we saw the traditional model of the corporation. Shareholders, as owners, elect and remove directors and have a voice in approving fundamental corporate changes. In Chapter 15, we will consider the shareholder's role in vindicating corporate claims through derivative suits. In Chapter 13, we will discuss shareholder's receipt of distributions from the corporation. In this Chapter, we focus on some nuts-and-bolts issues of how shareholders do what they do.

To vote or to receive a dividend, a shareholder must be the "record owner" as of the "record date" (*see* § 6.2). The shareholders act as a group (*see* § 6.3), which means that they usually must act through votes at meetings (*see* § 6.4). Much of this Chapter deals with the mechanics of voting at such meetings, including the requirement of a quorum (*see* § 6.4) and specialized topics of cumulative voting (*see* § 6.5), voting by proxy (*see* § 6.6), and ways to pool shareholder voting power (*see* § 6.7). We also address transferability of stock, including the possible limitation of one's ability to transfer to "outsiders" and provisions requiring a "buy back" of stock upon specified events (*see* § 6.8). In § 6.9, we discuss the shareholders' right to inspect corporate books and records.

## § 6.2 RECORD OWNER AND RECORD DATE

To be eligible to vote or to receive a distribution, generally one must be a record owner as of the record date. The concept of the record owner is not difficult. Basically, your name must appear in the corporate records. Every corporation keeps a record (called the "stock transfer book" or the "share register") of those to whom it has issued shares. Historically, one's ownership interest was represented by a stock certificate. Many feature impressive artwork, such as Disney's certificate, which features a picture of Walt Disney and various characters, including Bambi and Winnie the Pooh. Statutes prescribe the content of the certificates. *See, e.g.*, MBCA § 6.25(b).

In theory, when the record owner transfers her stock, she endorses the stock certificate and delivers it to the transferee. That person then submits the endorsed certificate to the corporation and requests that it issue a new certificate in her name. She becomes the record owner and the old certificate is canceled. A transferee who does not follow this procedure is not a record owner. Instead, she is considered the "beneficial" owner of the stock.

This procedure bears no semblance to reality in public corporations today. Few shareholders of publicly-traded companies ever see a stock certificate. In the 1960s, faced with a daunting volume of daily trades, firms developed the "book entry" or "street name registration" system. Under this system, stock certificates are largely irrelevant. Most stock certificates are stored in the vaults of the Depository Trust Company (DTC) and its clearing offices. Most of the shares are registered in the name "Cede & Co.," which is the registered owner of most publicly-traded stock. Stock ownership is recorded by brokerage firms, like UBS or Charles Schwab, and not in the share transfer books of the corporations. More recently, the SEC approved a variation that permits direct book entries of ownership in the records of the corporation itself.

The book entry system involves two sets of intermediaries between the owner of shares and the corporation. The system is efficient not only for trading but also for the distribution of dividends, which are transferred by wire from the company to brokerage firms on the day the dividend is payable. The broker deposits the dividend into its customer's account the same day.

Many states permit the corporation to issue certificateless shares. *See*, *e.g.*, MBCA § 6.26. With these, the corporation keeps records of share ownership and provides new owners with a written statement of the information otherwise required on certificates.

The record date is an arbitrary cut off, set as a convenience for the corporation.

- Corporation sets its annual shareholder meeting for May 30, and establishes a record date of May 10. S is the record owner of the stock on May 10, and on May 11 sells the stock to B. At the meeting on May 30, S has the right to vote those shares. Even though at the meeting she no longer owns the stock, she was the record owner on the record date. (The same would be true for a dividend declared on May 10 but not paid until May 30; S will get the dividend.)

Record dates can be set in the bylaws. More often, though, the board sets the record dates. Statutes usually set boundaries on when the record date may be set. They vary somewhat. MBCA § 7.07 is typical, and provides that the record date may not be more than 70 days before the meeting. This interim period allows the corporation to give proper notice of the meeting, to prepare a voting list, and to establish who is entitled to vote. It also permits management and other shareholders to solicit votes informally before the meeting. If the action involves the payment of a dividend, the record date determines who will receive the dividend.

If the board does not formally set a record date (which often occurs in closely held corporations), the record date is usually deemed to be the date the notice of the meeting is sent.

## § 6.3  SHAREHOLDERS MUST ACT AS A GROUP (IN ONE OF TWO WAYS)

Shareholders must act as a group. An individual shareholder has no power, simply by virtue of that position, to take any act entrusted to the shareholders. Usually, that means the shareholders will act at a meeting, which must satisfy statutory requirements for notice, quorum, and voting. On the other hand, statutes also authorize shareholders to take action by written consent without holding a meeting. Such provisions are especially helpful in closely-held corporations, where many shareholder decisions will be unanimous, and where the requirement of a formal meeting would be a waste of effort.

Most of these statutes require unanimity—that all shareholders agree in writing to the act that will be taken without a meeting. Some states, including Delaware, have gone further and authorize an act by the written consent of the holders of the number of shares that would be needed to take an act if a meeting were held. *See* Del. § 228.

## § 6.4 SHAREHOLDER ACTION AT MEETINGS: NOTICE, QUORUM AND VOTING

A. *Types of Meetings.* There are two types of shareholder meetings: annual and special. Meetings can be held anywhere, and need not be held in the state of incorporation. The principal purpose of the annual meeting is to elect directors, but the annual meeting may address other issues as well. The annual meeting is required, but failure to hold it does not affect the validity of any corporate action. A shareholder can seek a court order requiring the corporation to hold the annual meeting within the time set by statute. A typical provision is MBCA § 7.03(a)(1), which permits shareholders to seek an order if no annual meeting has been held "within the earlier of 6 months after the end of the [last] fiscal year or 15 months after its last annual meeting."

A special meeting is any meeting other than an annual meeting. It may be called by the persons specified in the statute or in the bylaws of the corporation. Statutes often permit the board, president, or the holders of at least ten percent of the outstanding stock to call such a meeting. The latter provision is somewhat controversial because it permits a vocal minority to call repetitive meetings to consider matters that have no chance of passing.

B. *Notice of Meetings.* MBCA § 7.05 requires that the corporation give written notice to all shareholders entitled to vote for every meeting (annual or special). Increasingly, the requirement of written notice is satisfied by e-mail. Statutes set forth time limits for giving the notice. Under MBCA § 7.05, for instance, the notice must be given not fewer than 10 and not more than 60 days before the meeting. The notice must state the time and place of the meeting.

Must the notice state the purpose of the meeting? For special meetings, the answer is yes. And, generally, the stated purpose is all that the shareholders can act upon at that meeting; they cannot do anything else. MBCA §§ 7.02(d), 7.05(c).

- Corporation sends notice of a special meeting, the purpose of which is to vote on the removal of a particular director. That is the only item of business the shareholders can transact at the meeting. For example, they could not vote to approve a plan to merge Corporation with another business.

Notice of the annual meeting, in contrast, often does not need to state a purpose. *See*, *e.g.*, MBCA

§ 7.05(b). Everyone knows the shareholders will be electing directors at the annual meeting. Some statutes require that notice state whether certain issues will be considered at a meeting. For example, some require that the notice tell shareholders whenever they will be voting on whether to approve a fundamental corporate change, such as a merger. *See, e.g.,* MBCA § 12.02(d). If such an issue is to be considered at the annual meeting, the notice of the meeting must say so.

Failure to give the required notice to all shareholders entitled to vote will void whatever action is taken at the meeting, unless any shareholder not notified waives the defect. She can do this by filing a writing with the corporation anytime (even after the meeting), or by attending the meeting without objecting at the outset to the lack of notice.

C. *Quorum and Voting.* Assuming the required notice has been given, the shareholders can only act at a meeting if there is a quorum. Importantly, in determining a quorum (and when determining if the vote is sufficient to take an act), we look at the number of *shares, and not the number of shareholders.* Each outstanding share is entitled to one vote (unless the articles provide differently). To have a quorum, a majority of the outstanding shares must be present (or represented, as by proxy, *see* § 6.6) at the meeting.

- Corporation has 20,000 shares outstanding. Corporation has 700 shareholders. That latter fact may matter to the caterer, but is otherwise irrelevant legally. To have a quorum, at least 10,001 shares must be present or represented at the meeting. If a quorum is not present, the shareholders cannot take an act.

The quorum requirement can be changed in the articles, and in some states in the bylaws. For instance, a corporation could provide that a supermajority, such as two-thirds of the shares, constitutes a quorum. In most states, the quorum requirement can be reduced to lower than a majority, though some states prohibit this. In some states, the quorum can never consist of fewer than one-third of the shares entitled to vote.

If a quorum is initially present at the meeting, a disgruntled faction may fear that it will lose a vote, and leave the meeting in an effort to "break" the quorum and prevent a vote. Under the general rule, this will not work. For shareholder voting, once a quorum is present, it is deemed present throughout the meeting; the fact that shareholders leave the meeting is irrelevant. (The rule is different for directors' voting—there, a quorum can be lost if people leave the meeting (*see* § 7.5).)

Once there is a quorum, what vote is required for the shareholders to take an act? The answer depends on the issue being considered. First, if the shareholders are electing directors, all that is needed is a plurality. In other words, the highest vote-getter for each seat wins, even if she does not get a majority of the votes cast.

Second, for routine matters that may be put up for shareholder vote, most states today require only a majority of the *votes actually cast* on the issue. The older, traditional rule required a majority of the shares to be present or represented at the meeting. The older rule, then, essentially counted abstentions (shares not cast either for or against a proposal) as a vote of "no."

- Corporation has 20,000 shares outstanding. At a meeting, 12,000 shares are present. This constitutes a quorum (because a majority of the shares are present). Of those 12,000 shares present, only 10,000 actually vote on a particular proposal. Under the traditional rule, at least 6,001 would have to vote "yes" to pass a resolution—that is, a majority of shares present. Under the modern view, only 5,001 would have to vote "yes"—a majority of those that actually voted on the deal.

Third, if shareholders are voting to remove a director before her term expires, most states require the affirmative vote of a majority of the shares *entitled* to vote. This is a more stringent requirement than what we just saw.

- Corporation has 20,000 shares outstanding. At a meeting, 12,000 shares are present. Of those 12,000 shares present, 10,000 actually vote on whether a director should be removed before her term expires. The measure cannot pass. It must be approved by a majority of the shares *entitled to vote*—not a majority of shares present or a majority of shares that

actually vote. Because there are 20,000
outstanding shares, a majority of that
number—at least 10,001—would have to vote
in favor of removing the director. Because only
10,000 voted, the requirement cannot be met.

Fourth, if shareholders are voting to approve a
fundamental corporate change, such as a merger,
most states require the affirmative vote of a majority
of the shares entitled to vote. The traditional view
here (still followed in some states, including Texas
and Ohio) is that the fundamental change must be
approved by *two-thirds* of the shares entitled to vote.
On the other hand, in some other states, fundamental
changes are treated no differently from routine
matters. For example, in Pennsylvania, the
fundamental change need be approved only by a
majority of shares actually voting on the matter. We
will discuss this issue in detail in § 16.2.

Anytime shareholders will be voting, the
corporation must prepare a "voting list," which is the
roster of those entitled to vote. *See, e.g.,* MBCA
§ 7.20. In some states, the list must be made
available to shareholders before the meeting
(beginning two business days after the notice of
meeting is given) and during the meeting itself.

## § 6.5  CUMULATIVE VOTING

A.        *What It Is and How It Works.* Cumulative
voting is relevant when shareholders are electing
directors. It does not apply when shareholders are
voting on anything else. It is intended to increase the
chances for minority shareholders to gain

representation on the board. When shareholders vote to elect directors, they either use "straight" voting or cumulative voting. Either way, as we saw in the preceding section, a candidate for director will win with a plurality of votes; she is elected if she gets more votes than the other candidates, even if it is not a majority of the votes cast. Throughout this section, let us assume there is a quorum at the meeting.

What is the difference between straight and cumulative voting? With straight voting, each position on the board is filled in a separate election at the meeting. Suppose there are three positions on the board and that all three will be filled at the annual meeting. With straight voting, there will be three elections at the meeting, one for each seat on the board. And each shareholder gets one vote in each of the three elections for each share that she owns.

- X and Y are the only shareholders of Corporation. X has 74 shares and Y has 26 shares. They attend the annual meeting to elect three directors. For each of the three seats on the board of directors, X has proposed her candidates (probably herself for one and two pals for the others) and Y has proposed her candidates (also probably herself for one and two pals for the others). What happens?

- For Seat #1, X will cast 74 votes for herself and Y will cast 26 votes for herself. X wins.

- For Seat #2, X will cast 74 votes for her friend and Y will cast 26 votes for her friend. X's friend wins.

- For Seat #3, X will cast 74 votes for another friend and Y will cast 26 votes for another friend. X's friend wins.

With straight voting, then, the holder of the majority of shares wins all seats. She can outvote the minority shareholder(s) for each seat being elected. The same would have happened if X had 51 shares and Y had 49.

With cumulative voting, however, the shareholders do not vote seat-by-seat-by-seat. Rather, there is one *at-large* election. The shareholders cast their votes in one election, and the top three vote-getters are elected to the board. (If there were five directors being elected, it would be the top five vote-getters, etc.) Not only that, but each shareholder gets to multiply the number of shares owned times the number of directors to be elected. So in the preceding hypo, X would multiply her 74 shares times the three directorships up for election. That gives her 222 votes (74 x 3). And Y would multiply her 26 shares times the three directorships up for election. That gives Y a total of 78 votes (26 x 3). Each shareholder can allocate her votes in any way she sees fit.

Here, if Y is smart, she will be able to elect someone she wants (either herself or a pal) to the board. Why? Because by cumulating three seats' worth of votes on one person, she can ensure (on this fact pattern) that one of her candidates will finish in the top three if she gives all 78 of her votes to that single candidate. It is an at-large election, so finishing in the top three (or whatever the number of directors is that is up for election) is all you need.

- Let's say Y puts all of her 78 votes on herself. X can elect herself to the board by casting 79 votes for herself. X can also elect one of her pals to the board by casting 79 votes for her pal. After casting those votes (totaling 158), X has only 64 votes left. She cannot stop Y from being elected, because Y has 78 votes.

The difference between cumulative and straight voting may be vividly illustrated by the deadlock situation where all shares are owned equally by two shareholders—say fifty shares each. If straight voting is applied and each shareholder votes only for her own candidates, a deadlock is inevitable. If there are three seats to be filled on the board, X will vote 50 shares for herself, 50 shares for one of her pals, and 50 votes for another of her pals. Y will vote 50 shares for herself, 50 shares for one of her friends, and 50 shares for another of her friends. In this fact pattern, no one is elected because no candidate got more votes than anyone else.

Now let's try it with cumulative voting. Here, X and Y each have 150 votes to allocate as they see fit (50 shares multiplied by the three directorships to be filled). X can put 76 votes on herself and guarantee her own election. Why? Remember, all X must do is finish in the top three. Y, with 150 votes, cannot place more than 76 votes on three candidates.

Now suppose Y casts 76 votes for herself. That guarantees her election. Now, though, X and Y each have 74 votes left. If they place all 74 on their respective best friends, there will be a deadlock for the third seat on the board. It would have been smarter for Y to cast 75 for herself and 75 for her friend. Then Y and her friend would control the board. However, if both Y and X used this strategy, four candidates would be deadlocked for three directorships.

Cumulative voting requires intelligent allocation of votes. Suppose X cast 76 votes for herself and Y put 100 votes for herself. Now what happens? Both X and Y are elected, because they will finish in the top three. But here X will be able to elect her pal to the board, because she has 74 votes to put on her friend. Y, in contrast, has only 50 votes to cast for her friend (because she cast 100 for herself). Here, then, the three highest vote-getters are Y, X, and pal of X. Y made a mistake by casting more than she needed to guarantee her own election, and wasted votes she could have put on her friend.

The intelligent spreading of votes among multiple candidates through cumulative voting can become complex. Various formulae may be employed. This one determines the number of shares required to elect one director when cumulative voting is in effect. You need one *share* more than this fraction: shares voting divided by number of directors to be elected plus one.

- Assume that 500 shares will be voting at the meeting and three directors will be elected at the meeting. The fraction puts 500 in the numerator, divided by four. Why four?

Because that is the number of directors to be elected plus one. 500 divided by four equals 125. We need one *share* more than 125 to elect a director. In other words, we need 126 shares.

Another formula tells us how many shares we need to elect a certain number of directors (we will call that number "n"). You need one *share* more than this fraction: shares voting multiplied by the number of directors you want to elect, divided by the number of directors to be elected, plus one.

- Now let's say 500 shares will be voting at the meeting and five directors will be elected at the meeting. Say also that we want to elect three out of the five directors. The fraction puts 1500 in the numerator. Why? It is 500 shares to be voted times (multiplied by) the three directors we want to elect. The denominator is 6. Why? Because that is the number of directors to be elected plus one. So it's 1500 divided by 6, which equals 250. So we need one *share* more than 250 to elect three directors. In other words, if we have 251 shares, we can elect three directors.

Cumulative voting has a strong emotional appeal. The notion that persons with considerable but minority holdings should have a voice in management seems "fair" and brings diversity of viewpoint to the board. Moreover, the presence of a minority director on the board may discourage conflicts of interest or other abuse by the majority.

As a practical matter, cumulative voting in a factionalized close corporation may be of considerable importance. It is irrelevant, of course, in one-shareholder corporations or when parties readily agree upon who should serve on the board of directors. In large, publicly held corporations, cumulative voting is generally thought to be a nuisance. It complicates voting by proxy and rarely affects the actual outcome of an election.

B.     *When Does It Apply?* In a few states, cumulative voting is mandatory. For example, the Arizona Constitution requires corporations formed in that state to provide cumulative voting. In most states, however, it is a matter of choice. Most of these states have "opt in" provisions. That means that if the articles are silent, cumulative voting does not exist. The corporation can choose to adopt cumulative voting, but must provide for it in the articles. *See, e.g.*, MBCA § 7.28(b). Other states have "opt out" provisions, so that if the articles are silent, cumulative voting applies.

When cumulative voting does apply, some states impose a requirement that at least one shareholder give notice to the corporation of her intent to cumulate her votes. If one does so, then all have the right to vote cumulatively. This is a desirable provision, because it allows the shareholders to forego cumulative voting when no one wants to use it. In addition, it warns the shareholders of when it will apply, so they can dust off the formulae and vote intelligently.

C.    *Effect of a Staggered Board.* Corporations sometimes attempt to minimize the impact of cumulative voting. One way is to use a "staggered" board. Usually, the entire board of directors is elected each year at the annual meeting. But corporations may choose to give directors staggered terms by dividing the board in half or thirds (*see* § 7.3). Then, each year, only half or one-third of the seats are open for election. The result of reducing the number of directors to be elected is clear—it requires more votes to elect one person to the board.

We can prove this by revisiting the formula for determining how many shares are necessary to elect one director under cumulative voting. Recall that the denominator in that formula consisted of the number of directors to be elected plus one. Any time we reduce the denominator, we will increase the number needed to elect a director. Suppose there are 1,000 shares to be voted and we will be electing nine directors. To elect one director, we need one share more than 1,000 divided by 10 (the 10 consists of the nine directors to be elected plus one). So that means we need one share more than 100, or 101.

But suppose the board is staggered and we are only electing three directors this year. Here, the 1,000 shares voting is divided by four (three directors to be elected plus one). To elect one director, then, we need one share more than 250, or 251. So, by reducing the number of directors being elected each year, staggered boards blunt the impact of cumulative voting.

## § 6.6  VOTING BY PROXY

Shareholders can vote by proxy. This refers to an agency relationship by which the shareholder (as principal) engages an agent (the proxy) to vote for her. The word "proxy" can be confusing, because sometimes it is used to refer to the document that creates this authority, sometimes to refer to the person granted the power, and sometimes to the grant of authority itself. The MBCA limits use of the word "proxy" to the person with the power to vote. It refers to the grant of authority as the "appointment" of a proxy, and to the document creating the appointment as an "appointment form."

In publicly-traded corporations, nearly all shareholder voting is by proxy. Large companies with thousands of shareholders and over a billion outstanding shares would find it impossible to get enough shareholders together to constitute a quorum. The companies hold meetings, of course, but at those meetings most shares counted as "present" for quorum purposes and voting are represented by proxies. The process by which this is done in public corporations is regulated by § 12 of the Securities Exchange Act of 1934 (*see* § 11.4).

Our focus here is the state law of proxies. Every state permits shareholders to vote "in person or by proxy." *See*, *e.g.*, MBCA § 7.22(a). The proxy appointment must be in writing. Beyond that, however, the states are not picky about form. Courts have upheld appointments that omitted the name of the proxy, the date of the meeting, or the date on which they were executed. The person appointed as proxy need not be a shareholder.

In most states, appointment of a proxy is effective for 11 months unless the document states otherwise. In a few states, there is an absolute limit—say, seven years—beyond which a proxy would not be effective. In most states, though, a proxy is good for whatever time it states. If it is silent on duration, it is 11 months. *See*, *e.g.*, MBCA § 7.22(c). The theory is that a new appointment form should be executed before each annual meeting.

Because a proxy is an agent, the appointment is revocable at the pleasure of the shareholder. So, regardless of the stated duration of the proxy, it can be revoked at anytime. Revocation can be express or by implication. For example, the execution of a later proxy appointment constitutes a revocation of an earlier, inconsistent appointment. Because later proxy appointments revoke earlier ones, it is important that proxy documents be dated. Inspectors of elections, where there is a contest, must determine which is the latest appointment form executed by a specific shareholder to determine how the shares are to be voted. The shareholder's attendance at a meeting may also constitute revocation of a proxy appointment, though this depends on the intention of the shareholder. The shareholder may be required to express her intent to revoke at the meeting. Death of the shareholder will result in revocation of the appointment, at least when the corporation is informed of the fact.

Can a proxy appointment be made irrevocable? Generally, the mere statement in the appointment form that it is irrevocable is meaningless. But the Supreme Court established in *Hunt v. Rousmanier's Adm'rs*, 21 U.S. 174, 203–06 (1823) that an appointment purporting to be irrevocable will be irrevocable if it is "coupled with an interest." This means that the proxy has some interest in the stock other than the interest in voting as the shareholder's agent. For example, if the proxy appointment is given to someone to whom the stock has been pledged (for example, as collateral for a loan), it will be "coupled with an interest."

- S is a shareholder of Corporation on the record date of the annual meeting, and thus is entitled to vote at that meeting. After the record date, but before the meeting itself, S sells the stock to P. S executes a proxy appointment authorizing P to vote the shares at the annual meeting, which provides that it is irrevocable. This proxy is irrevocable because it says so and is "coupled with an interest"—the proxy owns the shares, and thus has an interest in it other than simply voting.

Though the "proxy coupled with an interest" doctrine developed at common law, in recent decades there has been a trend toward codification. For example, MBCA § 7.22(d) lists five non-exclusive situations in which a proxy holder will be considered to have a sufficient interest in the stock to support irrevocability. *See also* Cal. Corporation Code

§ 705(e); NY Bus. Corp. Law § 609(f) (listing the same situations, but appearing to consider them exclusive).

Finally, we emphasize that appointment of proxies is permitted for shareholder voting. It is not allowed, however, for director voting. Public policy requires that directors exercise their independent judgment in voting. Thus, proxies among directors for voting as directors are invalid (*see* § 7.4).

## § 6.7  VOTING TRUSTS AND VOTING AGREEMENTS

Shareholders, particularly in close corporations, may find it advantageous to pool their voting power. One way to do this is to solicit proxy appointments from other shareholders. A problem with this approach, as we saw in the preceding section, is that the shareholder can revoke the proxy. In this section, we consider two other methods for pooling shareholder voting power: the voting trust (which is effective, but cumbersome), and the voting agreement (which is easy, but often not very effective).

A.     *Voting Trusts.* This is a true trust, so it involves separation of legal and equitable title to stock. The shareholders transfer legal title of their stock to a voting trustee; the legal title vests in the trustee the power to vote the shares. The original shareholders retain the equitable (or beneficial) title to the stock. Often, this equitable interest is reflected in "trust certificates," which can be transferred. Though they no longer own the stock, the shareholders generally retain other shareholder rights, so they can bring derivative suits, inspect the books and records of the corporation, will receive declared dividends, etc. Like any trustee, the voting trustee is a fiduciary. She must vote the shares as instructed by the equitable owners. This arrangement is effective, because the voting trustee is required to act as instructed; a court can compel her to do so.

On the other hand, the voting trust is cumbersome. First, as noted, the parties must form a trust that spells out the voting arrangement or some method for telling the trustee how to vote. Under corporate laws, the trust agreement must be in writing. Second, the shareholders must transfer legal title to the trustee. Third, some aspect of the trust must be filed with the corporation—sometimes it is the agreement itself, sometimes it is the fact of legal ownership in the trustee and equitable ownership in the shareholders. That means the trust cannot be a secret because such documents are available for inspection by shareholders (*see* § 6.9). Fourth, in some states, there is a temporal limit on the lifespan of a voting trust (often 10 years) and in some states there are rather odd limitations about when the trust can be renewed—for instance, the trust can only be renewed in the last year of its original existence. In most states, however, the trust may be extended at any time during its existence. *See*, *e.g.*, MBCA § 7.20(c).

Parties sometimes try to avoid the requirements of the voting trust by calling the arrangement something else. Courts usually will impose the statutory requirements if the deal has the essential characteristics of a voting trust. For example, in *Hall v. Staha*, 800 S.W.2d 396, 402 (Ark. 1990), the parties formed a limited partnership to obtain voting control over a corporation. The court treated the limited partnership as a voting trust, which was invalid for failure to comply with the statutory requirements.

Voting trusts are usually used to pool voting power for the election of directors. They should be drafted carefully to avoid disputes about whether the trustee is to vote on other matters, such as fundamental corporate changes. The parties should also address issues such as whether the trustee can transfer shares to third parties, the trustee's compensation, and how the trustee may be replaced.

B. *Voting Agreements.* These are contracts between or among shareholders to vote their shares as a block on certain matters. These are usually called "pooling agreements," because they pool the voting power of the shares affected by the agreement. Voting agreements are far less cumbersome than voting trusts. First, there is no separation of legal and equitable title. The shareholders retain both, so there is no need to transfer anything and no disruption of ownership. Second, in most states, they need not be filed with the corporation, so these agreements can be kept secret. Third, most states do not impose a time limit on voting agreements (though some do).

The manner in which the shares are to be voted—for or against a specific proposal—may be specified in the voting agreement itself. The parties must anticipate disagreement and provide a method for determining how the shares will then be voted. Usually, they provide that all the stock must be voted as a majority decides. Agreements may provide for arbitration in the event of deadlock. Thus, though a party to a voting agreement retains legal and equitable title, she has bargained away her right to vote her shares as she pleases; she is required to vote as the agreement provides.

There is one huge drawback to voting agreements. In many states, they are not specifically enforceable. That means a court will not force a party to vote her shares in accordance with the agreement. In the famous case *Ringling Bros.-Barnum & Bailey Combined Shows v. Ringling*, 53 A.2d 441, 448 (Del. 1947), the Delaware Supreme Court held that the proper remedy for breach of a voting agreement is to ignore the votes of the breaching party. Under the circumstances, the result defeated the very purpose of the pooling agreement, because it left a minority shareholder (who was not a party to the agreement) with considerably more clout than the agreement called for.

In other states, such as New York, the remedy for breach of a voting agreement is not clear. Though the New York Business Corporation Law allows voting agreements, it is silent on remedies for breach, nor is there definitive case law.

Led by the MBCA, many states now expressly provide that voting agreements are specifically enforceable. *See* MBCA § 7.31(b). This means that the court may force the parties to vote according to their deal. It is the superior remedy, and avoids the uncertainty of the New York approach and the possible unfairness of the Delaware view. In states providing for specific performance, presumably, parties will never use the voting trust. The pooling agreement is far easier to execute than a trust, and the availability of specific performance means that it will work just as well.

It is important to note that a shareholders' pooling agreement can extend only to voting on matters that are within the province of shareholders, such as the election and removal of directors, or the approval of fundamental corporate changes. Directors are forbidden to tie themselves down with agreements on how they will vote as directors (*see* § 7.4). Such an agreement would violate the public policy that directors exercise their independent judgment on each issue. Thus, shareholders will generally not be permitted to bootstrap a voting agreement to acts to be taken if they are elected to the board of directors.

- Shareholders X and Y enter a pooling agreement to vote their stock to elect each other to the board of directors. That is fine, because shareholders elect directors. There would be a problem, however, if they also agreed what acts they would take as directors once they are on the board. Such an agreement would violate the public policy against voting agreements for director voting.

On the other hand, statutory developments in recent decades have permitted "shareholder management agreements," under which shareholders may seize management authority. Such agreements are possible only in close corporations (*see* § 10.3).

## § 6.8   STOCK TRANSFER RESTRICTIONS, INCLUDING BUY-SELL AGREEMENTS

A.   *In General.*   One advantage of the corporation is the transferability of the ownership interest. A shareholder can sell or give her stock away—*inter vivos* or by will. Sometimes, however, investors impose restrictions on the transferability of stock. Such stock transfer restrictions (STRs) usually are imposed in the articles or bylaws, though they may also be established by contract between the corporation and shareholders or among the shareholders.

Why would anyone do this? In public corporations, STRs may be used to ensure that an issuance of stock remains exempt from the requirements of registration for public sale (*see* § 11.2). STRs are more commonly found in close corporations. For example, a STR is helpful to keep outsiders out—for example, to ensure that a present shareholder does not transfer their stock to someone who will be disruptive or destructive. A right of first refusal can provide this protection, by requiring that a shareholder offer her stock first to the corporation (or to other shareholders) before selling to an outsider. Such an agreement can also ensure that a shareholder does not jeopardize S Corporation's status for income tax purposes, such as the requirement that S Corporation cannot have more than 100 shareholders (*see* § 1.10).

Another common STR in close corporations is the buy-sell agreement, which *requires* the corporation or other shareholders to buy a shareholder's stock. This is helpful, for example, when a shareholder retires from employment with the corporation or when a shareholder dies. Because there is no market for the stock of a close corporation, a buy-sell agreement allows the departing shareholder (or her estate) to receive a return on investment. We discuss this further in subpart C below.

B. *Requirements.* Historically, courts were somewhat hostile to STRs because they are restraints on alienation. The common law would enforce them only if they did "not unreasonably restrain or prohibit transferability." Under this test, an outright prohibition on transferability would certainly be invalid. Similarly, an STR that prohibited transfer without consent of directors or shareholders would be highly suspect because such consent could be withheld arbitrarily. Language in the STR that consent "will not be unreasonably withheld" might help.

Today, most states have statutes concerning the enforceability of STRs. For example, MBCA § 6.27(c)(3) requires that the purpose of an STR be "reasonable." Helpfully, it then creates a safe harbor for restrictions intended to maintain the status of the corporation when it is dependent on the number or identity of shareholders, and to preserve exemptions under federal or state securities law. Such restrictions are valid without investigation into their reasonableness. MBCA § 6.27(d) lists two types of restrictions—consent restrictions and prohibitory restrictions—that are valid if "not manifestly unreasonable." This last clause is taken directly from § 202 of the Delaware corporate law.

Statutes generally require that a reference to any STR restriction imposed in corporate documents be noted on the face or back of each stock certificate that is subject to the restriction. *See, e.g.*, MBCA § 6.27(b). This does not usually require that the entire text of the restriction appear, but only that its fact be noted. MBCA § 6.27(b) also requires that the notation be "conspicuous," which is defined in MBCA § 1.40 as "so written that a reasonable person against whom the writing is to operate should have noticed it."

Suppose a shareholder transfers stock to a third party in violation of a valid STR. Is the third party bound by the STR? The third party is not bound by a restriction if she did not actually know about it or is not charged with knowledge of it. A conspicuous notation of the existence of the STR on the stock certificate will charge the third party with such knowledge.

Generally, statutes do not impose a time limit on STRs. Restrictions may terminate before any stated term either by express agreement of the shareholders involved (e.g., when all decide to sell their shares to an outside purchaser despite a restriction against such a sale) or by abandonment. If shares are transferred in violation of an STR and without objection by other shareholders, a court may conclude that the restriction is no longer enforceable. Isolated sales in violation of the restriction may not support such a conclusion, though a person objecting to the current sale may be estopped if he or she participated in an earlier transaction.

C. *Buy-Sell Agreements.* As noted, a common STR in close corporations is the "buy-sell" agreement, which requires either the corporation or other shareholders to buy one's stock upon the occurrence of a specified event. Frequently, such provisions are triggered by a shareholder's leaving the business by retirement or death. The choice of whether the corporation or other shareholders will purchase the stock is a matter of preference. Often, the corporation's purchase of the stock is the better option. Not only might the company have readier access to cash, but the corporation's purchase of the stock does not affect the proportional ownership of the other shareholders. Such a repurchase by the corporation is a distribution, and will have to satisfy the legal requirements for such transactions (*see* § 13.6).

Buy-sell provisions requiring purchase by the other shareholders can lead to problems. For instance, one of them might be unable or unwilling to purchase. The agreement may require that the shares be offered to willing shareholders proportionately.

The price provisions of buy-sell agreements often raise problems. Because there is no market price for stock in a close corporation, there must be some other metric for valuation. There are various options, including a stated price, or the best offer by an outsider. A common method of valuation is "book value." This is computed by dividing the balance sheet value by the number of outstanding shares. Book value is relatively easy to calculate, but may have no relationship with the actual value of the stock. Why? Because basic accounting conventions require that assets be valued at cost and not be reappraised upward or downward to reflect current market values.

Thus, real estate acquired decades earlier at a low price may carry a book value that greatly understates its value today. Accounting conventions also allow corporations to include certain things as assets that may never be realized—for example, the costs of formation or the value of "good will" acquired in connection with the purchase of another business. When adjusting book values, it may be appropriate to eliminate such non-assets from the balance sheet before computing book value. Instead of using book value, the agreement may require that the value of the stock be appraised at the time of purchase. Appraising the values of stock in close corporations is often a difficult thing (*see* § 16.3).

Many STRs provide that the purchase price of shares is to be paid in periodic installments extending over several years following the shareholder's departure from the business. Such provisions allow the business to pay for the shares out of future profits or cash flow without incurring indebtedness. The agreement should address questions of whether the seller is entitled to interest on deferred payments and whether the aggregate price should be adjusted depending on the profitability of the business in the years following her departure.

## § 6.9  INSPECTION OF CORPORATE RECORDS

Each state requires corporations to maintain certain records. These vary from state to state, but commonly include articles, bylaws, lists of shareholders, officers and directors, records of actions taken at meetings of shareholders and of the board of directors, and financial information. *See, e.g.*, MBCA § 16.01. Because many small businesses do not have accountants, statutes require only basic financial statements, made on the basis of generally accepted accounting principles (*see* § 12.6). In contrast, federal law requires publicly-traded corporations to prepare and disseminate very detailed financial records (*see* §§ 11.2 & 11.3).

Here, we address the shareholders' authority to inspect records maintained by the corporation. As we will see, qualified shareholders must jump through statutory hoops to gain access to corporate records. Importantly, these rules do not apply to directors. Because directors are managers, they have broad access to the corporation's papers. Indeed, directors' fiduciary duties require that they be able to inspect the entire gamut of records in the corporation. Shareholders, in contrast, are owners but not managers, so their right to inspect is narrower.

Here are some common characteristics of most statutes:

- The shareholders' right to inspect records does not include a right to inspect physical operations. Shareholders do not have a right to go to the production line and look over the assembly line.

- The shareholders' right to inspect usually permits her to take an agent with her and to have copies made (though the corporation can charge her for the copies).

- The right to inspect is usually held by the beneficial, or equitable owner of the stock, not simply the record owner. A shareholder who has transferred legal title of the stock to a voting trustee (*see* § 6.7) will usually retain the right to inspect.

- There is often a common law right to inspect, existing alongside the statutory right. In most states, however, the scope of this common law right is ill-defined.

Beyond these points, statutes vary on key points. For one, they differ on which shareholders are eligible to demand access to the records. The traditional view—still followed in some states—requires that a shareholder meet certain minima of ownership. Usually, this means that she *either* has owned stock (of any amount) for at least six months, or that she currently owns at least five percent of the outstanding stock (for any length time). The modern view, typified by the MBCA, grants inspection rights to "any shareholder," regardless of how long she has owned her stock or how much she holds.

Assuming the shareholder is eligible, statutes also vary regarding procedure and the types of records she may review. In some states, a shareholder has a right to review some routine documents (like articles, bylaws, lists of officers and directors, and records of shareholder actions) simply by showing up at the corporate office during business hours and demanding to see them. In other states, however, she may see such routine documents only after making a written demand (usually five business days in advance) describing the documents sought.

To gain access to more sensitive materials, such as financial information and the record of directors' actions, most states require an eligible shareholder to make a written demand (usually at least five business days in advance) describing the documents desired *and stating a proper purpose for the inspection.* She may also be required to state how the requested documents relate to her proper purpose. In some states, this assertion of a proper purpose is required for *any* inspection, even of routine documents.

Whether a shareholder has stated a proper purpose is sometimes hotly contested. As a general rule, the corporation is likely to see a demand for access to the records, particularly sensitive records such as financial books and director actions, as hostile. For many years, corporations routinely rejected such demands, which forced the shareholder to seek an injunction to order access. Now, many statutes dissuade corporations from doing this by imposing upon the corporation or an officer a fine for improper denial of shareholder access. And in some states, the corporation that denies access bears the burden of demonstrating that the shareholder had an improper purpose in demanding access.

A "proper purpose" is one that relates to the shareholder's interest as a shareholder. It must relate to some role that shareholders play. For example, determining the value of the shareholder's interest in the corporation is a proper purpose. This purpose for inspection is most important in close corporations because there is no public market for the stock. Unless the shareholder can review the financial information, she will be unable to determine the value of her stock. *See, e.g., Kortum v. Webasto Sunroofs*, 769 A.2d 113, 115–25 (Del. Ch. 2000).

A proper purpose may be one that is hostile to management. For instance, it is proper to investigate the reason for a decline in profits or to ascertain whether there has been mismanagement or questionable transactions. Such things affect the value of the shareholder's stock. Moreover, as we see in Chapter 15, shareholders may bring derivative suits against directors and officers who breach fiduciary duties to the corporation, for example, by making egregious errors of judgment or engaging in self-dealing. Therefore, inspection may be important to the shareholders' right to sue derivatively. Similarly, it may be proper for a shareholder to gain access to the list of shareholders so she can seek proxy appointments to elect new directors (*see* § 11.5).

On the other hand, some demands are not proper and should be rejected. For example, inspections intended to harass managers or to obtain trade secrets for competitors are improper. One concern, especially in earlier days, was that a shareholder would gain access to the list of shareholders to sell it, for example, to marketers. Indeed, New York allows the corporation to require a shareholder demanding access to the shareholder list to give an affidavit that she has not sold a shareholder list in the recent past. NY Bus. Corp. Law § 624(c).

Ultimately, the issue of proper purpose boils down to subjective motivation, which is always tough to establish definitively. Courts are aware of the need to balance the shareholders' right of access with the corporation's right to be free from "fishing expeditions" by shareholders.

# CHAPTER 7

# DIRECTORS

## § 7.1 INTRODUCTION

Initial directors are either named in the articles or elected by the incorporators (*see* § 3.5). Thereafter, shareholders elect directors at the annual shareholders' meeting (*see* § 5.3). In this chapter, we discuss the nuts and bolts of how the board operates. Statutes give great leeway regarding the number of directors and their qualifications (*see* § 7.3), and permit election of the entire board each year or, instead, multiple-year terms with a "staggered board" (*see* § 7.3). The board acts as a group (*see* § 7.4), which means that it usually must act through meetings. The requirements for a formal meeting are technical (*see* § 7.5). We also address what happens when a director cannot serve out her term (*see* § 7.6), director compensation (*see* § 7.7), and how the board can delegate its authority to committees (*see* § 7.8).

## § 7.2 STATUTORY REQUIREMENTS

Historically, states required that a board of directors have at least three members. Today, every state seems to have rejected this requirement and now permits a board of "one or more" directors. *See, e.g.*, MBCA § 8.03(a). *If the articles and bylaws are silent*, some states set up a sliding scale: if there is one shareholder, the corporation may have one or more directors; if there are two shareholders, it must have at least two directors; and if there are three or more shareholders, it must have at least three directors. This sliding scale seems based on a presumption that every shareholder will be a director, which may be harmless enough in most close corporations. But the sliding scale can create unnecessary problems. Suppose we have a corporation with one shareholder, who is also the sole director. If she wants to give stock to her two children, as gifts, the sliding scale rule would require that the corporation elect two more directors, because (after the gift) there will be three shareholders. The way around this is to provide expressly in the appropriate document that there will be one director.

There is considerable variation among the states regarding where the number of directors is set. Many states provide, as does MBCA § 8.03(a), that the number may be "specified in or fixed in accordance with the articles of incorporation or the bylaws." Under some older statutes, the number must be set in the articles. This is a disadvantage, because amending articles is a fundamental corporate change and requires assent from both the board and the shareholders (*see* § 16.4). It is far easier to amend bylaws (*see* § 3.5). In a few states, such as Maryland, even though the number of directors is set in the articles, it can be amended by bylaw. Some states, such as Arizona, permit the articles to set up a variable-sized board, with the actual number within that range being set by the board itself. Wherever the number is set, most corporations have an odd number of directors. This lessens the possibility that the board will split evenly when voting on some measure.

For years, statutes routinely required that each director have certain qualifications, such as being a shareholder or a resident of the state. These requirements largely have been eliminated. So long as a person is of legal age, she can be a director. The corporation is free, of course, to impose qualifications for directors, such as stock ownership, usually in either the articles or the bylaws.

In the United States, directors must be human beings. This fact is reflected in provisions, such as MBCA § 8.03(a), that the board consist of "individuals." In some countries, corporations or other entities may serve as directors, but this practice never caught on in the United States.

Usually, the entire board is elected at the annual meeting of shareholders. Accordingly, the usual term for directors (unless the articles provide otherwise) is one year. We will see in the next section that directors will serve longer terms if the corporation has a *staggered board*. Whatever the length of the term, however, in all states a director holds office (even after expiration of the term) until her successor is "elected and qualified." *See, e.g.*, MBCA § 8.05(e). As a result, the failure to hold annual meetings of shareholders does not affect the power of a corporation to continue to transact its business; directors continue in office, with power to act.

## § 7.3   A "STAGGERED" (OR "CLASSIFIED") BOARD

Most states permit the establishment of a *staggered* (in some states called *classified*) board.

With this, the directorships are divided into two or three groups, with as nearly equal numbers as possible. Then, one half or one third of the board is elected each year. For example, if there are nine directorships, the board could be staggered into three classes of three directorships each. In Year 1, the shareholders would elect directors to seats A, B, and C. In Year 2, they would elect directors for seats D, E, and F. And in Year 3, they would elect directors for seats G, H, and I. In this example, each directorship term would be three years. (Or the nine directorships could be divided into two classes, with five elected in Year 1 and the other four in Year 2, and each directorship term being two years.)

Historically, statutes permitted staggered boards only if there were a relatively large number of directors, usually nine or more. Smaller boards could not be staggered, but were elected in full each year. This is still the law in some states. A trend, though, typified by MBCA § 8.06, permits a staggering a board of any size.

One theoretical justification for a staggered board is that it ensures experience on the board, because the directors serve longer terms. The real goal, however, may be to ensure continuity of leadership. With only a fraction of the directorships open for election each year, it is more difficult for an outsider to gain a foothold on the board. Thus, if an aggressor has acquired a majority of the stock, she will only be able to elect new directors to one-third (or one-half) of the seats in one year. The directors elected by the old regime will remain in office for another year or two. Moreover, a staggered board blunts the impact of cumulative voting (*see* § 6.5, subpart C).

In public corporations formed under Massachusetts law, a staggered board is required, apparently to promote this sort of continuity. On the other hand, shareholders usually can remove directors before their terms expire without cause (*see* § 5.3). Thus, the new majority shareholder would be able to purge the board and elect "her" people as directors. To counteract this, some states permit removal of directors in corporations with staggered boards only for cause.

We noted that some states refer to staggered boards as "classified" boards. There is some terminological confusion here, because "classified" can refer to something else. Sometimes, the articles will provide for different classes of stock. Under MBCA § 8.04 and statutes in many states, the articles can provide that a class of stock will elect a certain number of directors. So the articles may provide that Class A stock may elect a certain number of the directors. Some people call this a "classified" board. Sometimes, then, "classified" means the stock is divided into different classes, with each having the power to elect a given number of directors. On the other hand, sometimes "classified" is used to indicate that the directors serve staggered terms.

## § 7.4   THE BOARD MUST ACT AS A GROUP
## (IN ONE OF TWO WAYS)

The power invested in directors is held jointly, which means that directors can act only as a body— as a group. An individual director has no power, simply by virtue of that position, to bind the corporation or to take a corporate act. Board acts are usually taken at meetings, which must satisfy statutory requirements for notice, quorum, and voting. (We will see below in this section, though, that the board might act by unanimous written consent in lieu of a meeting.) The theory is that shareholders deserve a board decision that is reached after group discussion and deliberation. Views may be changed as a result of discussion, and the sharpening of minds as a result of joint deliberation improves the decisional process.

There are four corollaries to the requirement that the board must act as a group.

- First, separate agreements by directors will not work. Thus, if each of the directors agreed with a proposition in individual conversations, there is no valid board act; the group must decide *as a group.*

- Second, directors may not vote by proxy. To do so would violate public policy: each director owes non-delegable duties to the corporation, which require her independent exercise of judgment. (Remember, in contrast, that shareholders, who generally do not owe fiduciary duties to the corporation, can vote by proxy (*see* § 6.6). Remember too that one person might wear more than one hat at a time. So if one person is simultaneously a shareholder and a director, she may vote *as a shareholder* by proxy; she cannot vote, however, *as a director* by proxy.)

- Third, directors may not enter into voting agreements tying themselves down to how they will vote. Such an agreement would violate the public policy just discussed. (*Shareholders*, in contrast, may enter voting agreements on how to vote as shareholders (§ 6.7).)

- Fourth, the formalities about notice, quorum, and voting at directors' meetings are strictly enforced.

These corollaries make little sense in a close corporation in which the (few) shareholders are active in operating the business. There, even the requirement of a formal meeting of the board will likely be considered a meaningless formality. Accordingly, today, statutes permit shareholders in close corporations to abolish the board and adopt more informal decision-making. When this is not done, management rests in the board, and the proprietors and their lawyers should be scrupulous in following the rules.

The board can act in only two ways. One, addressed in the next section, is to approve a resolution at a meeting. The other, permitted in all states, is unanimous written consent to act without a meeting. Section 8.21(a) of the MBCA provides that unless the articles or bylaws require a meeting, a board action "may be taken without a meeting if each director signs a consent describing the action to be taken and delivers it to the corporation." Such consent is an act of the board, just as if the action had been taken after a formal meeting. MBCA § 8.21(b). Note that though all directors must agree to the action, not all need sign the same piece of paper. For instance, in a corporation with multiple directors, each could sign and file with the corporate records a separate document agreeing to the board act.

Statutes allowing such written consents are salutary. They permit approval of routine matters without a formal meeting. And by requiring unanimous approval, they do not stifle minority sentiment. Any director who is opposed to taking the action proposed, or who believes that the board would benefit from full discussion, can require a formal meeting by refusing to sign the written consent.

Because statutes require that these consents be signed and filed with the corporation, obviously, they must be in writing. An increasing number of states permit director consent by e-mail. For example, under the MBCA, § 1.40(22A) provides that a requirement of a signature "includes any manual, facsimile, conformed or electronic signature."

## § 7.5 BOARD MEETINGS: NOTICE, QUORUM AND VOTING

Unless the board acts through unanimous written consent (*see* § 7.4), it will take actions by adopting resolutions at meetings. Here, we discuss the formal requirements regarding board meetings.

A. *Types of Meetings.* There are two types of board meetings: regular and special. Any meeting may be held anywhere, and need not be held in the state of incorporation. The time and place of regular meetings usually are set in the bylaws, or the bylaws can empower the board to determine when to call such a meeting. Regular meetings are usually held at specific intervals, and the interval can be set for whatever makes sense for the particular board— weekly, monthly, quarterly, etc. As a general rule, public corporations tend to have fewer regular meetings than smaller corporations, with routine functions delegated to an executive committee (*see* § 7.8). It is customary to hold a regular meeting of directors immediately after the annual meeting of shareholders.

Any board meeting other than a regular meeting is a special meeting. The difference between regular and special meetings of the board has nothing to do with what matters may be considered. Rather, the difference concerns notice.

B. *Notice of Meetings.* The corporation is not required to give notice to directors of regular meetings. *See* MBCA § 8.22(a). But it is required to give notice to directors of special meetings. *See* MBCA § 8.22(b). The details of the notice requirement for special meetings varies from state to state, so one should be careful to consult the applicable law concerning three things: when is it given, how it is given, and what does it say.

Section 8.22(b) of the MBCA requires that the corporation give notice at least two days before the special meeting. The timing can be changed in the articles. Some states require five days' notice and New York law, while requiring notice of special meetings, says nothing about timing.

In terms of content, most statutes require that the notice state the date, time, and place of the meeting; it need not, however, state the purpose for which the meeting is called. (This is different from notice of shareholders' meetings, which requires a statement of purpose (*see* § 6.4).) The lack of a statement of purpose reflects the fact that the board must be free to discuss relevant matters that come up during the meeting, so a statement of the purpose of the meeting might be too constraining.

Section 8.22(b) of the MBCA says nothing about the form of the notice of special meeting. The Official Comments to the MBCA make clear, though, that the notice can be written or oral. This conclusion is consistent with MBCA § 1.41, which provides that notice "must be in writing unless oral notice is reasonable under the circumstances." That section provides that notice by electronic transmission constitutes written notice, which reflects increasing statutory approval of notice by e-mail. In some states, a director must expressly agree that e-mail notice is satisfactory.

What happens if the corporation fails to given the required notice? As with shareholders, any purported action taken at that meeting is void, unless those not given notice waive the defect. Directors may waive notice in writing anytime (before, during, or after the meeting), so long as it is in writing and filed with the corporate records. *See* MBCA § 8.23(a). In many corporations, it is routine to have directors sign waivers of notice at every meeting. In addition, a director waives any notice defect by attending or participating in a meeting unless she "objects to holding the meeting or transacting business at the meeting and does not thereafter vote for or assent to action taken at the meeting." MBCA § 8.23(b).

Though statutes are usually quite clear about who can call a special meeting of shareholders, most are silent about who may call a special meeting of the board. The matter is often addressed in the bylaws, which routinely provide that the chief executive officer can call such a meeting.

C. *Presiding Officer.* At all meetings of the board, regular and special, the corporation's senior executive officer presides. This officer usually holds the title "president" but might instead be the "chief executive officer" or "chairperson of the board." Her duties may be described in the bylaws but are largely determined by tradition and practice. She usually sets the agenda of the meeting and may also be involved in preparing the information to be distributed to the directors before the meeting. A vice-chair may be named to perform these functions when the chairperson is absent.

D. *Quorum and Voting.* Assuming any required notice has been given, generally the board cannot act unless a quorum is present at the meeting. (There is a minor exception to this: even if the number of directors in office does not constitute a quorum, a majority thereof may vote to fill vacant director positions (*see* § 7.4).) In determining a quorum and voting, we look at the number of directors. The number of shares of stock they may own is irrelevant. Indeed, they need not even own stock in the company. *See* § 7.2.

If the board is of a fixed size, a quorum consists of a majority of that fixed number. If the board does not have a fixed size—for example, if it has a variable range—a quorum consists of a majority of the directors in office immediately before the meeting begins. *See* MBCA § 8.24(a). The quorum figure can be changed in the articles. In some states, the quorum requirement can be raised but cannot be lowered. Thus, it cannot be set at fewer than a majority of the directors described above. *See*, *e.g.*, NY Bus. Corp. Law § 707. In an increasing number of states, reflected in MBCA § 8.24(b), the quorum requirement can be raised or lowered, but never to a number fewer than one-third of the directors described.

- Suppose the board has nine directors. The articles and bylaws are silent as to quorum. That means that at least five of the nine directors must show up at the meeting to have a quorum and conduct business. If only four show up, they might as well get out a deck of cards and play bridge, because they cannot conduct corporate business.

When a quorum is present, passing a resolution (remember, that is how the board takes an act at a meeting) requires the majority vote of the directors *present* at the meeting. The articles (and in some states the bylaws) can raise that requirement to a supermajority but generally cannot lower it to less than a majority. *See* MBCA § 8.24(c) ("the affirmative vote of a majority of directors present is the act of the board . . . unless the articles or bylaws require the vote of a greater number of directors.").

- The board has nine directors. This time five show up at the meeting, so we have a quorum. A resolution is presented and three directors vote (two do nothing but sit there), each of the three voting in favor. The resolution passes, because it was approved by a majority of the directors present (three out of five).

Section 8.24(c) of the MBCA, and the statutes of most states, require that a quorum actually be present when the vote is taken. In other words, under the general rule, a directors' quorum can be lost, or "broken." Once a quorum is no longer present, the board cannot take an act at that meeting.

- The board has nine directors. Five directors attend a meeting, so we have a quorum. They vote on various resolutions. Now one of the five leaves the meeting. That destroys the quorum, because only four of the nine are present. The remaining four cannot take a corporate act.

This latter rule is different from shareholder voting. With shareholders, once a quorum is present, it is deemed to exist throughout the meeting even if some shareholders leave the meeting (*see* § 6.4). The quorum rule for directors encourages management to present important issues early in the meeting (when a quorum is more likely to be present) rather than toward the end of the meeting when some directors may have left.

In some close corporations, the articles define a quorum as all directors and, further, require a unanimous vote to approve a resolution. Proprietors should think long and hard before adopting such provisions. They give each director a veto, and thus permit each to prevent the board from taking any act. This may not seem like a problem when the business is founded. Later, however, after the directors disagree on various issues, it may lead to spiteful acts and corporate paralysis. *See* § 10.2.

E. *Telephonic and Virtual Meetings.* States generally permit directors to participate in regular or special meetings through "any means of communication by which all directors participating may simultaneously hear each other during the meeting." MBCA § 8.20(b). Anyone so participating is deemed to be present at the meeting. The provision permits conference telephone calls and virtual meetings through voice-over-internet protocols. Accordingly, directors may be on different continents but can participate and be considered "present" at the meeting.

F. *Registering Dissent or Abstention.* If a director disagrees with a proposed resolution, she must ensure that her position is properly recorded in the corporate records. MBCA § 8.24(d), which reflects the common view, provides that any director who is present when corporate action is taken is "deemed to have assented to the action taken" unless she takes one of three affirmative acts.

First, under MBCA § 8.24(d)(1), the director may object (at the meeting) to the transaction of business. This is rare; an example is an objection because the corporation failed to give notice of a special meeting.* Second, under MBCA § 8.24(d)(2), the director can ensure that her "dissent or abstention from the action . . . is entered in the minutes of the meeting." Third, under MBCA § 8.24(d)(3), the director can "deliver[ ] written notice of [her] dissent or abstention to the presiding officer at the meeting before its conclusion or to the corporation immediately after adjournment of the meeting."

Thus, assuming the director did not object to the transaction of business, she must record her dissent or abstention either in the minutes (by requesting such entry at the meeting), or in writing to the presiding officer (for example, a note to the president during the meeting), or to the corporation itself (for example, a letter to the corporate secretary "immediately" after adjournment). Some states are more precise about the third option, and require a registered letter within a set time after adjournment.

---

\* Maybe the required notice was not given to the objecting director but she heard about the meeting from other directors and attended.

Note, then, that an oral dissent by itself will not protect a director from the presumption that she concurred with the adopted resolution.

- There are five directors on the board. All five attend the meeting. After discussion, they will vote on whether the corporation should pay a dividend. Director X, convinced that the dividend is legally improper, stands on a table and screams out that she is opposed to the dividend because it is unlawful. The directors vote four to zero in favor of the dividend. Unless Director X records her dissent in one of the ways permitted by statute, she will deemed to have approved the dividend and, if the dividend was improper, will share liability for it.

Filing a written dissent eliminates liability and obviates later questions of proof. It may also have a desirable psychological effect upon the other directors when they realize that one of their colleagues considers the action questionable. It gives notice to shareholders or others examining the corporate records that at least one director seriously questioned the propriety of the decision.

## § 7.6 VACANCIES ON THE BOARD

A director might fail to serve her full term. She might resign in writing (MBCA § 8.07(a)), or die, or be removed by shareholders. It is in the corporation's interest to elect someone to fill out the remainder of the term, so the board stays at full strength. Who selects the new person? States take different approaches here, but the clear modern trend, reflected in MBCA § 8.10(a), is to allow either the shareholders or the directors to elect the replacement director. In some states, the cause of the vacancy will determine who should elect the replacement. If a director dies or resigns, in some states, the remaining directors will select the person to fill out that director's term. If, on the other hand, the director is removed from office by the shareholders, some states required that the shareholders elect the replacement.

There is another possibility. A vacancy may be created by amendment to the articles or bylaws to increase the size of the board. If there are five directors and the articles or bylaws are changed to increase the board to seven, there are two "new vacancies." In some states, newly-created board positions must be filled by the shareholders. As noted, though, the modern and increasingly prevalent view is that the replacement for any vacancy (even one created by an increase in the number of directors) may be elected either by the shareholders or the directors. MBCA § 8.10(a) expressly makes this point.

If the directors are to select a replacement, we apply the general quorum and voting rules (*see* § 7.3). Sometimes, though, the vacancy will mean that fewer than a quorum of directors remains. Statutes usually address this potential problem by providing, as MBCA § 8.10(a)(3) does, for election "by the affirmative vote of a majority of all directors remaining in office."

- There are seven directorship positions on the board. All were filled but four directors leave office (perhaps through retirement or death). The remaining three directors do not constitute a quorum. Without a provision like MBCA § 8.10(a)(3), we would be concerned that the board would be helpless to act. That helpful provision allows action by a vote of two-to-one—that is, by a majority of those remaining in office, even though they are less than a quorum.

Once the replacement is properly elected (by whatever group), she fills out the remainder of the term of the person she replaces. MBCA § 8.05(b).

## § 7.7   COMPENSATION OF DIRECTORS

Remember that people may wear more than one hat at a time. A director who is also an officer is entitled to compensation as an *officer*. Here we speak of compensation as a *director*. Traditionally, directors were not paid for ordinary services in that role. The idea was that directors were acting as trustees or were motivated by their own interest in the corporation. The common law evolved, however, to permit director compensation if it was agreed to in advance or if a director performed some extraordinary services.

Things have changed, especially in the public corporation. Early in the twentieth century, corporations started paying small honoraria to "outside" directors for attending meetings. (Outside directors are those who are not employed by the company for their full-time job. "Inside" directors are those whose day job is with the corporation (invariably as a high-ranking officer, such as the CEO).) This practice grew, as did the payments. It is now universal for public corporations to provide substantial compensation to outside directors. Indeed, today such compensation in large corporations now averages over $250,000 per year. Some corporations also provide retirement plans for outside directors. The sense is that the business "gets what it pays for," and such compensation improves the quality and interest of outside directors.

Modern statutes expressly authorize director compensation. For example, under MBCA § 8.11, unless the articles or bylaws provide otherwise, "the board of directors may fix the compensation of directors." When a group sets its own payment, we get nervous about conflict of interest. Directors, as fiduciaries of the corporation, should not use this opportunity to line their pockets. They must act in good faith and the compensation must be reasonable (*see* § 9.7).

Directors' compensation was long paid in cash. Increasingly, public corporations pay directors in stock or options to buy stock. The theory is that stock ownership aligns the outside directors' interest with that of the shareholders. In Chapter 9, we discuss the duties directors owe to their corporation. Breaching a duty can expose a director (inside or outside) to significant potential liability.

## § 7.8 COMMITTEES OF THE BOARD

A corporation may have various committees. One type—not our focus—is the committee consisting of directors or officers or employees or others (even outsiders), which is intended to advise management on various matters or to provide perspective or assist it in considering business-related problems. The other type of committee—which is our focus—is one that actually exercises board power. There is something problematic about such committees. After all, the board is the repository of managerial power. If it can delegate its authority to a committee, the concern is that the board members are abdicating their responsibilities to a subset.

Reflecting this nervousness, the early common law allowed the board to delegate limited functions to a committee. Today, statutes have changed the rule dramatically. Statutes now start with the proposition that committees can do *anything* the board can do, and then carve out exceptions. The exceptions are non-delegable matters that must be decided by the full board. These vary from state to state, but MBCA § 8.25(e) is representative. It provides that a committee generally cannot (1) authorize distributions (like dividends), (2) recommend to shareholders a fundamental corporate change, (3) fill a board vacancy, or (4) amend or repeal bylaws. Several states add to this list that a committee cannot set director compensation.

Two observations are in order. First, just because a board may delegate does not mean that it will. The authority to create committees is voluntary, and need not be used. Second, though committees cannot *do* any of the tasks listed by statute as non-delegable, they can recommend them for full board action. Thus, the board may create a committee to determine whether dividends ought to be declared and, if so, how large they should be. Though the committee cannot actually declare the dividend, the full board might accept the committee's recommendation on the issue.

Corporations may have "standing" committees, which exist constantly. A common standing committee is the "executive committee," which performs the functions of the board between meetings of the full board. For instance, if the full board meets only a few times each year, the executive committee enables discharge of board functions without having to call the full board for special meetings. Executive committees are usually composed of inside directors (directors who are also employed by the corporation, usually as officers). Such people are most likely to be available on short notice.

Other standing committees are routine, especially in public corporations. Federal law requires an audit committee (*see* § 11.3). Public corporations have a compensation committee (*see* § 11.6) and usually a nominating committee, which screens candidates for the board. These groups are primarily or exclusively composed of "outside directors." (Outside directors are not otherwise employed by the company; their "day job" is somewhere else. Inside directors not only serve on the board, but are employed by the company (usually as an officer).) Other committees that may be composed predominantly of outside directors include strategic planning, public policy, environmental compliance, information technology, and employee benefits.

In addition to these standing committees, the board may create ad hoc committees to consider specific issues as they arise, such as derivative litigation filed by shareholders on behalf of the corporation (*see* § 15.6), requests for indemnification for expenses incurred by directors or officers in connection with that litigation (*see* § 15.7), or review of interested director transactions (*see* § 9.7).

Historically, statutes permitted committees of the board only if the articles permitted. That is true in only a few states today. The overwhelming majority position is that taken by MBCA § 8.25(a), which allows the board to create committees unless the articles or bylaws forbid it. Historically, statutes required that committees have at least two members. This rule, too, has been rejected by the clear majority, which, like MBCA § 8.25(a), provides that a committee consists of "one or more members of the board of directors."

Unless the articles or bylaws provide differently, the appointment of committees generally requires a majority vote of all directors in office, *and not* simply a majority of those present at a meeting at which there is a quorum. *See*, *e.g.*, MBCA § 8.25(b)(1). Committees are governed by the same quorum and voting requirements as the board itself. *See*, *e.g.*, MBCA § 8.25(c). And the creation of a committee does not relieve other directors of their duties to the corporation. *See* MBCA § 8.25(d). A director who is not a member of a committee still owes the fiduciary duties discussed in Chapter 9, and can be held liable for breaching them.

# CHAPTER 8
# OFFICERS

## § 8.1 INTRODUCTION

Officers are employees and agents of the corporation. In § 5.5, we discussed their role in the traditional model of corporate management. Here, we address officers in greater detail. We start with statutory requirements—how many and what types of officers are mandated (*see* § 8.2)? We then discuss the sources of officers' authority (*see* § 8.3). One key issue is whether an officer can bind the corporation in a transaction. The answer depends upon agency law, which we discussed in § 1.9 and will apply to the corporate context in § 8.4. As we will see, directors generally hire and fire the officers, and are responsible for monitoring them (*see* § 8.5). Section 8.6 is short but important. It concerns the fiduciary duties of officers. The section is short because these overlap with those owed by directors, which are so important that they command the entirety of Chapter 9.

## § 8.2 STATUTORY REQUIREMENTS

Traditionally, statutes required that every corporation have three or four officers: a president, a secretary, a treasurer, and in some states a vice president. The statutes have always permitted the corporation to name additional officers. It would be cumbersome (in fact, unworkable) in many close corporations actually to have three or four separate people serving as officers. Legislatures foresaw the problem and provided that one person may hold multiple offices simultaneously. Even here, though, statutes traditionally imposed a limitation: the president and secretary had to be different people. This restriction was based upon the idea that the law might require the president to sign a contract binding the corporation and the secretary to verify the president's signature. Some states still recognize this limitation, and some states impose other restrictions. In Maryland, one person can hold multiple offices only if the bylaws allow, but even then the same person cannot be president and vice president at the same time.

The modern view, reflected in MBCA § 8.40(d), is that "[t]he same individual may simultaneously hold more than one office in a corporation," without restriction from the corporate law. Moreover, contemporary statutes tend not to require three or four officers. Section 8.40(a) of the MBCA basically leaves the matter up to the corporation, providing that "[a] corporation has the offices described in its bylaws or designated by the board of directors in accordance with its bylaws." MBCA § 8.40(c) requires the existence of only one officer, who shall be responsible for "preparing minutes of the directors' and shareholders' meetings and for maintaining and authenticating the records of the corporation. . . ." Though these functions describe the corporate secretary, the MBCA does not require that the person be given that title.

Most close corporations tend to use the traditional titles for their officers. The senior executive is likely called the "president," the principal financial officer the "treasurer," and the keeper of the records the "secretary." In public corporations, as we saw in § 5.6, officers' titles usually reflect their executive function. Thus, the chief executive officer (CEO) is at the head of managerial control, responsible for a team that generally includes the chief financial officer (CFO), chief operating officer (COO), chief accounting officer (CAO), and chief legal officer (CLO or general counsel) (*see* § 5.6). In states still requiring a president, in public corporations it is usually an intermediate management position, though sometimes one person serves as both CEO and president.

Fortunately, there is no need with officers (as there was with shareholders and directors) to discuss meetings and quorum and voting. Though shareholders and directors act only as groups, officers are individuals. In the traditional view of the corporation, they carry out the orders of the board and thus administer the day-to-day affairs of the corporation subject to the direction and control of the board.

## § 8.3   SOURCES OF AUTHORITY

Statutes generally do not define the authority of an officer. Section 8.41 of the MBCA is typical; it provides that each officer "has the authority and shall perform the functions set forth in the bylaws or, to the extent consistent with the bylaws, the functions prescribed by the board of directors or by direction of an officer authorized by the board of directors to prescribe the duties of other officers." This statute gives the corporation freedom to handle the question of officer authority in bylaws or to delegate to an officer the task of prescribing what the other officers are to do.

Modern statutes do not require that the articles say anything about officers (*see* § 3.4). On the other hand, the articles *may* set forth any provision about running the corporation. So it is possible that the articles might contain provisions (such as spelling out responsibilities) concerning officers. Customarily, however, such provisions are found in the bylaws.

In public corporations, the roles of the CEO, CFO, COO, CAO, CLO, and others usually will not be described in the articles or bylaws. Instead, they are often found in organization manuals that describe the corporation's structure. These manuals typically are prepared by management and may be approved by the board of directors (*see* § 5.6).

In all likelihood, the important sources of authority for officers in a close corporation will be the bylaws and express resolutions by the board that authorize an officer to enter particular transactions approved by the board. The following are typical boilerplate descriptions of the roles of officers in many close corporations. Of course, the board (or bylaws) may assign additional duties to any officer, and may provide for other officers, such as an assistant treasurer.

The *president* is the principal executive officer of the corporation. Subject to the control of the board, she usually supervises and controls the business and affairs of the corporation. She is the proper officer to execute corporate contracts, certificates for securities, and other corporate instruments. The *vice president* performs the duties of the president when the president is absent or unable to perform. She may also execute stock certificates and other corporate instruments.

The corporate *secretary* has several functions. She keeps the minutes of the proceedings of both the board and the shareholders, and ensures that the required notice is given for meetings of those groups. She acts as custodian of the corporate records and of the corporate seal, and should affix the seal to all authorized documents. The secretary keeps a register of the name and address of each shareholder, and signs, along with the president or vice president, stock certificates. She is also in charge of recording transfers of the corporation's stock.

Finally, the *treasurer* generally has custody of (and is responsible for) the funds and securities of the corporation. She receives, gives receipts for, and deposits money payable to the corporation. The treasurer may be required to give a bond to ensure faithful performance.

## § 8.4  APPLICATION OF AGENCY LAW

Officers are agents of the corporation (and, of course, other employees may be agents of the corporation as well). As we saw in § 1.9, agency is the law of delegation, by which a principal (P) permits an agent (A) to act on its behalf in deals with a third party (TP). Here, the corporation is P and the officer is A. The officer, like any agent, may have any of the three types of *authority* to bind P to contracts with TP: actual authority, apparent authority, or inherent authority.

*Actual authority* is created by manifestations from P to A (*see* § 1.9). In the corporate context, such manifestations may be in the bylaws or by board act. Typically, the board will pass a resolution authorizing A to do something on the corporation's behalf, such as negotiate and enter a deal with TP to purchase supplies for the corporation.

In dealing with a representative of a corporation, TP has an interesting dilemma: how does she know whether the person can bind the corporation? If the corporation is not bound, TP can only look to A for satisfaction on the contract, and A may be a person of limited means. The best way is to insist that the putative agent produce a certified copy of a board resolution authorizing the deal. If the corporate secretary executes the resolution and affixed the corporate seal, the corporation will be estopped to deny the truthfulness of the facts stated. This method will not help TP on the many small transactions for which there is no board approval. In those cases, TP may be taking a bit of a chance. On the other hand, if the corporation accepts a benefit of the contract, it will be held to have ratified the deal and thus be liable.

*Apparent authority* is created by manifestations from P to TP (*see* § 1.9). In the corporate context, this means conduct by the corporation that would lead a reasonable TP to believe that the officer had authority to bind the corporation to the deal. If an officer has entered transactions with TP in the past, on which the corporation has paid the bills, TP is protected. The corporation will be liable on the new transaction because the officer had apparent authority to bind it. The corporation may be able to recover that amount, however, from the officer who exceeded her actual authority.

*Inherent authority* "goes with the territory." It exists by virtue of the position. There is an academic debate over whether inherent authority should be recognized as a basis of agency power (*see* § 1.9). Whether we see it as inherent authority (as the Restatement (Second) of Agency does) or as a branch of apparent authority (as the Restatement (Third) of Agency does), the question is whether an officer can bind the corporation by acts she takes in office. The big issue is the president. Most non-lawyers probably believe that the president has enormous inherent authority, because most people presume that the president is almost an alter ego of the business. Surprisingly, the traditional view was that the president had limited power to bind the corporation. Usually it did not extend beyond minor, routine transactions. So unless the board gives actual authority, in some states the president is without power to bind the company.

In most states today, though, the president has broader authority. Generally, she can bind the corporation to deals entered in the "ordinary course of business." Any unusual contracts—such as long term employment contracts or settlement of litigation—should be authorized by the board.

Other doctrines may be relevant when an officer purports to act on behalf of the corporation but lacks authority (actual, apparent, or inherent) to bind it. Suppose the board learns that an officer acted beyond her authority in entering into a contract (on behalf of the corporation) with TP. The corporation can *ratify* the contract by accepting it (despite the lack of authority). It will usually do so by board act. The corporation will then be liable on the deal.

What happens, instead, if the corporation does nothing? Generally, ratification requires an affirmative act by P. So if the corporation does nothing, it will not be bound by ratification. On the other hand, if the corporation accepts a benefit of the contract, a court will probably find that the corporation is liable on the contract. In doing so, the court may use terms such as "estoppel" or "unjust enrichment." Courts can be rather imprecise in using these terms, but the results of the cases are usually consistent with common sense. Suppose an officer enters a deal with TP that is beyond her actual authority—say, to purchase supplies greater than a certain dollar figure. The corporation then accepts and uses the supplies. Common sense tells us that the corporation should be liable on that deal.

Common law gets to that result, though the theoretical basis is often unclear.

We have considered whether an officer can bind the corporation to deals with TPs. Now we turn to a related question: will the officer be personally liable on these deals? The answer again is found in agency law. The starting point is always that the officer (or any agent of the corporation) who acts within her authority is not personally liable on the transaction. This is because she is acting as an agent for a disclosed principal, and thus, under agency law, is not a party to the contract.

An officer may incur personal liability, though, under a variety of theories. First, an officer may expressly guarantee the performance by the corporation. TPs often insist on such personal guarantees, which must be supported by consideration or reliance to be enforceable. Whether it must also be in writing depends on the statute of frauds.

Second, an agent may bind herself by creating the impression that she is negotiating as an individual, rather than as agent of the corporation. The proper way for a corporate officer or agent to execute a document in the name of, and on behalf of, a corporation is this:

XYZ Corporation

BY: _____

PRESIDENT

A variation from this form runs the risk of creating the impression that the individual is jointly liable with the entity. For example, this form is ambiguous:

XYZ Corporation

_____

PRESIDENT

Here, it is not clear whether (1) the corporation and the president are joint obligors or (2) the president is signing as agent of the corporation. The word "president" does not resolve the ambiguity because it may be either an identification of an individual co-obligor or an indication that she signed as an agent of the corporation.

Third, if an officer negotiates a transaction without disclosing that she is acting solely on behalf of the corporation, she will be personally liable to TP on general agency principles relating to undisclosed principals.

Fourth, if the agent is acting beyond the scope of her authority she may be personally liable on the transaction unless the corporation ratifies the transaction.

Fifth, liability might be imposed by statute. Depending on the state, failure to pay franchise taxes or to have a foreign corporation qualify to transact business may create individual as well as corporate liability.

Given that officers are agents of the corporation, can their knowledge be imputed to the corporation? Generally, the answer is yes. Knowledge acquired by an officer while acting in furtherance of the business or in the course of employment is imputed to the corporation. So if the president knows of a transaction, and the corporation accepts benefits of it, the corporation may become liable through estoppel, even though the directors and other officers were ignorant of the transaction. Similarly, service of process on an authorized agent of the corporation supports a default judgment against the corporation even though the agent fails to forward the papers to the corporation or its attorney.

As a general rule, an officer's wrongful intentions may also be imputed to a corporation, which may open the business to civil liability or even criminal prosecution. Often, any criminal prosecution will be for "white collar crime." There are some examples of corporations being indicted for "personal" crimes such as murder, but actual prosecutions are very rare. For a corporation to be prosecuted for such conduct, the conduct itself must have been connected with, or in furtherance of, the corporation's business and the officer's position with the corporation must have been such as to justify imputation of criminal intent to the corporation.

## § 8.5 SELECTION AND REMOVAL OF OFFICERS

Generally, the board of directors hires and fires officers. If the bylaws permit a corporate officer to appoint other officers, the appointing officer will have the authority to remove the officers. Section 8.43(b) of the MBCA is typical of modern statutes, and provides that "[a]n officer may be removed at any time with or without cause" either by the board or the appointing officer. Thus, officers serve at will. This point is emphasized by MBCA § 8.44(a), which declares that "[t]he appointment of an officer does not itself create contract rights."

On the other hand, an officer may have contract rights if she and the corporation enter an employment contract. If she can get such a deal, and the corporation breaches it, the corporation may be liable in contract, typically for damages and not reinstatement.

There is nuance to this situation, however. In close corporations, employment contracts are often part of the basic planning arrangement among shareholders. Terms relating to employment may be placed in shareholders' management agreements (*see* § 10.3). Courts appear to be more willing to order specific performance of such an agreement than of an employment contract *per se*.

There has been a good bit of litigation, especially in close corporations, concerning long-term or lifetime employment contracts. Bylaws usually provide that officers are appointed to one-year terms. Does such a bylaw limit the power of a corporation to grant an officer a longer-term employment contract? No. The board has the authority to bind the corporation to such a deal, even though it will tie the hands of future boards. Of course, as we said above, the corporation may be liable for breach of contract if it fires the officer before her contractual term is up.

What about lifetime contracts? There is nothing inherently illegal about them, as long as they are expressly authorized by the board. But most cases involving claims of lifetime contracts are based upon oral statements in family-run close corporations. When the facts are ambiguous, courts tend to be hostile to lifetime contracts. After all, things change, and the notion that someone should have the same position in the corporation for life may be unreasonable.

It is clear that an officer or employee with a valid employment contract may be discharged for cause without breaching the contract. "Cause" includes dishonesty, negligence, refusal to obey reasonable orders, refusal to follow reasonable rules, or a variety of other acts such as engaging in sexual harassment or an unprovoked fight. Such conduct constitutes a breach of an implied covenant in any employment contract. And, as noted, officers without a contract for term employment are at-will employees and may be discharged at any time.

The board is responsible for monitoring the officers. The level of detail involved in monitoring will depend upon the size and structure of the corporation. In public corporations, the board cannot engage in a hands-on, "I'm looking over your shoulder"-kind of monitoring. In close corporations, however, it can. In any corporation, however, the board must engage in appropriate review. Failure to do so can constitute a breach of the board's duty of care (*see* § 9.3).

Finally, matters of officer compensation, especially in large public corporations, have commanded a great deal of attention in recent years. Employment contracts for high-ranking personnel in public corporations often provide for deferred compensation, pension plan benefits, options to purchase shares at bargain prices, reimbursement of business expenses, and other tax-related benefits. The high level of compensation has become a political issue (*see* § 11.6).

## § 8.6 FIDUCIARY DUTIES OF OFFICERS

Chapter 9 is devoted to fiduciary duties traditionally referred to as "directors' duties." They include duties of care and loyalty and an obligation of good faith. It is clear, however, that these duties are owed not only by directors but by officers. Section 8.42(a) of the MBCA codifies the same standards for conduct of officers as § 8.31(a) does for directors. The Delaware Supreme Court has recognized that officers generally owe the same fiduciary duties as directors. *Gantler v. Stephens*, 965 A.2d 695, 709 (Del. 2009). Accordingly, Chapter 9 addresses potential liability of officers as well as directors.

Beyond these basic fiduciary duties, § 8.42(b) imposes on officers an important duty to inform superiors of information that is material to the superior or that involves "any actual or probable material violation of law involving the corporation or material breach of duty to the corporation. . . ."

Accordingly, an officer who becomes aware of corporate violations of law is required to blow the whistle. She cannot remain silent and at the same time remain faithful to her duty to the corporation.

# CHAPTER 9
# FIDUCIARY DUTIES

## § 9.1 INTRODUCTION

Those who are willing to assume positions of power must shoulder the responsibility that accompanies that power. In the corporate world, managers (those with power to direct the business) are fiduciaries of the business. A fiduciary is "[a] person who is required to act for the benefit of another person on all matters within the scope of their relationship. . . ." BLACK'S LAW DICTIONARY 743 (10th ed. 2014). A fiduciary owes to the business three generic duties: those of (1) good faith, (2) care, and (3) loyalty. (We will see in § 9.5 that there is some recent authority for holding that "good faith" is an "obligation" rather than a "duty.") Generically, we will call these three the "fiduciary duties" or simply "the duties." They are not hermetically sealed, and it is possible that a single act by a fiduciary may violate all three duties.

It is important to remember that the duties are owed *to the corporation*. Breach of the duties may harm the corporation. Hence, the corporation (and not the shareholders) will have a legal claim against its breaching fiduciaries, and may sue them to impose personal liability for the breach. Often, these claims are asserted in a "shareholders' derivative suit," which we study in Chapter 15.

## § 9.2 WHO OWES WHAT DUTIES TO WHOM?

A.    *Who Owes Duties?* Directors always owe fiduciary duties to the corporation. As we saw in § 8.6, officers generally owe the same duties. This is especially clear in large, publicly-traded corporations. There, the senior officers are managers. The board of directors sets broad guidelines for the business, within which officers make significant management decisions (*see* § 5.6). Because of this broad power, the law imposes fiduciary responsibilities on these officers.

What about lower level officers in the large corporation? Here, courts will look at the extent of control given the officer and the type of liability being imposed. Officers in subordinate positions typically owe a lesser degree of duty, though even the lowest agent owes the principal duties of care, skill, propriety of conduct, and loyalty, and good faith in matters relating to her employment. The duties owed by junior officers are largely defined by specific instructions from more senior officers or employees, job descriptions, organizational charts, and the law of agency.

Shareholders, as such, have no power to manage the business. Thus, the starting point is that they owe no fiduciary duties to the corporation or to other shareholders. In most instances, then, a shareholder is not required to act with the best interests of the business or other shareholders in mind. But some shareholders *do* owe fiduciary duties. In the close corporation, shareholders may abolish the board of directors and take over management (*see* § 10.3).

When they do so, they will owe fiduciary responsibilities. The question of who owe fiduciary duties to the business is answered functionally: those with power to manage owe the duties. For the sake of simplicity, we will speak of duties owed by "directors," though we realize that others may owe them as well.

B.      *What Are the Duties? An Overview.* Let's get one thing out of the way first: some cases talk about directors as "trustees" and, thus, as owing the duties of a trustee. Though directors and trustees are both fiduciaries, the characterization of directors *as* trustees has never been accurate. Trustees are required to preserve and maintain the assets under their control, for the interest of the beneficiaries. They are to be conservative and may be liable if they commit trust assets to speculative ventures. In contrast, directors are expected to maximize economic returns for the shareholders, which may require boldness, audacity, and risk-taking.

Historically, courts have spoken of three fiduciary duties: those of (1) good faith, (2) care, and (3) loyalty (which is sometimes called the duty of fair dealing).

For a long time, claims asserting lack of good faith were rare. That has changed in the past generation, as courts have been forced to deal with a torrent of such claims. We will see in § 9.5 that these cases have been driven by the proliferation of "exculpation statutes" passed in the wake of a famous duty of care case, *Smith v. Van Gorkom*, 488 A.2d 858 (Del. 1985) (*see* § 9.4). We will also see that there is authority for considering "good faith" not as a separate duty, but as part of the duty of loyalty (*see* § 9.5).

The duties of care and loyalty demand a good bit of our attention, as we see in the succeeding sections of this chapter. The purpose here is to define them and give an overview. The duty of care is aimed at ensuring that directors take their job seriously. Directors get in trouble under the duty of care by being lazy or causing the corporation to do something that loses money or otherwise hurts the business. Because judges are not business experts, they should not assess the substantive correctness of business decisions. Their job is to review the quality of the decision-making process used by the managers. Under the "business judgment rule," the court will police whether the decision-makers undertook sufficient consideration of the issue, and will not second-guess a decision made in good faith (even if the decision turns out to be a disaster for the company) (*see* § 9.4).

The duty of loyalty is implicated when a manager has a conflict of interest. Anytime she is in a position to put her own interest above that of the corporation, we have a duty of loyalty problem. For instance, if the corporation enters into a contract with a business owned by one of its directors (or the director's spouse), that director is torn both ways—she has an incentive to maximize the return on both sides of the deal. The business judgment rule never applies in conflict-of-interest cases. So courts are far more intrusive, far more inclined to review the substance of what was done, in duty of loyalty cases than in duty of care cases (*see* §§ 9.6–9.8).

C.     <u>*Where Do the Duties Come From?*</u> Fiduciary obligations of managers developed at common law. Increasingly, however, states have codified at least the basic framework. Even in such states, however, courts have had to work out important details. So though there may be legislation, good lawyers also look to case law.

The MBCA is typical of legislation addressing fiduciary duties, though it is important to appreciate that the wording of statutes differs from state to state. Section 8.30(a) provides that directors "shall act: (1) in good faith, and (2) in a manner the director reasonably believes to be in the best interests of the corporation." These two clauses codify, respectively, the duties of good faith and the duty of loyalty.

Section 8.30(b) codifies the duty of care. It provides that directors " . . . shall discharge their duties with the care that a person in a like position would reasonably believe appropriate under the circumstances." An earlier version of the MBCA spoke of the care that an "ordinarily prudent" person would use, and many states still use the prudent person standard, either in their statute or in case law. The present version of the MBCA deleted "ordinarily prudent" because the drafters feared that it made directors too conservative—afraid to be bold and to take appropriate risks. Moreover, they felt that a focus on prudent persons might lead courts to assess the substantive correctness of business decisions, which would undermine the business judgment rule. That rule, as we just said, ensures that courts evaluate the *process* by which directors make decisions, and not second-guess the substance of those decisions.

Section 8.30(b) makes clear that the duty of care applies to directors "when becoming informed in connection with their decision-making function or devoting attention to their oversight function." This is helpful language, because it points out that directors perform two sets of tasks. First, they take certain acts, such as declare distributions, recommend fundamental changes to shareholders, have the corporation issue stock, and hire and fire officers. Second, they oversee what others do. In § 5.6, we noted that management of a public corporation does not fit the traditional model of corporate governance, in which the board is presumed to be in charge of day-to-day affairs. The reference in § 8.30(b) to the board's "oversight function" is a legislative recognition of reality: directors of a large, publicly-traded company do not make day-to-day decisions. That function is for senior officers. The board must oversee, to monitor, and to ensure that those calling the day-to-day shots are doing so consistent with their duties. In a close corporation, in contrast, the board of directors may well make the nitty-gritty quotidian decisions, and thus have less of an oversight role.

Section 8.30(c) imposes on directors a duty to disclose information that is in their possession but which is not known by others on the board. The duty applies to such information "known by the director to be material to the discharge of their decision-making or oversight functions." The duty to disclose is likely most important in interested director transactions (*see* § 9.7). Not all states have a counterpart to § 8.30(c). Even in such states, however, the idea that a director who knows something material (and knows that the other directors do not know it) will disclose it should be seen as part of the overall requirement that a fiduciary act in good faith.

Section 8.30 lays out the duty of care and loyalty, but does not give the test for when directors will be found liable for breaching the duties. Section 8.31 does that. The titles of the sections make this clear: 8.30 deals with standards of "conduct," while § 8.31 addresses standards of "liability." Section 8.31(a)(2) provides for liability if the plaintiff shows any of five listed things. The list reflects the duties of good faith, care, and loyalty.

D.    *To Whom Are the Duties Owed?* Managers owe fiduciary duties *to the corporation.* Some courts say that managers owe these duties to the shareholders. By this, however, they mean shareholders collectively, and not individually. Thus, these statements should be seen as saying that managers owe fiduciary duties to the business. By discharging the duties owed to the corporation, the managers act for the benefit of the shareholders. (We are not saying that managers do not owe independent duties to shareholders; they do, as we see at various points (*see, e.g.*, § 9.11). But these bedrock fiduciary duties are best considered as being owed to the company itself.)

When managers breach a fiduciary duty and harm the company, the company will have a claim against them, to impose personal liability upon them for hurting the corporation.

Ordinarily, fiduciaries do not owe duties to the creditors of the corporation. There is some support for the notion that when a corporation is insolvent (or approaching insolvency), the managers must preserve business assets for the benefit of creditors. The Delaware Supreme Court rejected this position in *North American Catholic Educational Programming Foundation, Inc. v. Gheewalla*, 930 A.2d 92, 103 (Del. 2007). It held that before a corporation is insolvent, managers must continue to discharge duties to the corporation itself and owe no special duty to creditors. Even when a business is insolvent, the court held, creditors will have standing to bring derivative suits against managers—but only for breach of duties owed to the corporation itself. Creditors have no right to assert direct claims against the managers.

### § 9.3  THE DUTY OF CARE: INACTION, CAUSATION, AND OVERSIGHT

A.     *Background.* The duty of care evolved at common law, though many states now codify it. Statutes and common law vary somewhat in stating the standard, but the idea is universal: a director must take her job seriously. So, in the language of MBCA § 8.30(b), she must discharge her duties "with the care that a person in like position would reasonably believe appropriate under the circumstances." In some states, as noted above, it's the care that an "ordinarily prudent" person would use. Either way, managers get in trouble under the duty of care either by being lazy or by having the corporation do something really dumb. There are two ways to breach the duty of care: nonfeasance and misfeasance.

Nonfeasance is when a director does not do anything (or at least not very much) toward discharging the job. One well-known example is *Francis v. United Jersey Bank*, 432 A.2d 814, 825–29 (N.J. 1981), which involved a reinsurance business that had been run by a father and his sons. The father died, and his widow, Mrs. Pritchard (the sons' mother) was elected to the board of directors. She knew nothing about business generally and nothing about the reinsurance business in particular. Mrs. Pritchard attended no board meetings and did nothing to acquaint herself even with the rudiments of the business. She was a figurehead. With Dad out the way and Mom doing nothing, the sons allegedly proceeded to siphon large sums of money from the corporation, mostly through improper payments to other family members.

The company went bankrupt, and the trustee in bankruptcy sued Mrs. Pritchard for breach of the duty of care. (Actually, the trustee sued her estate, because she had died by this time.) The New Jersey Supreme Court upheld a judgment of more than $10,000,000 based upon Mrs. Pritchard's breach. Apparently, the sons' misdeeds were so obvious that a person in like position—paying *any* attention to the business—would have seen that there was something wrong and would have taken some action to stop the harm to the company.

It is easy to feel sorry for Mrs. Pritchard. She was elderly, alcoholic, and devastated by her husband's death. And she was at the mercy of her sons; Mr. Pritchard had once said that those boys "would take the shirt off my back." On the other hand, nobody made Mrs. Pritchard take a directorship position. The lesson is clear: if you are going to take the job, you have to do the work. She breached her duty of care to the corporation by failing to exercise the diligence, care, and skill that someone reasonably would use in that position.

B. _Causation._ In duty of care cases, the plaintiff has the burden of showing that the defendant failed to meet the standard of care. However, making that showing usually does not result in liability. In most states, the plaintiff must also show *causation*. That is, she must demonstrate that the defendant's failure to meet the duty of care *resulted in harm to the corporation.* In *Francis,* the court found causation. If Mrs. Pritchard had not been asleep at the switch, she would have seen that something was terribly wrong and taken ameliorative steps.

*Francis* is unusual. In many cases, the plaintiff cannot show causation. (In *Francis,* remember, Mrs. Pritchard had died, so the judgment would not come out of her pocket; it would come out of her estate, which otherwise probably would have gone to the sons who allegedly misappropriated business funds.)

More typical is *Barnes v. Andrews*, 298 F. 614, 616–17 (S.D.N.Y. 1924), a decision by the legendary Judge Learned Hand, applying New York law. The case involved a corporation formed to make engine starters for Ford motors. About a year after the company was formed, the defendant became a director. He served for nine months, at which point the company was put into receivership because it had no assets. When the defendant became a director, though, the company had money, a manufacturing plant, and employees. During his directorship, the company simply failed to produce starters, and used up all of its money in salaries. Apparently, there was in-fighting among the officers, which paralyzed the company.

The defendant had been put on the board as a favor to the president of the company, who was a friend. The two saw each other socially, but the defendant never bothered to ask or to investigate why a company so well capitalized and staffed was not producing any products. The receiver sued the defendant for breach of the duty of care, and tried to recover money for benefit of the corporation's creditors. The defendant clearly did breach the duty of care. The duty of care encompasses a requirement that the director "keep advised of the conduct of corporate affairs." The defendant failed to do this (or anything else). Faced with the fact that the company was not producing anything, he failed to ask questions or to investigate in any way. He thus failed to do what a reasonable (or prudent) person would have done under the circumstances.

But the defendant was not liable! Why? Because the plaintiff failed to show that "the performance of the defendant's duties would have avoided loss, and what loss it would have avoided." In other words, the plaintiff failed to show causation. Even if the defendant had done his job, it is not clear that it would have made a difference. The in-fighting among officers may have been intractable.

It is usually difficult for a plaintiff to show causation in a nonfeasance case, because often it is not clear that the director, had he paid attention, could have stopped the bad things from happening. In general, as Judge Hand explained in *Barnes*:

> Directors are not specialists, like lawyers or doctors. They must have good sense, perhaps they must have acquaintance with affairs; but they need not—indeed, perhaps they should not—have any technical talent. They are the general advisers of the business, and if they faithfully give such ability as they have ... it would not be lawful to hold them liable.

That said, if a director happens to have special expertise, she is expected to bring it to the table.

- Allen is a director, and is an expert in antitrust law. He fails to attend board meetings or to do anything to discharge his duty of care. The board approves a deal that violates the antitrust laws and creates liability for the company. Is Allen liable? Maybe. Certainly he breached the duty of care by not acting as a person reasonably would in like position. And here there might be causation. Given his expertise, had he been doing his job, he might have been able to stop the board from taking this act.

In *Barnes,* Judge Hand considered placing the burden regarding causation on the defendant, to require the defendant to show that his breach did not harm the company. He rejected the idea. *Barnes* is the majority view, and is embraced by MBCA § 8.31(b)(1)(ii), which requires the plaintiff to show proximate causation.

But it is not the universal view. Interestingly, Delaware does it differently. In *Cede & Co. v. Technicolor, Inc.*, 634 A.2d 345, 361 (Del. 1993), the Delaware Supreme Court set up a system of shifting burdens. The initial burden is on the plaintiff to show that the defendant breached the duty of care. If the plaintiff does this, the burden shifts to the defendant to show that her actions as a whole were fair to the corporation. The defendant need not show an absence of causation. In other words, she need not show that the company's loss was caused by something other than her actions. Rather, in Delaware, she must show that she dealt fairly with the corporation.

C.     *Failure to Monitor.* Above, we noted that directors must satisfy the duty of care both with their "decision-making function" and their "oversight function" (*see* § 9.2, subpart C). The decision-making function deals with major policy decisions vested in the board, such as declaring distributions, recommending fundamental changes to shareholders, issuing stock, and hiring and firing officers. The oversight function involves monitoring whether subordinates are discharging their duties. Directors can fail to discharge their duty of care by failing to oversee those below them.

- Mid-level employees engage in illegal price fixing while working for Corporation. Corporation and the employees are prosecuted under the antitrust laws. The individuals are jailed and Corporation is fined $10,000,000. Now a shareholder brings a derivative suit against the directors to recover that $10,000,000 on behalf of the corporation. The theory is that the directors failed to monitor what the employees were doing, and thereby breached the duty of care.

In *Graham v. Allis-Chalmers Mfg. Co.*, 188 A.2d 125, 128–30 (Del. 1963), the Delaware Supreme Court held that the directors in such a case were not liable. It noted that the corporation had over 30,000 employees in several states, and concluded that the board of directors could not be responsible for the actions of all those people. Rather, the board was responsible only for very broad policy issues, and not the immediate supervision of mid-level employees. The plaintiff argued that the directors had a duty to establish a monitoring system to uncover problems such as those that got the corporation in trouble. The court, in overly broad language, said the board had no responsibility to set up a monitoring system until it had reason to suspect that the employees were doing something bad.

That broad language in *Graham* is no longer the law in Delaware. The Delaware Chancery Court established a new approach in *In re Caremark Int'l, Inc. Derivative Litigation*, 698 A.2d 959, 970 (Del.Ch. 1996). There, criminal activity by underlings cost the corporation $250,000,000 in fines for violations of Medicare and Medicaid rules. In upholding a settlement of the resulting derivative suit against the directors, the court held that the board of directors must implement reporting or information systems to monitor operations. The board has great discretion in setting up such a system. Indeed, "the level of detail that is appropriate for such an information system is a question of business judgment." But, without question, there must be one, and the board must use it.

The Delaware Supreme Court embraced *Caremark* in *Stone v. Ritter*, 911 A.2d 362, 370 (Del. 2006). There, it held that directors can be held liable for breach of the duty of care for failing to monitor only if (1) they "utterly failed to implement any reporting or information system of controls," or (2) "consciously failed to monitor or oversee its operations, thus disabling themselves from being informed of risks or problems requiring their attention."

The board must ensure that there is a command structure and should have a succession strategy to replace officers. It must have accounting and reporting systems in place that assure that transactions are appropriately recorded and monitored by responsible managers. The board must also ensure that there is an information system that assures that responsible officers are informed about problem areas as they develop. And, of course, the board must monitor the performance of the CEO.

In § 5.6, we discussed "inside" and "outside" directors. They owe the same fiduciary duties to the corporation. In discharging those duties, however, their capacity is relevant. An inside director has readier access to the actual workings of the corporation than an outside director. Directors are entitled to rely in on information provided by officers, as long as the reliance is in good faith and reasonable under the circumstances. This does not mean that outside directors may bury their heads in the sand and avoid responsibility for bad board decisions. As the court explained in *Joy v. North,* 692 F.2d 880, 896 (2d Cir.1982): "[L]ack of knowledge is not necessarily a defense, if it is the result of an abdication of directional responsibility. Directors who willingly allow others to make major decisions affecting the future of the corporation wholly without supervision or oversight may not defend on their lack of knowledge, for that ignorance itself is a breach of fiduciary duty."

## § 9.4 MISFEASANCE AND THE BUSINESS JUDGMENT RULE (BJR)

A. *Background.* With misfeasance, the board of directors has done something. Perhaps it has decided to have the company take an act or perhaps it has decided that the company should not take an act. Whatever the board decided has hurt the corporation in some way. For example, maybe the board decided to have the company start a new product line (like "New Coke" in the 1980s or the Edsel automobile in the 1950s) that turns out to be a loser in the market. In these cases (unlike cases of nonfeasance), causation is clear: the board has done something that harmed the corporation.

Whenever that happens, a shareholder may sue the directors for breach of the duty of care. (This will be a shareholders' derivative suit, seen in Chapter 15.) Or maybe a new board of directors will have the corporation sue the former directors, on whose watch the disaster occurred. Either way, the plaintiff will assert that the directors failed to use that degree of skill and care and diligence that someone in their position (or that a prudent person) would reasonably have used. Assuming that there is no allegation of conflict of interest, the plaintiff in these cases faces an enormous obstacle: the business judgment rule (BJR).

The BJR means that as long as business decisions are based upon reasonable information and are not irrational, managers making them will not be held liable, even if the decisions turn out to be disastrous to the corporation. Directors are not guarantors of success. They do not have to be "right." They must act care and diligence. Directors make mistakes. And sometimes, no matter how careful managers are, unexpected events can change what looked like a good idea into a loser. So the law cannot require perfection; it can require only that directors do appropriate homework and come to a conclusion that is not irrational. As the Official Comment to MBCA

§ 8.31 notes, "as a general rule, a director is not exposed to personal liability ... for an unwise decision."

Without the BJR, directors could be sued for any decision that turned out badly for the company. The potential liability could be devastating, particularly in the publicly-traded corporation, where mistakes in the market may have huge consequences. Such potential liability would dissuade people from serving in management positions.

Some opinions speak of breach of the duty of care as "negligence." It is quite clear, however, that simple negligence will not suffice to impose liability. Instead, to overcome the BJR, the plaintiff must show gross negligence or recklessness. As one well-known opinion explains, using "negligence" is

> misleading. Whereas an automobile driver who makes a mistake in judgment as to speed or distance injuring a pedestrian will likely be called upon to respond in damages, a corporate [manager] who makes a mistake in judgment as to economic conditions, consumer tastes or production-line efficiency will rarely, if ever, be found liable for damages suffered by the corporation. Whatever the terminology, the fact is that liability is rarely imposed upon corporate directors or officers simply for bad judgment, and this reluctance to impose liability for unsuccessful business decisions has been doctrinally labeled the business judgment rule.

*Joy v. North*, 692 F.2d 880, 885 (2d Cir. 1982). Plaintiff thus must demonstrate gross negligence or recklessness or that the managers put the corporation in a "no-win" situation. An example of the latter is *Joy v. North,* in which directors continued to approve investment in a real estate development that had made no progress, with no hope of success. As the court said "there was a low ceiling on profits but only a distant floor for losses."

Because of the BJR, a court addressing a claim that a management decision breached the duty of care focuses on *process*, and not on *substance* of the decision. A good example is *Shlensky v. Wrigley*, 237 N.E.2d 776, 780 (Ill.App. 1968), in which a shareholder sued management of the Chicago Cubs, asserting that its decision not to play baseball games at night hurt business. Long after every other major league team installed lights and played night games, the Cubs clung to the allure of afternoon games. (The Cubs did not install lights at Wrigley Field until 1988. Lights have not helped—the Cubs have not been to the World Series since 1945 and have not won the World Series since 1908.) Plaintiff had statistics showing that attendance at night games was higher than that at day games. The court dismissed the claim under the BJR, and emphasized that it had no authority to review the substantive merit of the management decision. The court explained:

> [W]e do not mean to say that we have decided that the decision of the directors [to refuse to play night home games] was a correct one. That is beyond our jurisdiction and ability. We are

merely saying that the decision is properly one before directors and the motives alleged in the amended complaint showed no fraud, illegality or conflict of interest in their making of that decision.

Some courts have characterized the BJR as establishing "a presumption that in making a business decision the directors of a corporation acted on an informed basis, in good faith, and in the honest belief that the action taken was in the best interest of the company." *Aronson v. Lewis*, 473 A.2d 805, 812 (Del. 1984). This view is consistent with the heavy burden on the plaintiff to win duty of care cases.

B.    *The* Van Gorkom *Decision.* The most controversial BJR case is *Smith v. Van Gorkom*, 488 A.2d 858, 878–80 (Del. 1985), in which the Delaware Supreme Court imposed liability on directors of a publicly-traded corporation (Trans Union) for agreeing to sell the company in a deal that paid the corporation's shareholders $55 per share. That price was $18 more than the stock was selling for at the time, so the deal negotiated by the directors brought the shareholders what appeared to be a handsome profit. Nonetheless, the directors incurred enormous personal liability.

Van Gorkom was the CEO of Trans Union. He owned 75,000 shares (of 20,000,000 outstanding). While reviewing the future of the company, management considered various options, including selling the corporation to an outsider. Van Gorkom, who was approaching retirement age, reached an intuitive judgment based on his knowledge of the corporation that $55 per share would be a good price. Financial officers made studies to determine whether Trans Union generated enough cash flow to support a leveraged buy-out at $55 per share. (In an leveraged buy-out, the purchase of the company's stock is paid for by cash flow from the company being acquired (§ 11.5, subpart B).)

With no further investigation, and without seeking other possible buyers, Van Gorkom spoke with Jay Pritzker, a "well-known corporate takeover specialist and a social acquaintance." Pritzker offered to buy the corporation (in a deal structured as a cash-out merger) for $55 per share, but demanded a decision within a few days. Van Gorkom called a special meeting of the Trans Union board. Only Van Gorkom and the CFO had advance knowledge of the purpose of the meeting. With no documentation, and based upon Van Gorkom's 20-minute oral presentation, the board approved the deal. They were given no written summary of the terms of the merger and no documents supporting the $55 price as adequate. The board asked an investment bank to do a hurried evaluation of the price, but did not push Pritzker for more time. As we will see in § 16.5, mergers must be approved by the shareholders, and this one was— overwhelmingly. About 70 percent of the shares voted in favor, and about seven percent opposed (the rest did not vote).

The Delaware Supreme Court concluded that the directors had breached the duty of care. The Court confirmed that in Delaware, as in most states, under the BJR, "director liability is predicated upon concepts of gross negligence." *Aronson v. Lewis*, 473 A.2d 805, 885 (Del. 1984). The court concluded that the Trans Union directors were grossly negligent in failing to inform themselves of the value of the company and of the proposed transaction. The potential liability in this case was stunning. The matter was remanded to the trial court to determine what would have been a fair price for the merger. If that the court concluded that sale to another suitor would have fetched $60 per share, based upon the shares represented in the class action, the directors would have been jointly and severally liable for $64,000,000. The case apparently settled, apparently for around $22,000,000. The settlement was paid from a combination of insurance proceeds and contributions from Van Gorkom, and, in a display of great magnanimity, Pritzker.

A feisty dissent argued that the directors should have been permitted to evaluate a proposed sale based upon their experience and in reliance on Van Gorkom's representations. The directors were sophisticated business people. Most of the academic commentary about the *Van Gorkom* decision has been critical. One academic called it the worst decision in the history of corporate law. On the other hand, the decision to sell the company is the most important matter a board can ever face. Maybe such an important decision should not be made without investigation and in blind reliance on the judgment of a single person.

*Van Gorkom* should be understood as the court's disapproving the *process* by which the board of Trans

Union made its decision, and not of the substantive decision itself. Most observers agree that if the board had taken more time, gotten more reports (including less hurried assessments by investment bankers) and had tried to find other potential buyers, the court would have upheld the substantive decision to sell to Pritzker at $55 per share.

*Van Gorkom* sent shockwaves through the corporate world. One undeniable result of the case has been longer meetings and greater documentation of decisions. Another was that business interests lobbied legislatures to do something to limit potential liability. The Delaware legislature responded very quickly, and now every state has responded. In every state, corporations are permitted to place exculpatory clauses in their articles. The upshot of these is to limit (or even eliminate) personal liability for damages for breach of the duty of care. *See, e.g.*, Del. § 102(b)(7); MBCA § 2.02(b)(4). We discuss such statutes at § 15.8.

C.     *Statutes Relating to the BJR.* Courts, not legislatures, created the BJR. Increasingly, statutes address the topic and at least give guidance on the application of the BJR. The American Law Institute's *Principles of Corporate Governance* § 4.01(a) also sets forth the general duty of care. Section 4.01(c) states that a "director or officer who makes a business judgment in good faith fulfills his or her duty" under § 4.01(a) if she (1) "is not interested in subject of the business judgment," (2) "is informed with respect to the subject of the business judgment to the extent the director or officer reasonably believes to be

appropriate     under     the     circumstances," and
(3) "rationally believes that the business judgment is
in the best interests of the corporation."

Section 8.31(a)(2) of the MBCA reflects the BJR. In
cases not involving conflict of interest, it places on the
plaintiff     the     burden     to     demonstrate     that     a
managerial decision "was not informed to an extent
the director reasonably believed appropriate in the
circumstances" or that there was a "sustained failure
. . . to devote attention to ongoing oversight of the
business and affairs of the corporation. . . ."

## § 9.5  THE DUTY (OR "OBLIGATION") OF GOOD FAITH

It has always been clear that fiduciaries must act
in good faith. Historically, the duty of good faith had
little content beyond the rare, obvious case in which
a  fiduciary  acted  intentionally  to  harm  the
corporation. In the past generation, the duty of good
faith has been invigorated. The activity is the result
of statutes passed in reaction to *Smith v. Van
Gorkom* (§ 9.4, subpart B). These statutes allow
corporations to eliminate manager liability for
damages.     They     contain     exceptions,     however,
designed to limit such exculpation to cases involving
breach of the duty of care. The wording varies from
state to state, but most list as exceptions various
things that would violate the duty of loyalty. In
addition, many, like Delaware § 102(b)(7), also
provide that a corporation cannot exculpate "for acts
or omissions not in good faith." *See* § 15.8.

In reaction to exculpation clauses adopted under such statutes, plaintiffs began bringing claims for breach of the duty of good faith. As a consequence, there has been increased litigation and more case law about that duty. One important case is *In re The Walt Disney Company Derivative Litigation,* 906 A.2d 27, 67 (Del. 2006). There, the Delaware Supreme Court held that the directors of that corporation did not breach the duty of care or the duty of good faith in approving a deal that compensated Michael Ovitz $130,000,000 for a little more than one year's work as an officer (*see* § 11.6).

The court criticized the directors for not using "best practices" either in deciding to hire Ovitz or in setting his compensation package (and its lucrative severance terms). Nonetheless, unlike the directors of Trans Union in *Van Gorkom,* here the Disney board of directors had done enough homework and reviewed enough expert analyses to be protected by the BJR. The court also held that the defendants had not violated the duty of good faith and, more importantly for present purposes, defined the limits of that duty.

As a matter of logic, the duty of good faith and the duty of care cannot be co-extensive. If they were, the duty of good faith would have no independent status, and the legislature's reference to "acts or omissions not in good faith" in statutes such as Delaware § 102(b)(7), would be meaningless. In *Disney,* the court explained that an act is not in good faith (and therefore cannot be exculpated) if the defendant acted in "intentional dereliction of duty, [or with] a conscious disregard of one's responsibilities." It explained:

> A failure to act in good faith may be shown, for instance, where the fiduciary intentionally acts with a purpose other than that of advancing the best interests of the corporation, where the fiduciary acts with the intent to violate applicable positive law, or where the fiduciary intentionally fails to act in the face of a known duty to act, demonstrating a conscious disregard for his duties.

We noted before that the duties of good faith, care, and loyalty are not hermetically sealed. It is quite likely that acts or omissions that breach the duty of good faith will also breach the duty of care or the duty of loyalty, to which we now turn.

## § 9.6　THE DUTY OF LOYALTY: OVERVIEW AND THE PROBLEM OF COMPETING VENTURES

Duty of loyalty cases are easy to spot. The fiduciary has put herself in a conflict of interest situation, in which she is tempted to put her own interest above that of the corporation. In conflict of interest cases, the BJR does not apply. Therefore, once the plaintiff demonstrates the fiduciary's conflict of interest, the burden shifts to the fiduciary to show that she comported with the duty of loyalty.

The duty of loyalty developed at common law. The most famous case is *Meinhard v. Salmon*, 164 N.E. 545, 546–48 (N.Y. 1928), which arose in the partnership context. Meinhard and Salmon jointly ran a real estate development under a 20-year lease. Meinhard provided the money to upgrade the buildings and Salmon ran the day-to-day business. Toward the end of the lease, the person who owned the property offered Salmon a vastly expanded deal, which included the realty involved in the 20-year least plus a great deal more contiguous property. Salmon accepted the opportunity without informing Meinhard. The New York Court of Appeals, in a famous opinion by Judge (later Justice) Cardozo, held that Salmon breached a fiduciary duty he owed to his partner Meinhard. The opinion has stood the test of time and is in every casebook as the leading exposition of what it means to be a fiduciary not just in a partnership, but in any business. Thus, just as Salmon owed a duty of loyalty to Meinhard, so do corporate managers owe this duty to the corporation.

Legislation deals with at least some aspects of the duty of loyalty. Most states have a counterpart to MBCA § 8.30(a)(2), which defines the general duty of loyalty: a fiduciary must discharge her duties "in a manner [she] reasonably believes to be in the best interests of the corporation." Beyond this, most states also have rather detailed provisions about one classic duty-of-loyalty fact pattern, the interested-director transaction (or "self-dealing"). Some states have legislation on other aspects of the duty of loyalty. In general, though, topics other than self-dealing are addressed by case law.

Because of the ingenuity of selfish people, there are limitless ways to breach the duty of loyalty. A fiduciary who steals money from the business obviously cannot be acting in a way she "reasonably believes to be in the best interests of the corporation." She has breached the duty of loyalty. Speaking very generally, there are three classic duty of loyalty fact patterns: is self-dealing, which we discuss in § 9.7, usurpation of a "business opportunity," which we see in § 9.8, and competing ventures, which we discuss now.

It is acceptable for a person to have more than one business interest. A fiduciary for a corporation that makes widgets may also be engaged in a business that makes video games. A problem arises, though, when a fiduciary of the widget company simultaneously is assumes a fiduciary position in a competing widget company. In general, under the duty of loyalty, a fiduciary for Company A should not be a fiduciary for a business that competes directly with Company A. Doing so breaches the duty of loyalty because the person is not acting "in a manner [she] reasonably believes in the best interests of [Company A]."

Some courts say that a fiduciary may go into competition with her corporation, so long as she acts in good faith and does not injure her corporation. Or, some cases say, a fiduciary may compete with her company if she gets the approval of the company's disinterested directors. Neither scenario seems realistic. First, the point of going into competition would seem to be to hurt Company A: the fiduciary thinks she can make money by competing, and that money likely comes at the expense of Company A.

Second, it appears unrealistic that the disinterested directors would think this is a good idea. It is hard to imagine such directors saying: "Sure, Sally, we think it will be great if you form a competing venture and try to take money away from Company A." Directors who do that could be sued for breaching their own fiduciary duties to Company A.

Of course, a fiduciary for Company A is not required to work for Company A forever. And she certainly has a right to pursue other business interests. If a fiduciary resigns her position with Company A on Monday and forms Company B on Tuesday, she should not encounter any problems, at least not concerning the duty of loyalty (she might have a contractual problem if she is subject to a valid covenant not to compete, and must be careful not to commit a tort such as stealing trade secrets). But few people will make the break that cleanly; they will not be comfortable with such a leap of faith. Accordingly, courts generally allow people to "prepare to compete" before resigning from Company A. Common examples include forming a corporation, leasing office space, and arranging for telephone and Internet service.

But the duty of loyalty is implicated if a fiduciary recruits personnel and clients while still on the payroll of Company A. *Duane Jones Co., Inc. v. Burke*, 117 N.E.2d 237, 245 (N.Y. 1954) involved a successful Madison Avenue advertising agency. The company started to falter when its founder and leader began to act erratically. At that point, some of its directors and officers, while remaining employed at Duane Jones Co., set up a competing agency. Only after the new business was established and running did they resign their fiduciary positions at Duane Jones Co. Immediately, the new company started representing several of Duane Jones Co.'s, major clients, which implied that they had solicited the clients while still at Duane Jones Co. They also enticed many lower-level employees to jump ship. Duane Jones Co. sued the erstwhile directors and officers and won a substantial jury verdict. The New York Court of Appeals affirmed the judgment, and held that the defendants had breached their duty of loyalty to Duane Jones Co. Even though the new agency did not make any money until the defendants had left the plaintiff firm, they breached their duty by arranging everything (clients and employees included) at the expense of Duane Jones Co. while still working there.

Common sense tells us that no one will move to another (existing or new) business without some assurance from clients that they will go to the new firm. This happens in law firms and advertising agencies and probably everywhere else. The fiduciaries must be careful to ensure that the decision to employ the new firm is the client's, and that they did not use the old company's resources to recruit the clients (or employees). Being careful, however, is no guarantee that one will not be sued.

## § 9.7  SELF-DEALING ("INTERESTED DIRECTOR TRANSACTIONS")

A.     *Overview.* Self-dealing refers generically to *any* transaction in which a fiduciary is on both sides.

- X is a director of XYZ, Inc. X also owns Supply Corp. If XYZ, Inc. enters a contract with Supply Corp., there is self-dealing (and we have an interested director transaction), because X is on both sides of the deal.

The concern in cases of this sort is that X, in her role as director of XYZ, Inc., has an incentive to have XYZ overpay because doing so lines X's pockets in her role as owner of Supply Corp. Recognizing this conflict, the common law allowed XYZ to void the contract at will. But this rule did not fit business needs. Many self-dealing transactions are good for the corporation; a fiduciary may give her corporation a benefit it cannot get elsewhere. For example, a director might lend money to a corporation when its credit rating makes it impossible to get one from a bank. Such transactions should be encouraged.

Modern law does not allow the corporation to void a contract solely because of such a conflict. Instead, statutes provide that an interested director transaction is not voidable because of the conflict of interest *if the fiduciary shows one of three things*: (1) that the transaction was fair to the corporation when entered, or (2) that it was approved by disinterested directors, or (3) that it was approved by disinterested shareholders. Placing the burden on the defendant makes sense, as we said above, in all duty of loyalty cases. Because duty of loyalty cases involve a fiduciary with a conflict of interest, the BJR cannot not apply, so the burden must be on the fiduciary. (There are a few aberrations. In Arizona, the burden is on the plaintiff to show that none of the three things listed is true. Ariz. Rev. Stats. § 10–863(C).)

The leading approach is probably that found in MBCA §§ 8.60–8.63, which is known as Subchapter F of the MBCA. (A significant number of states, however, adopted an earlier version of the MBCA, from 1975, which codified the topic at § 8.31. In the "new" version of the MBCA, § 8.31 sets forth the standard of liability for directors (as we saw in § 9.2).) And several states have their own variations on these themes. Though the overall structure of these statutes generally is the same, there are some significant variations in the details, as we see below.

B. *What Transactions Are Covered?* The older version of the MBCA—still in effect in some states—defines a self-dealing transaction as one "with the corporation in which the director of the corporation has a direct or indirect interest." MBCA (1975) § 8.31(a). It provides that she had an "indirect interest" if the deal was between the corporation and "another entity in which [she] has a material financial interest" or in which she is a general partner, officer, or director. If the director had an "indirect interest," the transaction should be considered by the board of directors.

This last phrase addresses the problem of "interlocking directorates"—when one person is on the board of directors of both parties to a transaction. It recognizes that routine business transactions between large corporations should not be subject to attack simply because the two corporations happen to have a common director. In large corporations, even transactions involving millions of dollars may be routine, and not be reviewed by the board of directors.

The current version of the MBCA features a clearer, broader definition of self-dealing: it is any transaction to which the fiduciary (1) is a party or (2) in which she has a known "material financial interest," or (3) in which a "related person" is a party or has a material financial interest. MBCA § 8.60(1). A material financial interest is one that reasonably would be expected to impair one's objectivity. MBCA § 8.60(4). A related person includes the fiduciary's spouse or relative (defined very broadly in MBCA § 8.60(5(ii)) or even such a relative of a spouse, a person living in the fiduciary's home, and an entity controlled by the fiduciary. MBCA § 8.60(5).

This definition is helpful. It makes clear that a deal between the corporation and a director's spouse or sibling is self-dealing. Older statutes, with the reference only to "indirect interest" were not as clear on this, though case law in some states filled the gap. Such deals should be considered self-dealing, and the parties should know what steps might be taken to avoid having them voided. And by requiring a "material" financial interest, this statute also shields routine transactions in which the only possible self-dealing is that the two corporations have a common

director. Because the interest would not be material
for the director, it should not be subject to approval
under the statute.

C.     *Is There a Safe Harbor?* We saw in subpart
A above that the statutes permit a fiduciary to avoid
having an interested transaction set aside. The
statutes appear to give the fiduciary three choices. In
fact, some states do not interpret the language this
way.

One choice is to show that the transaction was fair
to the corporation when it was entered. The other two
deal with approval by either of two groups:
disinterested directors or disinterested shareholders.
The big question is whether approval by one of the
two groups is a "safe harbor" that "sanitizes" the deal
without consideration of underlying fairness. The
MBCA says yes. Section 8.61(b) provides that self-
dealing "may not be the subject" of suit by or on
behalf of the corporation if the deal was approved by
directors under § 8.62 or by shareholders under
§ 8.63. The Official Comment to § 8.61 refers to such
approvals as "safe harbors."

The older version of the MBCA (§ 8.31 of the 1975
statutes) did not provide for automatic "sanitization"
by disinterested directors or shareholders. In other
words, even if the deal were approved by one of those
groups, a court could still review the transaction for
fairness. This older MBCA approach is patterned on
§ 144 of the Delaware law. In *Kahn v. Lynch
Communication Systems*, 638 A.2d 1110, 1116 (Del.
1994), the Delaware Supreme Court held that
approval by disinterested directors or shareholders

under § 144 only has the "effect of shifting the burden of proof of unfairness to the plaintiffs."

In other words, in Delaware and states following the older version of the MBCA, if one of those groups approved the transaction, the burden is on the *plaintiff* to demonstrate that the deal was nonetheless unfair to the corporation. *See, e.g., Cooke v. Oolie*, 1997 WL 367034 *32 (Del.Ch.1997) (court reviewed fairness even though transaction approved by disinterested directors). This means the defendant will likely win, because fairness will be assessed under the BJR. The showing of approval by one of the two groups demonstrates that there is no conflict of interest, which, in turn, means that the BJR governs.

On the other hand, if neither group approved the deal, the burden is on the *defendant* to show that it was fair. And fairness in this situation is assessed by the "intrinsic fairness" (or "entire fairness") doctrine. Under this, the defendant must demonstrate that the (1) *process* followed was fair and the (2) *substantive terms* of the deal were fair to the corporation. This is a very difficult burden, and few defendants succeed. *See Weinberger v. UOP, Inc.*, 457 A.2d 701, 710 (Del. 1983) (must show "utmost good faith and the most scrupulous inherent fairness of the bargain").

A good example of the Delaware approach is *HMG/Courtland Properties, Inc. v. Gray*, 749 A.2d 94, 112–15 (Del.Ch. 1999). Here, HMG sold realty to a company called NAF. Gray and Fieber, two of the five directors of HMG, held substantial interests in NAF, so the transaction was self-dealing for those two. Not only that, but Gray negotiated the sale on behalf of HMG. Before the transaction, Fieber disclosed his conflicting interest, but Gray did not. Moreover, even though Fieber knew of Gray's conflicting interest, he did not disclose it to the HMG board. The board approved the sale by a vote of four to zero (Gray voted; Fieber did not). More than a decade later, the company became aware that Gray had been interested in the transaction. It sued Gray and Fieber for breach of fiduciary duty.

Gray was in hot water. Though the transaction was approved by disinterested directors, they were unaware of Gray's conflicting interest. Section 144 in Delaware, like all interested fiduciary statutes, requires that the approval by disinterested directors or shareholders be knowledgeable—that the conflict of interest be "known" or "disclosed." So Gray could not point to relevant approval by disinterested directors, and was stuck trying to argue that the deal was fair.

What about Fieber? He had disclosed his conflict of interest in the deal, after which the disinterested directors approved. The court held that this approval did not help Fieber, though, because he had not informed the board about *Gray's* interest. In other words, Fieber's disclosing his own conflict was not enough to gain protection of the BJR. He was aware of Gray's conflict and did not tell the board.

So Fieber and Gray had the burden of showing fairness under the entire fairness test. As noted, the first part of this test is to show that the process followed was fair. Neither Gray nor Fieber could satisfy this requirement because they did not inform the board of Gray's interest. So even if the price were substantively fair, Gray and Fieber lose.

Under the MBCA and in Delaware, then, it is a good idea to get approval for a self-dealing transaction. Under the MBCA, such approval is a safe harbor. In Delaware, it puts the burden of showing unfairness on the plaintiff, and clothes the defendant with the protection of the BJR.

D.    *Getting Approval for the Conflicting Transaction.* Approval by the disinterested directors or disinterested shareholders is handled differently under various statutes.

In Delaware, for board approval, the conflict of interest must be "disclosed or . . . known" and the deal approved by "a majority of the disinterested directors, even though the disinterested directors be less than a quorum." Del. § 144(a)(1). Interested directors count toward the quorum, Del. § 144(b), and may participate in the meeting and even vote (though their votes do not count toward approval).

- There are seven directors, four of whom are interested in a self-dealing contract. At the board meeting, the three disinterested directors and one of the interested directors show up. That means there is a quorum, because four of the seven total directors are in attendance. Assuming appropriate disclosure or knowledge, if the disinterested directors vote two to one (or three to zero) in favor of the deal, it is approved, because it was authorized by a "majority of the disinterested directors."

The fact that the disinterested directors do not constitute a quorum of the board (because there are only three disinterested directors, of seven board positions) does not matter. The presence of the interested director was important, because it ensured the quorum.

Assume that instead of board approval, we seek shareholder approval. Delaware law again requires that the conflict of interest be disclosed to or known by the shareholders. Then the deal must be approved by "the shareholders entitled to vote thereon." So the quorum and voting rules of a regular shareholder meeting (*see* § 6.4) would be followed. The phrase "shareholders entitled to vote thereon" is ambiguous. On the one hand, it might mean voting stock generally, which (presumably) would permit voting of the shares (if any) held by an interested fiduciary. On the other hand, it might mean that only shares held by disinterested persons can vote. This ambiguity is a feature of statutes in several states. More modern statutes, based upon the current version of the MBCA, avoid this ambiguity.

Under the MBCA, board approval under § 8.62 must be by "qualified" (as opposed to "disinterested") directors. This term is defined in § 1.43(a)(3), which provides that a qualified director is one who does not have a conflicting interest and does not have a "material relationship" with such a director. Material relationship, in turn, means "a familial, financial, professional, employment or other relationship that would reasonably be expected to impair the objectivity of [her] judgment." Such a relationship with a self-dealing fiduciary renders a director unqualified to approve the deal. Section 8.62 requires the self-dealing fiduciary to inform the qualified directors of her interest, unless it is "already known by such qualified directors."

In addition, the quorum and voting rules are different from those in Delaware. Section 8.62(a) requires that the transaction be approved by "a majority (but no fewer than two) of the qualified directors who voted on the transaction." Note that this does not require a majority of all the qualified directors on the board—only a majority of those on the board or committee who actually voted. Section 8.62(c) defines a quorum as "[a] majority (but no fewer than two) of all the qualified directors on the board of directors, or on the committee." Moreover, § 8.62(a)(1) makes it clear that the qualified directors must deliberate and vote outside the presence and without the participation of the non-qualified directors.

- There are seven directors, four of whom are interested in a self-dealing transaction. Assume that the other three are "qualified." Two of the three qualified directors show up at the meeting. That is a quorum under § 8.62(c), because all that is needed is a majority (at least two) of the *qualified* directors. If they vote two to zero to authorize the deal, it is approved, because it is passed by a majority of the qualified directors who actually vote on the deal.

Instead of director approval, we might try shareholder approval. For this, MBCA § 8.63 gives more guidance that Delaware and the other older statutes. It requires approval by a majority of the "votes cast" by the holders of "qualified shares." MBCA § 8.63(a). So we do not need a majority of all qualified shares—only of those actually voted. Qualified shares are those held by folks who are themselves qualified. MBCA § 8.63(c)(2). In other words, the MBCA makes it clear that the interested fiduciary's shares (if any) may not be voted. A quorum consists of a majority of the qualified shares. MBCA § 8.63(d).

- The corporation has 50,000 outstanding shares. The interested fiduciary holds 20,000 of these shares, so there are 30,000 "qualified shares." At the meeting 18,000 of the qualified shares are represented. That means there is a quorum, because a majority of the qualified shares is present. Of those 18,000 shares, only 14,000 actually vote—and they vote 7,500 in favor and 6,500 opposed. The transaction is approved, because it was approved by a majority of the qualified shares that actually voted on the deal.

E. *Compensation and Loans.* The board of directors is responsible for setting executive compensation, including the directors' own compensation. Though historically directors were not paid, this has changed over time, as we discussed in § 7.7. There is a clear conflict when directors set their own compensation. Courts are sometimes asked to second-guess such compensation. These cases arise in at least two ways. One is a challenge by the Internal Revenue Service. C Corporations (as opposed to S Corporations) must pay federal income taxes. In calculating their taxable income, they are entitled to deduct salaries, but cannot deduct dividends paid to shareholders. Thus, corporations have an incentive to label money paid to a director/officer/shareholder as "compensation," rather than as a dividend. The IRS occasionally claims that a corporation has over compensated someone, and thereby taken too generous a deduction.

For us, the more important challenge is that the directors have breached their duty of loyalty by overcompensating themselves. In general, director compensation is treated as other forms of self-dealing, and will be upheld if the relevant self-dealing statute is met. So assuming all directors are interested in the compensation issue, and that the shareholders do not vote on the compensation, the burden will be on the directors to show that the figure is fair. If it is excessive, directors may be liable for wasting corporate assets and thereby breaching the duty of loyalty. *Rogers v. Hill*, 289 U.S. 582, 591–92 (1933).

Courts are reluctant to second-guess executive compensation, especially when the corporation has used procedures—such as an independent compensation committee—that minimize the appearance of conflict of interest. *See, e.g., Heller v. Boylan*, 29 N.Y.S.2d 653, 679 (N.Y. 1941) ("Yes, the

Court possesses the power to prune these payments, but openness forces the confession that the pruning would be synthetic and artificial rather than analytic or scientific . . . Courts are ill-equipped to solve or even to grapple with these entangled economic problems. Indeed, their solution is not within the juridical province.").

Can a corporation make a loan to one of its directors? Every state seems to include in its list of general corporate powers the power "to lend money. . . ." MBCA § 3.02(8). But making a loan to a director makes us nervous, because the company is putting at risk corporate assets that otherwise would be available for something that would seem to benefit the shareholders more directly—such as dividends or to expand the business. In many states, these deals are treated as interested director transactions—so they will be upheld if the requirements discussed in the preceding section were met.

Some states, however, address these loans by specific statutes. Historically, these states permitted loans to directors (and in some states officers and other employees) only if approved by the shareholders. Usually, that meant approval by a majority of the disinterested shares (i.e., shares held by persons other than the person getting the loan). More recently, these states allow the board of directors to approve such loans if it concludes that the loan is reasonably expected to benefit the corporation. *See, e.g.,* Mich. § 450.1548(1). For example, perhaps the corporation may lend money to a fiduciary to help her pay for education that will help make her a better director. Some states offer a choice—approval by a majority of the disinterested shares or by board finding that the deal is reasonably expected to benefit the corporation. *See, e.g.,* Texas Bus. Org. Code § 2.101(13).

## § 9.8 USURPATION OF BUSINESS OPPORTUNITIES

• Corporation wants to expand its manufacturing capacity, and is looking for land on which to build. D, a director (or O, an officer), learns of some land that would be perfect for Corporation's needs, but buys it herself. Because there is no way D can reasonably believe that this act is "in the best interests of the corporation," MBCA § 8.30(a)(2), D has breached her duty of loyalty to the business. D has usurped a business (or "corporate") opportunity (or "expectancy").

Most of the law of business opportunities is judge-made. As we will see, there is substantial variation among states concerning several aspects of the law. When it comes to remedy, however, courts seem in accord—the corporation is entitled to a constructive trust on the property usurped. That means the fiduciary who usurps must put the corporation in the position it should have been in absent her breach. Specifically, there are two possibilities—(1) if she still has the property, she must sell it to the corporation at her cost; and (2) if she has sold it at a profit, the corporation is entitled to recover that profit.

Though everyone would probably agree that the land involved in the hypothetical above was a business opportunity, courts would find different ways to explain why. Courts have used many linguistic formulations to define a business opportunity. If a court concludes that something is a business opportunity, the fiduciary's taking it may breach the duty of loyalty. If it concludes that it is not a business opportunity, the fiduciary may take it. The classic case of *Meinhard v. Salmon,* discussed at § 9.6, is best understood as an example of usurpation of a business opportunity.

Over time, the definition of business opportunity has gotten broader. In earlier cases, some courts defined an opportunity as something "necessary" to the business, or required that the business have an interest in the specific property the fiduciary acquired (not, for example, an interest in real estate generally). Some earlier opinions insisted that the property be related to the actual business the corporation engaged in at the time, and not to some future expansion of the business. Some courts still use some of these phrases, but the trend is for a broader concept.

In deciding whether something was an opportunity courts can use a dizzying array of factors, most of which overlap on the facts of a given case. These include:

- Whether it was in the corporation's "business line." The idea is clear enough—something is a corporate opportunity if it is related to what the company does. And courts have been rather expansive here, looking not just to the present business, but also to possible business expansion.

- Whether the fiduciary discovered it on company time or with company resources. If so, courts are more likely to hold that the property is an opportunity.

- Whether the company has an "interest or expectancy" in it. Some courts interpret this this elastic phrase narrowly, to refer to something the corporation has an option to buy. Most courts interpret the phrase more broadly, to cover anything the company would be interested in. This inquiry obviously overlaps to a degree with the business line question.

- Whether, in view of all the circumstances, it is "fair" that the fiduciary took it.

- The degree to which the corporation needed it.

If a court concludes that something was a business opportunity, the fiduciary is not necessarily precluded from taking advantage of it. The corporation may relinquish it to permit a director or officer to exploit it. The relinquishment in favor of a fiduciary is a self-dealing transaction, subject to the statutory assessment discussed at § 9.7. Indeed, the most recent version of the MBCA has added § 8.70, which permits "qualified directors" (a term relevant in self-dealing too) or qualified shareholders "disclaim" the corporation's interest.

Moreover, courts will not impose liability if the corporation was incapable of taking advantage of the opportunity. For instance, perhaps the third party who is selling the opportunity would refuse to deal with the corporation.

The most controversial basis is when the fiduciary claims that the corporation could not have pursued the opportunity financially. This defense is troublesome, because a fiduciary should try to help her company raise or borrow the money to pursue the opportunity. So some courts seem to conclude that fiduciaries should never be permitted to assert the corporation's inability to pay for the opportunity as a defense. Others permit fiduciaries to take the opportunity if they can show that the corporation lacked independent assets to take advantage of the opportunity. The Oregon Supreme Court took an interesting approach in *Klinicki v. Lundgren*, 695 P.2d 906, 919–20 (Ore. 1985). It concluded that a director may not rely on the company's financial inability unless she first presented the opportunity to the corporation.

This case raises another point on which courts have different views: whether the fiduciary must offer the opportunity to the corporation before taking it. Courts that require this in essence treat an opportunity as something in which the corporation has a right of first refusal, which makes a good deal of sense.

In this regard, we contrast two schools of thought—Delaware and that embodied in § 5.05 of the American Law Institute's (ALI) *Principles of Corporate Governance.* The leading Delaware case is *Broz v. Cellular Information Systems, Inc.*, 673 A.2d 148, 154–55 (Del. 1996). There, the defendant was a director of CIS, a cellphone company that had abandoned operations in the Midwest. He also owned RFBC, a competing cellphone corporation. A third party held an FCC cellphone license to operate in a part of the Midwest, adjacent to that served by RFBC. The third party approached the defendant (in his RFBC capacity) about buying the license, and the defendant bought it without informing CIS. CIS sued him for usurpation.

The Delaware court laid out a four-part test for determining whether something is a corporate opportunity—(1) the corporation must be financially able to exploit it, (2) it must be within the corporation's business line, (3) the company must have an interest or expectancy in it, and (4) by taking it, the fiduciary puts herself in a position "inimical" to her duties to the corporation. The court had established these factors in *Guth v. Loft*, 5 A.2d 503, 513 (Del. 1939).

The last factor demonstrates how closely related the duty-of-loyalty fact patterns are. They can overlap. Part of showing that a fiduciary has usurped an opportunity is showing (under the fourth factor) that by taking it she is now engaged in a competing venture with her corporation.

The lower court in *Broz* held the defendant liable. The Delaware Supreme Court reversed. First, CIS was not able to exploit the license financially. Second, the defendant learned of the opportunity in his individual (not corporate capacity). Third, though the license was in CIS's business line, CIS had no expectancy because it had foregone business in the Midwest. And fourth, acquiring the license did not put the defendant into a competing venture with CIS. The court held that a fiduciary need not present the opportunity to the corporation before seizing it. Doing so will provide a "safe harbor," but failure to do so does not result in liability. Rather, it means the fiduciary must bear the burden of proof at trial.

The ALI takes a different approach. In many casebooks, this is set out in *Northeast Harbor Golf Club, Inc. v. Harris*, 661 A.2d 1146, 1149–51 (Me. 1995), in which the Maine Supreme Court rejected the Delaware case law and adopted § 5.05 of the ALI's *Principles*. Section 5.05(a) imposes an absolute requirement that the fiduciary present the opportunity to the corporation and wait for it to reject the opportunity. In addition, the rejection must be fair to the corporation or rejected by disinterested directors or shareholders. Section 5.05(b) defines corporate opportunity as either:

- Something the fiduciary becomes aware of in connection with performance of her function as a director or senior officer or through the use of company information or property; or

- Something she becomes aware of in any capacity that is "closely related to a business in which the corporation is engaged or expects to engage."

Under the ALI test, the corporation's financial inability to pay for the opportunity is not a defense.

Remember that different duty of loyalty scenarios may be raised in a single fact pattern. In fact, let's finish the section with a great exam question—

- After D usurps the corporate opportunity by buying the land (in the hypo at the beginning of this section), she then sells the land to the corporation. There are two duty of loyalty problems to discuss here: usurpation of corporate opportunity, followed by an interested director transaction.

## § 9.9  MANAGING AND CONTROLLING SHAREHOLDER ISSUES (AND PARENT-SUBSIDIARY RELATIONS)

When a close corporation is managed directly by shareholders (*see* § 10.3), the managing shareholders owe to the corporation the fiduciary duties we have discussed in this chapter. Beyond this, the traditional view is that shareholders of a corporation do not owe fiduciary duties *to each another*. In § 10.6, however, we will see that this notion has changed to a considerable degree. At least in some states, *controlling shareholders*—that is, those who hold enough stock to elect the majority of the managers— owe a fiduciary duty not to oppress minority shareholders or the corporation.

In this section, we focus on an aspect of this potential liability of controlling shareholders for oppressive behavior. Here, the controlling shareholder is another corporation, that is, a parent corporation, which holds enough stock in a subsidiary to control the subsidiary. The trouble arises when the parent does not own all of the stock of the subsidiary. Though dealings between parent and subsidiary corporations often do not fall within the statutory provisions for self-dealing (*see* § 9.7), they may raise questions concerning the treatment of the parent's treatment of the subsidiary and its minority shareholders.

In *Sinclair Oil Corp. v. Levien*, 280 A.2d 717, 720–23 (Del. 1971), Sinclair (the parent corporation) owned 97 percent of the stock of Sinclair of Venezuela (Sinven). Sinclair dominated Sinven completely; it elected several of the directors, who were also Sinclair people. Plaintiff owned some of the other three percent of Sinven. He brought a derivative suit on behalf of Sinven against Sinclair, and alleged that the parent had breached its fiduciary duty to its subsidiary. The court made clear that parent corporations owe fiduciary duties to their subsidiaries, and that dealings between the two companies are judged on whether they are fair.

Importantly, however, the court's fairness inquiry may take either of two forms. One, it might be assessed under the BJR, with the burden on the defendant to show that the parent's was guilty of "gross or palpable overreaching." Two, it might be assessed under the "entire" (which the court sometimes calls "intrinsic") fairness test, which we saw with regard to self-dealing in § 9.7. Under this test, once the plaintiff showed self-dealing, the burden shifts to the defendant to show that the entire transaction was fair, both procedurally and substantively. As a practical matter, the choice of which test to apply will determine who wins. If the court applies the BJR, the defendant will probably win, because that test puts such a difficult burden on the plaintiff. On the other hand, if the court applies the entire fairness test, the plaintiff will likely win, because that test puts such a strict burden on the defendant.

The dividing line is whether there is self-dealing by the parent. In *Sinclair,* the court defined this as the parent's receiving something the subsidiary did not. The facts are instructive. Plaintiff argued that Sinclair caused Sinven to declare huge (but legal) dividends. It did so, allegedly, because Sinclair needed cash. Having Sinven declare huge dividends allegedly robbed Sinven of any chance to expand its business. These allegations, according to the court, did not involve self-dealing, because the minority shareholders of Sinven received the same dividend per share as Sinclair. Because there was no self-dealing (no conflict of interest), fairness was assessed under the BJR, and Sinclair won on that claim.

Plaintiff also argued that Sinclair had usurped opportunities belonging to Sinven by buying land for oil exploration in other countries. The court concluded, however, that Plaintiff failed to show any opportunities that had been available in Venezuela.

Without such evidence, there was no self-dealing, and fairness was reviewed by the BJR. Again, Sinclair won.

But Plaintiff's third claim was the charm. There, he alleged that Sinclair had Sinven contract to sell all of its crude oil to another Sinclair subsidiary at set prices. According to Plaintiff, Sinclair caused its other subsidiary to breach the contract with Sinven by failing to pay on time and by failing to buy the minimum amounts required. This, the court concluded, did constitute self-dealing, because Sinclair (through its other subsidiary) received a benefit (not having to buy so much oil, and not paying on time) to the detriment of Sinven. The court applied the entire fairness test, and Sinclair lost. Sinclair failed to meet its burden of proving "that Sinven could not possibly have produced or in some way have obtained the contract minimums."

In *Weinberger v. UOP, Inc.*, 457 A.2d 701, 709 (Del. 1983), the Delaware Supreme Court held that a cash-out merger of a partially owned subsidiary did not satisfy the entire fairness test. Signal owned 50.5 percent of the stock of UOP, and wanted to acquire the remaining 49.5 percent. Signal dominated the UOP board of directors. Signal required two of its directors, who were also UOP directors, to undertake a feasibility study. The two concluded that acquiring the remaining UOP stock for up to $24 per share would be a good investment for Signal. The companies agreed on $21 per share, and, after approval, the UOP shareholders were cashed out at that price.

Plaintiff was a UOP stockholder, who brought a direct (not derivative) suit, claiming breach of fiduciary duty owed to minority shareholders. By the time the matter was before the court, the merger had been consummated. Thus, Plaintiff sought "rescissory damages" of $3 per share for the minority shares. The trial court held for the defendants, but the Delaware Supreme Court reversed. It set out factors to be assessed in an entire fairness review. First, on procedural fairness, the court noted that the parent corporation had initiated and structured the deal, and required its insiders to use information obtained from the subsidiary to extract a good price for the parent. Second, substantive fairness requires an examination of all economic and financial considerations that affect the intrinsic or inherent value of the subsidiary's stock. Fair dealing and fair price are not to be considered in a bifurcated fashion. Rather, "all aspects of the issue must be examined as a whole since the question is one of entire fairness." And, importantly, the parent corporation has the burden to establish entire fairness.

In an important footnote the court said that "the result here could have been entirely different" if the subsidiary had appointed an independent negotiating committee of outside directors to deal at arm's length with the parent. It added that "fairness in this context can be equated to conduct by a theoretical, wholly independent, board of directors acting upon the matter before them." In the parent-subsidiary context, then, the parent must show that the action would have been taken even if the parties had been unrelated and had dealt at arm's length.

Such facts would be "strong evidence" that the transaction is fair.

The message of *Weinberger* is that independent directors should be added to the boards of partially-owned subsidiaries to permit arms-length bargaining with the parent. Of course, these independent directors must discharge their duties to the subsidiary. In *Cinerama, Inc. v. Technicolor, Inc.*, 663 A.2d 1156, 1162 (Del. 1995), the court stated that in this context the BJR has both procedural and substantive aspects. It is "procedural" because it places the initial burden of proof on the defendants to establish that the BJR is applicable. If the defendants establish that the BJR was satisfied, the burden of proof shifts and the plaintiff must demonstrate the lack of intrinsic fairness. If the BJR is not satisfied, the burden does not shift and the defendants must establish the intrinsic fairness of the transaction.

## § 9.10  WHICH FIDUCIARIES ARE LIABLE FOR A BREACH OF DUTY?

We know that directors and other fiduciaries may be liable for breaching their duties to the corporation. Now we need to assess exactly *which* fiduciaries are liable. In § 7.5, we noted that all directors present at a board meeting are presumed to concur with any action taken at the meeting unless their dissent is in writing in the corporate records. Thus, if the board does something improper at a meeting, a director can escape liability by ensuring that her dissent is in writing.

Even a consenting director may avoid liability if she relied in good faith on the report or opinion of an appropriate person. Statutes in every state embody this notion, which is typified by MBCA § 8.30(e). That section provides that in discharging her duties, a director "is entitled to rely on information, opinions, reports or statements, including financial statements and other financial date, prepared or presented by any of the persons specified in subsection (f)." That subsection, in turn, allows reliance on employees, professionals (such as lawyers and accountants), and on a committee of which the relying director is not a member.

It bears emphasis that the statutes require *good faith* reliance, which means that the fiduciary must reasonably believe that the person on whom she relies is competent and acting within the scope of her expertise. MBCA § 8.30(f)(1) & (2). It is imperative that the director not have "knowledge that makes reliance unwarranted." MBCA § 8.30(e). Accordingly, a director cannot bury her head in the sand and rely on information or advice she knows to be problematic. Various defendants in *Van Gorkom* (*see* § 9.4, subpart B) attempted to raise the defense of good faith reliance by saying that they had a right to rely on the CEO's assessment of the appropriate merger price. The court rejected the defense, however, because the defendants should have been aware that the CEO had not done much homework in coming up with the number.

Section 8.30(e) also reflects the notion that while directors are usually generalists, each brings her own expertise with her to the directorship. For example, a director with a background in finance cannot simply check her profession at the door and rely blindly on what the financial people in the corporation tell the board. Such reliance will not be reliable if she knows something that makes reliance, for her (with her expertise), unwarranted (*see* § 9.3, subpart B).

Finally, recall that fiduciaries have a duty to disclose not only their own interest in a transaction, but any conflict of which they know (*see* § 9.7). So a director must be careful not only to dissent properly, but to disclose important information that she has reason to believe is not known to the others. MBCA § 8.30(c), discussed at § 9.2.

# CHAPTER 10

# SPECIAL ISSUES IN THE CLOSE CORPORATION

## § 10.1  INTRODUCTION

The "close" or "closely-held" corporation has few shareholders and there is no public market for its stock. Because they have relatively few owners, close corporations resemble partnerships in some ways. In particular, the owners may try to run the business as informally as one may run a partnership (*see* § 10.2). The problem is that the traditional model of the corporation (*see* § 5.6) is not very flexible. The tension between the way proprietors may want to run a close corporation and the requirements of corporation law surfaces in three areas, on which we focus in this chapter.

First is how close corporations may be managed. Importantly, states have relaxed the customary corporate law requirements regarding management, and now permit flexibility that was unheard-of a few decades ago (*see* § 10.3). Second is shareholder liability for business debts. Specifically, if shareholders want to run a corporation like a partnership, should they be subject to liability for business debts the same as partners are? Occasionally the answer is yes (*see* § 10.4). Third is the relationship among shareholders. If the business functions as a partnership, should the shareholders owe each other the fiduciary duties customarily applied to partners? In some circumstances, the answer is yes (*see* §§ 10.6 & 10.7).

## § 10.2   CHARACTERISTICS OF A CLOSE CORPORATION (AND "STATUTORY CLOSE CORPORATION")

A close corporation is a true corporation, formed under the statutes we discussed in Chapter 3 and subject to the requirements for shareholders, directors, and officers discussed in Chapters 6, 7, and 8. Historically, there has been no magic number of shareholders for defining a close corporation. In all states, there can be as few as one shareholder. Whenever someone might say that there is a maximum number, we could find a corporation with one shareholder more. Many of the cases in your casebook involve corporations with a handful (say four or five) shareholders.

In speaking of close and public corporations, we may get the impression that all corporations are either small Mom-and-Pop shops or Fortune 500 behemoths. In fact, many companies are in between, with scores of shareholders and some limited market for the stock. For us, the line of demarcation will be whether the company's stock is publicly traded, which means that its securities are registered for public sale under federal law (*see* § 11.2). If the company's stock is not publicly traded, we will consider it a close corporation.

Historically, the law of close corporations has been judge-made. In the past generation or so, about 20 states have passed "statutory close corporation" statutes. Most of these are not separate codes, but "supplements" to the general corporate law, with an express provision that the general law applies in areas not addressed by the supplement. The MBCA promulgated such a supplement in 1984. So here is our terminology:

- A "close corporation" is one formed under a state's general corporate law, the stock of which is not registered for public trading. There is no maximum number of shareholders, and much of the important law about governance and liability may be common law. A "closely-held corporation" is the equivalent.

- A "statutory close corporation" is one formed under special provisions, applicable in about 20 states. The stock is not registered for public trading. The requirements of formation are very simple, but include the mandate that the articles refer to the business expressly as a "statutory close corporation." Most of these statutes also impose a maximum number of shareholders, often 30 or 50. This number does not create much of a problem, because most close corporations have far fewer shareholders than that.

Having made this distinction, in many states we can pretty much ignore it now. Why? Statutory close corporation supplements are not exclusive, so people forming a business with few shareholders do not have to use them. Evidence suggests that very few businesses do. Why not? The principal advantage of statutory close corporations is the flexibility they provide for setting up management. Today, however, that advantage can be enjoyed without satisfying the statutory close corporation legislation because most states now provide for such flexibility in their general corporation codes (*see* § 10.3).

There are some areas in which statutory close corporations are different from close corporations, depending upon the state. For instance, in some states, including Pennsylvania and Texas, in a statutory close corporation, pre-emptive rights exist if the articles are silent. In contrast, in a non-statutory close corporation, pre-emptive rights exist only if the articles say so. Pre-emptive rights allow existing shareholders to maintain their percentage of ownership by buying more stock when the corporation issues new stock (*see* § 12.4). So in some states, election of the statutory close corporation will change the default provision on whether the shareholders have pre-emptive rights. Proper planning of a close corporation should address this question and, if need be, ensure that a provision for pre-emptive rights be included in the articles.

Proper planning will also address the transferability of shares in a close corporation. Close corporations often employ stock transfer restrictions to ensure that "outsiders" may become stockholders only in limited circumstances (*see* § 6.8). In some states, the statutory close corporation laws make certain restrictions automatic, such as a right of first refusal. In other states, these restrictions are not automatic and must be spelled out. So, as with pre-emptive rights, election of the statutory close corporation may affect the default provision on such matters.

In the close corporation, there is no public market for the stock. Among other things, this makes it difficult to buy and sell stock in the hope of making a profit. It also makes it difficult to determine what one's stock is worth. More pointedly, it may be impossible to find someone who will buy the stock. In view of these problems, why do people own stock in close corporations? Some may hope to get dividends (*see* § 13.2), which are distributions of business profits. But most close corporations do not pay dividends, at least not regularly. Usually, profits of a close corporation are plowed back into the business to make it grow. Many (and probably most) people who invest in close corporations intend to work directly in the business and earn a salary. So a significant motivating factor is money received *not as a shareholder, but as an employee. See Wilkes v. Springside Nursing Home, Inc.*, 353 N.E.2d 657, 662 (Mass. 1976) ("The minority stockholder typically depends on his salary as the principal return on his investment, since the earnings of a close corporation . . . are distributed in major part in salaries, bonus, and retirement benefits.")

It is imperative in forming any business to anticipate problems and plan around them. Among other things, the lawyer for the business should force the proprietors to think about what happens in case of disagreement, retirement, or death. When starting the business, everyone is getting along fine. But often in the real world (and almost always on exam questions), this relationship collapses.

- X, Y, and Z form XYZ Corp., a close corporation. Each owns 100 shares of the 300 issued shares of the stock. Each is a director on the three-person board. Each has a job with the corporation and draws a salary. Everything goes great for a while. Then there is a disagreement about some business policy. X is on one side of the dispute, while Y and Z are on the other.

- On every matter considered by the board, X will lose by a vote of two-to-one. On every matter considered by shareholders, X will lose by a vote of 200–100.

- Now the corporation terminates X's employment. She argues that the corporation should declare a dividend for shareholders. But Y and Z vote to have the corporation use profits to expand the business instead (or maybe even to increase their own salaries).

X's situation here is not necessarily the result of ill will or a desire to oppress (though it might be). It could result from honest disagreement over business policy. Either way, though, X is only slightly better off than an orphan in a Dickens novel. She owns stock, but has no voice in management decisions. She is getting no financial return on her stock. She does not draw a salary. The only hope of return on investment for her is to sell her stock to somebody at a profit. But who would pay good money to be put in X's lamentable situation?

X could have avoided her problems. She might have negotiated an employment contract that required the corporation to employ her for a given period, terminable only for cause. She should have negotiated a "buy-sell" agreement, which would require the corporation to buy her stock upon some triggering event, such as when she got fired (*see* § 6.8). Note that these protections come not from the law of corporations, but from the law of contracts.

In setting up the business, the proprietors might consider corporate mechanisms that would avoid problems such as those faced by X. For instance, the articles could require unanimous attendance for a quorum or unanimous votes for various corporation acts. This poses its own risks, however, because it gives each shareholder a veto over every act. This, in turn, increases the possibility of deadlock: of the corporation's being unable to act because one shareholder refuses to play ball. Faced with deadlock, one faction may buy out the other, or the parties may agree to voluntary dissolution. If they cannot agree on that, one shareholder may petition a court for an order of involuntary dissolution of the corporation. Dissolution is not a great solution because it ends the corporate existence through sale of corporation assets. This not only puts an end to what may be a successful business, but usually obviates the chance to sell the entire business for its "going value." That value (what someone would be willing to pay to take the business over as is) is often greater than the sum that would be fetched if all the corporate assets were sold off in dissolution.

The point is simple: plan for the day when the proprietors disagree, retire, or pass away. Provide ways out, either in the corporate documents or by contract. Along the way, consider provisions for mandatory binding arbitration of intra-corporate disputes.

Sometimes, the minority shareholder in X's situation will have a common law claim. As we will see in § 10.6, some courts, analogizing the close corporation to the partnership, impose upon the shareholders the same responsibilities as a partner, which includes the duty of utmost good faith and loyalty *to each other*. In Chapter 9, we saw that fiduciaries owe duties of good faith, care, and loyalty *to the corporation*. If they breach one of those duties, they can be sued by (or on behalf of) the *corporation*. Here, we are talking about duties that run *from one shareholder to another*. This duty is breached by oppressive behavior, which can result in suit against the oppressor.

Not all courts recognize such a claim. Those that do are motivated by the fact that the minority shareholder in the close corporation has no exit from oppression because she cannot readily sell her stock. Many scholars, particularly of the law and economics school, decry such judicial intervention. To them, businesspeople are adults, able to negotiate to their own benefit or detriment. An investor who fails to protect herself contractually has no one to blame but herself. The law and economics (or "contractarian") school has been especially influential in changing the traditional rules about management of close corporations, which is our next topic.

## § 10.3  SHAREHOLDER MANAGEMENT

A.    *Background.* In the traditional model of corporate governance, discussed in Chapter 5, "shareholder management" would be an oxymoron. Shareholders do not manage; the board of directors does. Shareholders elect the directors and must approve fundamental changes, but they do not have a direct voice in running the corporation. The traditional model requires businesspeople to keep track of what hat they are wearing when they take particular acts. Businesspeople must separate their acting as shareholders from their acting as directors. This level of formality is cumbersome in the small corporation, in which the same few people wear both hats. Ultimately, in the close corporation, the traditional model has given way to one based upon flexibility and freedom of contract.

Because the traditional model vests management in the board of directors, it has long been clear that *directors* cannot enter voting agreements regarding how they will vote on the board (*see* § 7.4). Such an agreement is said to "sterilize" the board by robbing the corporation of the benefit of each director's independent judgment, which is to be forged in consultation with other directors at the board meetings. Voting agreements regarding director action violate this public policy, and thus are void.

On the other hand, *shareholders* have always been able to enter voting agreements, usually to require the parties to the agreement to vote their shares in a particular way. Often, these agreements will be to vote their shares to elect each other as directors. Such agreements are common and appropriate (*see* § 6.7).

Problems arise when shareholders attempt to agree not only on what to do as shareholders, but on what they will do when elected to the board. Under standard doctrine, these agreements are void. The classic example is *McQuade v. Stoneham*, 189 N.E. 234, 236 (N.Y. 1934), which involved an agreement among three of the (very few) shareholders of the New York Giants baseball team. The three shareholders agreed to vote their stock to elect each other to the board of directors, and then, as directors, to appoint each other to specified positions as officers, at set salaries.

The agreement to vote as shareholders to elect each other to the board was fine. But the agreement to appoint themselves as officers (and setting their salaries) was void. This is a board matter, to be determined by the board at a meeting, based upon independent judgment. These decisions cannot be subject to an agreement of shareholders. *McQuade* showed no tolerance for such "sterilization" agreements. But the judicial attitude was about to change, to a degree.

B.    *Common Law Inroads on the Traditional Model.* Just two years later, the New York Court of Appeals relented a bit in *Clark v. Dodge*, 199 N.E.

641, 642 (N.Y. 1936). There, Clark owned 25 percent and Dodge owned 75 percent of the stock of two corporations manufacturing medicinal preparations by secret formulae. Dodge was a passive investor. Clark actively managed the business, and was the only one who knew the formulae. The two agreed, as shareholders, that Clark would be general manager of the business and would receive one-fourth of the business's income. Clark, in turn, agreed to disclose the secret formulae to Dodge's son and, upon Clark's death without issue, to bequeath his interest in the corporation to Dodge's wife and children.

This sensible business arrangement runs afoul of *McQuade*, because the two shareholders were making decisions the directors should make: whom to hire as an officer and how much to pay him. Nonetheless, the court upheld the agreement. It criticized *McQuade* by saying that its doctrinal basis was "nebulous." The court continued: "If the enforcement of a particular contract damages nobody—not even, in any perceptible degree, the public—one sees no reason for holding it illegal, even though it impinges slightly upon the broad provision [vesting directors with the sole powers of management]. Damage suffered or threatened is a logical and practical test and has come to be the one generally adopted." Clark and Dodge were the only shareholders in the corporation, so their agreement could not hurt anyone aside from themselves. And any harm to the traditional model of corporate governance was "so slight as to be negligible."

The court in *Clark v. Dodge* did not overrule *McQuade*, but limited the older case to its facts. The ultimate reach of *Clark* has been debated, but it seems to permit a "sterilization" agreement if *all* shareholders agree to it.

Other courts addressed shareholder efforts to wrest management from the board. In *Burnett v. Word, Inc.*, 412 S.W.2d 792, 795 (Tex. Civ. App. 1967) the court took a hard line. There, shareholders agreed that the business could only borrow beyond a certain amount of money if the shareholders approved unanimously. The agreement required each party to vote *as shareholder and as director* to accomplish this goal. The court invalidated that portion of the agreement relating to the directors: "An agreement by which directors abdicate or bargain away in advance the judgment the law contemplates they shall exercise over the corporation is void. The agreement of the parties to bind themselves as directors is void."

On the other hand, in *Galler v. Galler*, 203 N.E.2d 577, 585 (Ill. 1964), the Illinois Supreme Court rejected *McQuade* and enforced a complex shareholders' agreement containing various impingements on managerial power. Among them was a requirement that the corporation pay a dividend. The court upheld the agreement and concluded that "any arrangements concerning the management of the corporation which are agreeable to all" should be enforced if (1) no minority shareholder complains, (2) there is no fraud or injury to the public or creditors, and (3) no clearly prohibitory statutory language is violated. It is not readily apparent what constitutes "clearly prohibitory statutory language" and why that phrase would not include the statutory requirement that management be discharged by the board of directors.

By the end of the 1960s, the state of the common law around the country was unclear. Some legislatures then stepped in to make the next move.

C.  _Legislative Inroads—Statutory Close Corporations._ In the _Galler_ case (see two paragraphs above), the court urged a legislative solution. The Illinois legislature responded with the first "statutory close corporation" statute. These statutes (_see_ § 10.2), adopted today in about 20 states, not only authorized "sterilization" agreements, but allowed the complete abolition of the board of directors! Shareholders now can manage the corporation directly, and doing so will not impose upon them personal liability for business debts. By the terms of these statutes, however, this flexibility was permitted only if the business was formed expressly as a "statutory close corporation."

What happened if proprietors set up shareholder management in the guise of a "regular" close corporation (one that did not qualify as a "statutory close corporation")? States took different approaches. In New York, it didn't matter. In _Zion v. Kurtz_, 410 N.E.2d 760 (N.Y. 1980), the Court of Appeals held that the flexibility allowed for statutory close corporations could be claimed by "regular" close corporations. Delaware reached the opposite conclusion in _Nixon v. Blackwell_, 626 A.2d 1366 (Del.

1993). There, the Delaware Supreme Court refused to apply "statutory close corporation" rules to a corporation that had failed expressly to elect them.

Ultimately, statutory close corporations may be less important than they could have been. Increasingly, liberal provisions regarding shareholder management are found in states' general corporation law, making them available to any close corporation.

D.    *The Ultimate Legislative Rejection of the Traditional Model.* General corporation laws today tend to embrace non-traditional governance in close corporations. These statutes usually refer to governance by "shareholder agreements." To avoid confusion with shareholder voting agreements (*see* § 6.7), perhaps it is a good idea to call them shareholder *management* agreements (SMAs).

The provisions vary from state to state, but there are common themes. We will focus on § 7.32 of the MBCA. Though these statutes do not require the corporation to call itself a close corporation, they apply only in such companies. Indeed, the only statutory qualification to take advantage of SMAs is that the stock of the corporation not be publicly traded. MBCA § 7.32(d) provides that an SMA "shall cease to be effective when the corporation becomes a public corporation."

Under § 7.32(a), an SMA is effective even though it is "inconsistent with one or more other provisions of this Act." This is a reference to those parts of corporation law that vest management authority in the board of directors. The statute lays out a series of stunning usurpations of board power, which, the Official Comment to § 7.32(a) makes clear, are simply illustrative and not exhaustive.

These statutes embody the rejection of the traditional model of corporate governance in the close corporation. The proprietors can do away with the board and vest management in shareholders or in others (e.g., hire a professional manager). They need not do so. They can retain a board structure and, even then, can have various issues, such as hiring officers or declaring dividends, decided by shareholder agreement. These sorts of agreements would have been unthinkable a few decades ago.

To a degree, statutes such as MBCA § 7.32 reflect the influence of law and economics scholars, who have long argued that businesspeople ought to be free to structure their business in the way that makes most sense to them. The freedom reflected in the MBCA makes the close corporation much more like the partnership in terms of management choice.

That freedom, however, is not absolute. Section 7.32(a)(8) of the MBCA provides that an agreement may not violate public policy. For example, the Official Comment spells out that an agreement providing that managers owe no duties of care nor loyalty to the corporation would not be upheld. Not only is it different in kind from the examples in § 7.32(a), but it would clearly violate public policy.

Statutes in every state impose strict rules about the permissible forms an SMA must take. Section

7.32(b) is typical, and gives two choices. First, it may be set in the articles or bylaws, but only if approved by all shareholders. Second, it can be set forth in a written agreement (separate from the articles or bylaws), but only if it is signed by all shareholders. Either way, then, the SMA must be in writing and must be adopted unanimously by those who are then shareholders.

*Villar v. Kernan*, 695 A.2d 1221, 1221–22 (Me. 1997) is a dramatic example of the importance of a written SMA. There, all three shareholders agreed orally that none of them would receive a salary from the business. After a falling out, the board of directors (dominated by Shareholders A and B) voted a salary to Shareholder A. Shareholder C (the one on the outs) sued, arguing that the three had entered into a binding SMA providing for no salaries. The court held that the agreement was unenforceable because it was oral. Accordingly, the traditional model of governance was in place. The board could vote a salary for Shareholder A, and there was nothing Shareholder C could do about it.

In many states, SMAs may be amended only by unanimous agreement. Many states provide that SMAs are valid for 10 years, unless the agreement says otherwise. Most states also require that the existence of the SMA be noted on the stock certificates, though failure to comply with this requirement usually will not affect the validity of the agreement. MBCA § 7.32(c).

Importantly, § 7.32(e) provides that if the SMA eliminates the board of directors, those who actually do run the show owe the fiduciary duties (discussed in Chapter 9) to the corporation. Whoever manages the corporation, including shareholders under an SMA, must do so in consonance with those duties.

It bears repeating that provisions of the type discussed here are part of the general corporation law. One need not form a statutory close corporation to take advantage of them. On the other hand, statutory close corporation statutes may provide some benefits. In Texas, for example, a statutory close corporation may file a statement with the secretary of state noting that governance is by SMA. Doing so constitutes notice to the world that the traditional model of governance is not followed. Thus, transferees of the company's stock are bound by the SMA, even if they lacked knowledge of it. Texas Bus. Org. Code § 21.701 et seq.

Finally, most statutes provide expressly that individuals who manage the corporation under an SMA are not personally liable for business debts. The entity is still a corporation, and the entity (not the individual proprietors) is liable for what it does. MBCA § 7.32(f). This means that an SMA, by itself, is not a basis for imposing personal liability on the shareholders through the doctrine of piercing the corporate veil.

## § 10.4  SHAREHOLDER LIABILITY— PIERCING THE CORPORATE VEIL (PCV)

A.  *Background and Policy.* The principal advantage of the corporation over both the sole proprietorship and the partnership is limited liability. The owners are not liable for debts incurred by the business. This is true even if there is only one shareholder; the entity (not the shareholder) is liable for debts incurred by the business. Shareholders may lose the money they invested if the business does poorly, but they will not be personally liable if the corporation commits a tort, breaches a contract, or otherwise incurs liability. A creditor generally must seek payment only from the corporation.

There are ways around this general rule. For example, a shareholder may voluntarily guarantee the performance of a corporation's obligation. Many owners of small businesses learn that merchants and lenders will not extend credit to the business unless the proprietors personally guarantee payment. A shareholder, like anyone else, is liable for torts she commits and contracts she breaches in her individual capacity.

The focus of this section is "piercing the corporate veil" (PCV), a long-recognized exception to the principle of limited liability. Under PCV, a court may impose personal liability on shareholders for business debts. PCV is an apt description of what happens: a plaintiff is allowed to reach through the corporation and impose personal liability directly on shareholders. Plaintiffs will attempt this only when the corporation itself lacks assets to pay the business debt. In these cases, then, the question for the court will be whether to have the loss fall on the plaintiff (by recognizing the corporate entity) or on the shareholders (by ignoring the corporate entity by invoking PCV).

At the outset, let's emphasize four points. First, PCV is exceptional. It happens rarely, because it is antithetical to the theory of the corporation as an entity (*see* § 2.2). It applies only when shareholders have abused the privilege of incorporation in some way so that a court concludes that the corporation should not be recognized as a separate entity.

Second, PCV applies only to impose liability on *shareholders,* not directors or officers. True, a shareholder may also be a director or officer at the same time, but PCV is imposed for acts taken by shareholders in their shareholder capacity. Directors and officers may incur personal liability for various things, including breaching their fiduciary duties, as we saw in Chapter 9.

Third, PCV occurs only in close corporations. One empirical study shows that it has never been applied in a corporation with more than nine shareholders.

Fourth, the case law on PCV is impossible to reconcile, and uses a dizzying array of terminology. Many courts say that they will PCV to "avoid fraud or to achieve equity," or to "avoid illegality," or something equally imprecise. They speak of PCV when the corporation is the "alter ego" of shareholders, or is a "mere instrumentality," or when there is "unity of ownership," or "excessive control" or "domination," or when the corporation is a "dummy" or a "shell" or a "sham." None of these terms have any content. Judge (later Justice) Cardozo said the entire area is "enveloped in the mists of metaphor." *Berkey v. Third Avenue R. Co.,* 155 N.E. 58, 61 (N.Y. 1926).

Each phrase is a conclusion for when a court might impose personal liability on shareholders.

Though the case law makes it impossible to predict whether a court will PCV on given facts, certain policy bases for the doctrine seem clear. They suggest different approaches to contract and tort cases. In a contract case, the plaintiff usually has dealt directly with the corporation. In the absence of fraud, then, she assumes the risk of loss. She could have insisted on a personal guarantee from the shareholders. If she did not, it is not clear why shareholders should bear the loss.

Tort is different. Here, the plaintiff interacted with the corporation involuntarily—for instance, by getting struck by the business's delivery truck. The question here is whether the shareholders should be able to transfer a risk of injury to members of the general public. The answer should depend on whether the corporation was adequately capitalized to cover the reasonably foreseeable risks in its particular business. If the corporation was plainly undercapitalized, perhaps the plaintiff should be able to PCV and pursue her judgment against the personal assets of the shareholders.

Policy thus suggests (1) that contract and tort cases should be treated differently and (2) that capitalization of the corporation should be the central factor in determining whether to PCV. Many (probably most) cases are consistent with these conclusions. Unfortunately, however, several cases are not.

B. *Case Law.* As we might expect, cases routinely address capitalization as a factor in PCV, as we will see below. The case law is notable, however, for discussing a great deal more. Many courts adopt what has been called a "template" approach under which they list a variety of factors, seeing how many are present in the case, and deciding whether those factors justify PCV. This approach is unpredictable because courts use different factors and there are no clear rules for how they should be weighted.

Anyone reading PCV cases will be struck by the emphasis on corporate formalities, on whether those running the corporation ran it by the book. Countless opinions, in contract and tort cases, bemoan the failure to follow procedures such as appointing officers, holding board and shareholder meetings, keeping financial records, and maintaining corporate assets separate from those of the shareholders. Based upon such things, courts may conclude that the corporation was the "alter ego" or "mere instrumentality" of the shareholders. Essentially, by failing to respect the separate corporate form, shareholders equate themselves with the business. Courts may then permit the plaintiff to equate the shareholders with the business and sue the shareholders directly for the business debts.

There are two significant problems with these alter ego cases. First, the list of factors used is often redundant and nonsensical. Many casebooks include *Dewitt Truck Brokers, Inc. v. W. Ray Flemming Fruit Co.*, 540 F.2d 681, 686–87 (4th Cir. 1976). There, fruit growers engaged Corporation to sell their fruit, for which Corporation received a commission. Corporation hired plaintiff to haul the fruit, but failed to pay, so plaintiff sued the principal shareholder of Corporation (at this point, Corporation had no assets). The court applied PCV and imposed personal liability.

Setting aside the question of capitalization, the *Dewitt Truck Brokers* court noted these factors: (1) failure to observe corporate formalities, (2) nonpayment of dividends, (3) insolvency of Corporation when the claim arose, (4) siphoning of corporate assets by the principal shareholder, (5) "nonfunctioning" of the officers or directors, (6) absence of corporate records, and (7) Corporation was a façade for the dominant shareholder. That seems like a daunting list, but look again. Factors 1, 5, and 6 are the same: failure to run the business by the book. Factor 7 is a conclusion, not a fact. Factor 3 is meaningless; of course the corporation is insolvent now. (If it were not, it would pay the bill and there would be no need to PCV.) And Factor 2 is absurd; the fact that the corporation does *not* pay dividends is great news for the creditors. It means there is more money in the corporate coffers instead of in shareholders' pockets. The only remaining factor, then, was siphoning of assets, which may relate to inadequate capitalization (which is what we thought was the key anyway).

This demonstrates the second problem with the alter ego cases: it is not clear why informality in running the corporation should result in liability. In most cases, the fact that the business is poorly run has nothing to do with the claim being asserted. For this reason, some courts refuse to PCV for mere sloppiness regarding formalities. One may argue that PCV is appropriate when the corporation is not run by the book because shareholders should not be allowed to ignore the rules of corporate behavior and then, when sued, claim the advantage of the corporate shield. In the absence of harm to anyone *from that behavior,* though, it is difficult to understand why the premise should lead to this conclusion. Moreover, the modern relaxed view toward corporate governance (*see* § 10.3) should make it more difficult to demonstrate that the managers have not played by the rules.

To be sure, if a failure to follow procedures results in harm, PCV would be appropriate. For instance, if activities in the business are so undifferentiated that a person reasonably believes she is dealing with a shareholder *individually* rather than with the corporation, personal liability may make sense. Fraud should also support PCV. For example, a shareholder may mislead the plaintiff regarding the financial status of the corporation so she enters into a deal. That shareholder should be personally liable.

As suggested above, the most significant issue in PCV cases is (or should be) whether the corporation was adequately capitalized. In subpart A of this section, we noted that this should be more important in tort than contract cases. After all, a contract claimant had the right, before entering the deal, to demand assurance that the corporation had sufficient assets (or to demand a personal guarantee from a shareholder). Surprisingly, though, many judges list "inadequate capitalization" as a factor for PCV in contract and tort cases.

Academics long assumed that courts would PCV more readily in tort than in contract cases. Some empirical research suggests, surprisingly, that courts are actually less likely to PCV in tort than in contract or statutory cases. *See*, *e.g.*, John H. Matheson, *Why Courts Pierce: An Empirical Study of Piercing the Corporate Veil*, 7 BERKELEY BUS. L. J. 1, 20 (2009); Robert B. Thompson, *Piercing the Corporate Veil: An Empirical Study*, 76 CORNELL L. REV. 1036, 1068–70 (1991).

Inadequate capitalization (usually referred to as "undercapitalization") means that the company lacks sufficient resources to cover prospective risks. It is assessed based upon likely economic needs in that particular business. It seems clear that the company need not be capitalized to ensure that it can pay for every conceivable liability. Capitalization should be reasonable in light of the nature and risks of the particular business. In making the assessment, courts agree that liability insurance "counts" as capital because it is available to compensate members of the public injured by the business.

There is a serious question as to when the adequacy of capital should be measured. There are two possibilities, each of which reflect different views of the duty to capitalize a corporation. Suppose a corporation was adequately capitalized initially, but suffered losses and now is unable to pay its debts.

The first view is to measure adequacy of capitalization at the time the company was formed (or perhaps when it expands into a new line of business). Under this view, the corporation was not undercapitalized and PCV would not be appropriate. Implicit in this view is the idea that the law does not guarantee that every creditor will be paid. Instead, shareholders "purchase" limited liability by parting with sufficient capital (reasonably related to potential risks in the business) when they form the corporation.

The second view assesses adequacy of capital when the claim arises. This approach seems almost to guarantee PCV. As noted, if the corporation were not undercapitalized *now,* the plaintiff would not be trying to PCV; her claim could be paid by the corporation. This view assumes that shareholders have an ongoing duty to *maintain* adequate capital for the nature of their operations, at the risk of personal liability. There is case law support for both of these approaches.

A powerful factor supporting PCV is when shareholders have siphoned off for themselves (maybe through salaries or dividends) the capital that could have been used to buy insurance or retained in the business. This was a factor in *Dewitt Truck Brokers.* In alter ego cases, courts sometimes stress that the shareholders *commingled* their own assets with corporate funds. Often, this is just a sign of sloppiness, unrelated to the plaintiff's claim. On the other hand, it may show "stripping" of corporate assets; shareholders may be draining business assets for their personal use. This enrichment of shareholders at the expense of creditors may justify PCV. Conversely, evidence that the corporation made a reasonable effort to provide a cushion for creditors will likely protect shareholders.

Two additional points are important. First, merely showing that there is an alter ego problem or undercapitalization, alone or together, will not support PCV. Though courts say this in different ways, PCV is appropriate only when recognition of the separate corporate existence will lead to injustice or an unfair or inequitable result. So it's not enough that there was questionable behavior in capitalizing or running the corporation. That behavior must have harmed the plaintiff so that recognition of limited liability would constitute fundamental unfairness.

Second, courts PCV to impose liability on "active" (and not "passive") shareholders. For example, in *Dewitt,* only the principal shareholder (who actually ran the corporation) was found liable. The other shareholders enjoyed limited liability.

C.      *Choice of Law Issues.* The courts of some states PCV more often than others. Delaware and New York are known as difficult states in which to get a court to PCV. Texas has codified aspects of PCV law in response to a liberal application of PCV by the Texas Supreme Court. Under Texas law, failure to follow corporate formalities will not support a finding of shareholder liability. And in Texas, to PCV in contract cases, the plaintiff must show actual fraud for the personal benefit of the shareholder. Tex. Bus. Org. Code § 21.223(b).

- Corporation is incorporated in State A, where it is difficult for the plaintiff to invoke PCV. Corporation does business in various states, including State B, where it is relatively easy to PCV. Plaintiff's claim arises in State B, and she sues in State B on a PCV theory. Which state's law applies regarding PCV?

There is surprisingly little case law on this choice-of-law issue. In most cases, courts appear to assume that they should apply the law of the state of incorporation, and in some cases will expressly apply the internal affairs doctrine to reach that conclusion. *See, e.g., Judson Atkinson Candies, Inc. v. Latini-Hohberger Dhimantec*, 529 F.3d 371, 378 (7th Cir. 2008) ("Texas has the same choice-of-law rule for veil-piercing claims as Illinois, namely that the law of the state of incorporation governs such claims.") That doctrine provides that the law of the state of incorporation will govern internal corporate affairs (*see* § 3.2). Arguably, the law of shareholder liability is an "internal affair." In some states, statutes prescribe that the liability of shareholders of corporations formed out of state is governed by the law of the state where the company was formed.

There is increasing recognition, however, that the internal affairs doctrine might not apply to the law of PCV. Choice-of-law rules generally provide for application of the law of the state with the most significant relationship to a dispute. It is not clear that a corporation should be able to "capture" favorable PCV law by forming in one state and therefore avoid PCV for activities in another state where it does business. The law seems to be moving in this direction. *See* Gregory S. Crespi, *Choice of Law in Veil-Piercing Litigation: Why Courts Should Discard the Internal Affairs Rule and Embrace General Choice-of-Law Principles,* 64 N.Y.U. ANN. SURV. AM. L. 85 (2008).

## § 10.5  SPECIAL APPLICATIONS OF PCV (AND ENTERPRISE LIABILITY)

A.    *PCV in the Parent-Subsidiary Situation.* PCV imposes liability on shareholders. Those shareholders might be other corporations. Indeed, one fairly common fact pattern is to PCV to impose upon a parent corporation liability incurred by a subsidiary. In general, courts look to the same sorts of factors here as they do in "regular" PCV cases.

In *In re Silicone Gel Breast Implants Liability Litigation*, 887 F.Supp. 1447, 1452–53 (N.D.Ala. 1995), the subsidiary, MEC, manufactured breast implants. The parent, Bristol (which owned 100 percent of the stock of MEC), did not manufacture breast implants. Plaintiffs sued Bristol on a PCV theory for product liability concerning the implants manufactured by MEC. The court permitted the claim to proceed. It stressed that MEC's board of directors was controlled by Bristol (many people didn't know MEC even had a board), MEC budgets were approved by Bristol, cash received by MEC went into an account maintained by Bristol, which also set employment policies and wage scales for MEC. The court additionally noted that the subsidiary may have been inadequately capitalized in view of the business risks in manufacturing breast implants. Based on the "totality of the circumstances," the court concluded that it would be "inequitable and unjust" to allow Bristol to have the limited liability ordinarily enjoyed by shareholders.

Other cases have used PCV to hold the parent liable when it operates the subsidiary in an "unfair manner," such as allocating subsidiary profits to the parent and losses to the subsidiary. This is the functional equivalent of undercapitalization, which we saw in § 10.4, subpart B. The parent that impoverishes the subsidiary in this way may be required to answer for debts incurred by the subsidiary.

The lesson of such cases is clear: the corporations should delineate between the affairs, assets, and operations of the parent and subsidiary. In many instances, ties between the two companies are inherently close. They may be housed in the same offices, share common employees, auditors, and lawyers. These ties are not necessarily inconsistent with the separate existence of the subsidiary, but problems can arise from carelessness or from being too casual about the separateness of the entity.

B.    *Reverse PCV.* PCV involves a plaintiff trying to impose liability for corporate debts on a shareholder. Sometimes the shoe is on the other foot: the shareholder wants the court to ignore that there is a corporation. This is "reverse PCV," a doctrine of questionable legitimacy.

In *Cargill, Inc. v. Hedge*, 375 N.W.2d 477, 480 (Minn. 1985), a family formed a corporation to own its farm. The family encountered financial trouble, and a creditor sued and won a judgment against the corporation. When the judgment was not paid, the plaintiff sought to have the farm sold to satisfy the judgment. Minnesota has a statute making farms exempt from execution, but only if they are owned by individuals. The statute did not apply on the facts, because this farm was owned by a corporation, and not by individuals. Nonetheless, the Minnesota Supreme Court applied "reverse PCV" and held that the corporation did not exist because the family members owned the farm. Perhaps recognizing the creativity it had displayed, the court said that the doctrine should be carefully limited.

Other courts seem skeptical, on the theory that one who forms a corporation must take the bad with the good. In *Sims v. Western Waste Industries*, 918 S.W.2d 682, 686 (Tex.App. 1996), the court refused to invoke reverse PCV. There, an employee of a subsidiary sued the parent corporation. Under workers' compensation law, an employee cannot sue her employer. The parent corporation was not the employer, but argued that it should be seen as the employer under reverse PCV (and, therefore, that it should be immune from suit). The court pointed out that the parent had "accepted the benefits of establishing a subsidiary corporation in Texas and will not be allowed to disregard that entity now that it is in [its] gain to do so."

C. *Enterprise Liability.* This is a theory under which separate corporations are treated as one economic unit, so a plaintiff may attempt to recover against the aggregate assets of all the companies, even though she only dealt with one.

- Karl is the sole shareholder of 10 corporations, each of which is properly formed. Each corporation owns one taxicab and holds the minimum insurance required by state law for operating a taxicab. The 10 corporations operate their cabs from a single garage and use a common dispatching system. The cabs are driven by hired drivers (who have no assets). The cab owned by Karl's Cab Co. is driven negligently and strikes Plaintiff. Suppose Plaintiff's claim vastly exceeds the assets (including insurance) of Karl's Cab Co.

Plaintiff might try to PCV and impose liability on Karl. She might have a decent claim for this if the corporation had been undercapitalized, and the claim might be strengthened if the corporation had not been run assiduously, and if Karl personally drained assets out of the business. Enterprise liability is different. It would allow Plaintiff to treat all 10 of Karl's corporations as one entity and recover from the aggregated assets of all the corporations, including Karl's Classy Cabs, Inc., Karl's Quality Cabs Corp., Karl's Colossal Cab Co., Karl's Cool Cabs, Inc., etc. This would allow Plaintiff to recover from the assets (including insurance) of all 10 companies. In essence, it erases the walls of one corporation not to go after the assets of a shareholder, but to go after the assets of all related companies.

The theoretical underpinning of enterprise liability makes great sense: in economic reality, this is one business, and the law should not allow the owner to subdivide his liability by chopping the business into small parts. Some courts have approved of the theory. The leading case is *Walkovszky v. Carlton*, 223 N.E.2d 6, 10 (N.Y. 1966), though the holding of that case is not as clear as it might be. Because the parties settled their dispute in that case, there was no court order permitting satisfaction of judgment from the combined assets of the separate corporations.

D.    *The Deep Rock Doctrine.* We saw in § 10.4, subpart B, that courts may PCV based upon undercapitalization of the corporation. The Deep Rock doctrine allows the court an alternative: it applies *only* in cases which the shareholder who would be liable under PCV is also a debt holder of the corporation. That means that the shareholder had (in addition to holding stock) made a loan to the company.

Under the Deep Rock doctrine, a court will "subordinate" the shareholder's debt to that of other creditors. That means it will put the shareholder last in line when it comes to paying creditors. This can be done even if the shareholder's loan is secured. The court has broad equitable power to subordinate the shareholder's claim to general and secured creditors. This notion was founded in bankruptcy proceedings, but is sometimes applied by state courts in insolvency cases. (BTW, the name of this doctrine comes from the Deep Rock Oil Corp., which was the subsidiary in the leading case of *Taylor v. Standard Gas & Electric Co.*, 306 U.S. 307, 309 (1939)).

## § 10.6  FIDUCIARY DUTY AND OPPRESSION

A.  *Background.* In § 1.4, we saw that in a *partnership* the partners owe each other a duty of utmost good faith and fair dealing. In the corporation, the traditional view is that shareholders do not owe fiduciary duties to one another. And in the close corporation, the standard notion is that the managers owe no special fiduciary duty to minority shareholders. But these views have changed significantly in the past few decades, as courts and legislatures recognize the potential plight of the minority shareholder in the close corporation. In § 9.9, we discussed one aspect of this change, specifically the duties of parent corporations to their subsidiaries. Here, we deal with the more typical plight of the minority shareholder in a close corporation.

Let us return to § 10.2, to the hypo involving X, the minority shareholder in a close corporation. She owns stock but has no voice in corporate management because she was fired. She is receiving no return on her investment and no salary. And because it is a close corporation, she has no way out. (If things go badly in a public corporation, at least a shareholder can sell her stock and get some return on her investment. But in the close corporation, there is no public market on which to sell one's stock.)

Remember that X could have protected herself with a buy-sell agreement. If she did not, she is in a very difficult position, at the mercy of the controlling shareholders (Y and Z in our hypo).

Y and Z may buy X's stock, but could do so for a very low price (because there is no other potential buyer). Doing so might actually be a good idea for Y and Z, simply to get rid of the nettlesome minority shareholder. X's ownership entitles her to inspect corporate books and records (*see* § 6.9) and, if Y and Z are guilty of breaching duties to the corporation, X has the right to bring a derivative suit on behalf of the entity (Chapter 15). Moreover, buying out X's interest at a bargain-basement price might allow Y and Z later to dissolve the corporation without having to give X her proportionate interest at liquidation.

B.    *Common Law Recognition of a Fiduciary Duty.* In the 1960s, courts started comparing the close corporation to the partnership, and addressing the possibility that partner-type fiduciary duties should apply in closely-held entities. The *Galler* case, discussed at § 10.3, subpart B, was influential in seeing the close corporation as the functional analog of the partnership. Some courts even refer to close corporations as "incorporated partnerships." No state has been more protective of minority shareholders in the close corporation than Massachusetts.

The leading case is *Donahue v. Rodd Electrotype Co.*, 328 N.E.2d 505, 508–19 (Mass. 1975), in which management had the corporation buy about half the stock owned by the founder of the company. The founder was 77 years old, wanted to retire, and needed money to do so. Management, which consisted of the founder's children, was happy to oblige, and had the corporation pay $36,000 to buy their father's stock. Then, a minority shareholder offered to sell her stock back to the corporation at the same price per share. Management refused, and the minority shareholder sued the managers. The Massachusetts Supreme Judicial Court held that shareholders in a close corporation owe *to each other* a fiduciary duty of utmost good faith and fair dealing. Among other things, this duty requires the corporation to provide an "equal opportunity" (or "equal access") to the minority shareholder to resell her stock. This gives her the same chance for a return on investment as management gave to their father.

There is a great deal of case law about the treatment of minority shareholders in the close corporation. Courts are somewhat imprecise with terminology, sometimes using "oppression," "freeze out," and "squeeze out" interchangeably. Generally, "oppression" describes any unfair deprivation by controlling shareholders of a minority shareholder's rights of participation. It may be participation in governance, distributions, employment, or almost any perquisite of ownership. An example is the unequal distributions of corporate assets to repurchase stock in *Donahue*. Another example is in mergers that unfairly cash out minority shareholders (*see* § 16.5, subpart B).

"Squeeze out" usually refers to the corporation's issuing more stock on a non-proportionate basis to dilute the interest of minority shareholders. For example, suppose the controlling shareholder makes a loan to the corporation to finance its operations. Now she has the corporation issue new stock at a set price to all shareholders, including the minority. So far, it looks fair. Then, however, the controlling shareholder pays for her additional stock by forgiving the debt to the corporation. The minority shareholder now has to come up with cash to buy her new stock. If she does not, her holdings will be diluted when the company issues new stock to the controlling shareholder.

Similarly, in *Byelick v. Vivadelli*, 79 F.Supp.2d 610, 627 (E.D. Va. 1999), majority shareholders engineered an amendment that reduced the plaintiff's ownership from 10 percent to 1 percent. The court held that the "dilutive transaction can be challenged under the Virginia common law of fiduciaries," and imposed upon the defendants the burden of demonstrating that the amendment was fair.

Courts use "oppression," "freeze out," and "squeeze out" pejoratively, to label behavior that breaches the fiduciary duty of utmost good faith and fair dealing. It is important to remember, though, that not every disadvantage to minority shareholders is the result of a breach of duty. To a considerable degree, a person holding a minority stake in a close corporation takes the chance that she will be outvoted on matters of management, that there will be no dividends, and that it will be difficult to sell her shares. That is why proper planning (including the negotiation of a buy-sell agreement) is so important (*see* § 10.2). That is also why some scholars argue that courts should not step in here; the shareholder should have taken steps to protect herself.

Indeed, the principle of the *Donahue* case creates a risk of judicial overreaching by permitting courts to review business decisions. Consider again the hypo from § 10.2 involving X, the minority shareholder who was fired from her employment with the corporation. It is possible, of course, that she was fired oppressively, as part of a freeze out. But it is also possible that the firing was justified; maybe she was incompetent, maybe the company did not need that many employees, or maybe different skills were required in the job. These are all business decisions, to which courts usually extend a presumption of correctness through the business judgment rule (*see* § 9.4). Broad application of *Donahue* would convert these from matters of business judgment to litigable matters of fiduciary duty.

The Massachusetts Supreme Judicial Court recognized this problem and recalibrated the fiduciary duty concept in *Wilkes v. Springside Nursing Home, Inc.*, 353 N.E.2d 657, 663 (Mass. 1976). There, the court said that an "untempered application of the strict good faith standard" might impose undesirable "limitations on legitimate action by the controlling group ... which will unduly hamper its effectiveness in managing the corporation in the best interests of all concerned." In other words, management in a close corporation "ha[s] certain rights to what has been termed 'selfish ownership' in the corporation which should be balanced against the concept of their fiduciary duty."

In *Wilkes,* the plaintiff was one of four shareholders, all of whom were employed by the corporation. After a disagreement, the other three had the plaintiff fired. He sued, under *Donahue,* and the court set up a regime of shifting burdens. First, the plaintiff must show that the controlling shareholders treated her oppressively. Second, if she shows oppression, the burden shifts to the defendants to show a legitimate business reason for the action. This step protects management prerogatives, such as firing for cause or because of the need to downsize. Third, if the defendants make such a showing, the plaintiff may still win if she shows that the legitimate business purpose may be realized through a less restrictive alternative. In other words, is there some way the corporation could achieve its purpose without harming the plaintiff? To this extent, then, Massachusetts has retreated from a strict reading of *Donahue.*

Several states have rejected the principle that shareholders owe each other a fiduciary duty in the close corporation. For example, in *Nixon v. Blackwell*, 626 A.2d 1366, 1377 (Del. 1993), the Delaware Supreme Court concluded that creation of such a claim should be left to the legislature. Similarly, in *Giannotti v. Hamway*, 387 S.E.2d 725, 734 (Va. 1990), the Virginia Supreme Court rejected a common law claim for oppression. The legislature had provided a right to petition for involuntary dissolution of the corporation in cases of "oppression."

According to the court, this amounted to a legislative determination that dissolution was the exclusive remedy; courts were not free to fashion a common law right of action for oppression. In many states, it is unclear whether shareholders in a close corporation owe each other a common law fiduciary duty.

Michigan has legislated a claim for oppression in the close corporation, and permits suit for "illegal, fraudulent, or willfully unfair and oppressive" behavior. The victim may sue either for harm to herself or harm to the corporation, and may seek a variety of remedies, including damages, purchase of her stock, or involuntary dissolution of the company. Mich. Bus. Corp. Act § 489(1).

Where a claim is recognized, cases will almost always involve oppressive behavior by the controlling shareholders against the minority shareholder. After all, the controlling shareholders have the power. It is possible, however, that a minority shareholder may breach the duty of utmost good faith and fair dealing. For example, if the corporate documents require unanimous approval for decisions, even a minority shareholder will have the power to harm the others by acting in bad faith. Doing so may breach a duty to the other shareholders.

The situation we are addressing—duties owed *to other shareholders*—should be distinguished from the traditional fiduciaries owed by directors in all corporations, which are discussed in detail in Chapter 9. In a close corporation operated under a shareholder management agreement, the managing shareholders owe those duties. Some of the behavior seen in cases like *Donahue* may well breach the traditional duty of loyalty, and open the managers to liability. Those claims, however, are brought by or on behalf of the corporation. The claims addressed here are brought by the oppressed shareholder.

C.    *The Effect of Involuntary Dissolution Statutes.* Today, statutes in every state provide that shareholders may petition for involuntary dissolution (or to have a receiver appointed to run the company) in specified situations (*see* § 16.8). These statutes, of which MBCA § 14.30(2) is typical, allow a shareholder to petition for involuntary dissolution, *inter alia,* if directors are deadlocked and shareholders cannot break the deadlock, while the corporation is suffering irreparable injury, or if management is engaged in "illegal, oppressive, or fraudulent" behavior. We make four points about these statutes.

First, because there was no right to involuntary dissolution at common law, the quoted language (especially the word "oppressive") might be interpreted narrowly. There was an early tendency in this direction, but over time courts have come to equate "oppressive" in the statutes with the common law fiduciary duty discussed above in § 10.6, subpart B. So conduct that is inconsistent with legitimate expectations of the shareholders as to their roles in the corporation may be found oppressive.

Second, because the statutes usually provide that the court "may" order dissolution, the matter is in the court's discretion. The statutes generally do not *require* a court to order involuntary dissolution upon finding one of the statutory standards are met. In an old case, the court refused to order dissolution because it was likely that one shareholder would form a new business and capture the goodwill created by all the shareholders in the current business. By refusing to order dissolution, the court probably forced the dominant shareholder to buy out the others. *In re Radom & Neidorff, Inc.*, 119 N.E.2d 563, 565 (N.Y. 1954).

Third, involuntary dissolution is not a preferred remedy for deadlock or oppression because it requires the dissolution of what may be a thriving business. It would make more sense to auction off the business as a going concern and distribute the proceeds, or to arrange for a buy-out of the shareholder petitioning for dissolution at a court-determined price. A few decades ago, some courts started ordering such buy-outs. In some states, they were aided by statutory close corporation statutes that provided for this remedy (though only in corporations qualifying for statutory close corporation status (*see* § 10.2)).

Fourth, the clear trend is toward statutory provisions allowing the court to order a buy-out at a "fair value" (to be set by the court). Section 14.34 of the MBCA is an example: the statute is triggered by involuntary dissolution, so the petitioning shareholder will have to make a showing (such as oppressive behavior) that would justify an order of dissolution. Moreover, the statutes seem to permit a buy-out *only* of the petitioning shareholder, and not of the other shareholders. So suing for involuntary dissolution is a bit of a gamble; if the court orders a buy-out instead of dissolution, it is the petitioning shareholder who will be bought out. The court generally does not have the authority to allow her to buy out the other shareholders.

## § 10.7  TRANSFER OF CONTROLLING INTEREST

A.  *Background.*  For our purposes, a "controlling shareholder" is one who owns either (1) an outright majority of the voting stock or (2) a substantial minority of the stock with the rest so dispersed that she is able to select the majority of management. (A group of shareholders who command either position can collectively be considered a "controlling shareholder.") Though controlling shareholders are encountered most frequently in close corporations, it is possible to have such a powerful owner in a public corporation, as we will see. In this section, we are concerned with the controlling shareholder's transferring her stock to a third party.

The controlling shareholder will be able to sell her stock (the "control block") for more than its value simply as an economic matter. Suppose the net asset value of the business is $1,000,000 and the controlling shareholder owns 51 percent of the stock. The economic value of that stock is $510,000. But because owning that much stock carries the ability to run the corporation, a buyer will pay more than that. The excess over the raw economic value is the "control premium."

Generally, there is no problem with the controlling shareholder's being paid a control premium. Some scholars have argued that minority shareholders should share in such a premium. The confusing opinion in *Perlman v. Feldmann*, 219 F.2d 173 (2d Cir. 1955), discussed in subpart D below, hinted at a fiduciary duty to the corporation and minority shareholders in this situation. But it is clear today that the controlling shareholder can keep the money. She has no obligation to minority shareholders to offer them a chance to sell their stock or to share in the control premium.

B.    *Looting.* Though most transfers of control appear to benefit minority shareholders by bringing in fresh and effective leadership, sometimes they result in disaster. For example, the buyer might be a thief who uses the newly-bought control to run the company for personal gain. She converts corporate assets to cash (which she pockets), fails to have the corporation pay bills, has the corporation run up debts, and generally runs the corporation into the ground. Does the controlling shareholder who sold to this "looter" bear any responsibility?

Yes, if she failed to make a reasonable investigation of the character and reputation of the third party. Everyone agrees that the controlling shareholder has a duty when selling control. There is some debate, though, about the scope of that duty. Some have suggested that it is merely a duty to disclose to the corporation and other shareholders if it is apparent that the third party is likely to violate the duty of fair dealing. Courts seem to be more exacting. If the selling shareholder's investigation raises red flags about whether the third party is a crook, the controlling shareholder should take further steps to allay the fears, or should refuse to sell to that person. There are various red flags, such as the third party's willingness to pay an excessive price, or a heightened interest in the liquid or immediately sellable assets of the business.

A classic example is *DeBaun v. First Western Bank & Trust*, 120 Cal.Rptr. 354, 355 (Cal. App. 1975). There, the seller was aware that the buyer had 38 unsatisfied judgments against him, including at least one for fraud and punitive damages. The buyer could not pay the purchase price without using the corporation's assets. Yet, in part because the buyer was an impressive luncheon companion, the seller sold to him. Any reasonable person would either have demanded explanations or walked away from the deal. In less than a year, the buyer took a company worth $220,000 and turned it into one that owed $218,000.

A seller who breaches the duty by selling a controlling interest to a looter is liable for all harm caused, which is usually the amount looted. There is some confusion, however, about who the plaintiff ought to be. In other words, there is confusion about to whom the controlling shareholder owes the duty of reasonable investigation. Some cases seem to say it is owed to the corporation. If so, the corporation (or, more likely, a receiver) should be able to sue and recover the full amount necessary to make it whole. Some cases, however, seem to say the duty is owed to the minority shareholders. If so, they should be able to sue to recover directly for the pro-rata harm done to their interests.

C.     *Sale Accompanied by Director Resignations.*
Imagine a sale of the controlling interest in which there is no looting. As part of the deal, the controlling shareholder agrees that both she and the directors friendly to her will resign. This practice of delivering a "stacked" board to the buyer allows the buyer to vote her shares and elect new directors immediately. The option would be for the buyer to call a shareholders' meeting to remove the sitting directors without cause. When the sale is accompanied by resignations, there is an argument that the control premium was paid to obtain the resignations. This makes it look as though the buyer "bought" seats on the board, which seems antithetical to public policy. Arguably, the premium should be recovered by the corporation for the benefit of the minority owners.

Delivering a stacked board is not a problem when the seller transfers a *majority* of the stock. In that instance, the buyer has the power to remove the incumbent directors and replace them with her friends. The situation becomes questionable when she sells less than a majority. Case law seems to permit the concomitant resignations if the court is convinced that the amount sold (though less than a majority) would truly enable its owner to control the board. In one case, dealing with the sale of 28 percent of the stock in a widely-held public corporation, the three judges on the appellate panel took three different positions. One judge concluded that 28 percent was enough because the other stock was so widely held. The second judge concluded that such deals were acceptable only if they involve a true majority. The third judge thought the matter should be remanded for trial. *Essex Universal Corp. v. Yates*, 305 F.2d 572, 579, 580, 583 (2d Cir. 1962).

Another case was easier: the president of the corporation, who owned four percent of the stock, sold his shares as part of an agreement to resign and to have the buyer's friends appointed as president and to two director positions. The court found the sale contrary to public policy as a sale of office, because the ownership of four percent would not allow the buyer legitimately to install that many managers. *Brecher v. Gregg*, 392 N.Y.S.2d 776, 779 (Sup. Ct. 1975).

D.    *Two Famous Cases.* We finish with two cases that arguably involve payments of a control premium. We say "arguably" because neither opinion is a model of clarity. At least one is likely in your casebook. In *Jones v. H. F. Ahmanson & Co.*, 460 P.2d 464, 476 (Cal.1969), defendants owned 87 percent of the stock in a savings and loan association (S&L), which was closely held. The defendants wanted to have the stock publicly traded, which would probably increase the value of their holding and guarantee a public market should they want to sell. They could have had the S&L "go public," but came up with a different plan.

Defendants created a holding company, which is a corporation that does not "do" anything; it just owns a majority of the stock of different companies. They transferred their stock in the S&L to the holding company. In exchange, they received the stock of the holding company. The minority shareholders of the S&L were not permitted to participate in this deal. The holding company then "went public," which created a public market for its stock. So now the defendants had stock (in the holding company) that could be cashed in on the public market. The minority shareholders of the S&L, in contrast, remained locked into a minority position (13 percent) in a subsidiary of the closely-held holding company.

The minority shareholders sued, and the California Supreme Court held that the defendants had breached a fiduciary duty owed directly to those shareholders. The duty imposed, then, was of the *Donahue* variety because it was owed by one shareholder to another, and not to the corporation. According to the court, there is a "comprehensive rule of good faith and inherent fairness to the minority in any transaction where control of the corporation is material." Even if the defendants had offered the plaintiffs a chance to sell their stock to the holding company, the court said, they would have to demonstrate good faith or a strong business reason for doing things the way they did.

In *Perlman v. Feldmann*, 219 F.2d 173, 176 (2d Cir. 1955), Newport was a company that manufactured steel during the Korean War, when supplies were scarce because of military need. Feldmann and his family owned 37 percent of Newport. Newport was publicly traded, and the 37 percent stake permitted Feldmann to elect a majority of the board (because the rest of the stock was held by so many people). Feldmann ran the show, and devised a brilliant plan to help Newport compete in the tough market. Under the plan, Newport would agree to sell steel, but only to buyers who make interest free loans to Newport, which it uses to expand its capacity. Feldmann sold his 37 percent stake to Wilport for $20 per share. The market price for the stock at the time was $12, so the control premium was $8 per share. It was worrisome that Feldmann earlier rejected an offer by Wilport to merge (essentially to buy out all shareholders) and then turned around to negotiate a sale of his family's stock.

Minority shareholders sued derivatively (that is, asserting a claim belonging to the corporation, not to them). They claimed that the sale of control to Wilport was essentially a sale of a corporation asset. Specifically, he sold the ability to control the allocation of steel in a period of short supply. As such, plaintiffs argued, the control premium belonged to the corporation.

The *Perlman* opinion is not a model of lucidity. It meanders through a discussion of fiduciary duties and also speaks of usurpation of corporate opportunities (which is a breach of the duty of loyalty, *see* § 9.8). The court goes out of its way to note that "[w]e have here no fraud, no misuse of confidential information, and no outright looting of a helpless corporation." Yet we have liability. And though the case was derivative, for reasons not made clear, the court allowed recovery directly by the minority shareholders. (As we will see in Chapter 15, the judgment in a derivative suit usually is recovered by the corporation, not the shareholders.)

To the extent the court was saying that a fiduciary cannot sell something that belongs to the corporation and pocket the proceeds, it makes sense. The remedy there, though, would be recovery by the corporation, not the minority shareholders. Indeed, such a case would be a garden-variety breach of the duty of loyalty owed to the corporation. So it is tough to see why *Perlman* has gotten the attention it has. It is a strange and confused opinion, with the confusion probably attributable to its unique facts.

# CHAPTER 11

# SPECIAL ISSUES IN THE PUBLIC CORPORATION

## § 11.1  INTRODUCTION

A "public" (or "publicly-traded" or "publicly-held") corporation is one whose securities are registered under federal law for public sale. Public corporations include what most people think of when they hear the word "corporation"—millions of dollars in assets, thousands of employees, and millions of shares owned by tens of thousands of shareholders. The 500 largest companies in the world, measured by revenue, comprise the "Fortune 500," which includes such iconic businesses as Ford, McDonald's, and Procter & Gamble. Not all public corporations are this large. Many are mid-sized and even smaller. In this chapter, we address the public market for stocks and special problems faced by public corporations.

These entities must go through a rigorous process to register their securities for public trading, and must routinely report publicly (*see* § 11.2). Pressures on management of public corporations has given rise to some spectacular cases of fraud, which led to passage of federal regulation of aspects of accounting practice in 2002 (*see* § 11.3). Because stock ownership is so widely dispersed, most shareholder voting in public corporations is done by proxy. Federal proxy regulations are an important area of potential civil and criminal trouble for public corporations (*see* § 11.4). Section 11.5 addresses methods by which one corporation may take over another, and the fireworks that can result from such efforts. Finally, § 11.6 addresses executive compensation in public corporations.

## § 11.2   PUBLIC TRADING OF SECURITIES, REGISTRATION, AND REPORTING

A.     *Securities and Markets.* The most obvious characteristic of a public corporation is that there is a public market for its securities. "Securities" are investments. As we shall discuss in § 12.2, securities might be "debt" or "equity." Debt means a loan: the company issues a debt instrument (often called a bond) to an investor, in return for her lending money to the corporation. Holders of such instruments are creditors (but not owners) of the business. Equity means ownership: the company issues stock to an investor, in return for her purchasing that stock with an appropriate form and amount of consideration. Shareholders, as we have seen, are owners (but not creditors) of the business. Though what we discuss here applies to all securities (debt or equity) for convenience, we will refer to stock.

Registration is part of the federal regulation of securities. When a corporation sells securities, it is an "issuance," and the corporation is called the "issuer" or "issuing company." When you and I sell stock, that sale is not an issuance; it is only an issuance if the company is selling its stock (*see* § 12.3). Whenever there is an issuance—to the public or to a few people, in a private placement—the consideration goes to the corporation. Indeed, the company issues stock expressly for the purpose of raising capital. But subsequent sales of that stock do not bring money to the company. It's like buying and selling a car. If you buy a new Ford Explorer from a Ford dealer, Ford Motor Company gets the net income from that sale. But when you sell that car to your cousin, Ford does not get that money; you do.

The same thing happens with stock. After the issuance by the corporation, the shareholder can dispose of the stock as she sees fit. She can give it away or she can sell it. If it is a close corporation, she may have trouble finding a buyer. If it is publicly traded, though, she can sell it on the stock market. Either way, the corporation will not get anything from these subsequent sales. Why, then, do public companies care about the price at which their stock sells?

Healthy stock prices are seen as good signs for companies. Managers may adopt strategies to ensure a robust price. One example is the announcement that a corporation will buy back some of its shares from on the public. This is often seen as a signal to the market that management believes the stock is undervalued. In addition, managers of public companies often are rewarded with bonuses or stock options, sometimes triggered by a high stock price. These incentives can lead to fraudulent reporting of financial numbers. Indeed, fraud in some public corporations in the early part of the twenty-first century contributed to a financial crisis, which led to passage of the Sarbanes-Oxley Act (*see* § 11.3). The problem is not that management takes an interest in the company's stock price. The problem is that some people cheat.

How does the public market work? The stock in public corporations is traded on stock *exchanges*, such as the New York Stock Exchange and NASDAQ. These entities provide facilities for people to buy and sell stock. Suppose you want to buy 100 shares of stock in McDonald's (MCD). You put in an order— through a broker (who is your agent for the deal), which may be an online brokerage service—for 100 shares of MCD. The stock exchange matches your "buy" with someone who wants to sell her stock in MCD. You pay the sales price to your broker, who takes a commission, and the seller gets the proceeds of the deal. You have no idea who that seller is. The exchange matched you up. Stock exchanges are a "secondary market" for stock; they facilitate these re-sales of stock. Each trading day, hundreds of millions of shares trade hands on these markets.

These public markets set prices in each stock on each trading day, based upon supply and demand. People willing to buy at a certain price will coax out shareholders willing to sell at that price. Historically, public stock trades were handled through professional brokerage firms, which charged substantial commissions. Technology has had a huge impact, with most trades today executed online, for minimal commissions. Online trading made it possible to engage in "day trading," in which speculators execute numerous transactions during the day in an effort to capture profits from modest variations in securities prices.

Not all stock transactions are consummated through an exchange. Stocks in smaller companies, for which there is a limited market, are traded "over-the-counter," or OTC. OTC trading is made possible by "market makers," who are broker-dealers who actually own an inventory of stock in various companies. You buy from (or sell to) the broker-dealer, not from (or to) a faceless third person. The broker-dealer is a "market maker" because it is trying to generate profits by buying and selling its inventories of stock for its own account. "Dealer" refers to the company's buying and selling stock that it actually owns. It is distinguished from the company's "broker" function, when it acts as an agent for someone else in a transaction involving stock owned by others.

Many OTC transactions are recorded on the "Pink Sheets." This is an electronic system that displays prices for "bid" and "ask" (prices at which dealers will buy and sell). Back in the old days, these numbers were published on pink paper—hence the name. OTC trading is episodic.

B.     _Federal Regulation._ In reaction to the stock market crash of 1929, Congress passed the Securities Act of 1933 ("the '33 Act") and the Securities Exchange Act of 1934 ("the '34 Act"). Speaking broadly, the '33 Act concerns the initial issuance of securities by the corporation, and the '34 Act focuses more on the stock exchanges and re-sales of securities. The theory underlying American securities regulation is disclosure—that an informed public can protect itself, at least to some degree. As

Justice Brandeis said, "sunlight is said to be the best disinfectant." Louis D. Brandeis, *What Publicity Can Do*, in OTHER PEOPLE'S MONEY AND HOW THE BANKERS USE IT 92, 92 (1914). The Securities and Exchange Commission (SEC), formed by the '34 Act, is responsible for enforcing the federal securities laws, which consist of several statutes in addition to the '33 and '34 Acts, including Sarbanes-Oxley. The SEC may bring civil suits against persons or companies for violating the law. It also works with the Department of Justice in prosecutions of those violating the criminal provisions of the securities laws.

The SEC promulgates rules for the administration of the various statutes. The most important is Rule 10b–5, which is a broad antifraud provision (*see* § 14.3). Here, our focus is SEC oversight of registration and reporting of public companies. Before a company can offer stock to the public, it must "register" the securities to be offered, unless it qualifies for an exemption from registration. (Note that it is the securities that are registered, not the company.) Registration is an exacting and expensive process, undertaken by lawyers who specialize in the area. The lawyers' and auditors' fees and related costs of registration can easily total $1,000,000. Selling securities publicly without registering them or qualifying for an exemption can open the company and responsible individuals to civil liability and criminal prosecution.

Registration is very intrusive. The company must place a great deal of information before the public. It must file an extensive "registration statement" with the SEC. It must also provide a copy of the "prospectus," which is part of the registration statement and will be given to potential purchasers. The prospectus describes the security being sold, the issuing company, and discusses the risks of investing. The SEC staff reviews the registration statement before permitting the company to offer securities to the public.

Originally, only companies with securities traded on a "national securities exchange" were required to register. The requirement was expanded in the 1960s. In addition to those on a national exchange, a corporation must register if it has (1) a class of securities with at least 500 stockholders and (2) $10,000,000 in assets. It is not the total number of security holders that is significant, but the number of holders of the specific class of security for which registration is required. For example, a corporation with 400 shareholders of one class of stock and 450 shareholders of a different class of stock is not required to register either class.

There are exemptions to the registration requirement. For example, an "intrastate" issuance need not be registered. Neither must a "private offering" of securities. Qualifying for these or the other exemptions is difficult, and is the specialty of very sophisticated practitioners.

Registration is just the beginning of the disclosure requirements. All "reporting" corporations must file a "10-K," which is a detailed annual report of the business and financial performance, and includes such information as stock options awarded to executives. Each corporation files a "10–Q," which is a quarterly report of similar information. And each must report within a matter of days certain specified events, such as the resignation of a director, in an "8–K" filing.

In the filings, the company must divulge the bad with the good. The goal is public access to relevant data. A central feature of 10–K is the "management discussion and analysis of financial conditions and results of operations," or "MD&A." The SEC makes the disclosures available to the public through a database called EDGAR.

The company and responsible individuals take these disclosures very seriously. Section 11 of the '33 Act imposes strict liability on the company for any "untrue statement of material fact" in the registration process. Though individuals are not strictly liable (they can defend based upon "due diligence") they want to avoid being on the wrong side of the SEC.

In addition to these federal laws on registration and reporting, an issuing company may have to comply with various state-law requirements under state "blue sky" laws. The name comes from early attempts by crooks to sell pieces of the blue sky to an unsuspecting and naïve public. A significant part of state regulation of new issuances was pre-empted by the National Securities Market Improvement Act (NSMIA) in 1996.

C.     *State Law.* Though most regulation of disclosure by public corporations is federal, *Malone v. Brincat*, 722 A.2d 5, 10 (Del. 1998) reminds us that there may be a role for state law. In that case, the Delaware Supreme Court held that when a corporation communicates with shareholders about corporate affairs generally (and not in connection with a request for shareholder action), fiduciary duties require the board to be truthful. The knowing dissemination of false information is actionable under state law, though the court was not clear whether a breach gave rise to a claim by the corporation or by shareholders.

## § 11.3  THE SARBANES-OXLEY ACT AND FINANCIAL ACCOUNTABILITY

The American economy was rocked in the early part of the twenty-first century by accounting scandals in several public corporations, most infamously Enron and WorldCom. These companies had engaged in fraudulent accounting practices in an effort to paint a rosy picture, which, they hoped, would keep their stock prices high. Managers of public corporations have an incentive to report good financial numbers—not only because it creates good publicity, but because many managers earn bonuses based upon financial results. They also usually own stock in the company, so anything that increases the stock price increases their personal wealth.

In § 12.6, we will review the basic accounting documents, including the balance sheet. Companies at the center of the accounting scandal engaged in "off-balance-sheet" accounting, which was an effort to remove liabilities from the balance sheet through a series of complicated accounting steps. Though each step may have had some legitimacy, the overall result clearly misrepresented the corporate financial health. This fraud was pervasive. Not only did it permeate various layers of management, but the internal and external auditors turned a blind eye to the shenanigans. For one thing, external accounting firms that were hired to oversee the auditing were permitted to provide other services to the corporations. This created an incentive not to blow the whistle. An accounting firm had an incentive to ignore accounting irregularities so it would not jeopardize this other lucrative business.

When the house of cards fell, and the financial reality became apparent, the price of the stock of these corporations plummeted. Retirement funds were wiped out. Lives were ruined. Throughout the companies, the finger-pointing began: the CEO did not know what was going on because he relied on what the CFO told him; the CFO did not know what was going on because he relied on the auditors to catch things, etc.

Congress reacted in 2002 with the Sarbanes-Oxley Act, or "Sarbox," or "SOX." It applies only to public corporations. Though partnerships and close corporations can be wracked by fraudulent accounting practices, Congress was principally concerned with fraud perpetrated on the public. SOX is aimed at financial accountability and corporate governance. It was intended to clarify responsibilities of various players and to impose process and responsibility.

Under SOX, every public corporation must have an audit committee. In fact, all public companies have long had such committees; the only question is whether they were effective. Under SOX, each company must state that it has an "audit committee financial expert" on the committee, and that all other members of the committee have a degree of financial literacy. Section 404 of SOX requires the corporation to evaluate its internal audit controls with a set of procedures to review the design of audit controls and to test their effectiveness. It also requires the company to hire a public accounting firm to undertake external audits of the internal controls. The CEO and CFO must attest to the accuracy of the financial statements by signing a document under threat of criminal liability. Other parts of SOX address the potential conflict of interest in accounting firms by limiting the amount of non-auditing work they can do for the corporation.

SOX also created the Public Company Accounting Oversight Board. This is a private, non-profit corporation that acts as an agency supervised by the SEC. The Board sets standards for the public accounting firms and reviews their work, with authority to discipline them. Under SOX, members of the Board can be removed by the SEC only for cause. In *Free Enterprise Fund v. Public Company Accounting Oversight Board*, 561 U.S. 477, 492 (2010), the Supreme Court declared the Board unconstitutional, under principles of separation of powers. The Board was too independent of the executive branch of the federal government. Rather than abolish the Board or undermine SOX broadly, however, the Court held that the SEC may remove members of the Board without cause. With this change just noted, the Court held that the Board members would not be insulated unduly from control of the executive branch.

The *Free Enterprise* decision is a disappointment to the critics of SOX, some of whom have engineered litigation efforts to challenge the legislation on separation-of-powers grounds. After the decision, SOX remains in place. Even the Board remains in place, with the change that the SEC can remove its members with or without cause.

Though many agreed that the accounting scandals required some federal legislative response, it is widely thought that SOX imposes greater costs than it brings benefits. In particular, many relatively small publicly-traded companies found the expense of the internal control and employment of the external auditing firm especially difficult. There is anecdotal evidence that some such corporations have "gone private"—that is, ceased being publicly traded, to avoid SOX. Solid data on this point, however, does not exist. Whatever the outcome on that argument, SOX represents a change in philosophy in federal securities regulation from ensuring disclosure to actually prescribing specific corporate practices.

## § 11.4  FEDERAL REGULATION
## OF PROXY SOLICITATION

A.     *Background and Federal Regulation.* In
§ 6.6, we discussed shareholders' voting by proxy.
"Proxy" usually refers to the person appointed to vote
the shares for the record shareholder at the
shareholder meeting. The rules for appointing a
proxy are prescribed by state law and are quite
uniform. In many close corporations, proxies are
rare; the shareholders usually attend the meeting
personally and vote their own shares.

Things are different in the public corporation. For
any shareholder meeting for any kind of corporation,
there must be a quorum. That is, a majority of the
shares entitled to vote must be represented at the
meeting (*see* § 6.4). Otherwise, no action can be
taken. In public corporations, usually the
shareholders who show up do not represent anything
close to a majority of the shares entitled to vote.
Therefore, management must solicit proxy
appointments to ensure that there will be a quorum.
When management does this, it will be asking the
shareholders to vote in a particular way on the
various issues to be considered at the meeting.
Federal law attempts to ensure that the corporation
provides accurate information in this process.

Specifically, § 14(a) of the '34 Act allows the SEC
to develop regulations "necessary or appropriate in
the public interest or for the protection of investors"
in connection with the solicitation of proxy
appointments in registered corporations. Section 14
makes it unlawful for any person to use an

instrumentality of interstate commerce or the facilities of a national securities exchange "in contravention of" such regulations. As a practical matter, it is impossible to solicit proxies in a registered corporation without using an instrumentality of interstate commerce. Congress gave the SEC this broad and undefined rulemaking authority because it was concerned about abuses in the proxy process, but was uncertain about remedies.

The SEC has issued detailed regulations under § 14, including Rule 14a–3, which requires that solicitations be accompanied by a "proxy statement." This is an important source of shareholder information about corporate affairs. It gives detailed facts about the business, background of directors and nominees (including their compensation), and about other issues to be voted upon at the meeting. Rule 14a–3(b) provides that if a solicitation is made on behalf of management for an annual meeting at which directors will be elected, the proxy statement must be accompanied by an annual report of the corporation. These Rules are good examples of the '34 Act's reliance on protecting investors by providing information. Rule 14a–9 makes it unlawful to distribute a false or misleading proxy solicitation. As we will see below, violation of this Rule can give rise to a private right of action for damages. Beyond this, the SEC can assess penalties and seek other remedies for non-compliance with its Rules.

B.      *Shareholder Proposals.* Rule 14a–8 permits qualified *shareholders* to submit proposals for inclusion in the company's proxy solicitation material. A qualified shareholder is one who has owned $2000 worth of stock (or one percent of the outstanding stock) for at least one year. If the proposal deals with something appropriate to shareholder action, and is submitted on time, the corporation *must* include the proposal, even if management is opposed to it. This mechanism gives minority shareholders an effective way to communicate with all other shareholders. Shareholder proposals have addressed a variety of topics—including executive compensation, affirmative action policies, and environmental concerns. For example, one proposal asked for shareholders to vote to force the corporation to comply with various human rights provisions in its dealings in China.

Shareholder proposals almost never "win"—that is, they almost never get the support of a majority of the shares voted at the meeting. Winning in this sense is often not the point. Management must take a position on the proposal. Usually, it solicits proxies to vote against it. This process of engaging management is the shareholder's goal. Even unsuccessful proposals, then, may call management's attention to an issue. Sometimes, when management receives a serious shareholder proposal, it will reach a mutually agreeable accommodation, obviating the need to send the proposal to all shareholders.

The most famous practitioner of Rule 14a–8 was Lewis Gilbert, a shareholder of various corporations, who submitted proposals about corporate governance and generally nettled management for over half a century. In *SEC v. Transamerica Corp*, 163 F.2d 511 (3d Cir. 1947), he won his fight to require the corporation to include in its proxy materials his proposal that shareholders (rather than the board) select the company's external financial auditors.

Rule 14a–8 is subject to express exceptions. Recognizing that many users of the proposal mechanism will not be trained in the law, the SEC drafted them in "plain English" and in a question-and-answer format. For example, the corporation may omit shareholder proposals that address a personal grievance of the shareholder, or deal with something not significantly related to corporate business, or relate to specific amounts of dividends, or when substantially the same proposal has been made within five years and failed to garner significant support.

Another exception is for a proposal that "related to an election to office." In *AFSCME v. American International Group, Inc.*, 462 F.3d 121, 130 (2d Cir. 2006), the court held that a proposal seeking to amend bylaws to allow shareholder-nominated candidates on the ballot for director did not "relate[ ] to an election" and thus had to be included. The SEC reacted by amending Rule 14a–8(i)(8) to exclude shareholder proposals of particular nominees for the board of directors. (When shareholders want to propose alternative candidates for the board, they can engage in a "proxy contest," which we discuss in § 11.5, subpart C.)

If management concludes that the shareholder proposal falls within an exception and thus need not be included in the proxy materials, it may seek a "no-action letter" from the SEC. This letter reflects a decision by the SEC staff that it will recommend to the SEC itself that no action be taken if the proposal is omitted. A no-action letter does not offer watertight protection. In some circumstances, a disgruntled shareholder may be able to sue. If a proposal opposed by management is included in the proxy statement, the proposing shareholder may include a statement of not more than 500 words supporting the proposal. Management is free to explain its opposition to the proposal, with no word limit.

C.    *Private Right of Action.* It is important to remember our context. Here, management is sending out proxy *solicitations*: it is asking shareholders to give it their proxy to vote in a particular way on a particular issue. Management will try to "sell" the shareholders on the idea by telling them why the shareholders should go along. Sometimes, management will lie.

Rule 14a–9 makes it unlawful to distribute proxy solicitation information that contains "any statement which, at the time and in the light of the circumstances under which it is made, is false or misleading with respect to any material fact, or which omits to state any material fact necessary in order to make the statements therein not false or misleading." (We will see very similar language in Rule 10b–5 (*see* § 14.3).) In passing § 14, Congress said nothing about a private claim for violation of that provision or any rule promulgated pursuant to it.

Nonetheless, in *J.I. Case Co. v. Borak*, 377 U.S. 426, 435 (1964), the Supreme Court found an implied right of action to sue for violation of Rule 14a–9. The Court concluded that "private enforcement of the proxy rules provides a necessary supplement to Commission action. As in antitrust treble damage litigation, the possibility of civil damages or injunctive relief serves as a most effective weapon in the enforcement of the proxy requirements." *Borak* led to a considerable amount of litigation, and to three more significant Supreme Court cases.

First, in *TSC Industries, Inc. v. Northway, Inc.*, 426 U.S. 438, 438 (1976), the Court held that a fact omitted from a proxy statement is "material" if "there is a substantial likelihood that a reasonable shareholder would consider it important in deciding how to vote." (The Court has adopted this definition of materiality for Rule 10b–5 as well (*see* § 14.3).) The holding rejected a competing test, which would have defined "material" as anything "a reasonable shareholder *might* consider appropriate." This distinction sent a message to lower federal courts to limit Rule 14a–9 to substantial misstatements. Earlier, some courts had found very minor misstatements or omissions to be "material" under Rule 14a–9.

Second, in *Mills v. Electric Auto-Lite Co.*, 396 U.S. 375, 386 (1970), the Court held that shareholder reliance on the misstatement or omission in the proxy materials is presumed. A contrary holding would make it impossible to proceed in most cases: the plaintiff would be required to show that each shareholder read the proxy materials and relied upon the misstatement of omission in deciding to give her proxy to management. Under *Mills,* the plaintiff must show only that the misstatement or omission in the proxy statement was material and that the proxy solicitation was an essential step in the transaction being challenged.

Third is the interesting case of *Virginia Bankshares, Inc. v. Sandberg,* 501 U.S. 1083, 1090 (1991). There, Virginia Bankshares (VB) owed 85 percent of the stock of a bank, and wanted to acquire the other 15 percent. It proposed a cash merger, which was approved by the boards of both corporations. Under the merger, VB would pay $42 per share for the remaining 15 percent of the bank's stock. Virginia law did not require approval by the bank's minority shareholders. Nonetheless, VB insisted on having the matter put to a vote by those shareholders. Management sent proxy solicitations to them that said the board had approved the plan "because it provides an opportunity for the Bank's public shareholders to achieve a high value for their shares."

This statement was misleading. The $42 merger price was more than the stock was trading for, and was more than its book value, but there was a credible estimate that the stock was actually worth $60 per share. The merger was approved, and the plaintiff, a minority shareholder who refused to give her proxy, sued for violation of Rule 14a–9. She sought damages consisting of the difference between the merger price and the true value of the stock. There was no question that the misstatement in the proxy statement was material—the board's conclusion that $42 was "high value" for their shares is something a reasonable investor would consider important.

Defendants argued that the statement did not violate Rule 14a–9. That rule addresses, *inter alia,* misstatements "with respect to any material *fact*." Defendants contended that the statement that the merger price gave "high value" was not a statement of fact, but of *opinion*, and therefore not within Rule 14a–9. The Court rejected the contention. A plaintiff may complain about a statement of opinion in proxy materials. Such a plaintiff must show: (1) that the board disbelieved the opinion and (2) that the opinion was not supported by fact. The plaintiff prevailed on these points at trial, as the jury concluded that the directors did not believe that $42 was "high value" and the facts simply did not support that figure.

Ultimately, however, the plaintiff lost in *Virginia Bankshares*. Because applicable law did not require the shareholders' approval for the merger, the plaintiff could not show *causation*. The merger would have gone through anyway, even if no proxies had been solicited and the shareholders had not voted.

## § 11.5  HOSTILE TAKEOVERS

A.    *Background.* A "hostile takeover" is exactly what it sounds like. An outsider—called the "aggressor" or "bidder" or "acquirer" (or "insurgent" or "raider" or "shark," depending on one's point of view)—tries to oust the incumbent board of a "target" corporation. Hostile takeover activity tends to go in waves. There is a good deal of such activity when the economy is hot and not so much when the markets are uncertain. When the target is a public corporation, there are two basic methods of takeover: the tender offer and the proxy fight.

B.     *The Tender Offer.* Here, the aggressor makes a public offer of cash (or, if it is a corporation itself, perhaps of its stock) to the shareholders of the target. Those who accept the offer tender their stock to the aggressor for the tender price. They do this because the tender price is substantially higher than the market price. The goal for the aggressor is to obtain a majority of the stock, so the tender offers are conditioned upon a given percentage of the shares' actually being tendered. If that number is not reached, the deal fails and the aggressor does not buy the stock.

When a cash tender offer is made, the open market price for the target company's stock will rise. Speculators known as "arbitrageurs" buy the target company's stock in the open market and tender it at the offer price, making a profit on the difference between the two prices. This activity also drives up the market price of the target's stock.

Tender offers are deals between the aggressor and the individual shareholders of the target. They are not fundamental corporate changes for the target. So, unlike a merger or a sale of substantially all the assets of the corporation, tender offers do not require the target board's approval. That is why they are "hostile": the aggressor acquires a majority of the voting stock, right under the nose of the board of directors of the target company. In subpart D of this section, we will see defensive measures the target's board might use to avoid the takeover.

In a wave of cash tender offers in the 1960s, the incumbent management never got a chance to employ defensive tactics. The aggressor made the tender offer and snapped up enough shares to seize control before management knew what hit them. Congress largely eliminated this possibility with the Williams Act in 1968. This legislation, which amends the '34 Act, requires anyone making a cash tender offer for registered securities to disclose various things, including the source of funds used in the offer, the purpose for which the offer is made, and any contracts or understandings the acquirer has regarding the target. The target company must respond publicly to the offer. The Act also imposes miscellaneous substantive restrictions on the mechanics of these offers, and includes a broad prohibition against the use of false, misleading, or incomplete statements.

The 1980s brought the "leveraged buyout," or LBO. With this, the aggressor got the money to buy shares of the target by issuing "junk bonds" and through temporary ("bridge") loans from commercial banks. The junk bonds were IOUs from the aggressor to the lender, and were (as the name implies) quite risky. If the takeover worked, the bonds and other loans would be repaid by the cash flow of the target corporation. .LBOs are "bootstrap" acquisitions: the target company provides the funds to finance its own purchase. In many instances, incumbent management participated in the buyout, and managed the business after public ownership was eliminated.

The era of LBOs ended in the late 1980s. Many companies failed after being acquired in this fashion, because their cash flow was not sufficient to carry the debt load of the LBO. When sources of cash for such takeover bids dried up, proxy contests started to look more attractive.

C.    *The Proxy Contest (or Proxy Fight).* Here, the aggressor competes with the incumbent management of the target to obtain enough proxy appointments to elect a majority of the board. Fights of this sort usually occur in relatively small public corporations. They are sometimes used (or at least threatened) to encourage the incumbent board to consider a consensual merger of the target into the aggressor. CEOs sometimes receive "golden parachutes," which are severance packages: the officer loses the job but gets a huge amount of money. The corporation pays this money to induce officers not to oppose takeover attempts that would benefit shareholders.

A proxy contest may be used in conjunction with a tender offer or with purchases on the market. For example, a bidder may buy a substantial minority position in the target through the stock market. Then, having a toehold in the corporation, the acquirer can use a proxy contest to obtain enough additional shares to replace incumbent management. Or it may gain an initial toehold by waging a proxy fight and complete the takeover by through a tender offer.

Proxy fights for registered corporations cannot be undertaken with stealth. A solicitation from more than ten shareholders requires compliance with the SEC proxy regulations (*see* § 11.4). Other SEC regulations require that "participants" (other than management) file information with the SEC and the securities exchanges at least five days before a solicitation begins. "Participant" includes anyone who contributes more than $500 to finance the contest. The information that must be disclosed relates to the identity and background of the participants, their interests in the corporation, participation in other proxy contests, and understandings with respect to future employment with the corporation. In addition, the Williams Act requires anyone who acquires more than five percent of the voting stock of a public corporation to file a disclosure statement within ten days thereafter. These requirements, again, reflect the theory underlying the '34 Act generally—that widely dispersed information provides the best protection for the investing public.

Those waging a proxy contest are waging an uphill battle. Incumbent management has access to corporate assets to fight the contest, and usually has access to defensive tactics discussed in the next subpart. Moreover, shareholder apathy generally favors management. Many shareholders who might respond to a cash tender offer for their stock may be less likely to answer a call for their proxy.

The expenses of a proxy contest—of soliciting thousands of shareholders for their proxies—can be daunting. It seems clear that the corporation should pay for printing and mailing the notice of meeting, the proxy statement required by federal law, and the proxy appointments themselves. These are legitimate corporate expenses, because without the proxy solicitation it is unlikely that the quorum requirement can be met. Many courts have allowed the corporation to pay the reasonable expenses of defending against the bidder. If the bidder is successful, it may ask that the corporation reimburse it for its expenses. Some courts have allowed this if the dispute involved policy rather than personalities and if the shareholders approve. In such cases, the corporation ends up paying the expenses of both sides of the dispute, because the losing management will normally reimburse itself before leaving office.

D. *Defensive Tactics.* Through the years, innovative lawyers have devised various ways for their clients to fend off hostile takeover attempts. These methods are occasionally referred to generically as "shark repellants." They include

- Finding a more congenial bidder (a "white knight").

- Buying a business that increases the chances that the threatened takeover will give rise to antitrust problems by concentrating too much power in a business area.

- Adopting voting procedures that make it difficult for a bidder who acquires a majority of the voting shares to replace the board of directors.

- Suing for an injunction to stop the proposed takeover, alleging violations of the Williams Act or antitrust laws (or anything else you can plausibly claim).

- Issuing additional shares to friendly persons to make a takeover more difficult (a "lockup").

- Increasing the dividend or otherwise driving up the price of shares to make the takeover price unattractive.

- Buying off the bidder (by paying "greenmail").

- Repurchasing the corporation's stock in the market to drive up the price (thereby hopefully making it too expensive for the acquirer to get control).

- Running up debt obligations to make seizing the company less attractive.

The most effective (and best named) defensive tactic is the "poison pill," which is also called a "shareholder rights plan." This provides that upon a triggering event (which is usually the aggressor's acquiring a given percentage of the corporation's stock) the corporation will issue debt or equity securities to the remaining shareholders at a bargain price. This dilutes the aggressor's ownership interest and makes it impractical for the aggressor to take control. Poison pills usually provide that the board of directors of the target corporation may voluntarily "disarm" the pill before it is triggered. This ingenious device forces the aggressor to negotiate with the incumbent management of the target.

Theoretically, a bidder could buy shares slightly below the number that triggers the pill, and then seek by a proxy fight to replace enough directors to cause the target to disarm the pill. To prevent this maneuver, lawyers have added a "dead hand" provision, to the effect that only the directors in office at the time the plan was approved may vote to disarm the poison pill. In *Quickturn Design Systems v. Shapiro*, 721 A.2d 1281, 1286 (Del. 1998), the Delaware Supreme Court held that such a "dead hand" feature violates the basic principle that the current board of directors has control of corporate affairs. Courts in other states, however, have upheld "dead hand" plans. Some corporations have adopted a "no hands" poison pill, which cannot be disarmed by anyone. And there is a "chewable poison pill," which gives the target's board a set time to negotiate before the pill becomes effective.

Board reactions to takeover attempts raise an important question. On the one hand, they look like any other business decision, so the board's choice should be protected by the business judgment rule (*see* § 9.4). On the other hand, though, the defensive tactics might be seen as directors' trying to hold onto their own jobs. After all, if the aggressor is successful, she will replace the present management. So fending off a hostile takeover might be seen as a conflict-of-interest situation, in which the business judgment rule would not apply (*see* § 9.6).

So what have courts done? Many have simply applied the business judgment rule. In *Panter v. Marshall Field & Co.*, 646 F.2d 271, 298–301 (7th Cir. 1981), a department store chain defeated an unwanted takeover bid by another retail chain. It did so by acquiring additional stores that created serious antitrust problems for the aggressor. Specifically, if the aggressor had succeeded, it would have gotten into trouble for having too much concentrated business power in that field. The aggressor withdrew the offer. Then the price of the target company's stock plummeted, in part because it spent so much to acquire the additional stores. Minority shareholders sued the directors. The majority opinion exonerated the board by applying the business judgment rule. A vigorous dissent argued, however, that incumbent managers should not be able to entrench themselves in office to the detriment of shareholders.

The Delaware Supreme Court has addressed takeover defenses more than any other court. The remainder of this subsection is devoted to opinions by that court. It is fair to say that the Delaware court has not earned high marks for its efforts. Many observers, including Delaware lower court judges, conclude that the Delaware high court has not provided clear guidance. *See In re Gaylord Container Corp. Shareholders Litig.*, 753 A.2d 462, 476 n. 46 (Del.Ch. 2000) ("Delaware's doctrinal approach [to defensive tactics] is premised on the assumption that the world can be viewed clearly by simultaneously wearing three pairs of eye glasses with different prescriptions (*Unocal,* business judgment, and entire fairness). It is not apparent that this approach works any better in the law than it does in the field of optics.").

For starters, in *Moran v. Household International, Inc.,* 500 A.2d 1346, 1356–57 (Del.1985), the Delaware Supreme Court upheld directors' adoption of a poison pill before any specific takeover attempt had arisen. Because there was no suggestion that the pill had been adopted to entrench the board, the matter was simply one of the directors' business judgment. The case was rather odd, since it dealt with an abstract poison pill plan, and not in the context of an actual hostile bid.

In *Unocal Corp. v. Mesa Petroleum Co.,* 493 A.2d 946, 957 (Del.1985), the court addressed a defensive tactic taken in response to an actual takeover threat. The board of the target, having concluded that a tender offer was inadequate, instituted a selective stock repurchase plan, the clear purpose of which was to defeat the tender offer. The repurchase offered stockholders considerably more than the aggressor was offering, and was not made to the aggressor (hence "selective stock repurchase"). The idea was to drive up the price of the stock so much as to make it impossible for the aggressor to complete the takeover. The court upheld the effort. Though it spoke of the board's "duty" to oppose a takeover it considered harmful to the corporate enterprise, the court noted the inherent danger that directors might be protecting their jobs by undertaking a defense.

Accordingly, the court in *Unocal* imposed "enhanced judicial scrutiny." It shifts the burden to directors to show a justification for their conduct. In addition, it requires the that the board have "reasonable" grounds for believing a threat existed, and that the defense adopted would be "reasonable" in relating to that threat. It thus injects the notion of "balance": if a defensive measure is to be upheld, "it must be reasonable in relation to the threat posed. This entails an analysis by the directors of the nature of the takeover bid and its effect on the corporate enterprise." The board may act to avoid danger to "corporate policy and effectiveness." *Unocal* appears to call for a review of the board decision under a rather objective standard, and is less deferential to the board than the business judgment rule.

The court discussed the balancing aspect of *Unocal* in *Unitrin, Inc. v. American General Corp.*, 651 A.2d 1361, 1391 (Del.1995). There, the board of the target initiated a repurchase of it stock in the open market to fend off a merger proposal. The lower court enjoined the tactic as disproportionate to the minimal threat actually posed by the aggressor. The Delaware Supreme Court reversed. When considering proportionality, it said, a court must first determine whether the board's response to a takeover attempt is "coercive" of shareholders or "preclusive." The latter term means that the board's effort would make a later tender offer impossible. If so, the court may enjoin the board's reaction to the takeover attempt. If the board's act is not coercive of preclusive, however, the court may enjoin it only if it is outside the "range of reasonableness" under the circumstances.

The Delaware high court adopted another twist in *Revlon, Inc. v. MacAndrews & Forbes Holdings, Inc.*, 506 A.2d 173, 182 (Del.1986). There, despite efforts to thwart a takeover, it became clear to the board of Revlon that sale of the company to one of two aggressors was inevitable. The court held that in this situation, the board may not exercise business judgment to prefer one bidder over the other. Instead, its role becomes that of auctioneer, and its duty is to obtain the best possible price for the company. The board's decision to defeat a higher bidder and favor a lower bidder violates this "*Revlon* duty."

Courts and commentators speak of a "*Revlon* claim," which is brought to enforce the *Revlon* duty to maximize price. If *Revlon* applies, the board cannot favor one bidder over another, but must treat them on an equal basis, in an effort to maximize the sale price. The Delaware court has not been clear, however, about when this duty applies. In *Paramount Communications, Inc. v. Time, Inc.*, 571 A.2d 1140, 1153–54 (Del. 1989), Time negotiated a stock-for-stock merger with Warner. After the agreement, but before consummation, Paramount showed up with an uninvited (and unwelcome) cash offer to buy Time stock. Time and Warner restructured their deal to have Time launch a tender offer to acquire 51 percent of the Warner stock for cash.

Plaintiffs argued that the original Time-Warner stock merger triggered *Revlon,* because it resulted in change of control. Thus, they asserted, Time management could not take sides, but had to treat Paramount equally. The defensive tactics, according to plaintiffs, breached the *Revlon* duty to maximize the sale price for the company. The court concluded that *Revlon* did not apply, and limited it to cases in which (1) the target initiates active bidding to sell itself or to effect a reorganization resulting in "a clear break-up" of the company, or (2) the target reacts to a takeover bid by abandoning its long-term strategy and seeks another transaction that involves the break-up of the company. The Time-Warner merger may have put Time "in play," but did not result in its break-up. Under *Unocal,* then, the defensive tactic was upheld.

Four years later, the court was back at it in *Paramount Communications, Inc. v. QVC Network, Inc.*, 637 A.2d 34, 51 (Del. 1994), in which the target board favored one of the competing aggressors and installed defensive mechanisms. The court concluded that *Revlon* applied, because the target pursued a deal that would result in a "change of control."

In *Lyondell Chemical Co. v. Ryan*, 970 A.2d 235, 242 (Del. 2009), the court emphasized that "there is only one *Revlon* duty—to [get] the best price for the stockholders at a sale of the company." It explained when that duty arises: "*Revlon* duties do not arise simply because a company is 'in play.' The duty to seek the best available price applies only when a company embarks on a transaction—on its own initiative or in response to an unsolicited offer—that will result in a change of control." Because the board of the target had adopted a wait-and-see attitude to a proposed takeover, it had not taken any act that would result in change of control. The court upheld the action under the business judgment rule.

The court reaffirmed its *Lyondell* holding in *RBC Capital Markets, LLC v. Jervis*, 129 A.3d 816, 852 (Del. 2015). In that case, a committee of the board initiated an active bidding process to sell the company in December 2010. It had no authority to do so, and the full board did not ratify the action until March 2011. Nonetheless, the court held that the *Revlon* duty was triggered by the committee action in 2010.

In 2014, the Delaware Supreme Court reminded observers that cases such as *Revlon* and *QVC* "primarily involve[ ] board resistance to a competing bid after the board had agreed to a change of control, which threatened to impede the emergence of another higher-priced deal." *C&J Energy Servs., Inc. v. City of Miami Gen. Employees' & Sanitation Employees' Ret. Trust*, 107 A.3d 1049, 1053 (Del. 2014).

E.     *State Anti-Takeover Law.* In § 11.4, subpart B, we discussed the Williams Act, which is federal law requiring various disclosures by potential aggressors in takeovers. The Act also contains substantive rules against fraud and high-pressure tactics in takeover efforts. Here we discuss state law on takeovers. States have long been interested in avoiding takeovers of "their" businesses, particularly by out-of-state corporations. States have thus enacted anti-takeover statutes. The first generation of these was aimed largely at notification by potential bidders, review and approval or rejection by a state. The Supreme Court dealt these a serious blow in *Edgar v. MITE Corp.*, 457 U.S. 624, 628 (1982), which invalidated the Illinois statute of this type as violating the Commerce Clause.

States shifted gears and passed a second generation of protective statutes. These "control share acquisition" laws provide that a purchaser of stock who increased her percentage of ownership above a certain level would be prohibited from voting those additional shares without approval of the board or other shareholders. Of course, if the bidder could not vote the stock that made her a majority owner, there was no possibility of a takeover. The Supreme Court upheld Indiana's version of such a statute in *CTS Corporation v. Dynamics Corp. of America*, 481 U.S. 69, 91–93 (1987). The Court rejected the argument that the Commerce Clause creates an area concerning the market for corporate control that is beyond state regulation. It also held that the Williams Act did not pre-empt the Indiana statute. In the wake of *CTS,* nearly every state now has adopted such a statute to thwart the takeover of public corporations formed there.

There is now a third generation: called "business combination" statutes. These restrict persons who acquire more than a specified percentage of stock from engaging in certain transactions (such as mergers) with the corporation for a specified period (usually three years) without the consent of the pre-acquisition board of directors. *See, e.g.,* Delaware

§ 203. States have adopted these statutes widely. So far, based largely on the reasoning of *CTS,* courts have generally concluded that these statutes pass muster. They do not violate the Commerce Clause and are not pre-empted by the Williams Act. *See, e.g., Amanda Acquisition Corp. v. Universal Foods Corp.,* 877 F.2d 496, 509 (7th Cir. 1989) (upholding the Wisconsin statute).

## § 11.6  EXECUTIVE COMPENSATION

The level of compensation paid to officers in public corporations (particularly to CEOs) has become a political issue from time to time. From 1993 to 2008, CEO compensation in the Fortune 500 companies quadrupled. According to Forbes magazine, the CEOs of the Fortune 500 corporations made an average of $10,500,000 in 2012 (which was down from $11,400,000 in 2008). This figure includes salary, bonus, and stock options. Politicians point out that the gap between CEO's compensation and that of the average workers in the company also increased. In 1993, CEOs made 131 times as much as the average worker. In 2013, CEOs of the 350 largest companies made 273 times as much as the average workers.

For many years, the federal government has tried to curb executive pay. The SEC required greater disclosure of executive compensation, on the theory that increased awareness of the stunning numbers would curb excess. The backfired. If anything, CEOs came to demand greater compensation when they found out what their competitors were making.

The government also tried to limit "golden parachute" severance packages (see § 11.5, subpart C) by imposing taxes on them. Again, the effort failed, as increased publicity apparently caused more executives to demand such deals.

Public corporations pay income tax on their net income. In calculating that figure, they are permitted to deduct compensation they pay. For over two decades, Congress has limited the income tax deductibility of executive salaries. This effort also has failed to curb compensation.

In the wake of the financial crisis in the first decade of the twenty-first century, some corporations received government "bail outs." For instance, under the Troubled Asset Relief Program (TARP), the United States Treasury purchased assets and stock of companies that had lent money on "subprime" mortgages. (These were mortgages that were unlikely to be repaid.) TARP was aimed at keeping such companies afloat and allowing them to restructure so they could make money and repay the federal funds. One aspect of the law limits compensation of the five highest-paid executives of corporations that received significant TARP funds. Federal law now requires that public corporations have compensation committees consisting of outside directors. These committees are required to develop performance criteria at the beginning of the performance period. The compensation arrangement must be adequately disclosed to, and approved by, shareholders. In addition, the outside directors must certify in writing that the performance criteria have been met before compensation is paid.

Critics argue, however, that compensation committees are ineffective. They tend to hire consultants and to follow the consultant's recommendations. Then the board tends to rubber-stamp what the committee says. Warren Buffett has famously characterized compensation committees as "tail-wagging puppy dogs meekly following recommendations by consultants." Lublin & Thurm, *Behind Startling Executive Pay, Decades of Failed Restraints,* WALL STREET J., Oct. 6, 2006, at A–1.

Are corporate executives overpaid? Consider the case of Harvey Golub, who was CEO of American Express from 1993 to 2000. For his efforts over those years he was paid $250,000,000. During his tenure, however, the market value of the corporation's stock increased more than six times, from $10,000,000,000 to $65,000,000,000. Golub recognized that he became wealthy, but noted "[m]y stockholders became even wealthier." He asked "How much of the $55,000,000,000 [increase in value] should I get?" Golub's payday was dwarfed, however, by Michael Eisner, who as CEO of Walt Disney Company, received $576,000,000 in a single year (1998)!

Speaking of Disney, the Delaware Supreme Court issued a long-awaited opinion in 2006, capping nine years of litigation about compensation to Eisner's hand-picked successor. After Eisner had suffered a heart attack, he urged the board to hire Michael Ovitz, one of the founders of the leading Hollywood talent agency. Ovitz negotiated a deal that included a severance package if he were fired without cause. After 14 months, Disney fired Ovitz without cause; things were just not working out. Disney paid Ovitz $130,000,000 as severance pay. Shareholders sued, claiming that the board had wasted corporate assets in paying this sum for fourteen months of unsuccessful service. The court held that the Disney board had not breached any duties in approving the compensation. *In re Walt Disney Company Derivative Litig.*, 906 A.2d 27, 70 (Del. 2006).

At least Disney and American Express had done well while these highly-paid executives were in the saddle. Home Depot once paid a CEO $245,000,000 over five years. During those years, the company's stock declined 12 percent in value while that of its archrival, Lowe's, had increased 176 percent!

One might well ask why compensation of corporate executives draws the attention of politicians while that of entertainers and athletes seem to go unquestioned. Oprah Winfrey routinely makes over $100,000,000 per year, including $385,000,000 in 2008. Robert Downey, Jr. reportedly made $50,000,000 for a single film. Actors in breakout television shows can make $1,000,000 per episode. Major league baseball players can make over $25,000,000 per year. Their efforts are not increasing the value of stock held by shareholders. Yet we do not see articles about how much more these people make than the average member of their audience.

# CHAPTER 12
# FINANCING THE CORPORATION

## § 12.1 INTRODUCTION

Every business needs money (or, more formally, "capital"). Whether it is a front-yard lemonade stand or a multinational conglomerate, the business cannot get started without money. It needs to buy supplies, to purchase or rent office or retail space, pay employees, etc. In general, there are two ways a business can get capital: it can borrow it or it can allow investors to buy ownership interests (in the corporation, these are shares of stock). These two sources of funds represent "debt" interests and "equity" interests in the business. In § 12.2, we will define the debt and equity and discuss how businesses use each.

Even after a business is up and running, it may need more money to maintain or expand operations. At that point, it may be generating earnings that it can "plow back" into the business for these purposes. Even then, though, it may seek capital from the outside, and the question will be the same as it was initially: do we borrow or do we sell ownership interests in the business? In other words, do we use debt or equity financing (or a combination)?

There are rules in every state about raising capital by issuing stock (*see* § 12.3). Existing shareholders may worry when the corporation issues new stock to others, because their interests in the business will be diluted. They may be protected by pre-emptive rights, which permit them to buy stock in the new issuance (*see* § 12.4). Some corporations are able to sell stock to the public, which raises a host of financial and legal issues. We saw the legal issues raised by the public issuance of stock in § 11.2, and address the financial issues here (*see* § 12.5). Finally, we will need some facility with basic accounting and financial records, which help measure the fiscal health of the business (*see* § 12.6).

## § 12.2   DEBT AND EQUITY FINANCING AND SECURITIES

A.      *Background and Definitions.* Debt in the corporate world means exactly what it means in our everyday world: you borrowed, and you have to pay it back, with interest, on terms specified in the contract. Whoever lends capital to the business is a creditor, not an owner, of that business. She is entitled to be repaid, but not to share in the profits if the business does well. Whether the business thrives or does poorly, the creditor has a right to be repaid.

Equity, in contrast, is ownership. The holder of stock is an owner of the corporation, and not a creditor. She is entitled to share in the success of the business, but will receive nothing if the business does poorly. In fact, she may lose her investment if the company does poorly. On the other hand, if the business is successful, she will share in that success.

Suppose your friend is forming a corporation to manufacture widgets. She needs $20,000 to get the business going. She will put in $10,000 of her own money and wants you to invest the other $10,000.

You agree. Do you lend the money to the business or do you buy stock in the business?

First, let's say you lend $10,000 to the corporation. The corporation will issue a document (probably called a bond, *see* subsection C) that obligates it to repay you $10,000 plus interest, due on demand one year from now.

- Say your friend forms the corporation and the business does poorly—it makes no money at all. A year from now, you have a right to demand payment on your loan.

- But let's say your friend forms that business and it does spectacularly well. Your friend sells the business for a million dollars. Do you share in that good fortune? No. You are not an equity holder. You are a debt holder. You get your $10,000 plus interest. Your friend gets the million dollars (minus the payment to you).

Second, let's say instead of lending, you invested the $10,000 in stock. You get 50 percent of the stock in the corporation (your friend, who also invested $10,000, gets the other 50 percent).

- The business fails completely. It not only does not make money, but uses up the $20,000 you and your friend invested. You get nothing. You were an equity holder and you have no right to payment. You have lost $10,000.

- But let's say the business does spectacularly well—and is sold for a million dollars. As an owner, you share in the good fortune. You own half the company, and therefore you get $500,000.

Most businesses use a combination of debt and equity financing. Our purpose is to understand the basics. Hitting the right mix of financing for a given business is very sophisticated work, and is the focus of the course on Corporate Finance. We should also know that the line between debt and equity is not always clear. Corporations can issue "hybrid" interests that have some characteristics of one and some of the other. The taxation consequences of these hybrids are often subject to debate. But that is beyond our scope in this class.

We need two more terms. First, a "security" is an investment. So we will speak of "debt securities" (which are loans to the corporation) and "equity securities" (which are ownership interests (stock) in the corporation). Second, when a corporation takes a loan or sells an ownership interest, it "issues" the security. So "issuance" is a sale by the corporation itself, and the "issuer" is the corporation. The corporation may issue debt securities or equity securities (or both).

B.    *Advantages and Disadvantages.* Debt is riskier for the business because it must be repaid. On the other hand, if the business does great, the good fortune does not have to be shared with the lender. Equity is riskier for the investor because she can lose her investment. So why wouldn't businesses always use equity financing? For one thing, it may be tough to get. People (and banks) may be more willing to lend to an unproven business than to own a piece of it. For another, owners of stock usually have the right to vote. So issuing stock means sharing power with others. A founder of a business may want to retain control and thus refuse to have the corporation issue stock to others.

There are tax consequences to the choices as well. In computing its income tax liability, the corporation is permitted to deduct interest payments on debt, but cannot deduct distributions, such as dividends, that are made to shareholders. So interest payments reduce the corporation's income tax liability, but dividend payments do not.

Debt financing allows the corporation to use "leverage"—that is, to use the borrowed money to increase its *rate of return* on investment. Assume that a business was started with $200,000 and generates an annual income of $20,000. Suppose you invested the initial $200,000 yourself. It was your money. The business generates $20,000 per year, which is 10 percent of the investment. You are making a 10 percent return on your investment.

Now let's say you started that business with $100,000 of your own money and $100,000 that you borrowed. Assume you borrowed that $100,000 at five percent interest. The business generates $20,000 per year. Of that $20,000, you have to pay $5,000 to the person from whom you borrowed the $100,000. That means you "netted" $15,000 income. But you only put at risk $100,000 of your own money. So your return on investment is $15,000 on a $100,000 investment; that is a return of 15 percent. So by using borrowed money, you "levered" your *rate of return* on the investment you made from your own funds from 10 percent to 15 percent.

This sounds great, but remember the risk of using debt financing. The loan has to be repaid, with interest. If the business's cash flow falls to $5,000 one year, you will be getting no return on your investment, because that $5,000 goes to pay interest on the loan.

C.    *Types of Debt Securities.* Debt securities, as we saw above, are loans to the corporation. Like any loan, repayment of a debt security may be secured or unsecured. There are two main types of debt securities: the debenture and the bond. The debenture is an unsecured corporate obligation, while repayment of a bond is secured by a lien or mortgage on some (or all) of the corporate property. In practice, though, many use "bond" as a generic term for debt securities. An "indenture" is the contract that defines the rights of the holders of the bonds or debentures. Typical debt securities are issued in multiples of $1,000, pay interest at a fixed rate for the life of the security, and have a specified maturity date that may be many years in the future.

Historically, debentures and bonds were reflected by certificates printed on heavy paper with elaborate and intricate designs, lettering, and figures. The purpose was to deter forgeries. They were "bearer" instruments, payable to the person who held them. All the holder had to do was deliver the certificate to the corporation at the maturity date, which would allow her to collect the face value of the bond. Interest payments were represented by coupons on the certificate. The bearer "clipped" the coupons with scissors as they matured, and submitted each to the company for payment, usually through a bank or broker.

Because debt instruments were payable to the bearer it was difficult for the government to ensure that income tax was being paid on the interest. So Congress stepped in to deny corporations an income-tax deductions for interest they paid on bearer instruments. As a result, ownership of these instruments is now reflected either by certificates registered in the name of the owner and transferable only by endorsement, or by book entries on the records of the corporation or brokerage firms.

Interest payments on debt securities are usually fixed obligations, expressed as a percentage of the face amount of the security. So a four percent bond means that a $1,000 investment will pay $40 per year. Not all debt instruments carry a fixed interest rate. Some corporations have issued "income bonds," on which the obligation to pay interest is conditioned on adequate corporate earnings. Somewhat rarer are "participating bonds," with which the amount of interest increases or decreases with corporate earnings. Such bonds start to look like equity investments.

Indeed, debt securities may have rights analogous to those provided for preferred stock. Preferred stock has the right to be paid first, before distributions are made to other shares (*see* § 13.4). Similarly, bonds with a "sinking fund" provision require the corporation to set aside cash to redeem a part of the issue each year. And sometimes the line between debt and equity is further blurred because holders of debt securities are given the right to vote for directors, usually on some contingency, such as failure to pay interest on bonds. Many debentures are made convertible into equity securities, usually common stock, on some predetermined conversion ratio. When convertible debentures are converted, they (and the debt they represent) disappear and the new equity securities take their place.

D. *Types of Equity Securities.* Most courses spend more time on equity securities than debt. We already know that "equity security" means stock, and represents an ownership interest in the corporation. Now we focus on other terminology.

*Authorized stock* is the maximum number of shares the corporation can issue. This number is set in the articles. There is no statutory limitation on the number of shares that may be authorized by a corporation and no requirement that all the authorized shares actually be issued. The number of authorized shares should be high enough to accommodate future efforts to raise capital. On the other hand, there are practical constraints on setting the number too high. Some states may impose franchise taxes based upon the number of authorized shares. Setting the number too high increases this tax with no corresponding benefit. Moreover, setting a large number of authorized shares may make investors nervous that their interests could be diluted if a great many shares are sold to other people later. The persons drafting the articles balance such factors.

*Issued stock* is the number of shares the corporation actually does sell. The corporation does not have to issue all of its authorized shares; what it actually does sell is called issued. Whether and when to issue stock is a management decision, usually made by the board of directors, which also sets the price at which stock is issued (*see* § 12.3, subpart E).

*Outstanding stock* consists of shares that the corporation has issued and not re-acquired. Often, this is the same number as issued. Assume the corporation has 10,000 authorized shares. It issues 4,000 shares and has not re-acquired any of them. The number of issued shares and the number of outstanding shares are the same: 4,000. Now assume that the corporation re-acquires 500 of the shares it has issued (the corporation can repurchase its stock from shareholders (*see* § 13.5)). Here, the number of issued shares is 4,000. The number of outstanding shares is 3,500. Stated another way, issued stock is historical; it is the number of shares the corporation has sold over time. Outstanding stock, in contrast, is a snapshot of how many shares are held at this moment by persons other than the corporation itself.

*Treasury stock* consists of shares the corporation has issued and then re-acquired. In the hypo we just did, the 500 shares that the corporation re-acquired would be treasury stock. The theory is that the corporation gets the stock and puts it in its "treasury." This is a strange theory, because there is no such thing as the treasury. Economically, treasury stock is the equivalent of authorized and unissued stock. Thus, the corporation can re-issue this stock. Until it is re-issued (if it ever is), the corporation holds this treasury stock. But the corporation does not vote these shares at shareholder meetings (nobody does) and it does not get any dividend on that stock (nobody does).

- Marjorie owns 100 shares of stock in Corporation. On June 8, Corporation buys Marjorie's stock. June 10 is the record date for voting at the annual meeting and for a dividend. Because Marjorie is not the record owner on June 10, she has no right to vote at the annual meeting and has no right to the dividend. Though Corporation owns this "treasury" or "reacquired" stock on the record date, the stock is considered unissued. Thus, Corporation it is not entitled to vote the stock or to receive a dividend.

MBCA § 6.31(a) has abolished the term "treasury," and simply treats all "re-acquired" stock as authorized and unissued, consistent with the rules we just discussed.

Every state permits the corporation to establish different *classes* of stock. The principal distinction is between *common stock* and *preferred stock*. This distinction is important when we get to distributions in Chapter 13. Distributions are payments by the corporation to shareholders. The best example is the dividend. Preferred stock is entitled to be paid first, before any other shares. The other stock (without the right to be paid first) is called common stock, and it is entitled to the rest of the distribution. The details on that are in § 13.4. For now, it is enough to know that we set up the different classes of stock in the articles.

If there is only one class of stock, by default it is common stock. It has the right to receive distributions (if there are any) and the right to vote—one vote per share. Indeed, there must be at least one class of stock entitled to receive distributions and one entitled to vote. Though these do not have to be the same class of stock, they usually are—common stock.

The corporation can have non-voting stock. The corporation can have weighted voting stock—for example, with two votes per share, as opposed to one. While this usually happens in close corporations, it can be used in public corporations as well. A good example is the corporation that published the New York Times. Though publicly traded, this corporation was long associated with a single family. The corporation had a special class of stock, held by family members, with super voting power. This helped ensure that the family could continue to run the business. The Securities and Exchange Commission adopted rule 19c–4 (the "one share one vote rule" or "all holders' rule") to prevent such unequal divisions in voting power in public corporations, but did not affect companies that were already doing such things. The District of Columbia Circuit held the rule invalid, though, as exceeding the power of the Commission. *See The Business Roundtable v. S.E.C.*, 905 F.2d 406, 417 (D.C. Cir. 1990).

A *series* of stock is a sub-class. A corporation desiring to give different characteristics within a class of stock may sub-divide that class into, say, Series A and Series B.

As noted, all the information about characteristics of various classes and series of stock is included in the articles. So the persons forming the corporation need to have a good sense of the capitalization needs and types of securities the corporation will need.

Corporations can give *options* to employees, as an incentive. The option gives the holder the right to purchase stock at the option price. She does not become a shareholder, however, until she exercises the option and pays the purchase price. At that point, the corporation issues the stock to her. *Puts* and *calls* are particular kinds of options. A *put* is the option to sell stock to at a set price. A *call* is the option to buy stock at a set price.

## § 12.3  ISSUANCE OF STOCK—DEFINITION, LIMITATIONS ON CONSIDERATION, AND "WATERED" STOCK

A.     *What Is an Issuance?* "Issuance" is a term of art. It refers to the corporation's selling its own stock. It is, as we know, a way to raise capital for the business. The corporation sells the stock (maybe to a small group, maybe to the public) and gets consideration for that issuance. This is to be contrasted with buying and selling stock on a stock market. When you go online and buy stock, say, in Burger King, the corporation does not get the money you pay. Why? Because, as we discussed in § 11.2, subpart A, that was not an issuance. You did not buy from Burger King, but from some member of the trading public. Only the initial sale by Burger King was an issuance.

Corporations often issue stock through subscriptions. These are offers to buy stock from the corporation. We discussed these in detail, including the general rule limiting revocation of pre-incorporation subscriptions, in § 4.4.

B.     *Form of Consideration for an Issuance.* We usually think of a corporation's selling its stock to get money. But the company may issue stock to get other forms of consideration as well. Maybe the corporation needs a building or services. Traditionally, a corporation could issue stock for any of three forms of consideration: (1) money, (2) tangible or intangible property, or (3) services that had already been performed for the corporation. These forms of consideration are still permitted in every state. The relevant question will be whether other forms are also permitted.

"Money" includes cash or its equivalent (like a check). "Intangible property" is also construed broadly, and usually is held to include patents, goodwill, contract rights, and computer software.

There is some debate about whether services rendered *before* the corporation is actually formed can constitute services "performed for the corporation." For instance, can a corporation issue stock to lawyer as compensation for doing the pre-incorporation work to form it? Some courts may conclude that the answer is no, because when the work was done, there was no corporation in existence. Most courts, however, appear to conclude that the answer is yes. In New York, a statute expressly provides that a corporation may issue stock as payment for pre-incorporation services. NY Bus. Corp. Law § 504(a).

Under the historic view, a corporation could not issue stock in exchange for a promise of future payment (i.e., a promissory note) or for a promise of future services. If the corporation purported to do so, the stock was said to be "unpaid," with liability imposed as it is with "watered" stock (subpart D below). A generation ago, these limitations were virtually universal. Indeed, in Texas, these rules about the form of consideration for an issuance were in the state constitution!

As noted three paragraphs above, the three classic forms of consideration (money, tangible or intangible property, and services already performed for the corporation) are acceptable in every state. In addition, in most states today, it is also permissible to issue stock for promissory notes and future services. This is because the majority view is that an issuance can be made for "any tangible or intangible property or benefit to the corporation." MBCA § 6.21. (In some states, the relevant provision says simply "tangible or intangible benefit to the corporation," which obviously includes property). So today, in most states, promissory notes and future services are acceptable, as is the discharge of a debt, and release of a claim—*anything* that constitutes a benefit to the corporation.

This change recognized the commercial reality that sometimes there is a legitimate need to issue stock in exchange for future services. For instance, assume that Movie Star agrees to make a film in exchange for a 20 percent interest in the film. Though a bank would probably lend millions of dollars to a new corporation to make the film, the historical rules on consideration would not permit the corporation to pay Movie Star in stock.

What happens if the corporation issues stock for a promissory note or for a promise of future services and the note is never paid or the services never performed? The shares are considered outstanding and validly issued, and the corporation has whatever claims it can assert for the future benefits or under the contract. MBCA § 6.21(e) permits the corporation to place the stock in escrow until the note is paid or the services performed, and to cancel the shares if there is a default.

A few states continue to adhere to the historical limitations and thus do not permit issuances for promissory notes or future services. Arizona provides an especially interesting example. Though it adopts the MBCA phrase on this point—"any tangible or intangible property or interest"—the statute then specifically provides that promissory notes and future services are prohibited. Ariz. Rev. Stats. § 10–621(B).

- Trick question: Louise Shareholder gives her stock in XYZ Corp. to her daughter Courtney as a gift—for *no consideration*. Is this valid? Yes. Remember, the rules in this section are "issuance" rules, so they apply only when there is an issuance—that is, only when the corporation is selling its own stock. They do not apply to transfers by anyone other than the corporation itself.

C.    *Amount of Consideration for an Issuance.* Assuming the issuance is made for a valid form of consideration, the next question is whether it was made for a proper amount of consideration. This brings us to "par" and "no-par" stock. Traditionally, corporations were required to have at least some par stock. Today, par is not required, though corporations can always elect to have it. If we do, the par value (like other characteristics of stock) is set in the articles.

In any issuance, the board of directors will decide the issuance price—that is, the price at which the corporation will sell the stock. In setting the issuance price, the board must be mindful about whether it is issuing "par" stock. Par means that there is a minimum price for the issuance. Not surprisingly, "no-par" means there is no minimum price at which the stock can be issued. When par stock exists, the par number is an arbitrary figure that has no necessary correlation with the actual value (or even the issuance price) of the stock.

- XYZ Corp. issues 1,000 shares of $2 par stock. It must receive at least $2,000 for this issuance. If it receives less than $2,000, there will be liability for "watered stock" (subpart D below). Par means minimum, not maximum. So the corporation can issue the 1,000 shares of $2 par for a billion dollars a share (if it can get a buyer). The board will set the actual issuance price when it authorizes the issuance, and the only limitation is that the company must receive at least $2 per share.

- Trick question. Bee buys some of that $2 par stock from the corporation. She pays $2 for it. A month later, she sells it to Patti for $1.50 per share. Is there a problem because Bee sold it for less than $2? No! Remember, par—like every rule in this section of the book—is an issuance rule. And issuance rules apply only when the corporation is selling its stock. Par is relevant only the price at which the corporation initially sells the stock. It is irrelevant to later sales.

- The board of XYZ Corp. authorizes the corporation to issue 5,000 shares of no-par stock. It will set the price at which the issuance is made, and there is no minimum. It can be issued for any amount.

In theory, par stock is a device used to protect creditors. How? The par value of any issuance goes into a fund called "stated capital," which cannot be used to pay a distribution (like a dividend) to shareholders. So stated capital is essentially a fund, a cushion, from which creditors can be paid. The problem is that the law never required par to be a particular amount. So corporations are free to set par at a nominal amount—say, at one tenth of a penny. Setting a low par gives for the board greater flexibility in setting the actual issuance price, and avoids potential liability for "watered" stock. It also means that the "stated capital" fund might be very small and offer little protection to creditors. Recognizing this, most states, led by the MBCA, have replaced the "stated capital" requirement with "insolvency" limitations on distributions (*see* § 13.6).

Historically, corporations could only issue par stock; there was no such thing as no-par. This started to change in the early twentieth century, and eventually the universal law became that the articles may provide for par and no-par stock, or a combination. The MBCA has basically abolished the notion of par stock, though corporations can still opt to have it. But if par stock is no longer required, why would anybody still have it? One reason is that old habits die hard. For generations, lawyers have drafted articles with par stock, and it's tough for them to get away from that. But par is a concept of waning importance.

Generally, the board of directors is responsible for determining the "value" of consideration received for an issuance. This meant that the board had to "fix" the "consideration, expressed in dollars" that the company was to receive. Historically, the board's determination on this score was conclusive as to actual value, so long as the board acted in good faith (or, in some states, without fraud) in making it. This rule protected directors from liability if the board

acted in good faith but set an erroneously high
valuation.

- The board of directors authorizes XYZ Corp.
  to issue 10,000 shares of $2 par stock to Collin
  in exchange for land. The board undertakes a
  valuation of the land and concludes in good
  faith that it is worth at least $20,000. The
  company issues the stock and gets the land. It
  turns out, however, that the land is only worth
  $16,000. As long as the board acted in good
  faith (or, in some states, without fraud) in
  fixing the value of the property, there is no
  problem. The valuation is conclusive. (On the
  other hand, if the board knowingly authorized
  the issuance of $20,000 worth of par stock for
  $16,000, we would have liability for "watered
  stock" (subpart D below).)

The modern trend, typified by MCBA § 6.21(c),
does not require the board actually to set a price tag
on consideration received for an issuance. Rather, it
must merely determine that the amount of
consideration to be received "is adequate." Moreover,
this determination of adequacy is presumed when the
board authorizes issuance at a given price.

- The board of directors authorizes XYZ Corp.
  to issue 10,000 shares of stock to Collin in
  exchange for a parcel of land that she owns.
  By authorizing the issuance, the board is
  deemed to have determined that the land "is
  adequate" as the amount of consideration for
  the issuance.

Not only that, but this determination "is conclusive insofar as the adequacy of consideration for the issuance of shares relates to whether the shares are validly issued, fully paid, and nonassessable." MBCA § 6.21(c). Thus, in a state adopting this modern view, the concept of par is not meaningful.

- The board authorizes the corporation to issue 10,000 shares of $2 par to Collin in exchange for land worth $16,000. The board's approving the issuance constitutes a finding that the land is "adequate" consideration for the issuance, and that finding is conclusive. So the issuance is valid and the stock is fully paid.

What about the issuance of treasury (or "re-acquired") stock? The corporation might re-acquire some of the stock it has issued. That stock is then considered unissued, so the company can re-sell this stock. There is never—and has never been—a minimum issuance price for the issuance of treasury stock. This is true even if the original issuance was of par stock.

- XYZ Corp. issued $2 par stock for $2 per share. Later, the corporation re-acquired this stock. Now the corporation wants to issue this treasury stock. There is no minimum issuance price. The fact that this was $2 par stock was relevant to its original issuance, but is irrelevant now. This is an issuance of treasury stock, not par stock.

D.     *Watered Stock.* We have just seen that the concept of par is less important than it used to be. In states not adopting the modern view on valuation (which we saw immediately above), however, issuance of par stock gives rise to the classic problem of watered stock. Indeed, even under modern statutes, there is an analog to liability in this area.

Watered stock is a generic term, applicable when the corporation issues stock for an improper form of consideration or issues par stock for less than par value. Technically, courts have used different terms for the various situations. So "unpaid" or "bonus" stock is issued for no consideration or an improper form (such as for future services in a state that does not permit that form of payment for an issuance). "Discount" stock is par stock issued for money for less than par value, and "watered" is (technically) par stock issued for property for less than par value. These specific terms are rarely used anymore; most people refer to all of these situations as "watered."

- The board of XYZ Corp. authorizes the issuance of 10,000 shares of $2 par stock to Collin for $16,000. Under the par rules, the corporation should have received $20,000. It actually received $16,000. So there is $4,000 of "water." The corporation can sue to recover that amount. Or, if the corporation is insolvent, creditors can sue to recover the $4,000.

Who is liable for the water? In other words, from whom can the $4,000 be recovered? First, directors who approved the issuance are jointly and severally liable. Second, the purchaser is also jointly and severally liable, even if she did not know about the par value. Because par value is established in the articles, and because it is printed on the stock certificates, the purchaser has no defense; he is charged with notice of the par value. Third, a transferee from the purchaser is not liable if she acts in good faith. That means that she did not know about the issuance problem. She is not required to pay value for the stock; for example, she might receive the stock by gift from the purchaser. As long as she is unaware of the problem, she is not liable for the water.

At common law, these liability rules were clear, though the theoretical basis for liability of the purchaser was not. Some courts spoke of par value creating a "trust fund" for the benefit of creditors and others imposed liability because the corporation has "held out" that the stock would not be issued for less than par. The theory is less important today, because any liability is imposed by statute.

Section 6.22(a) of the MBCA provides that a shareholder who buys stock from the corporation is not liable to the corporation or its creditors "except to pay the consideration for which the shares were authorized to be issued" or to which she and corporation agreed in a subscription agreement. This means that the shareholder is liable if she pays less for the stock than the consideration set by the board when it authorized the issuance. So it imposes liability for the *issuance* price, not for par value. The provision is not surprising. It simply means you must pay what you agreed to pay.

E.     *Determining Issuance Price and the Problem of Dilution.* Within the limitations seen above, the board determines the price at which the corporation will issue stock. The board has great discretion here.

- The articles of YZ Corporation authorize it to issue 2,000 shares. Suppose the business wants initial capitalization of $100,000. Y and Z—the individuals engaged in the business— agree that each will invest $50,000 and each will own one half of the stock. The board may issue each person one share, at an issuance price of $50,000. Or it might issue each person 10 shares, at an issuance price of $5,000. Or it might issue each person 100 shares, at an issuance price of $500. Or 1,000 shares at an issuance price of $50. (This last scenario is probably not a good idea, because it would exhaust the authorized stock and the corporation could not sell any more unless it amended the articles to provide for more authorized stock.)

The point is this: in any of these scenarios, Y and Z would each own half the outstanding stock, and the corporation would have received $100,000 ($50,000 from each investor). The individual shareholders probably do not care how many shares they have for their investment—just so they each get the same number of shares for the same investment.

Let's say Y and Z each get 100 shares, at the issuance price of $500 per share. Now let's say the corporation needs more capital to maintain or expand operations. Do Y and Z care what the issuance price is? Absolutely. Suppose the corporation sells 100 shares to A at $50 per share. So A gets 100 shares for $5,000. A will be a one-third owner of the corporation because he owns one-third of the outstanding stock. He thus has one-third of the voting power, and is entitled to one-third of any declared dividends. A will have as much economic benefit and voting power as Y and as Z. But he will have paid $5,000, which is only one-tenth as much as Y and Z paid. This is an example of "dilution." The value of Y and Z's stock has been diluted dramatically by this bargain-basement issuance to A.

To a degree, this is simply a risk an investor takes. But management may go too far if its dilutive issuance is oppressive. To a degree, this depends on the slippery notion of intent. An example is *Byelick v. Vivadelli*, 79 F.Supp.2d 610, 630 (E.D. Va. 1999), which involved a corporation with three shareholders. Plaintiff owned 10 percent of the stock and defendants (a married couple) owned the other 90 percent. Defendants were the only directors, and there was clearly bad blood between the married couple, on the one hand, and the plaintiff, on the other. Defendants had the corporation issue additional stock, but only to themselves. The result was to reduce plaintiff's ownership from 10 percent to one percent. In denying summary judgment for the defendants, the court held that managers owed the minority shareholder a fiduciary duty not to cause the corporation to take an act that benefits themselves at the expense of the minority. This "dilutive transaction" was such an act.

## § 12.4  PRE-EMPTIVE RIGHTS

We just saw that a shareholder's interest will be diluted if the corporation issues stock to other people. One way the existing shareholder might be protected from dilution is with pre-emptive rights. These allow a shareholder to maintain her percentage of ownership by buying stock when there is a new issuance. She may buy her proportionate share of the new issuance. She is not required to do so, however, and may waive her pre-emptive rights in writing. And if she exercises her right, she does not have to do so fully. So if she now owns 20 percent of the stock, she may buy 20 percent or less of the new issuance. Like anyone else, she must pay the issuance price for the stock, as set by the board.

- X owns 1,000 shares of XYZ Corp. There are 4,000 shares outstanding. The board of directors of XYZ Corp. announces that it will have a new issuance of 1,000 shares. Right now, X owns 25 percent of the stock of the company: 1,000 out of 4,000 outstanding shares. If the new issuance is made to third-parties, X's percentage of ownership will be diluted to 20 percent: she will own 1,000 out of 5,000 outstanding shares. But if X has pre-emptive rights, she may buy her current percentage (25 percent) of the new issuance. The new issuance is 1,000 shares, and 25 percent of that is 250 shares. So X may buy 250 shares of the new issuance.

Pre-emptive rights developed at common law. They are now a matter of statute in all states. In most states, pre-emptive rights are permissive, so they exist only if the articles provide for them (if the company "opts in"). *See, e.g.,* MBCA § 6.30(a). In some states, however, the opposite is true: pre-emptive rights exist unless the articles take them away (if the company "opts out"). In those states having special provisions for "statutory close corporations," (*see* § 10.2) legislation usually provides that pre-emptive rights exist unless the company opts out of them. *See, e.g.,* Pa. Rev. Stat. § 2321(b).

Even if pre-emptive rights do not apply, directors must be mindful of the equitable principles against oppressive dilutive issuances, which we saw in the preceding section. And even if pre-emptive rights do not exist, there is nothing to stop the board from issuing new stock to existing shareholders in their present percentages.

The argument in favor of pre-emptive rights is a democratic one: those who buy the initial issuance should be entitled to maintain their percentage interest. Many times, however, pre-emptive rights are a nuisance. For example, suppose a corporation with a fairly large number of shareholders needs capital on short notice, and wants to obtain it by issuing stock. Having to offer it first to existing shareholders (to honor their pre-emptive rights) can be cumbersome. Accordingly, pre-emptive rights tend to be used only in small close corporations.

Moreover, as a practical matter, the protection afforded by pre-emptive rights is sometimes illusory. A minority shareholder may not be able to pay for the additional stock. Sometimes, the dominant shareholder will have lent money to the business. She can buy her allotment of a new issuance by forgiving that debt; that way, she exercises her pre-emptive rights without need for direct cash outlay. The minority shareholder may not be in that position. Unless she can make a plausible claim of oppression, the minority shareholder who cannot afford to pay for the additional shares is just out of luck; her interest will be diluted.

In addition, we must be mindful of five common statutory restrictions on pre-emptive rights. These vary somewhat from state to state, but here are some typical limitations, applicable unless the articles provide otherwise. First, pre-emptive rights generally do not apply between different classes of stock. For instance, a holder of preferred shares will not have a pre-emptive right to buy common stock. *See* MBCA § 6.30(b)(4) & (5).

Second, there is a split of authority as to whether pre-emptive rights attach to the issuance of treasury stock (*see* § 12.2). Some states deny pre-emptive rights on the issuance of treasury stock. Today, the majority view appears to be that pre-emptive rights attach to the issuance of "unissued" stock. Because treasury shares are "unissued," pre-emptive rights do attach.

Third, pre-emptive rights often do not apply to the issuance of stock originally authorized in the articles and issued within six months of incorporation. *See, e.g.,* MBCA § 6.30(b)(3)(ii). This permits the corporation to raise initial capital with multiple issuances without having to worry about honoring pre-emptive rights.

Fourth, pre-emptive rights generally do not attach to the issuance of "shares sold otherwise than for money." MBCA § 6.30(b)(3)(iii). Applying pre-emptive rights when there is an issuance for property or services would be almost impossible, and would frustrate the corporation's ability to issue stock in exchange for specific property or services. A few cases have imposed pre-emptive rights in such cases unless the corporation shows a need for particular property and that issuing stock (as opposed to paying cash) is the only feasible way to get it. In many situations, the corporation can simply pay cash to get property, so might be able to issue stock for money, thereby honoring pre-emptive rights.

Fifth, pre-emptive rights usually do not apply to stock issued as compensation to directors, officers, or other employees. This includes stock issued pursuant to options held by such people MBCA § 6.30(b)(3)(i) & (ii). Without this limitation, existing shareholders could claim the stock that is intended as compensation for particular people.

- Here is a great exam question. The articles of the corporation provide for 5,000 authorized shares. The company is formed on February 1. On March 1, it issues 1,000 shares to Y and

1,000 shares to Z. On July 1, the corporation wants to issue 2,000 shares to A to acquire A's real property, which is the ideal location for the business. A insists that she will not sell for cash, but wants a 50 percent stake in the company. Y and Z object to the new issuance (because it will dilute them from holding 50 percent each to 25 percent each). They assert pre-emptive rights. Result?

This hypothetical raises three points. First, the articles are silent about pre-emptive rights. In most states, then, there are no pre-emptive rights. As noted, in most states, pre-emptive rights exist only if the articles provide for them. Second, even if pre-emptive rights do exist (as they do in some states when the articles are silent), this issuance is not for money, so pre-emptive rights do not attach. Even courts that find ways around that statutory limitation will not do so here because the corporation needs this particular property and cannot get it except by issuing stock. Third, the issuance to A is an issuance of stock originally authorized in the articles and sold within six months of formation, so pre-emptive rights do not attach.

## § 12.5   FUNDING FROM VENTURE CAPITAL OR PUBLIC ISSUANCE

Most businesses, including the overwhelming majority of corporations, are small affairs, with at most a handful of owners. Issuance of securities (debt or equity) is a decision made by management as the need arises. Sometimes, corporations receive funding of "venture capital" (VC). This is a potential equity financing vehicle for a non-public company. Though VC funding was instrumental in high-tech companies for many years, it is not limited to them. VC is most often used to get businesses started when other sources of funds cannot be had. So if the bank will not make a loan and there is insufficient interest among the entrepreneur's circle of friends to get the business started, one might turn to VC.

A VC firm buys a large portion of the company's stock. The issuance is private (not on the public market) and the VC firm is gambling that the business will succeed. Many do not. As a rule of thumb, one-third of VC-backed companies fail, one-third succeed, and one-third end up in "limbo"— getting by, but not excelling. George W. Dent, *Venture Capital and the Future of Corporate Finance,* 70 WASH. U.L.Q. 1029 (1992). Because of the poor batting average, VC firms insist on high rates of return and demand a voice in management, which is usually guaranteed by their holding the majority of the voting stock.

The largest potential source of funding for business is the public. Companies "go public" to have access to the public for raising capital. Usually, such companies have a track record and profitability that warrants the sense that the public will buy the stock. So though the company has issued stock before, those were private placements. Now it plans its initial public offering (IPO).

We have seen the *legal* issues relating to registering securities for public trading (*see* § 11.2).

Here, we look at the *financial* issues involved: determining how much money the company needs to raise and how many shares to offer. This process is more difficult than it may sound, because the company will attempt to hit a "sweet spot" for pricing in the market. It also must be careful to raise enough money without overreaching. It is devastating for a corporation to announce an issuance and then fail to meet its capitalization goal.

The company must also select an underwriter. This is typically an investment bank, which manages the process of drafting the offering memorandum to be filed with the Securities and Exchange Committee. The underwriter advises on structuring the offering, pricing, and maintaining a market for the company's stock. The underwriter and the corporate heavy-hitters go "on the road" to speak with potential large institutional buyers of the stock, such as mutual funds and hedge funds.

The underwriter acts on either a "firm commitment" or on a "best efforts" basis. In a "firm commitment" underwriting, the underwriter itself buys all the stock in the public offering at the issuance price (minus a negotiated discount). The underwriter then resells to the stock to the public. Here, the underwriter bears the risk that the public will not buy the stock at the offering price. It reduces the risk by making sure that the price is not set until the last possible moment, when it has the best information on market interest. In a "best efforts" underwriting, the money to purchase the stock comes directly from the public, and not the underwriter.

Here, the corporation bears the risk that the stock will not fetch the offering price.

## § 12.6  ACCOUNTING AND FINANCIAL RECORDS

Every corporation is required to keep "appropriate accounting records," which are among those that are available for shareholder inspection (*see* § 6.9). MBCA § 16.01(b). Without accurate financial accounting, managers may fail to see problems until it is too late. There are three basic financial statements, and it is important to understand not only what they tell us about the business's fiscal health, but their limitations as well.

A.      *The Income Statement.* This tells whether the business was profitable over a given period—usually one year. It tells us if the business is "making money." The goal is to determine the profit before taxes (PBT) of our business, which is revenue minus costs. Revenue is the income generated by the business for the year. Costs are what the business paid out to generate that revenue.

Assume that Courtney's Widgets Corporation (CWC) buys widgets at wholesale and sells them at retail. Assume for a given year that CWC sold 10,000 widgets at $5 apiece. It had purchased those 10,000 widgets for $3 apiece. CWC's revenue for the year was $50,000 (10,000 widgets multiplied by $5). Its cost for those widgets was $30,000 (10,000 widgets multiplied by $3). CWC's PBT was $20,000, and its income statement would look like this:

| | |
|---|---|
| Revenue | $50,000 |
| minus Costs | $30,000 |
| PBT | $20,000 |

Of course, we cannot ignore taxes. Let's say the business was subject to income tax of 30 percent. Based upon its profit of $20,000 for this year, the tax would be $6,000. So to determine net income, we would take PBT ($20,000) minus taxes ($6,000), with the result being $14,000.

Assume the next year CWC purchases a widget-making machine for $25,000. The machine will last for five years. If we did the income statement as we did for the preceding year, we would subtract a cost of $25,000. This would be misleading, though, because even though CWC spent $25,000 on the machine, it will be using the machine for five years. So it is not accurate to "cost" the entire machine this year. Instead, CWC will use *depreciation*: it will record only one-fifth of the cost of the machine this year, and one-fifth next year, and so on for five years. This ensures that the income statement reflects that part of the machine "used up" each year.

This method is called "straight-line" depreciation, with equal amounts recorded each year for the five years. There is "accelerated" depreciation that would be more appropriate for equipment that is "used up" unevenly, with more of the cost recorded in earlier years than later. Straight-line depreciation is sufficient for our hypo.

Now let's assume CWC bought the machine for $25,000 and will depreciate it over five years. It manufactured and sold 40,000 widgets at $5 apiece, paid $35,000 for raw materials and $60,000 in salary. The income statement of this year would look like this:

| Revenue | $200,000 | (40,000 widgets at $5) |
|---|---|---|
| minus Costs | $35,000 | (raw materials) |
| minus Salary | $60,000 | |
| minus Depreciation | $5,000 | |
| PBT | $100,000 | |
| minus Taxes | $30,000 | (30 percent) |
| Net Income | $70,000 | |

The income statement is helpful, but has an important limitation: it does not necessarily tell us how much cash the business has on hand. This statement shows the company made $70,000 in the year. But the company does not have $70,000 in the bank. Why? Because it spent $25,000 on the widget-making machine, but only depreciated $5,000 of it. So it was out of pocket $20,000 more than appears in the income statement. To capture that reality, we need a second document.

B.        *The Cash Flow Statement.* This tells us how much more (or less) cash the business has at the end of the year than it did from the beginning of the year. The cash flow statement and the income statement will be identical except when we have an item, like the widget-making machine, for which we take depreciation. In such cases, the cash flow statement *adjusts the income statement*. We need to adjust it to reflect that we depreciated a portion of the expense of the machine, but were actually out-of-pocket substantially more than that amount.

Here is the formula for converting an income statement into a cash flow statement: start with the income statement's bottom line (net income), then *add* the amount recorded as depreciation, then *subtract* the amount paid for the machine.

In the business just discussed, we start with $70,000, which was the net income figure for the year. We then add to that the depreciation we took on the income statement. Because that was $5,000, we now have $75,000. Now, we subtract the amount actually paid for the machine—the out-of-pocket cost—which was $25,000. So the figure we end up with is $50,000. That means that though the corporation made a profit of $70,000 during the year, it only has $50,000 cash on hand at the end of the year.

Now assume that the company performs in exactly the same way the following year. Its revenue is $200,000, from which we deduct costs of $35,000 and salary of $60,000 and depreciation of $5,000. As last year, that gives us a PBT of $100,000. We pay the same tax as last year, $30,000. Thus, the net income of $70,000 is the same as it was last year.

So far, we see that the income statements for the two years are identical. But what about the cash flow statement for this more recent year? Start with the net income of $70,000. Then add the amount we took in depreciation, which was $5,000, so we are at $75,000. Now subtract the amount we were out-of-pocket for the widget-making machine this year. That number is *zero because we did not pay a nickel for that machine this year.* The entire cost was out-of-pocket last year. So our bottom line on the cash flow statement is $75,000.

In sum, then, the company was equally profitable in each year. But its cash flow posture was much better in the second year. Though it had $50,000 cash on hand after the first year, it has $75,000 cash on hand after the second year. The difference is due to its getting the benefit of the widget-making machine for which it paid last year.

C.        *The Balance Sheet.* The income and cash flow statements measure fiscal health over a period, usually a year. The balance sheet, in contrast, is a picture of how things stand at a particular moment. The income and cash flow statements are videos, showing progress. The balance sheet is a snapshot, and it records three things.

First are the corporate *assets.* In this part of the balance sheet, we total the value of all of the business's "stuff"—its cash, land, buildings, accounts receivable, equipment (minus any amount of depreciation on it that was reflected on the income statement). In other words, we list the value of everything the business owns. Accounts receivable consist of the money owed to the company by its customers. They are not depreciated, but may be "written off" (taken off the balance sheet as an asset) if one of the customers has filed for bankruptcy.

Second are the corporation's *liabilities*. This consists of everything the company owes, such as accounts payable, wages owed to employees, indebtedness from borrowing, etc.

Third is the *equity* in the business. This is what is left after we deduct liabilities from assets. It is equity because it is what the owners of the business (the shareholders) "own."

We put the assets on the left side of the balance sheet. Then put the liabilities on the right side. Under the liabilities, also on the right side, we put the equity. It is a "balance" sheet because the left side (assets) and the right side (liabilities plus equity) always balance. By definition, they must balance, because equity is the difference between the assets and the liabilities.

Suppose we start a business with $10,000 invested by shareholders. The business's assets consist of the $10,000 the shareholders paid for their stock. That figure appears on the left side of the balance sheet. What are the liabilities? Zero. We did not borrow the money, so we created no debt. Liabilities are recorded on the right side of the balance sheet as zero. What, then, is the equity? It is $10,000 (assets minus zero liabilities). So the balance sheet looks like this:

Assets                                    Liabilities

    Cash    $10,000                              $0

                                          Equity

                                               $10,000

Instead, let's say the business started with $10,000, which it *borrowed*. As before, the business's assets consist of $10,000 cash, entered on the left side of the balance sheet. On the right side, the $10,000 is a liability, because the company borrowed it and thus created a debt of $10,000. Borrowing money, then, increases the business's assets (because it gives the business money). But it creates a liability too. The balance sheet would look like this:

Assets                                    Liabilities

    Cash    $10,000                              $10,000

                                          Equity

                                               $0

In the first scenario, if the business were liquidated today, the shareholder(s) would get the $10,000 in equity. In the second, the shareholders would get nothing. The balance sheet tells us the relationship of assets to liabilities at a specific moment. Using it in combination with the income statement and cash flow statement will give a sophisticated observer a great deal of information about the value and viability of a business.

# CHAPTER 13

# DIVIDENDS AND OTHER DISTRIBUTIONS

## § 13.1  INTRODUCTION

A distribution is a payment made by the corporation to a shareholder *because* she is a shareholder. Suppose a shareholder also happens to be an employee of the corporation. The corporation's paying wages to her is not a distribution, because it is not being paid in her *capacity* as a shareholder. There are four generic types of distributions: dividends, repurchases of stock, redemptions of stock, and a liquidating distribution. In this Chapter, we deal with the first three. (The fourth, the liquidating distribution, is made to shareholders during dissolution, after creditors have been paid. We discuss it in § 16.8.)

A dividend is a payment of corporate wealth that could otherwise be used by the business (*see* §§ 13.2–13.4). A repurchase is exactly what it sounds like: the corporation pays a shareholder to repurchase her stock (*see* § 13.5). A redemption is closely related: the corporation buys stock back from shareholders, but here the corporation's right to do so (and the price at which the purchase takes place) is set in the articles (*see* § 13.5). Some states do not employ different terms for the different types of distributions. For instance, the MBCA does not use "dividend" at all, referring generically only to distributions. MBCA § 1.40(6). Importantly, each state imposes statutory limits on when a corporation can make a distribution (*see* § 13.7).

## § 13.2   DIVIDENDS—IN GENERAL

When a business is profitable, it must make a choice about what to do with the profits. It might spend that money to invigorate the business, perhaps to upgrade machinery or expand into different cities or product lines. It might invest the profits, for example, in securities. Or it might make pay a dividend to its shareholders. The decision of what to do with profits is made by the board of directors. A dividend is a distribution of earnings to the shareholders. It is paid pro-rata by share, so someone with 100 shares will get five times more in dividend payments than someone with 20 shares (assuming they hold stock in the same class).

Generally, dividends are paid by large public corporations. But not all big companies pay dividends. Google, for example, has never paid dividends, and for many years, neither did Microsoft. When you invest in such companies, then, you hope to make money by selling the stock for more than you paid for it. Many public companies, though—usually in more "traditional" businesses—have long histories of paying dividends. McDonald's, Consolidated Edison, Procter & Gamble are a few of hundreds that have consistently paid dividends, which make the stock more attractive to investors. Not only might an investor make money by appreciation of the stock price, but the company will pay you in the meantime. Some dividends beat returns on such mundane investments as money markets and certificates of deposit. In early 2016, for example, Consolidated Edison paid a dividend of 3.8 percent.

Those public corporations that pay dividends usually do so every quarter, though some pay every six months and a few pay every month. These are called "regular" dividends. A "special" dividend, in contrast, is a one-shot, non-recurring payment. A special dividend that accompanies the payment of a regular dividend is called an "extra."

Most close corporations do not pay dividends. But, again, this is a management decision, and the owners of a small business may have the company declare dividends if they wish (assuming the legal tests (*see* § 13.6) are met).

Dividends are usually paid in cash, but they can be paid in property (sometimes called "in kind" dividends). Regular dividends are almost always in cash, and special dividends are often in property. Property dividends must be paid in fungible property, such as shares of stock in a subsidiary or of some other company in which the corporation has an investment. Or the corporation may issue debt instruments (essentially IOUs) to the stockholders, making them creditors for that amount.

Dividends may also be paid, however, in additional shares of the corporation itself. This "share dividend" is not a true distribution because no assets leave the corporation. With cash and property dividends, the corporation is actually giving up something of value. With share dividends, it is not. Instead, the share dividend merely increases the number of ownership units outstanding without affecting the corporate assets and liabilities. If a shareholder receiving a share dividend sells the new shares, she may view the transaction essentially as a cash dividend, because she will end up owning the same number of shares as before and has, in addition, the cash received from the sale of the new shares. In fact, though, she now owns a slightly smaller percentage of the enterprise than she owned before the dividend (since the number of outstanding shares has increased by the number of new shares distributed). In most cases, this dilution will be so slight as to be unimportant.

Instead of a share dividend, the corporation might issue "rights" or "warrants." These are options to buy additional shares from the corporation at a set price (usually below the current market price). Like share dividends, these are also not true distributions. The shareholder who exercises the option must give capital to the corporation to maintain her percentage of ownership. If she does not do so, or if she sells the option (there is a public market for rights and options in public corporations), her interest in the business will be diluted.

Finally, a share dividend should be distinguished from a stock "split." With a split, the corporation issues more stock to the shareholders, but the price of each share is correspondingly lowered. Indeed, public companies often use stock splits to maneuver their stock price into its historical trading range. The economic effect of a stock split is nil.

- Corporation has 1,000,000 outstanding shares, trading at $90 per share. This gives it a market capitalization of $90 million (outstanding shares multiplied by price per share). Corporation approves a two-for-one split. Each shareholder will get an additional share for each share she now owns, but the market price of the stock is cut in half: from $90 per share to $45 per share. Before and after the split, then, the market capitalization is $90,000,000. And the value of each shareholder's stock remains the same. Instead of having one share worth $90, after the split a shareholder would have two shares, each of which is worth $45.

## § 13.3  SHAREHOLDERS' "RIGHT" TO A DIVIDEND

Shareholders have no right to a dividend until the management declares it. At that point, the dividend becomes a debt of the corporation and cannot be rescinded. The corporation owes the payment to the shareholders; they are creditors to that extent.

If management declares a dividend, it is payable to those who were shareholders on the "record date." We discussed record dates with regard to shareholder eligibility to vote in § 6.4, where we noted that the same concept governed who would be eligible to receive a dividend. If the board fails to fix a record date, the date on which it authorized the dividend will be treated as the record date. *See, e.g.*, MBCA § 6.40(b).

Especially in public corporations, there will be a gap between the record date and the "payable date," which is when payment is actually made. Usually this gap is two or three weeks.

- The board of Corporation declares a dividend on April 7, to be paid on April 24. Chuck owns stock in Corporation on April 7, and sells it on April 8 to Harry. On April 24, Corporation will pay Chuck, because he owned the stock on the record date. The fact that Harry owns it as of the payable date does not matter.

The board's determination of whether to pay dividends is reviewed under the business judgment rule (*see* § 9.4). Courts are reluctant to second-guess dividend decisions. Judges realize that they are not trained to know what the optimal dividend policy might be in a particular business. Accordingly, shareholders who sue to compel the declaration of a dividend are fighting an uphill battle.

On the other hand, the business judgment rule can be overcome in cases of self-dealing, bad faith, or other egregious circumstances. So it is possible for a minority shareholder to prevail, but only on a strong showing of abuse. For instance, if she can show that the corporation is thriving and the board continually refuses to declare dividends while paying its members large bonuses, she might convince a court to compel the declaration of a dividend. In such a case, the majority is oppressing the minority by diverting earnings to themselves at the expense of the minority.

There appears to be only one case in which a court forced the declaration of a dividend without a strong showing of abuse or bad faith. It involved the relatively early days of the stunningly successful Ford Motor Company. For years, Ford paid phenomenal regular and special dividends. Abruptly, Henry Ford had the company stop making the distributions. He wanted to use the profits to expand manufacturing capacity dramatically. Two shareholders, brothers named Dodge, sued to force Ford to resume payment of dividends. They were using the massive Ford dividends (for them, over $1,000,000 per year) to get their own automobile company rolling (OK—a bad pun). That competing company was Dodge Motors, which, after the brothers' deaths, became a division of Chrysler.

In *Dodge v. Ford Motor Co.*, 170 N.W. 668, 685 (Mich. 1919), the Michigan Supreme Court ordered Ford to pay dividends. The case is unique, however. In part, Henry Ford sealed his own fate when he testified at that his desire was not to make money but to do social good. Had he testified that the company would make more money if it invested profits in expanded capacity, it is unlikely that any court would have compelled the dividend. But Ford, obsessed with his legacy and with not being seen as a robber baron, testified that it was his social duty to make low-priced cars, and said little about business judgment. That, combined with the court's own view of desirable social policy, sealed the result.

## § 13.4   CLASSES OF STOCK (PREFERRED, CUMULATIVE, REDEEMABLE, ETC.)

A.     *Background.* All corporations issue stock. In most, there is only one class, called common stock. Unless the articles provide otherwise, each share carries one vote on those matters on which shareholders get to vote, and if there is a dividend, each share gets a pro-rata part of it.

But the articles can create different classes of stock with different voting rights. Thus, the articles may provide for a class of non-voting stock, or for a class with weighted voting rights (e.g., Class A gets two votes per share and Class B gets one). They can also create classes of stock that affect shareholders' right to any declared distribution. That is the focus of this section.

Note that even though the business can have different classes of stock, at least one class must have unlimited voting rights and at least one class must have the right to receive the net assets upon dissolution. In other words, the articles cannot deny voting rights to all shares, nor can they provide that when the company dissolves no shareholders will get what is left after creditors are paid off. Usually, the class that is entitled to vote and the class that is entitled to net assets upon dissolution are the same class (common stock), but this need not be so.

There are some important terms relating to dividends: preferred, participating, and cumulative. Stock that is not given one (or more) of these characteristics in the articles is common stock.

B.    *Preferred Stock.* "Preferred" means "pay first." It does not mean "pay more." So a class of stock with a dividend preference must be paid first, before the common stock. Depending upon the size of the dividend pool, the preferred shares may end up getting more than the common shares, or perhaps not. That is irrelevant. What matters is that the preferred shares are paid first. The preference can be stated in dollar terms.

- Corporation declares a dividend of $40,000. It has a class of preferred stock with a dividend preference of $2; there are 2,000 outstanding shares in this class. Corporation also has 10,000 common shares outstanding. The 2,000 preferred shares are entitled to their $2 preference first, before the holders of common stock receive anything. Multiply the 2,000 shares times the $2 preference. This is a total of $4,000, which is paid to the preferred shares. That leaves $36,000 (from the pool of $40,000). That $36,000 goes to the common shares. Because there are 10,000 of those, each common share gets $3.60.

In this hypo, then, the common shares get more money than the preferred. That is fine; remember, preferred does not mean pay more. But if that is the case, why do people want to hold preferred stock? Because they know that they are first in line. Suppose, for example, in this hypo, Corporation declared a dividend of $10,000. There, the preferred shares would get the first $4,000, as we just saw. That would leave $6,000 for the common stock.

Because there are 10,000 such shares, the common would only get 60 cents per share. Whether the preferred shares get more money than common will depend upon the size of the dividend pool. Holders of preferred stock have the comfort of knowing that they are first in line if the corporation pays a dividend.

Remember, there is no right to a dividend until the board declares it; so having preferred dividend stock does not entitle the shareholder to compel payment. It is not like holding debt, in which case the holder is a creditor and can demand payment in accordance with the debt agreement (*see* § 12.2). In practice, dividend-preferred stock usually does not carry voting rights, but the articles can provide whatever the corporation wants in this regard.

A preference on payment can be relevant not only with dividends, but when the corporation is dissolving. As we will see in § 16.8, dissolution involves the process of liquidation, by which corporate assets are gathered and converted to cash, after which creditors are paid. The amount remaining after creditors are paid will go to the shareholders, pro-rata by share. But here, too, we may have preferred stock, and it works same way as it does with dividends. Suppose during liquidation the corporation has $20,000 left after paying creditors. Suppose further that it has 2,000 shares of preferred stock with a $2 *liquidation* (or *dissolution*) preference (as opposed to a *dividend*) preference and 10,000 shares of common stock. As with the dividend hypo above, the first $4,000 goes to the preferred stock (2,000 shares multiplied by their $2 preference). The remaining $16,000 goes to the 10,000 common shares, so they get $1.60 per share.

The articles must state whether a class has a dividend or liquidation preference (or both). It would be a problem for the articles to say that there will be "10,000 authorized shares of $2 preferred stock" without indicating whether the preference was for dividends or for liquidation. The good news, of course, is that they work exactly the same way—they just come up at different times—one when there is a dividend and one when the corporation is being dissolved.

Preferred stock can also have other characteristics. Specifically, it can be participating or cumulative, as we discuss in the next two subsections.

C. *Preferred Participating Stock.* Roughly speaking, participating means "pay again." So preferred participating stock not only gets paid first, it also gets paid again, which means that it participates with the common shares after the preference has been paid.

- Corporation declares a dividend of $40,000. It has a class of preferred stock with a dividend preference of $2 *that is also participating*; there are 2,000 outstanding shares in this class. Corporation also has 10,000 common shares outstanding. The 2,000 preferred shares are entitled to their $2 preference first, before the common shares get anything. So we multiply the 2,000 shares times the $2 preference. This is a total of $4,000, which is

paid to the preferred shares. That leaves
$36,000 (from the pool of $40,000).

- Here, the $36,000 does not go to the common
  stock alone (as it did in the hypo we did
  before). Instead, because the 2,000 shares of
  preferred are *also* participating, they
  participate with the common stock in the
  $36,000. So that $36,000 is divided by 12,000
  shares, which this consists of the 10,000
  common *plus* the 2,000 preferred
  participating. Dividing $36,000 by 12,000
  shares equals $3 per share. So here, the
  common get $3 per share. The preferred
  participating get $5 per share. Why? Because
  they got $2 in their preferred capacity and $3
  more in their participating capacity.

Holders of common stock do not like it when
preferred shares also participate. They must share
"their" dividend with shareholders who have already
been paid. And holders of preferred stock would love
to have it be participating as well, because then they
not only get paid a set amount first, but get to share
in what is left. Again, all of this is set up in the
articles.

D.    *Preferred Cumulative Stock.* Cumulative
means that a preferred dividend accrues from year-
to-year. Most dividends are not cumulative, which
means that if a dividend is not declared for a
particular year, the shareholder never gets it. But
with preferred cumulative dividends, the "meter is
running" on their preference, so it adds up each year
until the board finally does order a dividend.

- Corporation declares a dividend of $40,000. It has a class of preferred stock with a dividend preference of $2 *that is also cumulative*; there are 2,000 outstanding shares in this class. Corporation also has 10,000 common shares outstanding. The corporation does not pay a dividend in 2016, 2017, and 2018. It finally declares a dividend in 2019. Those 2,000 shares of preferred cumulative stock are entitled to be paid first (before the common shares), and they are entitled to be paid for *four years of their $2 preference*. Their $2 preference was adding up for 2016, 2017, and 2018—plus the corporation owes them the preference for 2019, when it declared the dividend).

- Now let's do the math. The corporation owes the preferred cumulative shares $8 each (that is, four years multiplied by the $2 preference). There are 2,000 such shares. Multiply the 2,000 shares times the $8 per share, and we get a total of $16,000. So the first $16,000 of the declared dividend pool of $40,000 goes to the preferred cumulative stock. That leaves $24,000 (from the pool of $40,000). That $24,000 goes to the common stock. There are 10,000 common shares, so they get $2.40 per share.

If we wanted to do so (and provided for it in the articles), we could also give those preferred cumulative shares a right to participate. There, the $24,000 left after paying the cumulative preferred dividend would be divided by 12,000 shares: the 10,000 common plus the 2,000 preferred cumulative participating shares.

Again, there is no right to a dividend until it is declared. So unpaid cumulative preferred dividends are not a debt owed by the corporation. The board of directors may defer preferred cumulative dividends indefinitely if it is willing to forego dividends on the common shares as well. Usually, common stock is the only voting stock, so doing so may make the electorate angry. On the other hand, it is possible to provide in the articles that holders of preferred cumulative stock have the right to elect a certain number of directors if dividends are not paid for a specified period.

E. *Other Terminology—Series, Convertible, Redeemable.* A corporation may have *series* of preferred stock. A series is essentially a sub-class, so the corporation could have preferred stock "series A" and "series B," etc. The difference between a series and a class is usually is the manner of creation. Classes of preferred stock are created in the articles, while series may be in the articles or created by the board on its own (if the articles allow).

When the board creates a series, it carves out a sub-class of preferred shares from an authorized class of preferred stock. Such shares are also called "blank shares" because no terms are specified in the articles provision that creates the class. The board may vary the substantive terms of each series to take into account changing economic conditions. The power to create series of preferred shares is important as part of the "poison pill" defensive tactic against unwanted takeover attempts (*see* § 11.5, subpart D). When an outside aggressor acquires a given percentage of the corporation's stock, the corporation issues a new series of preferred stock to existing shareholders (but not to the aggressor). Doing so dilutes the percentage of stock held by the aggressor, and makes it more difficult for her to take over the corporation.

Preferred stock may be *convertible* into common shares at a specified price or specified ratio. Typically, the original conversion ratio is established when the class of preferred is created. The conversion price is usually set at a level that requires the common to appreciate substantially in value before it becomes profitable to convert the preferred.

Shares can be made *redeemable* at a specified price. The redemption is usually at the behest of the corporation and allows the corporation to force the holders of redeemable stock to sell their shares to the corporation at the price set in the articles. When the board exercises the redemption power, the shareholders' rights shift from holding an equity interest in the corporation to holding a contractual right to receive the redemption price. Preferred stock may also be made redeemable at the option of the *shareholder* at a specified price. This gives the shareholder the right to force the corporation to buy her stock at that price. Such stock has the general economic characteristics of a demand promissory note, so it is an example of an equity security that looks like a debt security (*see* § 12.2).

Historically, only preferred stock could be redeemable. The fear with redeemable common stock is that management could call for redemption to eliminate antagonistic shareholders. The MBCA does not prohibit redeemable common stock. Remember also that every corporation must always have at least one class of stock entitled to receive the net corporate assets upon dissolution. So no corporation can have all its stock subject to redemption.

## § 13.5  CORPORATE REPURCHASE OR REDEMPTION OF ITS OWN STOCK

We just saw that stock may be *redeemable*, which usually means that the corporation can demand that that class of stock be reacquired for a price set in the articles. Another way the corporation can repurchase its stock is simply to enter deals with individual stockholders. These repurchases are not set in the articles, and are individually negotiated. Redemptions and repurchases deal only with a corporation's buying back its *own* stock, and not its investment in stock of other companies.

When the corporation reacquires stock, it makes a distribution. That is, it pays a shareholder because of her status as a shareholder; it pays her to buy the stock she holds. The transaction decreases the worth of the corporation, because it makes a distribution to the shareholder and gets no asset in return. It receives what is now unsold stock. If the corporation reacquires a proportional part each shareholder's stock, the result is the equivalent of a dividend: each shareholder gets a pro-rata distribution.

Redemptions generally must be exercised proportionately within the class of stock involved. So if there are ten shareholders in the redeemable class, the corporation cannot redeem the stock of a few and not others. Its call for redemption must be equal to all in the class.

That is not true, however, with repurchases. These are individually negotiated, and usually are not proportional. The result is to increase the proportional ownership of those shareholders whose stock is not repurchased.

- U, V, W, X, and Y each own 20 percent of the stock of Corporation. If Corporation buys back all of U's stock, the remaining four shareholders will each own 25 percent of the stock. Why? Because the stock that U owned is no longer outstanding. All the outstanding stock is now owned equally by each of four shareholders. Thus, the unequal repurchase from one shareholder increases the ownership stake of the others.

Close corporations must be careful not to engage in unfair behavior in repurchasing stock. Under the "equal opportunity" or "equal access" rule, a corporation offering to buy back one shareholder's stock generally must make the same proportional offer to others. The leading case on this point is *Donahue v. Rodd Electrotype Company of New England, Inc.*, 328 N.E.2d 505, 508–19 (Mass. 1975) (*see* § 10.6, subpart B). Not all states follow this rule.

Publicly held corporations may repurchase their own shares to retire them. Here, management concludes that the market has for some reason underpriced the company's stock. Retiring the shares at a bargain price will increase the earnings per share of the remaining shares. Doing so also often results in raising the price of the stock because the market sees the buy-back as a statement of confidence by management. On the other hand, a public corporation may buy its own stock for other reasons, such as to evade a hostile takeover (*see* § 11.5).

## § 13.6  STATUTORY RESTRICTIONS ON DISTRIBUTIONS AND LIABILITY FOR IMPROPER DISTRIBUTIONS

A.    *Background.* All states limit a corporation's power to declare distributions. In some states, the rules vary a bit depending on the type of distribution, so the rules for dividends are slightly different from those for redemptions and repurchases. In general, however, the limitations are the same for all forms of distribution, be it dividend, redemption, or repurchase.

The limitations are intended to protect creditors. In theory, they ensure that the corporation cannot dole out money to its shareholders to the detriment of creditors. The starting point is the same in every state: a distribution cannot be made if the corporation is insolvent or the distribution would render it insolvent. "Insolvent" here generally means the "equity" test: that the company is unable to pay its debts as they come due. In some states, there is an alternative ("bankruptcy") test for insolvency (subpart C below).

Beyond this, there is a significant split of authority. Some states apply the traditional "fund" restrictions on when a corporation can declare a distribution. Though the number of states in this camp is waning, most courses cover it because some important states, including Texas, New York, and Delaware, still use it. The modern approach, spearheaded by the MBCA, does not address funds, but imposes only insolvency limitations

B.    *Traditional ("Fund") Limitations on Distributions.* Fewer and fewer states continue to apply the fund restrictions. Even among them, unfortunately, there is some variation. What we discuss here is the typical model. (You should be careful, however, to adhere closely to the model your professor assigns.) In this approach, there are three funds: earned surplus, stated capital, and capital surplus. To start with a conclusion, distributions can be paid from earned surplus and capital surplus, but not from stated capital.

These funds require us to focus on two ways in which a business can make money. One, it can do well in the business world, by selling a lot of widgets (or doing whatever the company does). This is the creation of earned surplus (it is "earned" from conducting business). Two, it can raise capital by issuing stock. Stated capital and capital surplus are related to the second of these.

*Earned surplus* consists of all earnings minus all losses minus distributions previously made (essentially the amount of cash the corporation earns from doing business). If a corporation has earned surplus, it is doing well in the real world. Distributions can be paid from earned surplus.

*Stated capital and capital surplus* are generated by issuance of stock. Issuance is when the corporation sells its own stock, and it must receive consideration from that sale (*see* § 12.3). Every penny of that consideration is allocated between stated capital and capital surplus. The allocation is important because capital surplus may be used for a distribution, but stated capital cannot. How is the allocation made?

If the distribution is of par stock, the par value of the issuance goes into stated capital and the excess over par value goes into capital surplus. If it is a no-par issuance, the board allocates the consideration between stated capital and capital surplus. Usually, the board must act within a given period (typically 60 days) after the issuance and may allocate any part, but not all, to capital surplus. If the board does not act within that period, the entire consideration from the no-par issuance is allocated to stated capital.

- Corporation issues 10,000 shares of $2 par stock for $50,000. Of this, $20,000 is allocated to stated capital. Why? Because it is the par value of the issuance (10,000 shares multiplied by $2 par). The excess over par value (here, $30,000) goes into capital surplus.

- Corporation issues 4,000 shares of no-par stock for $40,000. If the board does nothing, the entire $40,000 will be allocated to stated capital. If it desires, however, the board can allocate any part but not all of the $40,000 as it sees fit between stated capital and capital surplus.

Stated capital cannot be used for a distribution because it is a cushion to protect creditors. But it might not be much of a cushion. The corporation might set par value of par stock at a fraction of a penny (In Delaware, par values can be as low as $0.0001). Or it may simply issue no-par stock and allocate the vast majority of the issuance to capital surplus.

Under the fund approach, distributions are proper from "surplus"—either earned surplus or capital surplus. Again, remember the difference. Earned surplus is generated by business success, while capital surplus is generated by issuing stock. A distribution may always be paid from earned surplus. But some states impose restrictions on use of capital surplus. Commonly, the shareholders must be informed if their distribution is being paid from capital surplus. In some states, the articles must provide that distributions may be paid from capital surplus. One typical use of capital surplus is to pay holders of cumulative preferred stock to discharge the cumulative rights. This permits the company to avoid building up preferred arrearages during the early years of operation when there may be no earned surplus.

In some states, there is no distinction between "earned" and "capital" surplus. Instead, there is just "surplus" and "stated capital." Surplus consists of net assets minus stated capital. Distributions may be paid from surplus but not from stated capital.

Some states permit distributions from current profits even if there is an earnings deficit from operations for prior periods. In other words, even though there is no earned surplus, the company is making some money currently. Payment of a dividend from this current profit is called a "nimble dividend." The leading case is *Goodnow v. American Writing Paper Co.*, 69 A. 1014, 1016 (N.J.1908), which permitted the corporation to use current earnings to pay a dividend rather than pay down debts. Some states do not permit nimble dividends.

C.     *The Modern Approach.* The MBCA has changed the law on distributions dramatically. Most states now adopt the MBCA approach, in which the various funds we just considered are irrelevant. Under the MBCA, the fund limitations are replaced by insolvency limitations. Thus, a distribution is improper only if the corporation is insolvent or if the distribution will render it insolvent. MBCA § 6.40(c)(1) & (2).

Importantly, though, the MBCA prescribes two tests for insolvency. They are alternatives, so the distribution is improper if either is met at the time of the distribution. First is the equity test for insolvency, which we noted above: the corporation is insolvent if it is unable to pay its debts as they become due in the ordinary course of business.

Second is the "bankruptcy" or "balance sheet" test for insolvency: the distribution is unlawful if the corporation's assets do not exceed its liabilities plus the amount that would be needed to pay liquidation preferences if the company dissolved today. A preference means that this class of stock is to be paid first, before other shares (*see* § 13.4, subpart B). A liquidation preference is paid when the corporation dissolves, after it has paid its creditors.

- Corporation has assets of $250,000 and liabilities of $200,000. Corporation has a class of stock of 1,000 shares with a $5 liquidation preference. If Corporation dissolved today, it would need $5,000 to pay the liquidation preferences (1,000 shares multiplied by $5 preference). The balance sheet test for insolvency equates liquidation preferences with liabilities. So Corporation has $250,000 in assets. It has liabilities of $200,000 and the liquidation preference would be $5,000. Assets ($250,000) minus liabilities plus liquidation preferences ($205,000) equals $45,000. So under this test, Corporation can make a distribution of up to $45,000.

D.    *Liability   for   Improper   Distributions.* Directors who assent to the declaration of a distribution are liable to the extent the distribution is improper. For instance, in the hypothetical immediately above, Corporation may properly declare a distribution of $45,000. Suppose the board of directors approved a distribution of $60,000. The distribution would be unlawful to the extent of

$15,000. Directors would be jointly and severally liable for that $15,000. The money recovered from directors would be returned to the corporation. If a plaintiff sued one of several directors, and recovered on behalf of the corporation, that director could seek contribution from other directors who also assented to the distribution.

Directors are presumed to have concurred with board action unless they dissent in writing (*see* § 7.5). So any director who dissented in writing would not be liable. In addition, directors may rely in good faith on information provided by officers and professionals. Thus, a director who relied in good faith and reasonably on what the corporate financial people told the board about funding available for a distribution may be protected from liability (*see* § 9.10).

Historically, directors have been strictly liable for improper distributions. That is still the rule in many states. There is a trend, however, led by the MBCA, toward holding directors liable only upon proof that they breached a duty to the corporation by making the distribution. MBCA § 8.33(a) provides that directors who approved what turns out to be an unlawful distribution are liable only if the plaintiff "establishes that when taking the action, the director did not comply with section 8.30," which, as we saw in Chapter 9, imposes the duties of good faith, care and loyalty.

Shareholders generally are liable for unlawful distributions only to the extent that they knew *when they received it* that it was improper. To that extent, the shareholder must return the distribution to the corporation. If a shareholder finds after the fact that the distribution was unlawful, she does not have to return it.

E. *Contractual Provisions Concerning Distributions.* What we considered in subsection C above are statutory limitations on distributions. Many restrictions, however, will be contractual. Creditors of a corporation may be nervous about dissipation of corporate assets through distributions. It is common, therefore, for corporations entering deals or borrowing money to agree to restrict distributions. Such restrictions vary widely. If the corporation is publicly held with an established history of regular dividend payments, the agreement may permit dividends of specified amounts provided that certain ratios are maintained between assets and liabilities, or between current assets and current liabilities. Close corporations may agree to forego all distributions (or even to impose restrictions on salaries) as a condition of entering a contract or getting a loan.

The corporation's articles may address distributions. For example, they may protect preferred shares by limiting the amount that can be paid to common shares, or by requiring that a portion of earnings to be set aside as a "sinking fund" to be used to retire a portion of the preferred dividend each year. (A sinking fund is one set up with regular deposits for the purpose of paying off a debt or, in this case, to keep relatively current on preferred dividends.) Otherwise, holders of preferred stock have scant protection, because, as we saw above, claims to dividends, even preferred cumulative dividends, are not corporate debts. They are merely a priority position in future distributions that may never be declared.

# CHAPTER 14

# POTENTIAL LIABILITY IN SECURITIES TRANSACTIONS

## § 14.1  INTRODUCTION

In Chapter 11, we addressed aspects of federal securities law in the public corporation: registration and reporting requirements (*see* § 11.2), Sarbanes-Oxley (*see* § 11.3), proxy solicitation (*see* § 11.4) and hostile takeover rules (*see* § 11.5). We noted that the underlying policy of federal securities law is disclosure. The idea is that truthful information protects the investing public. In this chapter we focus on state and federal law aimed at fraudulent behavior in the trading of securities—not only the initial issuance by the corporation, but in the secondary market for re-selling as well.

Common law fraud allows one to sue if another has made a material misrepresentation (a lie), on which the victim reasonably relies to her detriment. This applies in securities transactions as much as in the sale of cars. But common law fraud does not apply to someone who trades without disclosing information she possesses that the other party does not possess. We will call this "inside information." When someone trades on the basis of inside information, she is not telling a lie. Indeed, she says nothing, so she cannot be liable for common law fraud.

The law developed, however, to impose liability on insider trading. State common law made the first steps here, and federal law has gone farther. They have done so by imposing upon the "insider" (and we will define that) a duty either to disclose what she knows or to forego the trade.

The first cousin to insider trading is "tipping." Here, the insider does not use the information to trade on her own account. Instead, she "tips" a friend or acquaintance, who then trades on the tip. State and federal law may impose liability on the "tipper" and the "tippee."

We start with state law (*see* § 14.2). Then we address two important federal provisions: Rule 10b–5, promulgated by the SEC under § 10(b) of the 1934 Act as a general anti-fraud measure, and § 16(b) of the same Act. Section 16(b) is expressly aimed at insider trading. Rule 10b–5 was not (at least not as a general matter), but has been interpreted to proscribe insider trading and tipping far more broadly than § 16(b). Rule 10b–5 has generated a tremendous amount of case law. Fears about baseless claims led Congress, through legislation like the Private Securities Litigation Reform Act (PSLRA), to impose procedural hurdles in such cases to weed out baseless cases. The Securities Litigation Uniform Standards Act (SLUSA) imposes restrictions on securities fraud class actions.

## § 14.2  STATE LAW

A.    *From Fraud to a Fiduciary Duty to Disclose Nonpublic Information.* The state law of securities fraud is largely common law. The starting point is the basic claim for fraud. As noted above, this is a claim for someone victimized by a misrepresentation on which she reasonably relied to her detriment. It is a difficult claim to win. The plaintiff must show that the defendant *knowingly* misrepresented a *material* fact, with the *intent* to induce reliance, that she (the plaintiff) *reasonably* *relied* upon the misrepresentation, and suffered damage as a consequence.

- X owns stock in a close corporation. The stock is worth $1,000. X tells a friend: "I own stock in this corporation. This company is about to take off because of a new product. I need some cash right away, so I need to sell the stock, and because you are my pal, I'll let you have it for $10,000." The friend buys the stock, which turns out to be worth only $1,000. The friend can sue X for fraud, and seek recovery of $9,000.

Fraud works well when, as here, the defendant lies. But what if she does not make a misstatement?

- Dot is a director. Because of her position, she learns that the company has developed a new product that will revolutionize the market. The financial officers at the company estimate that the company's value will double within weeks of the introduction of the new product. Dot is playing golf with Louise Shareholder, who owns $10,000 worth of stock in the company. Louise says "I don't think the company's doing anything great; I'd like to sell my stock." Dot says "OK. I'll buy it for $10,000." Louise sells to Dot. A month later, the new product hits the market and the value of everybody's stock doubles.

Louise cannot sue Dot for fraud, because Dot did not tell a lie. Instead, Dot used her superior knowledge (nonpublic information gained by being a director) to buy Louise's stock. The starting point is the traditional common law view—that the insider owes no duty to the shareholder. This view reflects a conclusion that fiduciaries owe duties when they manage, but not when they are engaged in personal financial transactions. Under this view, Louise cannot sue Dot.

Courts have moved to amend this traditional rule. Some courts take a very strict view, and conclude that an insider (like a director or officer, and probably a managing shareholder of a close corporation) holds nonpublic information "in trust" for the benefit of shareholders. These courts impose a duty on the insider to disclose the nonpublic information to the shareholder before dealing with her. If she cannot divulge the information, she must abstain from trading.

This view is usually called the "Kansas rule," after cases like *Hotchkiss v. Fischer*, 16 P.2d 531, 536 (Kan. 1932), which held that a director has a duty to shareholders "to communicate . . . all material facts in connection with the transaction which the [director] knows or should know." Kansas has not retreated from the rule. *Sampson v. Hunt*, 564 P.2d 489, 492 (Kan. 1977). There is some old case law in other states supporting this strict view. *See, e.g., Taylor v. Wright*, 159 P.2d 980, 985 (Cal.App. 1945);

*Oliver v. Oliver*, 45 S.E. 232, 234 (Ga. 1903). This view tells fiduciaries that they owe duties not only to the corporation while managing, but even to shareholders when trading in their personal account.

Other courts take a position between the Kansas rule and the traditional common law approach. They impose upon insiders a duty to disclose "special facts" (sometime called "special circumstances"). The leading case is *Strong v. Repide*, 213 U.S. 419, 431 (1909). There, the director of a sugar company in the Philippines knew that the company planned to sell its land to the United States at great profit (in fact, he helped negotiate the deal), then dissolve and distribute cash to the shareholders. The plaintiff was a shareholder, who was ignorant of this inside information. The plaintiff sold his stock to the director. In this deal, the director did not disclose the inside information. The Court held that the defendant breached a duty to disclose "special facts" in dealing with shareholders. The Court was less than clear about what constituted a special fact. It is an elastic concept, but certainly includes information, like that known by the defendant in *Strong*, that would have a dramatic effect on the value of the stock. The fact that the defendant was an insider, which he failed to disclose to the seller, was also a special fact.

One can find cases embracing all three of these approaches: the common law view (*see, e.g.*, *Fleetwood Corp. v. Mirich*, 404 N.E.2d 38, 46 (Ind.App. 1980) (no duty to disclose)), the Kansas rule, and the special facts doctrine (cases cited in the preceding two paragraphs). The majority view is probably the special facts approach. The notion of a special fact on which an insider should not trade mirrors a requirement under Federal Rule 10b–5 that a misstatement *or omission* concern a "material" fact. That term is interpreted meaning something a reasonable investor would consider important in making an investment decision (*see* § 14.3). This is also as good a definition of a "special fact" as any.

Importantly, the Kansas and "special facts" approaches hold that the insider owes a duty *to a shareholder*. If the person with whom the insider trades is not a shareholder, there is apparently no duty to disclose the nonpublic information.

- Dot is a director. Because of her position, she learns devastating corporate news. When the news goes public, the value of the company's stock will plummet. Dot is playing golf with Louise, who is *not* a shareholder. Louise says: "Dot, that company of yours seems interesting. I'd like to buy some stock." Dot says: "OK—I'll sell you some of mine." Louise buys the stock. The next day, the news goes public and the stock becomes worthless.

Again, Louise cannot sue for fraud, because Dot did not tell a lie. On the other hand, Dot plainly traded on the basis of nonpublic information and took advantage of Louise. But arguably neither the Kansas nor special facts rule applies. Why? Because Louise was not a shareholder at the time of the transaction, so Dot owed no duty to her. We are unlikely to get a definitive resolution on this score, because state law is not used much. Instead, cases such as this (and the earlier hypo when Louise was a shareholder) can be pursued under Federal Rule 10b–5.

B.  *Insider Trading in the Market.*  The examples addressed in the preceding subpart involved face-to-face transactions. What happens if the insider trades on a market? In *Goodwin v. Agassiz*, 186 N.E. 659, 661–63 (Mass. 1933), the plaintiff sold stock in a mining company on a stock exchange. These are faceless transactions, so usually one has no idea who is on the other side of the trade. By going back through the records, however, the plaintiff was able to find that the person who bought his stock was an insider of the mining company. As an insider, the defendant had learned of a geology report indicating that an area in Michigan was likely rich in ore; the company was trying to buy up land there and then to mine the ore. The plaintiff sued under the "special facts" doctrine.

The defendant won for two reasons. First, the geology report was so speculative that it did not constitute a special "fact." It was, instead, merely an "opinion." Second, and more importantly, the court refused to permit suit for trades on a public exchange. Doing so would impose an untenable burden: an insider, before trading, would have to seek out the person on the other side of the deal and inform her of the inside information. Thus, the common law claims under the Kansas and special facts rules appear not to apply when the insider trades on a public exchange. So the person on the other side of her trade cannot sue.

In New York, the *corporation* may sue insiders who trade in its stock on a public market. In *Diamond v. Oreamuno*, 248 N.E.2d 910, 911 (N.Y. 1969), a director and an officer had inside information of impending bad news for the corporation. They unloaded their stock on the public market before the bad news was made public. They sold at $28 per share. After the bad corporate news became public, the stock price fell to $11. The New York Court of Appeals held that the two insiders had breached a duty owed *to the corporation* and were liable for the $17 per share that they "saved" by selling before the news became public. The court concluded that even though the defendants' acts did not harm the corporation financially, they harmed the company's reputation, which made the conduct actionable. It is not clear that *Diamond* has gathered much of a following.

## § 14.3   RULE 10b–5:
## BACKGROUND AND ELEMENTS

A.        *The Provision and Who Can Enforce It.*
Federal Rule 10b–5, promulgated by the SEC in 1948 under § 10(b) of the Securities Exchange Act of 1934, is an antifraud provision. It has been interpreted and applied in thousands of cases. Its language is deceptively simple, and is worth studying:

> *It shall be unlawful for any person, directly or indirectly, by the use of any means or instrumentality of interstate commerce, or of the*

*mails or of any facility of any national securities exchange,*

*(1)   to employ any device, scheme, or artifice to defraud;*

*(2)   to make any untrue statement of a material fact or to omit to state a material fact necessary in order to make the statements made, in light of the circumstances under which they were made, not misleading, or*

*(3)   to engage in any act, practice, or course of business which operates or would operate as a fraud or deceit upon any person,*

*in connection with the purchase or sale of any security.*

The SEC can enforce this provision by seeking civil penalties and injunctions. It can refer cases to the Department of Justice for criminal prosecution. The Rule says nothing, however, about whether a private citizen may sue for damages. Over time, the federal courts have inferred the existence of such a claim. *Basic, Inc. v. Levinson,* 485 U.S. 224, 230–31 (1988). There is, however, an important limitation on standing to bring a civil suit for damages: one may sue under 10b–5 only if she bought or sold securities because of some bad act by the defendant. In other words, if someone neither bought nor sold, she cannot sue. This rule was set forth in *Birnbaum v. Newport Steel Corp.,* 193 F.2d 461, 463–64 (2d Cir. 1952). The Supreme Court embraced it in *Blue Chip Stamps v. Manor Drug Stores,* 421 U.S. 723, 731 (1975).

- Courtney owns 100 shares of XYZ Corp. She is thinking about selling it, because the company has not been doing very well. The company issues a press release full of lies, saying that it has new business prospects and that the stock price will go up. In reliance on that press release, Courtney does not sell. After the lies are exposed, the value of the stock plummets. Courtney has been hurt by the bad act of XYZ Corp., but she cannot bring a private action for damages under 10b–5. She did not buy or sell securities in reliance on the misrepresentation, so she cannot sue.

Claims under Rule 10b–5 invoke exclusive federal jurisdiction. They may not be brought in state court. They are brought by the victim of fraudulent behavior in a securities transaction, who usually seeks damages for the harm caused. Punitive damages are not recoverable under Rule 10b–5. Because the claim belongs to the victim of the fraudulent activity, it is not a derivative suit. Claims under Rule 10b–5 are often brought as class actions, in which a representative plaintiff sues on behalf of a group of similarly situated investors. As we will see throughout this section, Congress has acted to curb what it considered abusive class action litigation.

B.    *Who Can Be Sued?* The Rule forbids "any person" from doing any of the things proscribed. This phrase includes individuals and entities. And though the *plaintiff* in a civil Rule 10b–5 case must have bought or sold securities, the same is not true of the defendant. A defendant might have traded—for example, someone who lies to another to get that person to buy her stock. But this is not required. A corporation that issues a misleading press release can violate Rule 10b–5, even though it did not buy or sell. So can a "tipper," who tells someone about inside information, allowing that person to trade and profit on the basis of the inside information.

Because it applies to "any person," 10b–5 is implicated in securities transactions of *any* business, including partnerships, close corporations, public corporations, and sole proprietorship. (This is different from § 16(b), which, as we will see in § 14.5, applies only in public corporations.)

C.    *Elements in a Rule 10b–5 Case.* What must the plaintiff (or the government, when it sues or prosecutes) establish in a Rule 10b–5 case? The key element will be that the defendant committed one of the types of fraudulent behavior prohibited by 10b–5. We will discuss these in detail in § 14.4. For now, let's just say that such behavior may involve a misrepresentation or an omission. The defendant may lie (make a misrepresentation) or, with insider trading, may fail to disclose something that the law requires her to disclose (an omission). Beyond that, here are the elements.

1.    *Instrumentality of Interstate Commerce.* Rule 10b–5 is triggered by the use of facilities of interstate commerce, including the mail or facilities of a national exchange. This is easy to meet. The transaction need not cross state lines; even *intrastate* phone calls meet the interstate nexus. Moreover, the fraudulent behavior itself need not engage an

instrumentality of interstate commerce. All that is required is that such an instrumentality be used at some point in the deal.

- A, a director of XYZ Corp., lies to B in a face-to-face meeting, in an effort to get B to buy stock in XYZ. B then goes online and buys XYZ stock. The interstate nexus is met by use of the Internet, even though that use occurred after commission of the fraudulent act.

- Suppose instead that A lied to B in a face-to-face meeting in an effort to get B to buy A's stock. Suppose B then writes a check to A to pay for the stock and A endorses the stock certificate to B. The interstate nexus is satisfied by the check because it must clear through banking channels.

About the only kind of transaction that would not satisfy the interstate nexus is a face-to-face meeting in which the buyer pays cash and the seller endorses the stock certificate. This probably does not happen very often (at least not in the real world; exam questions might be another thing).

2.      *Materiality.* The fraudulent behavior must concern a "material" fact. A fact is material if "there is a substantial likelihood that a reasonable [investor] would consider it important in deciding [whether to buy or sell securities]." *TSC Industries, Inc. v. Northway, Inc.*, 426 U.S. 438, 449 (1976) (this case was about proxy solicitation, but "material" is defined the same in all Rule 10b–5 cases). Materiality will usually be clear: the defendant will say (or fail to

disclose) something that a reasonable investor would consider important to the value of the stock.

Materiality may be problematic, however, when there are statements about something that *may* (not necessarily *will*) happen. In *Basic, Inc. v. Levinson*, 485 U.S. 224, 227–28 (1988), an aggressor corporation started buying up stock in a target, in hopes of merging. The target company issued misleading press releases denying that it was being pursued. (It did so to tamp down rumors of the possible acquisition; when such news gets out, the public would buy the target's stock and thereby drive the price up. This may stymie the deal.) When the acquisition was announced, those who had sold stock in the target when the press releases came out sued under 10b–5. They sought damages for the lost value, and alleged that if the target had told the truth, they would not have sold their stock, and would have gotten more money for their stock through the acquisition.

Were the misstatements in the press releases "material?" The Court adopted the reasoning of an influential lower court opinion that had addressed similar facts, *SEC v. Texas Gulf Sulphur Co.*, 401 F.2d 833, 849–50 (2d Cir. 1968). It employed a sliding scale approach that considers (1) the *probability* that the event will occur (e.g., the merger will go through) and (2) the *magnitude* of the possible event. Because a merger is of enormous magnitude (because it ends the life of the corporation), statements about it will become material at a lower level of probability. The

Court remanded the case to allow the district court to apply the standard.

In 1995, Congress passed the Private Securities Litigation Reform Act (PSLRA). It was concerned with securities class actions asserting marginal claims, which are aimed at extorting settlements from defendants. The PSLRA makes it more difficult for the plaintiff in Rule 10b–5 (and other securities) cases, whether brought as class actions or individually.

The PSLRA sets out a "safe harbor" for "forward-looking" oral or written statements that are "accompanied by meaningful cautionary statements identifying important factors that could cause actual results to differ materially from those in the forward-looking statements." The effect of such cautionary language is to render the statement non-material for purposes of 10b–5. The "forward-looking" statement must be about the future—for example, a projection of revenues or of plans for future operations. It must not be and not a statement of the current state of affairs.

In addition, the cautionary language (saying, essentially, that the forward-looking statement might be wrong) must be closely related to the forward-looking statement. It must be specific to the riskiness involved, and not simply some blanket warning like "hey, we don't have a clue if any of this will really happen." The safe harbor under the PSLRA applies only to public corporations, and has been the basis of motions to dismiss many Rule 10b–5 cases.

Some courts had imposed a similar common law requirement called the "bespeaks caution" doctrine, which will apply to all businesses. If there were specific warnings concerning statements of future performance, it would essentially tell the investor to go cautiously. *See, e.g., EP Medsystems, Inc. v. EchoCath, Inc.*, 235 F.3d 865, 874–80 (3d Cir. 2000). Such case law and the PSLRA have led to longer corporation documents, larded with cautionary language.

3.     *Reliance.* The plaintiff asserting common law fraud must demonstrate that she relied on the misstatement made by the defendant. Such reliance must be reasonable under the circumstances. Reasonable reliance is also an element in Rule 10b–5 cases. In claims of misrepresentation, indirect reliance is sufficient. For example, if you buy securities because your investment adviser recommends them, and she, in turn, recommends them because she has read some misrepresentation in corporate documents, you may claim reliance.

Indeed, courts go much further in cases of mass misrepresentation. In *Basic, Inc. v. Levinson,* 485 U.S. at 227–28, discussed immediately above regarding materiality, the Court adopted a "fraud on the market" theory, which applies only in cases involving public corporations. The theory establishes a presumption of reliance. That case was a class action on behalf of people who sold their stock after the company issued misleading press releases. Defendants argued that each member of the class should be required to show that she had read the press release and relied upon it when she sold her stock.

The Court rejected the defendant's argument and emphasized that all investors rely on the integrity of prices set by the securities exchanges. Because misleading statements affect prices in the public markets, they constitute a "fraud on the market." In such cases, the court will presume that each member of the class relied on the misrepresentation in making her decision to trade in securities. The defendant can rebut the presumption, but doing so seems difficult. For example, the court in *Basic* said the defendant could escape liability by showing that news of the merger discussion entered the market and "dissipated the effects of the misstatements."

The fraud-on-the-market theory is based upon economic research that suggests that efficient markets (including public markets on which securities are traded) set securities prices based upon the mix of publicly available information. Because this information includes a misleading public statement such as that alleged in *Basic*, the person who buys or sells on the public market is "relying" upon all the information that forms the basis for the price at which she buys or sells.

Some scholars criticized this economic theory, and in 2014 the Supreme Court entertained an argument that it should be rejected. In *Halliburton Co. v. Erica P. John Fund, Inc.,* 134 S.Ct. 2398, 2413–14 (2014), however, the Court refused to overrule the fraud-on-the-market theory. Thus the presumption of reliance established in *Basic* survives. The Court also reaffirmed, however, that the defendant may rebut the presumption. Indeed, *Halliburton* permits the defendant to attack reliance early in the litigation, when the court is considering whether to certify the case to proceed as a class action.

The Court has also created a presumption of reliance in cases of omission, in which the defendant fails to disclose something the law requires her to disclose. In such a case "proof of reliance is not a prerequisite to recover. All that is necessary is that the facts withheld be material. . . ." *Affiliated Ute Citizens of Utah v. United States*, 406 U.S. 128, 153 (1972).

4.          *Scienter.* Section 10(b) of the '34 Act, on which Rule 10b–5 is based, makes unlawful "manipulative or deceptive device or contrivance." Such language "connotes intentional conduct designed to deceive or defraud investors," and thus cannot cover mere negligence. *Ernst & Ernst v. Hochfelder*, 425 U.S. 185, 193, 199 (1976). Because an SEC Rule cannot exceed the scope of the statute on which it is based, Rule 10b–5 cases thus cannot be based upon negligence. Plaintiff must show scienter, which the Court described as an intent to "deceive, manipulate, or defraud."

In *Hochfelder,* the Court refused to decide whether recklessness could support a Rule 10b–5 claim. The majority view in the lower federal courts seems to accept that recklessness may suffice, though some courts appear to make it something like "recklessness plus." In one case, the court spoke of "an extreme departure from the standards of ordinary care, . . .

which presents a danger of misleading buyers and sellers that is either known to the defendant or is so obvious that the actor must have been aware of it." *Sundstrand Corp. v. Sun Chemical Corp.*, 553 F.2d 1033, 1045 (7th Cir. 1977).

Whatever standard of proof at trial, the PSLRA made it more difficult for plaintiffs even to get past the pleading stage by stating a claim. It imposes a requirement that the plaintiff must plead "with particularity facts giving rise to a strong inference that the defendant acted with the required state of mind." The requirement of particularity means details, not conclusions. In *Tellabs, Inc. v. Makor Issues & Rights, Ltd.*, 551 U.S. 308, 310 (2007), the Court held that a "strong" inference of scienter is more than merely plausible or reasonable. It must be cogent and at least as compelling as any inference of non-fraudulent intent.

5.      *Causation.* A plaintiff in a Rule 10b–5 case may be required to prove two types of causation. First is "but-for" causation, which developed in common law fraud cases. Here, the plaintiff must show that she did what she did (buy or sell securities) *because* the defendant engaged in fraudulent behavior.

The PSLRA (applicable only regarding public companies) adds another requirement: plaintiff must show "loss causation." This means that the defendant's fraudulent behavior caused the loss about which plaintiff complains. Suppose, for instance, that Corporation lies in its prospectus or annual report. Plaintiff reads the document and is induced by the lie to buy stock in Corporation. Later,

Corporation suffers huge losses for some totally unrelated reason, perhaps a downturn in the macroeconomic market or maybe because an executive stole all the assets. Plaintiff cannot show loss causation here. True, her investment has decreased in value, but that decrease had nothing to do with Corporation's lie.

6.    *"In Connection with the Purchase or Sale of Any Security."* Defendant's fraudulent behavior must be in connection with a buy or sell of securities. This requirement is reflected in the *Birnbaum* rule, seen in subpart A above, that a civil Rule 10b–5 plaintiff must have bought or have sold securities. In many cases of misrepresentation or omission, this will be clear. The defendant will have said something (or failed to disclose something she was required to disclose) that led directly to the plaintiff's buying or selling securities.

Sometimes, however, it is not as clear as this. In *SEC v. Zandford,* 535 U.S. 813, 819–25 (2002), a stock broker urged an elderly man to open an account and give a power of attorney to trade securities for the man and his handicapped daughter. The broker traded in the account and absconded with the proceeds. Each trade was part of the dealer's plan to bilk the clients, so the fraudulent scheme was "in connection with" securities transactions. It might have been different if the broker had decided, after trading in the account, to steal the money. In *Zandford,* the reason for the trades was the fraudulent scheme.

The purchase or sale may be of "any security." Though most cases involve transactions in equity securities (stock), Rule 10b–5 applies to deals concerning debt securities as well.

7.      *Other.* Privity is not a requirement under Rule 10b–5. Thus, the plaintiff need not have dealt directly with the defendant. This is one reason insider trading on the public exchanges can be actionable under Rule 10b–5, as we see in the next section.

## § 14.4   FRAUDULENT BEHAVIOR

A.      *Background.* We have just discussed the elements of a claim under Rule 10b–5. In this section, we focus on the types of behavior that can violate the Rule. All the elements we have just seen— materiality, scienter, reliance, causation, and the like—must concern some fraudulent act or omission. In this section, we will assume that the elements discussed above are satisfied, and will focus on the types of behavior violate Rule 10b–5. We start with two important points.

First, 10b–5 only prohibits *deception*, not unfairness. So a transaction (like a merger) that is adequately disclosed cannot be attacked under Rule 10b–5, even if its terms are unfair.

Second, there is no liability in a private Rule 10b–5 case for "aiding and abetting." Suppose a corporation violated 10b–5 by making misleading statements in its prospectus. Defrauded investors can sue the corporation. Because the corporation might have no assets, plaintiffs for years sued "secondary" or "collateral" participants, such as the accountants and bankers who may be said to have aided the corporation's fraud. The Supreme Court put a (surprising) end to the practice in *Central Bank of Denver, N.A. v. First Interstate Bank*, 511 U.S. 164, 191–92 (1994).

Congress changed this result in the PSLRA, but only for cases brought by the SEC. So aiding and abetting is not a viable theory in private actions brought under Rule 10b–5. The Court reiterated this point in *Stoneridge Investment Partners, LLC v. Scientific-Atlanta, Inc.*, 552 U.S. 148, 157–58 (2008).

B.    *Terms of the Rule.* Review the language of Rule 10b–5, which is set forth at § 14.3, subpart A. It has three parts. Parts (1) and (3) seem to be different ways to say "do not defraud folks." Clearly, behavior that would constitute common law fraud is actionable under Rule 10b–5.

- Close Corporation is issuing stock. President tells you that the company already has contracts to provide services for hundreds of clients. A brochure published by Close Corporation says the same thing. It is a lie. You buy the stock. You can sue Close Corporation and the President under 10b–5.

Nothing in the Rule limits its application to issuances (sales by the corporation itself). Indeed, it is likely that most cases involve re-sales of stock.

- Susie owns stock in Corporation. She tells you that the company is about to introduce a revolutionary new product and that the stock will increase in value. Because she needs cash, she says, she will sell it to you for "only" $10,000. You buy it. It turns out to be worthless. Everything Susie said was a lie. You can sue Susie under Rule 10b–5.

As we saw in § 14.3, the *defendant* in a 10b–5 case need not have bought or sold securities. So, for example, the corporation that issues a misleading press release violates the Rule and can be sued by all who buy or sell in reliance on the press release. (Indeed, reliance will be presumed in this type of case under the "fraud on the market" theory (§ 14.3, subpart C(2)).)

The most important developments under 10b–5 concern its application to insider trading. Again, look at the language of the Rule. The only part that seems related to insider trading is (2), and it seems quite limited at that. It imposes liability for "omit[ting] to state a material fact," but *only* if the fact would be necessary to make something already said "not misleading." In other words, if the defendant makes a statement that implies something material, the Rule expressly requires her to make an ameliorative statement.

- Close Corporation is issuing stock. The President tells you: "the last four quarterly reports by our accountants show profitability." This is literally true. What she does not say is that though the audit for the most recent quarter is not complete, it will show that the company lost a tremendous amount of money.

The President did not lie to you. But she made a statement that implied something that isn't so. To make what she said "not misleading," she should have told you about today's conversation with the accountant.

C.      *Insider Trading.* We just saw that Rule 10b–5, on its face anyway, seems to impose a duty to disclose only when the defendant has already said something. To fix a misunderstanding created by what she already said, the defendant should disclose something. Thus nothing in the Rule seems to apply to the classic insider trading case in which the defendant says nothing at all. Review the hypos in § 14.2, subpart A, involving Dot. They do not seem to implicate Rule 10b–5 as written.

But they do violate Rule 10b–5 as interpreted. This is the most important area of Rule 10b–5 jurisprudence, and it is the result of case law. The first hint that trading on the basis of inside information might violate Rule 10b–5 came in *In re Cady, Roberts & Co.*, 40 SEC 907, 912 (1961). The proceeding was an administrative discipline case against a broker, and the SEC concluded that anyone with direct or indirect access "to information intended to be available only for a corporate purpose" may not take "advantage of such information knowing it is unavailable to those with whom he is dealing," including the investing public.

The first major federal court case to apply Rule 10b–5 to insider trading was *SEC v. Texas Gulf Sulphur Co.*, 401 F.2d 833, 853–54 (2d Cir. 1968). There, a mining company (TGS) was looking for mineral sites in Canada. Core samples at one site were very favorable, and the company began buying up land in the area. The company wanted to keep news of the strike quiet so it could buy the land cheaply. At the same time, insiders bought TGS stock and call options based upon their inside information about the core sample. The court held that these insiders violated 10b–5 by stock trading on the inside information. Insiders cannot trade until the information is divulged and the market has a chance to digest the information.

In addition, the case involved "tipping." Insiders passed inside information to others so the others could buy TGS stock. The court found that this violated Rule 10b–5 as well. According to the court (and the SEC in *Cady, Roberts*), the purpose of 10b–5 is to assure that all traders have relatively equal access to information.

Development of the law now shifted to the Supreme Court. *Chiarella v. United States*, 445 U.S. 222, 224 (1980), was a criminal case brought against a blue-collar employee of a printing company. The defendant worked on documents relating to a tender offer. Though the names of the aggressor and target companies were left blank on the documents on which the defendant worked, he was able to determine (through research) the identities of the companies. He used this information to buy stock in the target on the public market. He made a handsome profit and was prosecuted and convicted.

The Court reversed the conviction. The defendant owed no duty to the general public to disclose the information he had obtained. Not everyone in possession of nonpublic information owes a duty to disclose it. Because the defendant was not an insider of the company whose stock he bought, Rule 10b–5 did not prohibit his trading. Stated another way, the "*Cady, Roberts* duty" (to disclose nonpublic information or else abstain from trading) did not attach to this defendant. According to the Court in *Chiarella,* the Rule 10b–5 proscription on insider trading does not arise because one has superior information. Rather, it arises from breach of a fiduciary duty.

Specifically, the Court held that the *Cady, Roberts* duty is imposed only on those persons who have a "relationship of trust and confidence [with the shareholders]" of the corporation. In other words, it applies to those whose jobs routinely give them access to inside information. Because Mr. Chiarella was not an insider of the company whose stock he bought, Rule 10b–5 did not prohibit him from trading on the basis of inside information.

Chief Justice Burger filed an important dissent in *Chiarella.* He argued that the defendant should be convicted under Rule 10b–5 because "a person who has misappropriated nonpublic information has an absolute duty to disclose that information or to refrain from trading." The majority of the Court did not consider this "misappropriation" argument, because the Justices concluded it was not properly raised in the trial court. We will see that a version of the misappropriation theory was to succeed later.

Shortly after *Chiarella*, the SEC adopted Rule 14e–3, which prohibits *anyone* from trading on the basis of undisclosed information about pending tender offers. It applies even to eavesdroppers who happen to hear about a tender offer and trade on that information. So the defendant in *Chiarella* today would run afoul of Rule 14e–3, even though he did not violate Rule 10b–5. (The Supreme Court upheld the validity of Rule 14e–3 in *United States v. O'Hagan*, 521 U.S. 642, 667 (1997).)

The next big case, *Dirks v. SEC*, 463 U.S. 646, 657 (1983), involved "tipping." Secrist was a former insider of Equity Funding Corporation, a life insurance and mutual fund company. He was concerned about massive fraud in the company. He contacted Dirks, who was a broker, to tell him about the fraud and ask him to investigate. Dirks did, and found that Secrist was right. Dirks advised his clients to sell their Equity Funding stock and "blew the whistle" by going to the SEC with evidence of the fraud. The SEC rewarded Dirks by charging him with violating 10b–5. (Some people think the SEC was being spiteful because it had failed to follow up on allegations about fraud at Equity Funding.)

Specifically, the SEC charged, Secrist was a "tipper" and Dirks was a "tippee" of nonpublic information. And when Dirks used that information to tell his clients to sell their Equity Funding stock, was a "tipper" and his clients were "tippees." The

SEC's theory, as in *Chiarella,* was that these people were using nonpublic information. The Court's holding, as in *Chiarella,* is that Rule 10b–5 is only implicated if there is a breach of fiduciary duty. The Rule does not "require equal information among all traders." Rather, "only some persons, under some circumstances, will be barred from trading while in possession of material nonpublic information."

*Dirks* sets out very clear rules. First, one is a tipper only if she passes along nonpublic information in breach of a duty to her corporation *and* receives some benefit for doing so. The benefit might be material (like money) or it might consist simply of making a gift or enhancing one's reputation. Federal courts of appeals have disagreed on what constitutes a "benefit" for these purposes. The Second Circuit requires that the tipper receive some personal gain. *U.S. v. Newman,* 773 F.3d 438, 446 (2d Cir. 2014), cert. denied, 136 S.Ct. 242 (2015). The Ninth Circuit has held that the tipper receives a benefit by passing inside information to a family member. *U.S. v. Salman,* 792 F.3d 1087, 1094 (9th Cir. 2015). The Supreme Court has agreed to review the Ninth Circuit decision, with oral argument scheduled in the October 2016 Term. *Salman v. U.S.,* 136 S.Ct. 899 (2016).

Whether one passes information in breach of duty is determined by the person's motivation. On the facts of the case, Secrist was not a tipper. His motivation was to expose fraud, not to line Dirks's pockets. Further, Secrist did not benefit from giving the tip.

Second, without a tipper, there can be no tippee. So once it determined that Secrist was not a tipper, Dirks cannot be in trouble as a tippee. If there had been a tipper, a tippee violates 10b–5 if he trades on the tip and knew or should have known the information was given to him wrongfully.

Third, while a tippee can "inherit" a fiduciary duty from a tipper and breach it by tipping a third party, that did not happen here. Dirks did not inherit a fiduciary duty from Secrist because Secrist violated no duty when he gave the information to Dirks. "[S]ome tippees must assume an insider's duty to the shareholders not because they receive inside information, but rather because it has been made available to them improperly."

In footnote 14, the Court in *Dirks* suggested that persons such as underwriters, accountants, attorneys, or consultants working for the corporation and who receive corporate information in a legitimate manner should be viewed as temporary insiders and not as tippees. Hence, if they disclose confidential information it is as a tipper and not a tippee.

*Carpenter v. United States*, 484 U.S. 19, 22–23 (1987) offered a chance to consider the "misappropriation theory" first suggested by Chief Justice Burger in *Chiarella*. In *Carpenter,* a reporter for the *Wall Street Journal*, Mr. Winans, wrote a daily column that discussed stocks. Favorable mention of a stock in this column usually led to a run-up in price of that stock. Winans gave information about which stocks he would feature to some associates, who bought stock before the column was published. The associates profited from these trades.

Because Winans received no information from the corporations themselves, he could not be held liable under the "traditional" or "classical" approach to insider trading under 10b–5. As we have seen, that applies only to persons with a relationship of trust and confidence with the shareholders of the corporation. The government prosecuted Winans under a misappropriation theory. Specifically, he was using information that "belonged" to the *Wall Street Journal*, not to the companies referred to in his column. Winans was convicted of criminal violations under the mail fraud statute, § 10(b), and Rule 10b–5. The Second Circuit affirmed. The Supreme Court affirmed the conviction under Rule 10b–5 by an equally divided court, thus leaving the status of the misappropriation theory unclear. At the same time, though, the Court unanimously upheld Winans's convictions for mail fraud.

Next is *United States v. O'Hagan*, 521 U.S. 642, 650–55 (1997). O'Hagan was a partner in a major Minneapolis law firm. The firm represented Grand Met, an English company, and was working with it in its effort to acquire Pillsbury through a tender offer. O'Hagan was not involved in that matter but learned about it from other members of the law firm. Based on this information, O'Hagan bought Pillsbury stock and options. When news of the takeover went public, he sold the stock at a profit of $4,300,000. After being disbarred and prosecuted in state court, O'Hagan was hit with a 57-count federal indictment, including violations of 10b–5 and 14e–3. The Court affirmed his convictions. For 10b–5, the case is significant for its adoption of a misappropriation theory.

As in *Carpenter,* the government could not proceed under the "traditional" or "classical" approach. O'Hagan was not an insider of Pillsbury, and thus cannot have violated any duty to it. (What O'Hagan did is sometimes called "outsider trading," because he trades in the stock of a company to which he owes no fiduciary duty.) Instead, he misappropriated information that belonged to his employer (the law firm) and to his employer's client (Grand Met). The Court took the case to resolve the split among lower courts about whether misappropriation is a viable theory for 10b–5 cases. It embraced the theory and reinstated O'Hagan's convictions under 10b–5.

We note two things about *O'Hagan.* First, the Court did not decide whether the misappropriation theory applies in private civil actions. It clearly applies in criminal prosecutions but, at least at the Supreme Court level, it is an open question whether it should apply in private cases.

Second, the version of the misappropriation doctrine adopted by the Court is narrower than that suggested by Chief Justice Burger in his dissent in *Chiarella.* He asserted that the duty not to trade on misappropriated information "ran to those with whom the misappropriator trades." In this view, O'Hagan would have violated some duty to those who were on the other side of his market trades in Pillsbury. In *O'Hagan,* the Court held that the obligation runs to "the source of the information"—in that case, the law firm and its client.

The development of the law of insider trading under Rule 10b–5 has implicated different policies. The SEC originally asserted that the prohibition of insider trading was based upon equality of access to information. The Court rejected this assertion in *Chiarella* and *Dirks*, and shifted the focus from equal access to preventing a breach of fiduciary duty owed to the company whose securities are traded. With misappropriation, liability is imposed on one who takes information in breach of a duty owed to someone unconnected with the corporation in whose securities she traded. Disclosure to the person on the other side of the trade is irrelevant. The breach of duty under this theory is the failure to disclose the proposed trading to the person with the proprietary right to the information. In other words, O'Hagan would not have committed a criminal violation if he had advised his law firm and Grand Met that he proposed to speculate in Pillsbury stock.

## § 14.5   SECTION 16(b)

In contrast to Rule 10b–5, § 16(b) of the '34 Act *expressly* addresses insider trading. Indeed, it applies to nothing but insider trading. But it embraces a strange definition of insider trading. Cases under § 16(b), like 10b–5 cases, must be brought in federal court. Beyond that, there are important differences between the two provisions.

*First*, § 16(b) applies only to trading in registered securities, which means it applies in public corporations. Rule 10b–5 applies to "any person," so can come up in public or closely-held businesses.

*Second*, § 16(b) applies only to trading in *equity* securities, while 10b–5 applies to "any security" (which would include debt securities).

*Third*, § 16(b) imposes *strict liability,* while 10b–5 requires a showing that the defendant acted with scienter. In § 16(b), intent of the defendant is irrelevant.

*Fourth*, § 16(b) creates a claim *for the corporation*, not for someone injured by fraudulent behavior. The claim can be asserted by the corporation itself or by a shareholder on the corporation's behalf. A shareholder suing under § 16(b) need not have owned stock when the claim arose. Note, then, that the SEC does not enforce § 16(b). The law relies on civil enforcement by or on behalf of the corporation.

*Fifth,* § 16(b) applies only to three kinds of defendants: directors, officers, and ten-percent shareholders. This is far more limited than Rule 10b–5, which applies to "any person."

Section 16(b) is invoked when the defendant buys *and* sells stock in her corporation within six months. This is called "short swing" trading. Under § 16(a), the three types of defendants in § 16(b) are required to report to the SEC any "purchase" or "sale" of the company's stock. This information must be posted to a publicly accessible website by the end of the following business day. Thus, the public has access to this information.

If the defendant makes a profit on her buying and selling within six months, the corporation is entitled to recover the profit. She is liable even if she had a compelling need to raise cash. The idea is to discourage the defendants from trading in their company's stock (at least within six months). It does this by taking away any profit they make. And because it is strict liability, the plaintiff need not show that the defendant used inside information. It is presumed that she did. It imposes strict liability.

- D is a director of Corporation. On February 1, he buys 100 shares of Corporation's stock at $30 per share. On August 5, he sells those shares at $40 per share. He is not liable under § 16(b), because his buy and sell were not within six months.

People paying attention to the calendar should never run into § 16(b) problems. Most violations are inadvertent, and seem to be based on confusion over what constitutes a "purchase" and a "sale" under the statute. For example, courts struggle with whether things like redemptions and exchanges pursuant to mergers constitute purchases and sales under the statute. Transactions involving options to buy or sell (puts or calls) are covered by section 16(b) if they have the effect of a buy and sell.

There are two tricky areas in § 16(b). The first is about the three types of defendants. A person is subject to § 16(b) as a director or officer if she held either role either at the time of purchase or sale. The SEC has made clear that "officer" refers to actual responsibility and function, not merely title.

- D is a director of Corporation on February 1, when she buys 100 shares of Corporation stock at $30 per share. She ceases being a director on April 1. She sells the stock on May 1 at $40 per share. She is liable to Corporation for her profit. The purchase and the sale were made within six months and the defendant was a director during one of those events (here, the purchase).

Here's the tricky part: one is covered as a ten percent shareholder only if she *holds more than ten percent both at the time she buys and the time she sells.* So though we speak of "ten percent" shareholder, she must actually own more than ten percent, at both "ends" of the buy and sell. To determine this status, courts use a "snap shot" approach. They ask how much stock the defendant owned immediately *before* the buy or immediately *before* the sell. We don't care about her status *after* the buy or the sell. (BTW, the typical 10 percent shareholder is an aggressor corporation trying to takeover a target by buying the target's stock in the public market.)

- S owns zero percent. She buys 11 percent. That purchase is not subject to § 16(b). Why? Because immediately *before* making this purchase, the defendant owned less than ten percent. (It does not matter that she owns more than ten percent *after* the purchase; we care about her status immediately *before* the event.

- Now assume that she buys six percent more. That purchase is covered by § 16(b). Why? Because immediately *before* making this purchase, she owned more than ten percent.

- Now let's say that within six months of this second purchase, the defendant sells some or all of the 17 percent that she now owns. Will that sale be covered by § 16(b)? Yes. Why? Because immediately before the sale, she owned more than ten percent of the corporation's stock.

- That means that we have a purchase and a sale—both covered by § 16(b) within six months. If she made a profit on that purchase and sale, she is liable the corporation for that profit.

How do we determine whether one has made a profit by buying and selling within six months? Here is the second tricky issue—watch for this on the exam.

Profit, we all know, means that you sell something for more than you bought it for. That is true under § 16(b). In the real world, though, those two things happen in this order: we buy first (say, for $5) and later we sell (say, for $7). That would be a profit of $2 per share, both in the real world and under § 16(b).

But here is the shocker: under § 16(b), something is considered a profit *regardless of the order of the purchase and the sale.* In other words, one can make a profit under § 16(b) *even if the sale is made before the purchase!* Just as long as the price you pay to buy the stock is lower than the price at which you sell it.

- D is a director of Corporation. Two years ago, she bought 2,000 shares of Corporation stock at $30. On February 1 of this year, she sold 2,000 shares at $25. On June 1 of this year, she bought 1,500 shares at $19.

In the real world, D has made no profit. She bought at $30 and sold at $25, which is a loss. Then has bought more stock at $19. She has not made any money. But under § 16(b) she has! She owes Corporation $9,000—strict liability.

Here's how to apply § 16(b). First, focus on the sale. Here the sale is February 1 of this year, when she sold at $25. Second, ask whether she *bought* for less than $25 within six months *either before or after that sale*. Here, she did nothing within six months before February 1. But within six months after that date (June 1), she bought at $19. So § 16(b) essentially says to her: "you bought at $19 and you sold at $25; that is a profit of $6 per share." We don't care that she sold before she bought and we don't care that the shares she bought on June 1 have not been sold.

The last step is to calculate the total "profit." Here, she "made" $6 per share, and we multiply that by 1,500 shares. Why? We use the largest number of shares that she both bought and sold within the six months. Within the six months, she sold 2,000 shares (on February 1) and she bought 1,500 shares (on June 1). We use the 1,500 because that is the largest number common both to the buy and the sell.

Suppose instead she had sold 2,000 shares on February 1 and bought only 500 on June 1. We would multiple by 500 shares, because 500 is the largest number common both to the buy and the sell.

# CHAPTER 15
# DERIVATIVE LITIGATION

## § 15.1  INTRODUCTION

As we have seen, shareholders are the owners of the corporation. That status allows them to do various things, including elect and remove directors, vote on fundamental changes, and inspect the books and records. In this chapter, we focus on a particularly interesting shareholder right: the right to bring a "shareholder's derivative suit." In such a case, the shareholder sues to vindicate the *corporation's* claim and not her own personal claim. The suit is "derivative" because the shareholder's right to bring it "derives" from the corporation's right to sue.

But why should a shareholder be able to do this? After all, whether to have the corporation assert a claim is a management decision, which should be made by the board of directors. In two situations, though, the board might not act. First, there might be good business reasons not to sue. For example, suppose the corporation has an ongoing relationship with a supplier, and a contract dispute arises. The corporation could sue, but it values the relationship with the supplier, and decides that the parties will work out the problem in the future. A derivative suit here seems questionable because it is second-guessing the kind of business decision directors are hired to make.

Second, the board may not sue because the directors (or some of them) would be defendants in the case. For example, suppose the claim is that the corporation has been harmed by the incumbent directors' breach of one of the fiduciary duties discussed in Chapter 9. Here, the board members have a conflict of interest. If the directors decide that the corporation should sue, they are approving a suit against themselves. In this situation, a derivative suit may make sense, because we have some question about whether the board will pursue such a claim with diligence.

The law permits a shareholder to initiate a derivative suit in either situation. It imposes strict procedural prerequisites on the plaintiff (*see* § 15.4). Even if a plaintiff may initiate suit, it is not always clear that she has a right to continue to pursue it; the corporation may move to dismiss if the claim is not in the company's best interest (*see* § 15.5). To avoid abusive derivative litigation, courts must approve their settlement or voluntary dismissal (*see* § 15.6). Derivative suits seek to impose personal liability on the defendants. One of the most significant developments in the law in the past generation is the availability of protection for directors and officers from liability and from the expense of such litigation (*see* §§ 15.7 & 15.8). We start, however, with the determination of whether a suit is derivative (*see* § 15.2) and an overview of such litigation (*see* § 15.3).

## § 15.2   DETERMINING WHETHER A CASE IS DERIVATIVE

Anytime a shareholder sues in her capacity as a shareholder (as opposed, for example, to her capacity as an employee), her suit will either be "derivative" or "direct." In a derivative suit, she is suing to vindicate the corporation's claim. In such a case, the corporation is the real party in interest. In contrast, a direct suit asserts the shareholder's own personal claim. If it is a derivative suit, the shareholder must satisfy the procedural requirements imposed in such cases (*see* § 15.4). In a direct suit, in contrast, the plaintiff need not jump through any special procedural hoops.

As a rule of thumb, to determine whether a claim is derivative, ask: could the corporation have brought this suit? If so, it is probably a derivative suit, because the plaintiff is vindicating the entity's claim.

- S, a shareholder of C Corp., sues Third Party because Third Party allegedly breached its contract with C Corp. This is derivative because C Corp. could sue Third Party.

Most derivative suits are brought against corporate managers and assert that they have breached one of the fiduciary duties we discussed in Chapter 9. Directors and officers owe these duties (of good faith, care, and loyalty) *to the corporation.* Hence, when they breach such a duty, the corporation is the aggrieved party. The suit against them seeks to impose personal liability on the managers— liability to the corporation. Here are two examples:

- The board of directors of XYZ Corp. approves a corporate purchase of land without undertaking any evaluation of the land. The property turns out to be worthless. This breach of the duty of care (*see* § 9.4) by the board has hurt XYZ Corp. A shareholder may bring a derivative suit to have the corporation recover from the directors for the losses suffered by the corporation.

- The board of directors of XYZ Corp. approves a contract to buy supplies from D Corp., which is wholly owned by a director of XYZ Corp. Under the deal, XYZ Corp. pays far more than the market price for such supplies. This interested director transaction constitutes a breach of the duty of loyalty and harms XYZ Corp. A shareholder may bring a derivative suit against the directors who approved the deal to have the corporation recover (from the directors) for the losses.

Occasionally, a derivative suit is brought against a third party who has allegedly caused harm to the corporation. Here's an example:

- XYZ Corp. enters into a contract to buy supplies from Third Party (TP). TP fails to provide the supplies, forcing XYZ Corp. to pay for the supplies from another company, at greater expense. The corporation has a claim against TP for breach of contract. If the corporation does not assert the claim, a shareholder might bring a derivative suit against TP.

If the answer to the question we posed above is no (in other words, if the corporation could not have asserted the claim) the shareholder is asserting her own right. This is a direct (not derivative) suit.

- S, a shareholder of C Corp., sues C Corp. because it issued stock without honoring her pre-emptive rights (*see* § 12.4). This is a direct suit. C Corp. could not bring this suit, because C Corp. has not been harmed. The harm is to the shareholder.

These claims would also be direct: a suit to force the corporation to allow a shareholder to inspect the books and records, a suit to honor a dividend preference when the corporation declared a dividend, and a suit for violation of Rule 10b–5 (*see* § 14.3). The latter is direct because it gives a private right of action for damages by a buyer or seller of securities who is defrauded by misleading statements or omissions. Notice that most direct suits are against the corporation itself; the claim is that the corporation is not living up to some agreement with the shareholder.

Sometimes it is not obvious whether a claim is derivative or direct. In such cases, the defendant will argue that it is a derivative suit. Why? To force the plaintiff to jump through the procedural hoops required of derivative suits. A famous example is *Eisenberg v. Flying Tiger Line, Inc.*, 451 F.2d 267, 272 (2d Cir. 1971). There, the plaintiff held stock in a corporation that operated an airline. After a series of mergers, the plaintiff ended up owning stock in a holding company that *owned* an airline. He challenged the mergers as depriving him (and other minority shareholders) of having a vote or influence on a corporation that ran an airline. He bought stock to participate in a company that *ran* an airline, not one that simply *owned* an airline. The defendant argued that this was a derivative suit, and that the plaintiff was required by statute to post a bond (this is a requirement for derivative suits in some states). Because the plaintiff refused to post a bond (of $35,000), the trial court dismissed the case.

The Second Circuit, applying New York law, reversed, and held the claim was direct. This meant that the plaintiff was not required to post the bond, and the case could proceed. The court emphasized that a derivative suit is one regarding injury to the corporation. Here, the injury (if any) was to minority shareholders. The court discussed *Gordon v. Elliman*, 119 N.E.2d 331, 339 (N.Y. 1954), in which the New York Court of Appeals held that a suit to force the board to declare a dividend was derivative. That court concluded that the failure to pay dividends was a failure to discharge a duty owed to the corporation, not the shareholders. The decision in *Gordon* was widely criticized, and led to a statutory change in New York to define a derivative suit as one in which plaintiff seeks a judgment "in [the corporation's] favor." NY Bus. Corp. Law § 626. This amendment legislatively overturned the result in *Gordon*. Today, a suit for the declaration of a dividend would be seen as direct, because it seeks to put money in the pockets of the shareholders, and not to assert a right belonging to the corporation.

It is important to distinguish between a derivative suit and a class action. In a class action, a representative sues on behalf of similarly situated persons to enforce their individual claims. In other words, a class action is a *direct* suit in which there are so many potential plaintiffs that they satisfy the class action requirements of Federal Rule of Civil Procedure 23 (or the state equivalent). *Eisenberg* was a class action, on behalf of other minority shareholders who opposed the mergers. All of those people had direct claims, and nobody was asserting the interest of the corporation. The corporation had not been wronged. A derivative suit is entirely different, because it is not brought by a representative on behalf of other shareholders who are similarly situated. It is brought by a shareholder on behalf of the *corporation.*

Derivative suits and class actions are alike, however, in that in each, someone purports to sue on behalf of someone else. In the class action, the fate of the class members' direct claims will sink or swim with the representative. In a derivative suit, the corporation's interest will sink or swim with the shareholder plaintiff.

Why does anyone (whether a plaintiff in a derivative suit or the representative in a class action) take on the burden of litigating for someone else? One answer is altruism: the plaintiff wants to do the right thing. Another possibility is that the moving force behind the litigation is the plaintiff's lawyer. In many cases, it is the lawyer who recruits a shareholder to bring the derivative suit (and it is often the lawyer who recruits the representative in a class action). We worry that the lawyer is motivated not by altruism, but by the desire to make money.

Such a case is called a "strike suit." The objective of the suit is to obtain a settlement that, in blunt terms, pays the plaintiff shareholder to ignore a corporate wrong and provides the attorney with a generous fee. The defendants may favor this result because they write a check and the case goes away. It may not matter to them that the lion's share of the check goes to the attorney, and not to the corporation.

In response to this potential for abuse, the law of every state imposes procedural safeguards, seen in § 15.4. In addition, as seen in § 15.6, a derivative suit can be settled only with court approval.

## § 15.3   DERIVATIVE LITIGATION: OVERVIEW

If the derivative suit is successful, the recovery goes to the corporation. This makes sense, because the suit asserted the corporation's claim. On the other hand, the shareholder did all the work of bringing and prosecuting the case. So what does the successful shareholder plaintiff recover? What is her reward for taking on this task and prevailing? As a general matter, she recovers her litigation costs from the other side. A common rule of civil procedure is that the prevailing party recovers her costs from the losing party. "Costs" is a term of art, and usually consists of various expenses of litigation (such as filing fees, discovery costs, and expert witness fees), but not attorney's fees.

Under the "American Rule," each party bears her own attorney's fees. One exception to this rule is found in derivative litigation. Because the successful derivative plaintiff conferred a benefit on the corporation (by vindicating the corporate claim), usually she will recover attorney's fees from the corporation, often from the recovery she won. Even if there was no monetary recovery (for example, a case that resulted in equitable relief) the shareholder plaintiff may be entitled to recover her attorney's fees from the corporation, so long as the suit conferred a benefit on the corporation. *See*, *e.g.*, MBCA § 7.46(1) (court may order the corporation to pay plaintiff's expenses and attorney's fees if the case "resulted in a substantial benefit to the corporation.").

In some cases involving close corporations, the derivative suit model does not make sense. For example, suppose a corporation has three shareholders—X, Y, and Z—each of whom owns one-third of the stock and each is a director. Let's say X is also president of the corporation, and has the company buy supplies from another business, which she owns. And suppose this interested director deal causes the corporation to overpay for supplies by $30,000. X has breached her duty of loyalty to the corporation, and has caused damage of $30,000. If another shareholder brings a derivative suit and wins, the $30,000 judgment will go to the corporation. Because X owns one-third of the corporation, however, this recovery in essence returns one-third of the judgment to X, the wrongdoer.

For this reason, some courts will treat the case as a direct suit, and allow the "innocent" shareholders to recover directly their pro-rata share of the harm done. Some commentators suggested this approach, and some states have adopted it. For example, in Texas, derivative claims in corporations having 35 or fewer shareholders may be treated as direct. Thus the plaintiffs need not satisfy the procedural requirements of a derivative suit, and the recovery goes to them, not to the corporation. Tex. Bus. Org. Code. § 21.563.

What happens if the shareholder plaintiff loses the derivative suit? First, she will bear her own attorney's fees and probably have to pay the defendant's litigation costs. Second, in most states, the court may order her to pay the defendant's attorney's fees if she sued "without reasonable cause or for an improper purpose." *See, e.g.,* MBCA § 7.46(2). And third, a judgment on the merits is entitled to claim preclusion (res judicata) effect, which means that no other shareholder can sue the same defendant on the same transaction or occurrence. This is because that claim, on behalf of the corporation, has already been asserted. Claim preclusion prohibits a second assertion of the same claim.

Is the corporation a party in the derivative suit? Yes, it must be joined. And though the suit is brought to assert the corporation's claim, the corporation is joined as a defendant. This is because the corporation did not actually sue, and the law has always been reluctant to force the joinder of an involuntary plaintiff. In the litigation itself, the corporation may play an active role or may be passive. It may side with the individual defendants and urge that their conduct did not harm the company, or it may champion the plaintiff's cause.

The New York Business Corporation Law has an interesting provision that allows a director or officer to sue another director or officer to force her to account for breach of a duty to the corporation. Such a plaintiff sues in her own name, though any recovery goes to the corporation, and need not satisfy the prerequisites of a derivative suit. NY Bus. Corp. Law § 720.

## § 15.4  PREREQUISITES FOR A DERIVATIVE SUIT

A.    *Contemporaneous Ownership.* In nearly every state, the person bringing a derivative suit must have owned stock *when the claim arose* or must have gotten stock "by operation of law" from someone who owned the stock when the claim arose. The purpose of this "contemporaneous ownership" requirement is to prevent someone from purchasing a lawsuit by buying a share of stock in the corporation after the claim becomes apparent.

Section 7.41(1) of MBCA is typical of the statutes imposing the contemporaneous ownership requirement, as is Rule 23.1 of the Federal Rule of Civil Procedure. Though statutes do not define "operation of law" for purposes of the rule, case law makes clear that it refers to things like inheritance or a divorce decree. The purchase of stock does not constitute a transfer by "operation of law."

- P brings a derivative suit to vindicate a claim belonging to XYZ Corp. P did not own stock in XYZ when the claim arose, but her uncle did. In the meantime, her uncle passed away and she inherited the stock from him. She has standing under the contemporaneous ownership requirement because she received the stock "by operation of law" from someone who owned the stock when the claim arose.

- In contrast, if P's uncle had not died, and P bought the stock from her uncle after the claim arose, P would not have standing to bring a derivative suit. She did not own the stock when the claim arose and did not obtain it "by operation of law" from someone who did.

When a claim occurs over time, some courts have adopted the "continuing wrong" theory to permit a shareholder to sue if she held stock (or got it by operation of law) at any point during a continuing wrong. For example, in *Palmer v. Morris*, 316 F.2d 649, 651 (5th Cir. 1963), the plaintiff bought stock after a wrongful transaction was entered, but before the payments under the deal were made. The court upheld standing. Section 800(b)(1) of the California Corporation Code embodies this approach, and permits a shareholder to sue if she owned stock during the alleged wrong "or any part thereof."

A handful of states do not always insist on contemporaneous ownership. For instance,

California permits a court to allow any shareholder to prosecute a derivative suit if various conditions are met, including a strong prima facie case in favor of the claim and the likelihood that no similar suit will be filed. Cal. Corp. Code § 800(b)(1). And in federal court, as we saw before, claims based on § 16(b) of the '34 Act may be brought by any current shareholder, even if she did not own stock when the claim arose (*see* § 14.5).

The contemporaneous ownership requirement does not mandate that the plaintiff own a particular amount of stock; neither does it require that the shareholder have known anything about the claim when it arose.

B.     *Adequacy of Representation.* In most states, the derivative plaintiff must *also* demonstrate that she will adequately represent the interests of the corporation. *See, e.g.*, MBCA § 7.41(2). Because the result of the litigation will bind the corporation, the plaintiff must demonstrate to the court that she has the proper motivation to pursue the case. The court should ensure that the plaintiff's lawyer is not real party in interest, and that the plaintiff shareholder has some legitimate interest in prosecuting the case.

Part of ensuring adequacy of representation is an ongoing interest. Thus, though statutes in many states are silent on the point, courts insist that the plaintiff continue to own stock when the case is brought and throughout the litigation. *Lewis v. Anderson*, 477 A.2d 1040, 1046 (Del. 1984). If the plaintiff divests her holding during the case, she loses standing, and the court might permit recruitment of another shareholder plaintiff.

C. *Security for Expenses.* In § 15.2, we noted the concern with "strike suits"—that is, derivative suits filed with the hope of extorting a settlement that benefits the plaintiff's lawyer. One way to dissuade plaintiffs from filing such suits is to force them to put up some of their own money as security for the defendants' litigation costs. Usually this means that the plaintiff would have to post a bond (deposit money with the court) from which the defendants may recover their litigation expenses (and maybe attorney's fees) if the derivative claim turns out to be a loser.

Several states still require security for expenses. Section 627 of the New York Business Corporation Law is perhaps the best known. It gives the corporation a right to demand that the plaintiff post security for expenses unless she owns at least five percent of any class of the corporation's stock or unless the stock she owns is worth at least $50,000. *See also* Pa. Cons. Stat. § 1782 (similar, with the exception if plaintiff's stock worth at least $200,000). The court sets the size of the bond, which depends upon the estimated expenses of suit. This figure may include expenses to individual defendants for which the corporation may be liable for indemnification (*see* § 15.7). The requirement is a significant hurdle for plaintiffs. Indeed, as we saw in *Eisenberg v. Flying Tiger Line, Inc.* in § 15.2, a plaintiff required to post a bond may well simply abandon the derivative suit.

Today most states do *not* require the plaintiff to post security for expenses.

D.    <u>*Demand That the Corporation Bring Suit.*</u> This is the major procedural prerequisite for derivative suits. The idea makes sense: whether the corporation should pursue litigation is a business decision, so a shareholder should not be permitted to proceed without giving corporate management a chance to pursue the claim. Statutes thus require the shareholder to make a written demand that the corporation bring suit. And because corporate decisions are made by the board, the demand must be made on it. (Some older statutes also required the plaintiff to make a demand on *shareholders* that the corporation bring suit. These shareholder-demand statutes are now a thing of the past.)

The demand on the board of directors must state with specificity what the claim is and against whom it exists. Must this demand always be made? There are two general views: (1) the traditional approach, which is still followed in many states, and (2) the MBCA "universal demand" approach.

1.    *The Traditional Approach.* Under this view, the plaintiff need not make a demand on the board of directors if such a demand would be "futile." The archetype is when a majority of the board is interested in the challenged transaction. For instance, suppose the derivative claim is against the incumbent directors for engaging in an interested director transaction or for lining their own pockets with excessive bonuses. Arguably, it is futile to demand that the board authorize the corporation to

sue. Why? Because in essence one is demanding that the board authorize suit against its own members.

Under Delaware law, the demand is futile if the plaintiff can allege detailed facts creating a "reasonable doubt" either that the directors were disinterested or that the challenged act was the product of valid business judgment. *Aronson v. Lewis*, 473 A.2d 805, 808 (Del. 1984). Moreover, in Delaware, the plaintiff cannot use discovery to ferret out facts supporting futility. Rather, she has may only employ her right to inspect corporate books and records (*see* § 6.9).

The New York Court of Appeals found the "reasonable doubt" language in Delaware law confusing, and rejects it. *Marx v. Akers*, 666 N.E.2d 1034, 1038 (N.Y. 1996). Beyond that, though, its definition of when a demand would be futile is consistent with that in Delaware. Demand is futile if the majority of the board is tainted or under the control of a tainted director. Or a board decision may be so bizarre that it cannot possibly be justified as consistent with the duty of care.

In these "demand excused" cases, the plaintiff files the derivative suit without making a demand on the board. But it would be easy for a plaintiff simply to allege that the board is tainted and thus that demand would be futile. So the law requires that the plaintiff's derivative complaint allege "with particularity" either her efforts to get the board to bring suit or her reasons for concluding that such demand was futile. Thus, she must allege in detail why board members could not be trusted with making the decision of whether to have the corporation sue. In addition, some states require that the complaint be "verified," which means that the shareholder plaintiff must sign it under penalty of perjury.

What are the consequences of the plaintiff's making a demand on the board? First, the board may accept it as a recommendation and authorize the corporation to bring suit. If this happens, the case is brought by the corporation itself and is not a derivative suit; then, there is no further role for the shareholder.

Second (and far likelier), the board may reject the demand. If this happens, either the shareholder will give up or assert that the board erred in concluding that the case should not be filed. This latter course is almost always a loser, because the shareholder is simply disagreeing with a decision by the board. The board's judgment will be upheld under the business judgment rule. That means that the shareholder would have to show that the board's decision was tainted by self-interest (and if that were true, the demand would have been excused in the first place).

Indeed, under Delaware law, the shareholder will always lose in this "demand rejected" scenario, because making the demand on directors constitutes an admission that the board was disinterested. *Spiegel v. Buntrock*, 571 A.2d 767, 777 (Del. 1990). This means that the board's decision is protected by the business judgment rule. As a consequence, it is almost impossible to find a case in Delaware in which the shareholder makes the demand.

What happens, though, if the plaintiff sues without making a demand on the board? Most likely, the board of directors, on behalf of the corporation, will move to dismiss the case on the ground that the plaintiff should have made the demand. On this motion, the court faces one issue: would a demand on the board have been futile? In other words, would demand have been excused?

In most cases, the decision on this issue will depend upon whether a majority of the directors was tainted. If a majority of directors is charged with the breach of duty alleged in the derivative suit (or is under control of directors who breached the duty), demand would be excused as futile. If the court determines that the demand was not futile (that it should have been made) the derivative suit will be dismissed. On the other hand, if it determines that the demand was excused, the derivative suit continues.

2.     *The MBCA "Universal Demand" Approach.* Under the modern approach, embodied in the MBCA, the plaintiff in a derivative suit must always make the demand on the board of directors. Under this approach, there is no such thing as a "demand excused" case. Section 7.42 of MBCA leads the way on this point. The universal demand requirement recognizes that (1) litigation over whether a demand is excused is expensive and time-consuming and (2) that making a demand—even if a majority of the board is tainted—will give the board a chance to consider the claim in the context of potential litigation and do the right thing.

Under MBCA § 7.42, the plaintiff must make the demand on the board of directors and then wait at least 90 days before filing the derivative suit. She may sue before 90 days if the board rejects the demand or if waiting that long will cause "irreparable injury" to the corporation. For example, if the statute of limitations on the claim is about to expire, or if the bad behavior of the proposed defendants threatens the company's existence, the plaintiff may be permitted to sue earlier. The corporation may accept the demand and have the corporation bring suit. Or, if the shareholder has filed suit, the corporation (through the board of directors) may take over the case. More likely, though, the board will reject the demand and have the corporation move to dismiss the derivative suit.

## § 15.5   MOTIONS TO DISMISS AND THE SPECIAL LITIGATION COMMITTEES (SLC)

Here, we assume a derivative suit is pending and the corporation wants it dismissed because, in the judgment of independent people, the case is not in the corporation's best interest. This might be true for a variety of reasons. For example, maybe the expense of litigation will exceed the anticipated recovery, or maybe corporate funds would be better spent on business activities, or maybe litigation will create publicity that will be harmful to the business. Such a determination must be made by disinterested, independent people, and not by those who are the defendants in the derivative suit. Usually these independent people will be outside directors serving on a committee.

Boards of directors may appoint committees (consisting of one or more directors) to perform various tasks (*see* § 7.4), including to consider whether litigation is in the company's best interest. A committee investigating this issue is usually called a "special litigation committee" (or SLC). Often, members of the committee will be new directors, brought onto the board specifically to serve on the SLC. This committee is required to investigate the facts and determine whether the case is in the company's best interest. If the SLC concludes that suit is not in that interest, the corporation may move to dismiss. In ruling on the motion to dismiss, what level of review does the court exercise?

There is an important clash of policies here. On the one hand, the law permits shareholders to file a derivative suit. On the other hand, whether the corporation should pursue the claim is a business decision, for which shareholders have no training. Rather, that decision is in the expertise of the board. But if the suit is against the board members, we are nervous that they will seek dismissal simply to save their own hides. So the law must balance the shareholder's undoubted right to *initiate* a derivative case with management's right, under proper circumstances, to determine whether the suit should *proceed*. This balance will be affected by the type of claim asserted.

When the derivative suit is against a third party, such as a supplier who breached a contract with the corporation, courts are very deferential to the SLC. In these cases no director or officer is a defendant, so the SLC's conclusion that the case should be dismissed is reviewed by the business judgment rule (*see* § 9.4). Unless the plaintiff can show that the SLC members were so lacking in diligence that they breached the duty of care, the court will honor the SLC conclusion and dismiss the case.

Derivative cases against directors or officers stand on a different footing. Again, we always insist that members of the SLC be independent and disinterested. Nonetheless, we are nervous that members of the SLC might try to help their fellow directors. This is the fear of "structural bias": that even independent directors will look at the defendants and say "there but for the Grace of God go I," and try to get the case dismissed.

Historically, everybody assumed that the plaintiff in a derivative suit against directors or officers simply had a right to initiate *and to pursue* litigation against a director or officer. A committee could not try to get the case dismissed. This view started changing, however, with *Gall v. Exxon Corp*, 418 F.Supp. 508, 517 (S.D.N.Y. 1976). In that case, a federal court permitted a disinterested SLC to seek dismissal based upon its conclusion that the case was not in the company's best interest. The court was properly concerned with whether the SLC was independent of the alleged wrongdoers. Rather than forbid the motion to dismiss, however, the court assessed whether the SLC consisted of truly disinterested persons and had undertaken a reasonable investigation.

Today, motions to dismiss derivative suits against directors or officers, based upon SLC determinations, are commonplace. But the level of intrusiveness of a court's inquiry in such motions varies from state to state. Under the traditional approach, the court's scope of review of the SLC decision is determined by whether demand on directors was required or excused (*see* § 15.4, subpart D). Recall that demand is excused if it would be futile (for example, if a majority of the board was accused of wrongdoing).

In Delaware, in a "demand required" case (one in which making the demand on the board was not futile) the court generally will grant the motion to dismiss based upon the SLC recommendation. This makes sense. If the demand was required, there was no conflict of interest and the board's decision should be protected by the business judgment rule.

Things are different, however, in a "demand excused" case (one in which making the demand on the board would have been futile). Here, under Delaware law, as established in *Zapata Corp. v. Maldonado*, 430 A.2d 779, 788–89 (Del. 1981), the court must assess two things, one of which is procedural and the other substantive.

First, the court must review the "the independence and good faith" of the SLC. The corporation has the burden on this point, and must show not only that members of the SLC were independent, but that the committee undertook a reasonable investigation and had reasonable bases for its findings and recommendation. The court may permit limited discovery on these topics. Second, assuming the first requirement is met, the court must undertake an independent review of the substance of the SLC's recommendation. The judge is to apply her "own independent business judgment" to determine whether the case is in the best interest of the corporation. This substantive assessment is surprising, because it requires the court to make precisely the types of business judgments courts are not trained to make.

Many states part company with Delaware on this second prong of its analysis is "demand excused" cases. That is, many courts in such cases will grant the motion to dismiss if they conclude that the SLC members were truly independent and undertook a reasonable investigation. Stated another way, these courts will dismiss the derivative suit if the first prong of the *Zapata* test is satisfied; they reject the second prong of Delaware's *Zapata* test.

Again, every state agrees that members of the SLC must be independent and disinterested. But who appoints them? Sometimes, the members of the SLC will be appointed by tainted directors (that is, by directors who are not independent and disinterested, such as defendants in the derivative suit). In a perfect world, this would not happen. In a perfect world, members of the SLC would be appointed by independent and disinterested directors. But ours is not a perfect world, and, pragmatically, we address our concern about such "structural bias" with the requirement that the members of the SLC be independent and disinterested.

Now let's review the procedure under the MBCA. Recall from § 15.4, subpart D, that demand on the board of directors is never excused under the MBCA. Accordingly, there is no bifurcation between "demand required" and "demand excused" cases. Section 7.44(a) of MBCA *requires* a court to dismiss if these underlying requirements are met: (1) an appropriate group determines (2) in good faith after a reasonable inquiry that (3) the derivative suit is not in the corporation's best interest. Unlike Delaware law in *Zapata,* the MBCA does not permit the court to undertake an independent investigation and use its own business judgment to determine whether the derivative litigation is in the company's best interest. It focuses wholly on the procedural components of independence and reasonable investigation.

MBCA § 7.44(b) defines the appropriate group who may make the recommendation to dismiss—and focuses on the notion of a "qualified" director. This is defined in MBCA § 1.43 as one without a material interest in the outcome and without a close relationship with such a person. In addition, MBCA § 7.44(e) permits the court, on motion by the corporation, to appoint a panel of qualified persons to make the determination. So if there are no qualified directors on the board, MBCA § 7.44(e) avoids the need to recruit new directors to serve on the SLC.

If the plaintiff filed the derivative suit after the board rejected her demand, § 7.44(c) requires that she allege in detail facts showing either that a majority of the board was tainted or that the underlying requirements of § 7.44(a) were not met.

More interestingly, § 7.44(d) allocates the burden of proof in a way reminiscent of the "demand required" and "demand excused" bifurcation under traditional law. If, when the board rejected the demand, a majority of the board was qualified, the plaintiff must prove that the underlying requirements of § 7.44(a) were not met. If, however, a majority of the board was tainted (and thus not qualified), the corporation must demonstrate that the requirements of § 7.44(a) were satisfied.

## § 15.6 DISCONTINUANCE OR SETTLEMENT OF A DERIVATIVE SUIT

Statutes uniformly provide that a derivative suit "may not be discontinued or settled without the court's approval." MBCA § 7.45. In addition, most statutes provide that if the court determines that a proposed discontinuance or settlement will "substantially affect" the interests of shareholders, "the court shall direct that notice be given to the shareholders affected."

Most derivative suits (like most cases generally) are settled and do not go to trial. In reviewing proposed settlements, courts consider all relevant factors, including the size of the potential recovery in litigation versus the size of the proposed settlement, the possibility of success in litigation, the financial position of the defendants, and the reasonableness of the proposed fee to be paid to the plaintiff's lawyer (who usually works on a contingent fee basis). The settlement should lay out responsibility for various litigation expenses.

One reason for giving notice to shareholders is to solicit their input on the terms of the proposed settlement. Shareholders may appear at the settlement hearing to object. The exercise, however, is not one in democracy; no vote is taken, and the decision whether to approve settlement is entirely for the judge. A court-approved settlement ordinarily has the same effect as a final judgment on the merits, though problems may arise as to whether shareholders are bound if they were not notified of the proposed settlement. So another reason for giving notice to shareholders is to ensure that the settlement will bind them.

## § 15.7 WHO REALLY PAYS? INDEMNIFICATION STATUTES

One should not lightly assume the responsibilities of serving as a director or officer. The jobs are rigorous and the fiduciary duties exacting. Moreover, such people are targets for litigation, sometimes justified and sometimes baseless. Litigation expenses and attorney's fees can be catastrophic, so many people refuse to serve in management positions unless they are protected from exposure—both to liability and to the costs of litigation. Every state permits corporations to protect directors and officers from such risks.

Corporations may provide three layers of protection. Whether to do so, and to what extent, are business decisions to be answered by each company. As a general rule, public corporations provide all three layers to the maximum extent permitted. One layer is a provision in the articles exculpating directors and officers from personal liability. The second is liability insurance. These are discussed in § 15.8. The focus here is the third layer of protection: indemnification statutes.

Indemnification means reimbursement; the corporation reimburses its director or officer for expenses and attorney's fees incurred in the suit against her. Usually, she will have been sued "by or on behalf of the corporation." This means that she was sued by the company or in a derivative suit for allegedly breaching a duty to the corporation. Indemnification statutes may apply in other cases as well, such as criminal prosecutions of a director or officer. But we are concerned mainly with civil litigation brought against someone *because of her role* as a director or officer.

Indemnification raises interesting public policy questions. Clearly, we should not use corporate funds to avoid the consequences of improper conduct. Directors and officers who misbehave should be liable for the judgment against them and should have to pay their legal expenses and attorney's fees too. On the other hand, one who is vindicated in litigation has a legitimate claim that the corporation should pay her expenses and attorney's fees. (What should we do, though, if the director or officer settled the case against her? Keep that one in mind as we consider the possibilities.)

These matters are handled by statute. Though the terms vary from state to state, the provisions of the MBCA are typical. If you study the provisions of particular states, however, be careful about whether they apply to both directors and officers. Though the MBCA provisions discussed below refer only to directors, MBCA § 8.56(a)(1) provides that a corporation may indemnify officers to the same extent. (So throughout our discussion we will refer to directors, but could also speak about officers.)

Let's assume that D has been sued for some alleged breach of duty as a director. She has incurred litigation expenses and attorney's fees. She may have settled the case, which means she will have written a check to the corporation in return for dismissal. Or perhaps the litigation resulted in her having to pay a judgment to the corporation or a fine to some regulatory body. She now turns to the corporation and seeks reimbursement for these expenditures. Her case will fall within one of three categories.

<u>Category 1: when is indemnification required?</u> Under MBCA § 8.52, the corporation must indemnify D if she "was wholly successful, on the merits or otherwise," in defending the suit brought against her. This means that in the underlying case brought against her, D won a judgment. It makes great sense that the corporation should be required to reimburse D all her expenses and fees. Though she was accused of wrongdoing, the litigation vindicated her.

Note that she did not have to win on the merits of the case. In other words, winning on a technicality, such as improper venue, or that the plaintiff lacked standing to bring a derivative suit, is just as good as winning a jury verdict. Notice also that under the MBCA she must win the entire case. Section 8.52

requires that she was "wholly successful" in the suit against her. Not all states are so stringent. In some, D is entitled to reimbursement "to the extent" that she was successful.

- D was sued on three claims. She won a judgment on two of those claims and settled the third. She does not qualify for mandatory indemnification under the MBCA, because she was not "wholly successful" (because she won on only two of three claims). But in states mandating indemnification "to the extent" she was successful, D would be entitled to reimbursement for all expenses and attorney's fees incurred in litigating the two claims she won.

<u>Category 2: when is indemnification prohibited?</u> In most states, the corporation is prohibited from indemnifying D is she was "held" or "adjudged" liable to the corporation. That means that the issue was actually adjudicated and there was a court finding of liability. In such a case, there was a finding that D breached a duty to the corporation. It makes sense that she should be personally liable for the judgment and her own expenses and attorney's fees.

Some state provisions are narrower in this regard, however. Under MBCA § 8.51(d)(2), the corporation cannot reimburse if D was "adjudged liable on the basis that [she] received a financial benefit to which [she] was not entitled." Thus, if the court found that D breached the duty of care (which does not involve an improper financial benefit to D), the corporation would not be prohibited from reimbursing D's litigation expenses and attorney's fees. (Under MBCA § 8.51(d)(1), however, the corporation could not reimburse D for the judgment against her.)

Category 3: when is indemnification permitted (or, in MBCA terms "permissible")? Every situation that does not satisfy Category 1 and does not satisfy Category 2 will fall into Category 3. One example, just noted, is when D is found liable for breach of the duty of care, but not for having received an improper financial benefit. Another example is when the case against D is settled.

- D is sued in a derivative suit and agrees to settle the case. Pursuant to the settlement, she paid $50,000 to the corporation. In the litigation, she incurred various legal expenses of $25,000 and attorney's fees of $200,000. Thus, D is out of pocket $275,000. She seeks reimbursement of that amount from the corporation.

This case does not fall within Category 1 because she did not win a judgment. It does not fall within Category 2 because the case settled, so there was no adjudication at all (and certainly no adjudication that she received an improper financial benefit). The case falls within Category 3, and the corporation may (but is not required to) reimburse her.

There are important questions as to whether the corporation should reimburse and, if so, for which amounts. To be eligible, D must show that she satisfied the standard for permissive indemnification. In most states, the standard is the same as in MBCA § 8.51(a)(1): D must demonstrate that (1) she acted in good faith and (2) with the reasonable belief that she acted in the corporation's best interest. By statute, the fact that the underlying case ended in settlement or a judgment or conviction is not itself determinative of whether D had met this standard. MBCA § 8.51(c). So none of those things creates a presumption that D did not act in good faith.

Every state specifies persons who may determine whether D is entitled to permissive indemnification. Under MBCA § 8.55(b), the decision is made by majority vote of qualified directors (or by a committee of two or more qualified directors). Instead, the decision may be made by vote of shareholders, not counting shares held by an interested director. Or, as another option, the decision may be made by special legal counsel.

If a proper group determines that D is entitled to permissive indemnification, what sums are reimbursed? Most statutes speak of "expenses" as including attorney's fees, so in the hypo above, D's $25,000 in expenses and $200,000 in attorney's fees could be reimbursed.

The bigger question concerns the amount she spent to settle the case. Settlements are inherently ambiguous; we do not know who would have won had the case been tried. Nonetheless, allowing D to recover the $50,000 she paid to settle the claim results in a strange circularity. D was accused of breaching a duty to the corporation. To settle the claim, she wrote a check to the corporation for

$50,000. If the corporation reimburses her for this, the corporation receives nothing as compensation for the alleged breach by D. Indeed, if the corporation pays D the full $275,000, it is actually worse off than if no suit had been brought; the corporation is out-of-pocket $275,000. If no suit had been brought, the corporation would have that $275,000 in its coffers.

Recognizing this problem, most states appear not to permit reimbursement for amounts paid to settle the underlying case, at least if the case against D was for breach of duty to the corporation (which it almost always will be). If the case was for something else—say, liability to a third party incurred in D's role as a director or officer—perhaps the corporation should reimburse her, assuming she meets the standard for permissive indemnification.

Section 8.51(d)(1) of the MBCA prohibits indemnification in a case brought by or on behalf of the corporation. It provides an exception, though, for reasonable "expenses," which can be reimbursed if D meets the standard for permissive indemnification. The Official Comment to that provision makes clear that expenses in this context do not include settlement amounts. (Under § 8.51(a), one can get indemnification from "liability," which includes settlement, but not in cases brought by or on behalf of the corporation.)

The indemnification statutes discussed to this point are augmented in most states by provisions allowing a *court* to order the corporation to indemnify a director. MBCA § 8.54(a)(3) is an example. It allows the court to order indemnification that would be "fair and reasonable" under the circumstances of the case. The authority to do so is strikingly broad. The court may order indemnification even of one who was adjudged liable to the corporation for breach of fiduciary duty! Such indemnity would be limited to expenses, including attorney's fees, and could not include the judgment entered against her.

Finally, states also permit (but do not require) the corporation to advance litigation expenses to a director during the litigation. This permits the defendant in a derivative case to avoid potentially enormous personal outlays for expenses and fees. The problem for the corporation is that advances are made before much is known about the merits of the litigation. The statutes permit such advances only if the director gives a written affirmation of her good faith belief that she has satisfied the requirements of permissive indemnification. In addition, she must make a written undertaking to repay funds advanced if it is determined that she did not. This undertaking need not be secured and the corporation may accept it without reference to the financial ability of the director to repay the advance. *See, e.g.,* MBCA § 8.53(b). The purpose of this latter provision is to avoid discrimination against less well-to-do directors.

Statutes also specify who may approve such advances. Under MBCA § 8.53(c), advances may be approved by qualified directors or by shareholders (not counting shares of the interested director). MBCA § 8.53(c). Corporations may make advances for expenses by a provision in the articles or bylaws, or by action by the directors or shareholders.

## § 15.8   EXCULPATORY PROVISIONS AND INSURANCE

*Smith v. Van Gorkom*, 488 A.2d 858 (Del. 1985) (§ 9.4, subpart B), sent shock waves through the corporate world because it imposed liability for breach of the duty of care in circumstances in which few observers expected it. In reaction to that decision, every state passed a statute permitting corporations to provide in their articles that directors (and in some states officers) will not be liable for damages in certain circumstances. These provisions vary from state to state, but MBCA § 2.02(b)(4) is typical. It says that the articles may include a provision "eliminating or limiting the liability of a director to the corporation or to its shareholders for money damages for any action taken, or any failure to take any action, as a director."

These "exculpation clauses" are widespread. Indeed, it is difficult to see why anyone would agree to serve as a director without such protection in the articles. In every state, though, the power to exculpate through such provisions is limited. Under the MBCA, exculpation is not permitted in cases involving (1) receipt of an improper financial benefit, (2) intentional infliction of harm on the corporation or shareholders, (3) approval of an unlawful distribution, or (4) intentional violation of criminal law. MBCA § 2.02(b)(4). Other states word the exceptions differently, but the upshot is similar everywhere: the articles can exculpate directors for liability for damages for breach of the duty of care, but not for breach of the duty of loyalty. (In § 9.5, we discussed case law concerning whether breach of the obligation of good faith could be exculpated.)

Corporations can also protect directors and officers with "D&O" liability insurance. This is purchased from third-party providers (insurance companies), but it is not cheap. However, such insurance can help at various levels. It can provide a source of money for a manager who is entitled to indemnification but whose corporation lack funds to pay it. It may also cover claims that the corporation elects not to indemnify.

The language of D&O policies varies considerably from issuer to issuer. Indeed, there is no standard-form policy for D&O insurance. Generally, D&O insurance can cover claims based on negligence, misconduct not involving dishonesty or knowing bad faith, and false or misleading statements in disclosure documents. Deliberately wrongful misconduct, dishonest acts, acts in bad faith, and violations of statutes such as § 16(b) (*see* § 14.5) are not covered. Applying for D&O policies requires broad disclosure of contingent or possible claims; failure to disclose known claims may permit the insurer to void the entire policy. Policies usually provide that expenses advanced by the insurer reduce the amount of insurance coverage provided.

Most states have statutes expressly permitting corporations to purchase D&O insurance. *See, e.g.*, MBCA § 8.57. Even without such authorization, the power to obtain such insurance is implicit in the universal corporate power to provide compensation for executives.

# CHAPTER 16

# FUNDAMENTAL
# CORPORATE CHANGES

## § 16.1  INTRODUCTION

This chapter addresses changes in the life of a corporation that are so profound that generally they cannot be approved merely by the board of directors. Unlike most management decisions, fundamental changes must also be approved by shareholders. In most states, these events are considered fundamental: (1) amendment of the articles of incorporation, (2) merging into another corporation, (3) acquisition of the company's stock in a "share exchange," (4) sale of substantially all the business assets, (5) conversion to another form or business, and (6) dissolution. We may add to this list involuntary dissolution, which is a fundamental change, but is the result of action not by the board and shareholders, but by a court or government official. Statutes on fundamental changes vary considerably from state to state, so one must be careful consult the appropriate legislation.

## § 16.2  PROCEDURE FOR
## FUNDAMENTAL CHANGES

In general, each fundamental corporate change except the involuntary dissolution is accomplished through a five-step process.

*First*, the board of directors approves the matter. In a few states, shareholders have the power to initiate amendment of the articles, but as a general rule there can be no fundamental change without the board's initiating it.

*Second*, the board must inform the shareholders that it recommends the fundamental change.

*Third*, the board calls a special meeting of shareholders to consider the change. If the shareholders approve, the change goes through. If they reject it, the fundamental change will not be made. In a few states, such as Ohio, the notice of the special meeting to consider a fundamental change must be sent to all shareholders—even those who do not have voting rights. In most states, however, notice goes to those shareholders entitled to vote.

Assuming that there is a quorum at the meeting of shareholders (*see* § 6.5), the shareholders will vote on whether to approve the fundamental change. On this issue, there are three approaches: the traditional, the majority, and the modern. Under the *traditional approach,* the change must be approved by *two-thirds of the shares entitled to vote*. This requirement is extraordinary for two reasons: it requires a supermajority (two-thirds), and it is a supermajority of the shares entitled to vote (and not simply of the shares present at the meeting).

- X Corp. has 6,000 shares entitled to vote on a fundamental change. Say 4,500 shares attend the meeting. At least 4,000 of those must vote "yes" to approve the proposal; we need two-thirds of the 6,000 entitled to vote, not two-thirds of the 4,500 present. Thus, if 3,800 shares attended the meeting, the deal could not be approved, because it would be impossible to get the "yes" votes of 4,000 shares.

Though the trend has been away from this supermajority requirement, several states, including Texas, Ohio, and Massachusetts, still adhere to it.

Under what appears to be the *majority approach,* the fundamental change must be approved by a *majority* of the shares *entitled to vote.* Note that the majority has to be of those *entitled* to vote, and not simply of those present or actually voting.

- X Corp. has 6,000 shares entitled to vote. At the meeting, 3,100 shares attend (so we have a quorum). At least 3,001 must vote "yes" to approve the fundamental change.

The *modern approach* is the most liberal, and is embraced by the MBCA. It requires approval by only a majority of the shares *actually voting* on the fundamental change. *See, e.g.,* MBCA §§ 10.03(e), 7.25(c).

- X Corp. has 6,000 shares entitled to vote. At the meeting, 3,100 shares attend (so we have a quorum), but only 2,800 shares actually vote on whether the fundamental change should be approved. All that is required under this view is for 1,401 shares to vote "yes."

*Fourth,* if the change is approved by shareholders, the corporation goes through with the change. But shareholders who opposed the change may have a "dissenting shareholders' right of appraisal," which allows them to force the corporation to buy their stock.

*Fifth*, in most fundamental changes, the corporation must inform the state by delivering a document summarizing the change, which is filed with the appropriate state officer.

## § 16.3  DISSENTING SHAREHOLDERS' RIGHT OF APPRAISAL

In the nineteenth century, fundamental corporate changes had to be approved by *every* shareholder. This gave each shareholder a right to veto; if even one shareholder voted "no," the transaction failed. Modern law rejects this idea and requires only approval by a designated percentage of the shares (*see* § 16.2). In lieu of a right to veto, modern law provides a shareholder who objects to the fundamental change a "right of appraisal."

This name is misleading. It is not a right to have your stock appraised. Instead, it is a right to force the corporation to buy your stock at "fair value." Statutes in each state create this right and prescribe detailed steps for exercising it. Failure to adhere to the (rather picky) rules will result in waiver of the right.

It is important to scour the relevant statutes to determine which fundamental changes will trigger the right of appraisal. This varies from state to state. For instance, in some states, an amendment of the articles (at least, one that will harm a class of shareholders) gives rise to a right of appraisal (for the shareholders harmed). In most states, though, amendment of the articles does not trigger the right of appraisal. In some states, shareholders of both corporations in a merger (the disappearing corporation and the surviving corporation) have the right of appraisal. In others, however, only the shareholders of the disappearing corporation will have it. In most states, only shareholders who were entitled to vote on the fundamental change will have the right of appraisal. In a few states, though, even holders of non-voting stock will be able to exercise the right.

Speaking very generally, the right exists for holders of voting stock in the disappearing corporation in a merger, for shareholders of a corporation that transfers substantially all its assets, and for shareholders of a company whose shares are acquired in a "share exchange."

But even if a corporation is engaged in one of these changes, there is an important limitation on the availability of the right of appraisal. In most states, the right of appraisal is not available if the company's stock is publicly traded or if the corporation has a large number of shareholders (usually 2,000 or more). This means that the right of appraisal exists in close corporations. And this makes sense. If the corporation's stock is publicly traded, or if there is a large number of shareholders, the disgruntled shareholder does not need a right of appraisal. She can simply sell her stock on the public market. This is why appraisal statutes speak of a shareholder's recovering the "fair value," and not the fair *market* value of her stock. In a close corporation, there is no *market* for the stock.

In most states, shareholders must take three steps to exercise their right of appraisal. First, before the shareholders vote on the matter, the dissenting shareholder must file with the corporation a statement of her objection to the proposed change and of her intent to demand payment if the deal is approved. Second, the shareholder must abstain or vote against the proposed change. And third, within a set time (usually 20 days) after official notification from the corporation that the change was approved, the shareholder must make a written demand to be bought out and tender her stock to the corporation. *See, e.g.*, Del. § 262; MBCA § 13.21.

The burden then falls to the corporation to accept or reject the shareholder's demand. The corporation may reject the demand and offer a lower figure. The shareholder may accept that lower figure or reject it. At some point, depending upon the statute, either the corporation or the shareholder will file suit for an appraisal. Often, the corporation must do this within 60 days of the shareholder's demand; failure to file suit may mean that the corporation is bound to pay the shareholder the amount she demanded. In some states, the shareholder must institute litigation if she and the corporation do not agree on the value of her stock.

When the matter is litigated, the courts in most states will appoint an appraiser to assess the value of the stock. But how does an appraiser or a judge set the value? The goal is to determine the value "immediately before" the fundamental change took place. For example, the court would assess the value of the shareholder's stock immediately before the company merged or before it sold off all its assets. After the litigation, courts in many states are empowered to award attorney's fees either to or against the corporation depending upon the good faith with which the parties set their estimates of fair value.

Delaware courts developed a method of assessing stock value called the "Delaware block" or "weighted averages" method. This method looks to three factors: net asset value, earnings per share, and market value of the company before the fundamental change took place. (Just because there is not a public market for the stock of a close corporation does not mean there is not a market for sale of the overall business; that is what the third factor looks at.) The court then weights these factors as it sees fit on the facts of the case. For instance, it might multiply net asset value by 40 percent, earnings per share by 30 percent, and market value of the company by 30 percent. Academic literature criticized this method, principally for being too subjective.

As a consequence, courts have moved away from the Delaware block method and embraced other accounting models for setting the appraisal price. Even the Delaware Supreme Court held that the block method shall no longer "exclusively control" in appraisal proceedings. *Weinberger v. UOP, Inc.*, 457 A.2d 701, 713 (Del. 1983). The court in that case instructed judges to take "a more liberal approach," including "proof of value by any techniques or methods which are generally considered acceptable in the financial community and otherwise admissible in court." The result is that valuation is set by models created not by lawyers but by accountants, and that are studied in detail not in law schools but in business schools. *See, e.g.*, Bernhard Grossfield, *Lawyers and Accountants: A Semiotic Competition*, 36 WAKE FOREST L. REV. 167 (2001).

After determining the value of the dissenting shareholder's stock, some courts discount that value in one of two ways. A "minority discount" punishes the shareholder for not having enough voting strength to affect corporate decision-making. A "lack of marketability" discount punishes the shareholder for the fact that there is no market on which she can sell her stock. Neither discount makes sense. By definition, the shareholder will hold a minority of the stock. If she held a majority, she could have blocked the fundamental change from being approved. And by definition, there is no market for her stock, because we are dealing here with close corporations. So both discounts are inconsistent with the statutory goal of setting the fair value of the stock, which should simply be the shareholder's pro-rata share of the value of the company. Accordingly, courts increasingly reject minority and lack-of-marketability discounts. *See, e.g., HMO-W, Inc. v. SSM Health Care System*, 611 N.W.2d 250, 255 (Wisc. 2000) (rejecting minority discount but not ruling on lack-of-marketability discount because not properly raised on appeal).

Is the right of appraisal the shareholder's exclusive remedy for any of the various fundamental changes? In some states, the answer is yes. In most, however, appraisal seems to be the exclusive remedy unless the action taken was fraudulent or oppressive. The typical argument is that a merger or other fundamental change was undertaken not for some legitimate corporate purpose, but to squeeze out minority shareholders. Shareholders in such a case will argue that they should be able to sue to rescind the merger (or other fundamental change), and should not be limited to the right of appraisal. If the fundamental change has already been realized, the shareholders may sue for "rescissory damages," which is a monetary recovery that would put them in the position they would be in had the change not been approved.

An example is *Coggins v. New England Patriots Football Club, Inc.*, 492 N.E.2d 1112, 1118–19 (Mass. 1986). In that case, Sullivan borrowed millions of dollars to purchase all the voting stock of the corporation that owned the New England Patriots. As a condition of the loan, however, banks insisted that Sullivan reorganize the corporation so its income would be devoted to repaying the loan. In addition, the lenders required that the loan had to be secured by corporate assets (and not only by the stock). To satisfy these conditions, Sullivan had to get rid of minority shareholders, all of whom owned nonvoting stock. He designed a merger under which the minority shareholders received a cash payment of $15 per share and no longer held any equity in the corporation. The merger was approved through the statutory procedure. A group of minority shareholders sued Sullivan for oppressive behavior. They asserted that Sullivan owed them a fiduciary obligation, and that he breached it by engineering the merger.

The Massachusetts Supreme Judicial Court held for the shareholders. First, the right of appraisal is not exclusive if plaintiffs show a breach of fiduciary duty. Second, the merger constituted such a breach because it was not supported by a legitimate business reason. The purpose of the merger was to permit Sullivan to get a personal loan so he could buy all the stock of the corporation. Thus, the court concluded, Sullivan, as controlling shareholder, breached a duty to the minority. Finally, while the normal remedy would be an injunction against the merger or rescission, on the facts of the case neither remedy would work. Why? The case did not get to the court until a decade after the merger, so undoing the deal was infeasible. Instead, the plaintiffs could recover "rescissory damages," which would be the present value of the minority shareholders' stock. Because the Patriots had increased markedly in value over that decade, the minority shareholders recovered far more than the $15 merger cash-out price.

Under *Coggins,* the plaintiff bears the initial burden of showing self-dealing by the defendant. If she makes this showing, the burden shifts to the defendant to show: (1) a legitimate business (as opposed to personal) purpose for the transaction and (2) that the transaction was fair to minority shareholders. Because Sullivan could not show a business reason for the merger, the court was not required to address the question of fairness.

Delaware courts also permit aggrieved minority shareholders to sue for breach of duty in the merger context. Unlike the Massachusetts court, though, courts in Delaware do not assess whether there was a business purpose for the transaction. Instead, as established in *Weinberger v. UOP, Inc.*, 457 A.2d 701, 709 (Del. 1983), after the plaintiff shows self-dealing, the defendant must assume the burden of showing that the deal was fair under the "entire fairness test" (sometimes called the "intrinsic fairness test"). This is a rigorous standard, under which the defendant must show that the transaction was: (1) procedurally fair (looking at the overall course of dealing, such as who initiated the deal) and (2) substantively fair (looking at the price).

It is worth emphasizing that not every objection to a fundamental change will justify a suit for rescission or rescissory damages. Indeed, as the Delaware Supreme Court recognized in *Weinberger*, if the shareholder's complaint is that the financial terms of a cash-out merger are inadequate, appraisal will be her only remedy. States also take differing approaches as to whether claims of fraudulent or otherwise unlawful behavior may be addressed in the appraisal proceeding or whether they have to be litigated separately. Most courts seem to reach the common-sense conclusion that the questions may be litigated in a single proceeding. *See, e.g., HMO-W, Inc. v. SSM Health Care System*, 611 N.W.2d 250, 259 (Wisc. 2000).

Finally, note that the assertion of appraisal rights can create severe cash drains for the corporation. Thus, it is common for merger and other agreements to provide an "out" if large numbers of shareholders assert their rights of appraisal.

## § 16.4  AMENDMENT TO THE ARTICLES OF INCORPORATION

An amendment to the articles is a fundamental corporate change. As such, it can be accomplished only though the procedure discussed in § 16.2. (In some states, relatively minor changes, such as changing the registered agent, may be accomplished by the board without shareholder approval.) Why would anyone want to amend the articles? One common reason is to increase the number of authorized shares. So if the corporation has issued all the stock authorized in its original articles, an amendment is necessary if the corporation is to raise capital by issuing more stock. Another common reason is to add an exculpatory clause to the articles (*see* § 15.8).

What happens if an amendment is harmful to a particular group of shareholders? For instance, the articles might be amended to delete dividend rights or voting rights for a specific class of stock. In relatively early times, some courts concluded that shareholders had a "contractual" or "vested" right in articles provisions, and that such provisions could not be amended over the objection of those shareholders. Modern law rejects this theory. MBCA § 10.01(b) is typical in providing that no shareholder has a "vested property right" to any articles provision.

This does not mean that shareholders are powerless in the face of amendments that hurt them. Most states seem to provide one of two protections. One is the right of appraisal (*see* § 16.3). Specifically, in some states, if an amendment "materially and adversely affects" a shareholder, she has the right to force the corporation to buy her out (assuming the various requirements of the appraisal statute are satisfied). The other protection, provided in lieu of a right of appraisal, is "class voting." This requires that the amendment be approved not only by the appropriate percentage of all shares, but by a like percentage of shares in the affected class. Under this regime, if the class to be affected by the amendment does not approve the amendment, it will not be made.

Beyond this, a shareholder aggrieved by an amendment may be able to sue for breach of fiduciary obligation. Some courts allow minority shareholders to sue concerning harmful amendments to articles that serve no purpose other than to harm them. An example is *Byelick v. Vivadelli*, 79 F.Supp.2d 610 (E.D. Va. 1999), which we discussed at § 12.3, subpart E. Some states would not permit suit, but would instead find the statutory protections of appraisal rights or class voting to be exclusive.

## § 16.5  MERGER, CONSOLIDATION, AND SHARE EXCHANGE

A.    *Terminology, Background, and Successor Liability.* This section addresses the ways in which separate business entities may be combined. Usually, such combinations are undertaken as a way for one company to acquire another. There are different ways to accomplish this goal. The choice will depend not only on corporate law, but on business and tax considerations, which are beyond our scope.

A *merger* involves two existing corporations, with one combining into the other. For instance, X Corp. merges into Y Corp. X Corp. disappears and Y Corp. survives. Technically, a *consolidation* involves two existing corporations, both of which disappear to form a new entity: X Corp. and Y Corp. consolidate to form Z Corp. X Corp. and Y Corp. disappears and Z Corp. survives. Increasingly, states consider the consolidation obsolete, because it is usually advantageous to have one of the extant corporations survive, and if a new entity is desired, it can simply be created and the existing corporations merged into it. Accordingly, the law in many states, and in the MBCA, simply does not provide for consolidations. On the other hand, Delaware retains the consolidation. *See* Del. § 251(a). (Throughout this section, we will refer to "mergers," but the discussion applies to consolidations as well.)

A merger is always a fundamental change for a corporation that will cease to exist. Thus, the transaction must be approved not only by the board of directors, but by the shareholders of that corporation, under the procedure detailed in § 16.2. Increasingly, as reflected in MBCA § 11.04(h)(1) (in prior versions this was 11.04(g)(1)), a merger or consolidation is not considered a fundamental change for the surviving corporation. Under the MBCA, then, the shareholders of that corporation will have no voice in whether the merger is approved. They cannot vote and will not have the right of appraisal. In some states, however, the merger or consolidation is a fundamental change for the surviving corporation unless specific statutory factors are met. For example, in Delaware, shareholders of a surviving corporation do not vote if the transaction will not amend that company's articles and if the corporation will not issue an additional 20 percent of stock in consummating the deal. Del. § 251(f).

One abiding characteristic of a merger is "successor liability." This means that the surviving company will succeed to the rights and liabilities of the disappearing company. The doctrine protects creditors; if they had a claim against a company that disappeared in a merger, successor liability assures that they now may assert that claim against the surviving company.

The classic merger is a stock-for-stock transaction in which two similarly-sized corporations combine. The shareholders of the disappearing corporation give up their stock in that company and receive stock of the surviving corporation. In fact, for generations, that was the only form a merger could take. Modern statutes are far more flexible, and permit paying off the shareholders of the disappearing corporation in stock or other securities, in options to acquire stock or other securities, or in "cash, other property, or any combination of the foregoing." MBCA § 11.02(c)(3).

B.     _Triangular and Reverse Triangular, Cash-Out, and Other Mergers._ Suppose one company (the "aggressor" company, or A Co.) wants to acquire another (called the "target" or T Co.). The two could set up a merger, with T Co. merging into A Co. Then, however, under the doctrine of successor liability, A Co. would assume the obligations of T Co.

Instead, the parties might engineer a _triangular merger_. Here, A Co. forms a wholly-owned subsidiary ("Sub Co."). A Co capitalizes Sub Co. with cash or with A Co. stock. A Co. owns all the stock of Sub Co. Then T Co. merges into Sub Co. The shareholders of T Co. receive the cash or A Co. stock with which Sub Co. was capitalized. Sub Co. receives all the stock of T Co. As a result, (1) A Co. acquires all the stock of T Co. (because A Co.'s subsidiary now owns all that stock); (2) the shareholders of T Co. get either stock in A Co. or cash (in which case they hold no stock in any of the companies); and (most importantly) (3) A Co. does not assume responsibility for the liabilities of T Co. (Sub Co., as survivor of the merger, does that).

Why go through all this? In most of these deals, A Co. and T Co. are publicly traded corporations with widely-held stock, and the subsidiary is formed solely to facilitate the acquisition. Thus, the transaction may be substantially cheaper than a direct merger between A Co. and T Co., because the parties do not have to pay for a shareholder vote in a public corporation. More significantly, as noted, A Co. acquires T Co. without assuming direct liability for T Co.'s obligations.

Another possibility is the *reverse triangular merger*. Here, A Co. forms a wholly-owned subsidiary (Sub Co.), but Sub Co. then merges *into* T Co. In the merger between Sub Co. and T Co., shareholders of T Co. get the stock of Sub Co., which is exchanged for cash or perhaps for stock in A Co. As a result, T Co. ends up being a wholly-owned subsidiary of A Co.

The critical point is that both triangular and reverse-triangular mergers involve three-way transactions by which T Co. becomes a wholly-owned subsidiary of A Co. without a transfer or assignment directly between the two. T Co.'s shareholders receive cash or shares of the A Co. even though the merger is with a subsidiary of that corporation.

A *cash-out merger* is exactly what it sounds like: shareholders of the target company give up their stock in the target in exchange for cash. Such transactions are also called *freeze out* or *squeeze out* mergers because they freeze or squeeze these shareholders out of their equity interest. Before the deal goes through, these persons are equity holders; afterward, they are not.

In a typical cash-out merger, X Corp. is merged into Y Corp. The majority shareholders of X Corp. receive stock in Y Corp and the minority shareholders of X Corp. receive cash or other property. This procedure can be used to force out unwanted minority shareholders, or to eliminate public ownership as part of a "going private" transaction (to cease being a publicly-traded company). There are legitimate reasons to cash out the minority shareholders, but such a transaction can also be oppressive. We address fiduciary issues raised in such cases in subpart D below.

Many mergers are between parent and subsidiary corporations. If the parent will be the surviving company, it is an *upstream merger*. If the subsidiary survives, it is a *downstream merger*. A downstream merger can be used to change the state of incorporation of a publicly held corporation. The corporation creates a wholly-owned subsidiary in the new state and then merges itself into its subsidiary. The stock and financial interests of the parent are mirrored in the stock and financial structure of the subsidiary. When the merger occurs, each shareholder and creditor of the old publicly held corporation incorporated in State A automatically becomes a shareholder and creditor of a corporation incorporated in State B.

Many states have adopted statutes that provide a special summary merger procedure, called a *short-form merger*, for upstream or downstream mergers in which the parent owns a large majority (usually 90 percent or more) of the stock of the subsidiary. The short-form merger allows a parent to merge its subsidiary into it (or vice versa) without a shareholder vote in either corporation. Moreover, the board of directors of the subsidiary is not required to approve the merger. *See* MBCA § 11.05.

The short-form procedure is based on the reality that the minority shareholders of the subsidiary cannot block approval of the merger. After all, the parent corporation already owns at least 90 percent of the stock of the subsidiary. In some states, the minority shareholders of the subsidiary will have appraisal rights, even though they did not vote on the deal.

C.    *Share Exchange.* Some states, following the lead of MBCA § 11.03, recognize a fundamental corporate change called the *share exchange.* It is a substitute for the reverse triangular merger, discussed in the preceding subsection. The name is misleading; it is not an exchange of shares, but a device that compels a sale of stock. In other words, it forces the shareholders of a target company (T Co.) to sell their stock to the acquiring company (A Co.). The result is that A Co. gets all the stock of T Co., and the T Co. shareholders end up with cash or other property.

The share exchange is a fundamental change only for the target company. Accordingly, the transaction must be approved through the procedure discussed in § 16.2. If it is, all shareholders must relinquish their stock under the terms of the exchange (even those who opposed the deal). A dissenting shareholder of the target company may assert appraisal rights. Because the share exchange is not a fundamental change for the acquiring company, its shareholders do not vote on the transaction and do not have a right of appraisal.

D.    *Fiduciary Issues in Mergers.* Mergers, like any fundamental change, can be used to oppress minority shareholders:

- X, Y, and Z are the shareholders of XYZ Corp. Each owns one-third of the stock. After a disagreement, X and Y cause XYZ Corp. to merge into XY Co., which they own. X, Y, and Z receive cash under the terms of the merger. X and Y run XY Corp., which now has acquired the former XYZ Co. Z is out of luck—she has some cash, but no equity position.

What can Z do? The starting point is his statutory right of appraisal, by which she can force the corporation to buy her stock for fair value, which may be a higher figure than the cash-out merger price she was paid. The big question will be whether the right of appraisal is the exclusive remedy. In some states, it is. In others, however, Z may be able to sue if the transaction was tinged with fraud or oppression (*see* § 16.3).

## § 16.6  DISPOSITION OF ALL OR SUBSTANTIALLY ALL ASSETS

A corporation's disposing of all (or "substantially all") of its assets, "not in the ordinary course of business," is a fundamental change. *See, e.g.*, MBCA § 12.02. As such, it must be approved by the procedure detailed in § 16.2. For starters, though, why would a corporation want to do this? Often, it will sell off its assets before undergoing a voluntary dissolution and going out of business. In the voluntary dissolution, it will (after paying creditors) distribute the proceeds of the sale of assets to its shareholders. So sometimes this course is the first step in ending the company's existence. Or, as another possibility, the business may sell its assets to raise cash, which it can then use to expand and grow.

Whatever the reason, this is a fundamental change only for the company disposing of its assets. It is *not a fundamental change for the company buying the assets.* This means that the buying corporation need not go through the procedure in § 16.2. Thus, the shareholders of the buying corporation do not get to vote on the deal, and do not have rights of appraisal. This makes sense, because when you own stock in a company, you expect it to go out and acquire things. But you do not expect your company to sell off all its assets. If your company does so, you as a shareholder would expect to have a vote, and would expect rights of appraisal if the deal goes through.

We now focus on three statutory terms. First, what is a "disposition" of all assets? Everyone agrees that a *sale* qualifies. Most states seem to agree that leasing or exchanging the assets for other property is a "disposition." On the other hand, mortgaging or pledging the assets (for a loan, for instance) is not a "disposition."

Second, while a disposition of "all" assets is covered, what would qualify as a disposition of "substantially all" the assets? Courts have not been consistent on this score, but have been flexible, and have required shareholder approval when significant components of the company are disposed of, even though other significant components are retained.

Third, note that disposition of all or substantially all assets is only a fundamental change if it is "not in the ordinary course of business." Some corporations are in the business of selling their assets. For example, a company that buys and sells real estate routinely sells its assets. But most businesses do not do this, and it will be obvious when a sale of assets is not in the ordinary course.

There is an important distinction between disposition of assets, on the one hand, and mergers and consolidations, on the other. As we saw in § 16.5, with such combinations, at least one business entity ceases to exist. Thus, we expect successor liability: the surviving company succeeds to the rights and liabilities of the entities that disappear. In the sale of assets, however, no entity disappears. The company that sold its assets still exists (and, indeed, now should have considerable cash, because it just sold all its assets). Because the company selling off its assets still exists, a creditor of the selling corporation can sue it. And if the selling corporation dissolves, it will have to discharge its liabilities before distributing assets to shareholders. Accordingly, as a general rule, we do *not* expect successor liability in a sale of assets.

There are exceptions to this rule. One is when the sale provides otherwise. Thus the company buying assets may agree in the sale to assume liabilities of the selling company. (Presumably, doing so will permit the buyer to buy the assets for a lower price.) Another exception is the "mere continuation" doctrine. Under this, if the corporation buying assets is a mere continuation of the selling company, the court will apply successor liability. For instance, if the buying company has the same management and engaged in the same business as the selling company, a court may equate the two corporations and find the buyer to have assumed the seller's obligations. Finally, another exception is the "de facto merger" doctrine, by which a court concludes that what was consummated as a sale of assets was "really" a merger.

Many cases dealing with these exceptions to the general rule involve product liability claims. In *Franklin v. USX Corp.*, 105 Cal.Rptr.2d 11, 17–19 (Cal.App. 2001), plaintiff's decedent died of lung cancer allegedly caused by her exposure to asbestos when she was a child. Her parents worked for Western Pipe & Steel Shipyard (WPS) in the 1940s, and allegedly were exposed to asbestos at work, which they brought home unwittingly on their clothing, thereby exposing the plaintiff's decedent. WPS sold its assets to Consolidated of California (Con Cal) in 1945 for $6.2 million in cash, and the buyer agreed to assume the liabilities of WPS. Con Cal sold its assets to Consolidated of Delaware (Con Del) in 1948 for $17 million. Later, Con Del was merged into United States Steel (USX). Plaintiff argued that the subsequent companies assumed WPS's liability from the 1940s. Thus, he asserted, USX was liable for the product liability claim filed decades later.

Clearly, Con Cal was liable for claims against WPS, since the deal between them said so. And clearly, USX was liable for Con Del's claims, because successor liability would attach to their deal (because it was a merger). The question was whether Con Del assumed the liabilities of Con Cal when it bought its assets in 1945. The trial court held that it did. Though the transaction was a sale of assets, and not a merger, the trial court found that it was a "de facto merger" and thus that successor liability attached.

The California Court of Appeal reversed. It reviewed the case law on "mere continuation" and "de facto merger" and reached an interesting conclusion: no case had ever imposed successor liability in a sale of assets if the sale was for adequate consideration. Stated another way, courts will impose successor liability in a sale of assets only if the sale was for inadequate capital. Reviewing the facts, the court found that the purchase of assets for $17 million in 1945 was adequate. Indeed, plaintiff did not argue that there was insufficient consideration to meet the claims of creditors at the time Con Cal sold to Con Del and subsequently dissolved.

Successor liability in a sale of assets might be analogized to piercing the corporate veil on the basis of undercapitalization (*see* § 10.4). Just as shareholders of a close corporation might be held personally liable for corporate debts if they failed to invest enough capital to cover prospective liabilities when forming the company, so a buyer of assets may incur successor liability if he failed to pay sufficient capital for the assets.

## § 16.7  CONVERSION

Historically, if we wanted to change business forms—say, from a corporation to a limited liability company or a partnership—we had to dissolve the corporation and form the new business. Increasingly, this is unnecessary, as states have begun to embrace a new fundamental change, the conversion. This device allows a corporation to convert to any other form of business by going through the procedure discussed in § 16.2. Those states permitting conversion provide that a dissenting shareholder has appraisal rights, which we discussed in § 16.3. Under the MBCA, the process is called "entity conversion," MBCA §§ 9.50–9.56, and it triggers appraisal rights, MBCA § 13.02(a)(8).

## § 16.8  DISSOLUTION

A.    *Background.* Dissolution is the ultimate fundamental change for a business. Though various events may trigger dissolution, dissolution is a *process* that may take considerable time to accomplish. At the end of the process, the corporate existence will cease. Some recent statutes, such as the Texas Business Organizations Code, § 11.101, use "termination" instead of dissolution, but the process is the same. We will discuss that process in subpart E below. There are three types of dissolution.

B.    *Voluntary Dissolution.* Here, the entity "decides" to dissolve. This is a fundamental change, and the procedure discussed in § 16.2 is followed. Thus, in most states, the board of directors and the shareholders must approve the voluntary dissolution. In some states, the pattern is different. For instance, in New York, voluntary dissolution is effected by vote of the shares, and does not require board of director action. NY Bus. Corp. Law § 1001(a).

However voluntary dissolution is triggered, at some point in the process, the corporation must give notice to creditors. This will ensure the orderly payment of obligations. Moreover, the board of directors must ensure that all franchise and other taxes have been paid. And, as we will see in subpart E below, creditors must be paid before shareholders receive liquidation distributions.

There is no right of appraisal from a voluntary dissolution. Because the corporation is ceasing its existence, it makes no sense to allow a shareholder to force the company to buy her stock.

Voluntary dissolution can be used (as mergers can be used) to freeze out minority shareholders unfairly. For example, controlling shareholders might cause dissolution in an effort to keep minority shareholders from sharing in a profitable business. Upon dissolution, some other entity, owned by the controlling shareholders, would take over the business. In such cases, courts should be willing to step in to provide protection for the minority by permitting them to sue for breach of fiduciary obligation owed to them.

C.    *Administrative Dissolution.* Here, the appropriate state officer decrees dissolution of the corporation. The officer is not required to go to court or to get a judicial order. It simply orders dissolution. The reasons and procedures vary from state to state, but administrative dissolution usually arises when the proprietors have abandoned a business and therefore have failed to pay franchise taxes, file annual reports, or to do other things that are required of corporations. The statutes mandate that the state officer give notice of the intention to order dissolution. If the proprietors fail to respond or to fix the problems, the corporation "forfeits" its charter, and thus ceases to exist. Statutes allow reinstatement of the corporation if the proprietors fix the problems within a set time.

D.    *Involuntary Dissolution.* Here, someone goes to court to seek an order dissolving the corporation. In most states, a creditor may do this if the corporation is insolvent and either the creditor has a judgment against the corporation or the company admits the debt in writing. *See, e.g.*, MBCA § 14.30(a)(3). In some states, but not under the MBCA, a director can petition for involuntary dissolution in limited circumstances.

Most important, however, are provisions permitting shareholders to petition for dissolution. In many states, as in MBCA § 14.30(a)(2), any shareholder may seek dissolution on various grounds, including (1) director deadlock, inability to break the deadlock, and the corporation is suffering or will suffer irreparable injury, (2) shareholder deadlock and inability for at least two consecutive annual meetings to fill a vacant seat on the board, (3) waste or misapplication of corporate assets, or (4) management is engaged in "illegal, oppressive, or fraudulent" behavior. We discussed such statutes in connection with oppressive behavior in § 10.6, subpart C.

Generally, a shareholder petition for involuntary dissolution is made in a close corporation. Indeed, under MBCA § 14.30(b), the shareholder petition is available *only* in close corporations. In some states, only specified percentages of shares can seek involuntary dissolution. In New York, for instance, the petition for involuntary dissolution based upon illegal, oppressive, or fraudulent acts must be brought by at least 40 percent of the shares.

Some states expressly provide that a shareholder petition for dissolution can be denied if the court approves a buy-out of the petitioning shareholder. NY Bus. Corp. Law § 1118. In some states, courts will permit the corporation or other shareholders to avoid dissolution by purchasing the complaining shareholder's stock for fair value, even if the statute does not expressly permit such a course.

E.     *The Liquidation Process.* As noted, dissolution is a process. After the triggering event (such as approval of voluntary dissolution or a court order of involuntary dissolution) the corporation remains in existence, but only for the process of liquidation (or "winding up"). The board of directors usually oversees this process, though the court may appoint a receiver to do so if the directors have been engaged in bad behavior.

The liquidation process consists of four steps. First, those in charge gather all corporate assets. This includes claims the corporation may have against others. The corporation may bring suit to perfect those claims and gather the assets. Second, they convert the assets to cash by selling them off. Third, they then pay creditors and set aside an appropriate amount to cover prospective claims. Finally, they distribute the remainder to shareholders. Note, then, that shareholders are last in line. As holders of the equity interest in the company, they can receive their liquidating distribution only after the creditors (the holders of debt interests) are paid off. Directors can be personally liable for distributions wrongfully made to shareholders before debts are discharged.

Shareholders receive the liquidating distribution just as they receive dividends: pro rata by share. The articles may provide for a "liquidation preference" for a particular class, which will work just as a dividend preference (*see* § 13.4): the preferred shares are paid first, before the common shares. We saw an example of liquidation preferences in discussing the modern definition of "insolvency" (*see* § 13.6, subpart C).

After the debts are paid, or provided for, and the remaining money distributed to shareholders, the directors certify these facts to the appropriate state officer, who then files a certificate formally ending the existence of the corporation.

# GLOSSARY

**ADOPTION** is a contract principle by which a person agrees to assume a contract previously made by someone else for her benefit. Adoption is effective only from the time such person agrees, in contrast to a "ratification," which relates back to the time the original contract was made. In corporation law, the concept is applied when a newly formed corporation accepts a pre-incorporation contract entered into by a promoter for the benefit of the corporation to be formed.

**ADVANCES FOR EXPENSES** refers to the payment of litigation expenses of a director or officer before there is any determination of whether she breached a duty to the corporation. *See* **INDEMNIFICATION**.

**AGGRESSOR CORPORATION** is one that attempts to obtain control of a publicly held corporation, often by tendering cash to the shareholders, but also possibly through a merger or other transaction that requires agreement of the target's management.

**ALL HOLDERS' RULE** is a rule adopted by SEC that prohibits a public offer by the issuer of shares that excludes designated shareholders.

**ALTER EGO** means "other self" and is a phrase widely used in piercing the corporate veil cases.

**AMOTION** is the common law procedure by which a director may be removed for cause by the shareholders.

**APPRAISAL** is a statutory right granted to shareholders who formally dissent from specified fundamental transactions, such as mergers. In an appraisal proceeding, a court determines the value of the dissenters' shares and the corporation must pay that value to the dissenting shareholders in cash.

**ARBITRAGEURS** are market investors who take off-setting positions in the same or similar securities to profit from small price variations. By taking advantage of momentary disparities in prices between markets, arbitrageurs may make markets more efficient.

**ARTICLES OF INCORPORATION** is the document that is filed in order to form a corporation under the MBCA. Under various state statutes, this document may be called a "certificate of incorporation," "articles of organization," "charter," or other similar name.

**AUTHORIZED SHARES** are the shares that a corporation may issue. The number is set in the articles.

**BENEFICIAL HOLDER (OR BENEFICIAL OWNER)** is one who holds beneficial title, but not legal title, to securities. An example is when stockholders transfer legal title of their stock to a voting trustee, who is given power to vote the stock in the manner decreed by the trust. The voting trustee holds the legal title to the stock, but the transferor retains beneficial title. *See* **VOTING TRUST**. Another example is the person who owns stock but whose name is not listed as owner in the records of the corporation. *See* **RECORD OWNER** and **STREET NAME.**

**BENEFIT CORPORATION ("B CORP")** is a for-profit corporation that also expressly commits to benefiting society, for example, by promoting environment-friendly policies.

**BIDDER CORPORATION** is another name for **AGGRESSOR CORPORATION.**

**BLUE SKY LAWS** are state statutes regulating the sale of securities to the public within the state. Most blue sky laws require the registration of new issues of securities with a state agency that reviews selling documents for accuracy and completeness. Blue sky laws also may regulate securities brokers and sellers of securities. The National Securities Markets Improvement Act, passed by Congress in 1995, pre-empts a significant portion of traditional blue sky law regulation.

**BONDS** are debt instruments secured by liens on corporate property. Historically, a bond was payable to bearer and interest coupons representing annual or semi-annual payments of interest were attached (to be "clipped" periodically and submitted for payment). Today, most bonds are issued in registered or book entry form, and interest is paid to the registered owner. The word bond is sometimes used more broadly to refer also to unsecured debt instruments, i.e., debentures.

**BONUS SHARES** are par value shares issued without consideration. They are a species of watered stock.

**BOOK ENTRY** describes the method of reflecting ownership of publicly traded securities in which customers of brokerage firms receive confirmations of transactions but not stock certificates. Brokerage firms also may reflect their customers' ownership of securities by book entry in the records of a central clearing corporation, principally Depository Trust Company (DTC). DTC reflects transactions between brokerage firms primarily by book entry in its records rather than by the physical movement of securities. Shares held by DTC are recorded in the name of its nominee, Cede and Company.

**BOOK VALUE** is the value of shares determined on the basis of the books of the corporation. Using the corporation's latest balance sheet, liabilities are subtracted from assets, and an appropriate amount is deducted to reflect the interest of senior securities. The resultant number is divided by the number of outstanding common shares, which then gives the book value per share.

**BROKER** in a securities transaction is a person who acts as an agent for a buyer or seller, or an intermediary between a buyer and seller, usually charging a commission. A broker who specializes in shares, bonds, commodities, or options must be registered with the exchange where the specific securities are traded. A broker differs from a dealer, who (unlike a broker) buys or sells for his own account. Securities firms typically act both as dealers and as brokers, depending on the transaction involved.

**BYLAWS** are formal rules of internal governance adopted by a corporation.

**CALLS** are options to buy securities at a stated price for a stated period. Calls are written on a variety of common shares, indexes, foreign currencies, and other securities. The person who commits himself to sell the security upon the request of the purchaser of the call is the "writer" of the call. The act of making the purchase of the securities pursuant to the option is the "exercise" of the option. The price at which the call is exercisable is the "strike price." *See also* **PUTS**.

**CAPITAL STOCK** is another phrase for common shares, often used when the corporation has only one class of shares outstanding.

**CAPITAL SURPLUS** is an equity or capital account that reflects the capital contributed for shares not allocated to stated capital. Capital surplus is traditionally the excess of issuance price over the par value of issued shares or the portion of consideration paid for no par shares that is not allocated to stated capital.

**CAPITALIZATION** is an imprecise term that usually refers to the funds received by a corporation for the issuance of its common and preferred shares. However, it may also refer to the proceeds of loans to a corporation made by its shareholders (which may be in lieu of capital contributions) or even to debt capital raised by the issuance of long-term bonds to third persons.

**CASH FLOW** refers to an analysis of the movement of cash through a business as contrasted with the earnings of the business. For example, a mandatory debt repayment is taken into account in a cash flow analysis even though such a repayment does not reduce earnings. *See* **NEGATIVE CASH FLOW**.

**CASH MERGER** is a merger transaction in which specified shareholders or interests in a corporation are required to accept cash for their shares.

**CASH TENDER OFFER** is a technique by which an aggressor seeks to acquire shares of a target corporation by making a public offer to purchase a specified fraction (usually a majority) of the target corporation's shares at an attractive price from persons who voluntarily tender their shares.

**C CORPORATION** is any corporation that has not elected S corporation tax status. The taxable income of a C corporation is subject to tax at the corporate level and dividends actually declared are taxed at the shareholder level. *See* **S CORPORATION**.

**CEO** stands for "chief executive officer."

**CFO** stands for "chief financial officer."

**CHARTER** may mean (i) the document filed with the Secretary of State, to create a corporation, or (ii) the grant by the state of the privilege of conducting business in corporate firm. "Charter" may also be used in a colloquial sense to refer to the basic constitutive documents of the corporation.

**CLASSIFIED BOARD OF DIRECTORS** may refer either (1) to a board of directors in which the individual members are elected by different classes of shares or (2) to a board of directors in which one-third or one-half of the directors are elected each year. *See* **STAGGERED BOARD**.

**CLO** stands for "chief legal officer," who may also be called "general counsel."

**CLOSE CORPORATION** or **CLOSELY HELD CORPORATION** is a corporation with relatively few shareholders and no public market for its shares. "Close" and "closely held" are synonymous.

**COMMON SHAREHOLDERS** are the ultimate owners of the residual interest in a corporation. Common shareholders typically have the right to select directors to manage the enterprise and to receive dividends out of the earnings of the enterprise when and as declared by the directors. They are also entitled to a per share distribution of the assets that remain upon dissolution after satisfying or making provisions for creditors and holders of senior securities

**CONSOLIDATION** is an amalgamation of two corporations pursuant to statutory provision in which both of the corporations disappear and a new corporation is formed. The MBCA eliminates the consolidation as a distinct type of corporate amalgamation. *See* **MERGERS**.

**CONTROL PREMIUM** describes the pricing phenomenon by which shares that carry the power of control over a corporation are more valuable per share than the shares that do not carry a power of control.

**CONVERTIBLE SECURITIES** are those that include the right of exchanging the convertible securities at the option of their holder for a designated number of shares of another class, called the conversion securities.

**COO** stands for "chief operations officer."

**CORPORATE OPPORTUNITY** is a fiduciary concept that limits the power of officers, directors, and employees to take personal advantage of opportunities that belong to the corporation.

**CORPORATION BY ESTOPPEL** is a doctrine that prevents a third person from holding someone acting for a nonexistent corporation personally liable on an obligation entered in the name of the nonexistent corporation. The theory is that the third person relied on the existence of the corporation and is now "estopped" from denying that the corporation existed.

**CUMULATIVE DIVIDENDS** on preferred shares carry over from one year to the next if a cumulative dividend is omitted. All omitted cumulative dividends must be made up in a later year before any dividend may be paid on the common shares in that year. Cumulative dividends are not debts of the corporation but merely a right to priority in future distributions.

**CUMULATIVE VOTING** is a method of voting that allows substantial minority shareholders to obtain representation on the board of directors. When voting cumulatively, a shareholder may multiply the number of shares he owns by the number of director positions to be filled at that election, and cast that number of votes for any one candidate or spread that number among two or more candidates.

**DEADLOCK** in a closely held corporation arises when a control structure permits one or more factions of shareholders to block corporate action if they disagree with some aspect of corporate policy. A deadlock usually arises with respect to the election of directors by an equal division of shares between two factions. A deadlock may also arise on the board if there are is even number of directors.

**DEALER.** *See* **BROKER.**

**DEBENTURES** are long term unsecured debt instruments. *See* **BONDS**.

**DEEP ROCK DOCTRINE** is a principle of bankruptcy law by which claims presented by controlling shareholders of bankrupt corporations may be subordinated to claims of general or trade creditors.

**DE FACTO CORPORATION** at common law is a partially formed corporation that provides a shield against personal liability of shareholders for corporate obligations. Such a corporation may be attacked only by the state.

**DE JURE CORPORATION** at common law is a corporation that is sufficiently formed that it is recognized as a corporation for all purposes. A de jure corporation may exist even though some minor statutory requirements have not been fully complied with. *See* **DIRECTORY REQUIREMENTS**.

**DERIVATIVE SUIT** is a suit brought by a shareholder in the name of a corporation to correct a wrong done to the corporation.

**DISSENTERS' RIGHT.** *See* **APPRAISAL**.

**DISTRIBUTION** is a payment to shareholders by a corporation.

**DIVIDEND** is a distribution to shareholders from or out of current or past earnings.

**DOUBLE TAXATION** refers to the structure of taxation under the Internal Revenue Code of 1954 that subjects income earned by a C corporation to a tax at the corporate level and a second tax at the shareholder level if dividends are paid.

**DOWN STREAM MERGER** is the merger of a parent corporation into its subsidiary.

**EQUITY** or **EQUITY INTEREST** in general refers to the extent of an ownership interest in a venture.

**EQUITY FINANCING** is raising money by the sale of common or preferred shares.

**EQUITY SECURITY** is a security that represents an ownership interest in the business, typically common or preferred shares.

**FORWARD LOOKING STATEMENT** is a public statement by a corporation that makes projections of financial data, estimates of future sales or profitability, discussion of management objectives and goals, or discussion of economic trends affecting the business.

**FREEZE-OUT** refers to any process by which minority shareholders are prevented from receiving financial return from the corporation in an effort to persuade them to liquidate their investment in the corporation on terms favorable to the controlling shareholders.

**FREEZE-OUT MERGER.** *See* **CASH MERGER**.

**GOLDEN PARACHUTE** is a lucrative contract given to an executive of a corporation that provides additional economic benefits in case control of the corporation changes hands and the executive leaves, either voluntarily or involuntarily. A golden parachute may include severance pay, stock options, or a bonus payable when the executive's employment at the corporation ends.

**GREENMAIL** is a slang term that refers to a payment by the target to an aggressor to purchase shares acquired by the aggressor at a premium over the price paid by the aggressor. The aggressor in exchange agrees to discontinue its takeover effort.

**HEDGE FUND** is a pooled investment vehicle with a limited clientele, which invests in more diverse ways than mutual funds. Instead of the traditional long-term holdings in stocks, bonds, and cash, these invest in a wide array of investments to "hedge" against the risks of traditional markets. Hedge funds are often volatile, because they engage in high-risk behavior, such as arbitrage and short-selling.

**HOLDING COMPANY** is a corporation that owns a majority of the shares of one or more other corporations. A holding company is not engaged in any business other than the ownership of shares. *See* **INVESTMENT COMPANIES**.

**INCORPORATORS** are the person or persons who execute the articles of incorporation to form a corporation.

**INDEMNIFICATION** is reimbursement by a corporation of expenses incurred by officers or directors who have been named as defendants in litigation relating to corporate affairs. In some instances, indemnification of amounts paid to satisfy judgments or settlement agreements also may be proper.

**INDENTURE** is the contract that defines the rights of holders of bonds or debentures as against the corporation. Typically, the contract is entered into between the corporation and an indenture trustee whose responsibility is to protect the bondholders.

**INDEPENDENT DIRECTOR** is a director of a publicly held corporation who has never been an employee of the corporation or any of its subsidiaries, is not a relative of any employee of the company, provides no services to the company, is not employed by any firm providing major services to the company, and receives no compensation from the company other than director fees. *See* **INSIDE DIRECTOR, OUTSIDE DIRECTOR**.

**INITIAL PUBLIC OFFERING (IPO)** is the first sale of equity securities to the general public by a startup business.

**INSIDE DIRECTOR** is a director of a publicly held corporation who holds executive positions with management. *See* **INDEPENDENT DIRECTOR, OUTSIDE DIRECTOR**.

**INSIDER** is a term of uncertain scope that refers to persons having a relationship with a corporation, its directors, officers, or senior employees.

**INSIDER TRADING** refers to unlawful transactions in shares of publicly held corporations by persons with inside or advance information on which the trading is based. Usually but not always the trader himself is an insider.

**INSOLVENCY** may be either "equity insolvency" or "insolvency in the bankruptcy sense." Equity insolvency means the business is unable to pay its debts as they mature while bankruptcy insolvency means the aggregate liabilities of the business exceeds its assets. It is not uncommon for a business to be unable to meet its debts as they mature and yet have assets that exceed in value its liabilities, or be able to meet its debts as they mature and yet have liabilities that exceed in value its assets.

**INSTITUTIONAL INVESTORS** are investors who largely invest other people's money, e.g. mutual funds, pension funds, and life insurance companies.

**INTERLOCKING DIRECTORS** are persons who serve simultaneously on the boards of directors of two or more corporations that have dealings with each other.

**INVESTMENT BANKERS** are commercial organizations chiefly involved in the business of handling the distribution of new issues of securities.

**INVESTMENT COMPANIES** are corporations involved in the business of investing in securities of other businesses. The most common kind of investment company is the mutual fund. An investment company differs from a holding company in that the latter seeks control of the ventures in which it invests while an investment company seeks investments for their own sake and normally diversifies against risks.

**ISSUED SHARES** are shares a corporation has actually issued and outstanding.

**LEVERAGE** refers to advantages that may accrue to a business through the use of debt obtained from third persons instead of additional contributed capital.

**LEVERAGED BUYOUT (LBO)** is a transaction in which an outside entity purchases all the shares of a public corporation primarily with borrowed funds. Ultimately the debt incurred to finance the takeover is assumed by the acquired business. If incumbent management has a significant financial and participatory interest in the outside entity, the transaction may be referred to as a management buyout (MBO).

**LIMITED LIABILITY COMPANY (LLC)** is an unincorporated business form that provides limited liability for its owners and may be taxed as a partnership. A certificate must be filed with a state official to create an LLC.

**LIMITED LIABILITY PARTNERSHIP (LLP)** is a general partnership that has elected to register under state statutes that provide protection against liability for actions of co-partners. To create an LLP, a certificate that is renewable annually must be filed with a state official. Limited liability partnerships may provide "partial shields" or "full shields" against liability, depending on state law.

**LIMITED LIABILITY LIMITED PARTNERSHIP (LLLP)** is a limited partnership that has elected to register under state statutes that provide protection for general partners against liability for actions of other general partners. To create an LLLP a certificate that is renewable annually must be filed with a state official.

**LIMITED PARTNERSHIP (LP)** is a partnership consisting of one or more limited partners (whose liability for partnership debts is limited to the amount invested) and one or more general partners who have unlimited liability. A limited partner who participates in the management of the partnership business may inadvertently assume the liability of a general partner. A certificate must be filed with a state official to create a limited partnership.

**LIQUIDATING DISTRIBUTION** or **LIQUIDATING DIVIDEND** is a distribution of assets to shareholders by a corporation that is reducing capital or going out of business. Such a payment may be made if management decides to sell off certain company assets and distribute the proceeds to shareholders.

**LIQUIDITY** refers to the market characteristic of a security or commodity that has enough units outstanding and publicly traded that purchases and sales occur routinely and usually without a substantial variation in price.

**MANAGEMENT'S DISCUSSION AND ANALYSIS OF FINANCIAL CONDITION AND RESULTS OF OPERATIONS** is an important portion of the annual report that must be distributed to shareholders by corporations registered under the Securities Exchange Act of 1934.

**MERGER** is an amalgamation of two corporations pursuant to statutory provision in which one of the corporations survives and the other disappears. Compare **CONSOLIDATION.**

**MUTUAL FUND** is a publicly held open end investment company. An "open end" investment company stands ready at all times to redeem its shares at net asset value. A mutual fund thus provides the advantages of liquidity, diversification of investment, and skilled investment advice for the small investor.

**NASDAQ** is an acronym for "National Association of Securities Dealers Automated Quotations," which is an obsolete name. NASDAQ is a stock exchange, with the highest daily trading volume in the world.

**NEGATIVE CASH FLOW** means the cash needs of a business exceed its cash intake. Short periods of negative cash flow create no problem for most businesses; longer periods of negative cash flow may require additional capital investment if the business is to avoid insolvency.

**NIMBLE DIVIDENDS** are dividends paid out of current earnings at a time when there is a deficit in earned surplus. Some state statutes do not permit nimble dividends. The concept of nimble dividends has application only under traditional legal capital statutes.

**NOMINEE REGISTRATION** is a form of securities registration widely used by institutional investors and fiduciaries to avoid onerous registration or disclosure requirements. Nominee registration usually is in the form of "and Company," e.g. "Smith and Company."

**NO-PAR SHARES** are shares issued under a traditional par value statute that are stated to have no par value. Such shares may be issued for any consideration designated by the board of directors. In other respects no par shares do not differ significantly from par value shares. In states that have abolished par value, the concept of no par shares is obsolete.

**NOVATION** is a contract principle by which a third person takes over the rights and duties of a party to a contract and that party is released from the contract. A novation requires the consent of the other party to the contract, but that consent may be implied from the circumstances.

**NYSE** is an acronym for the New York Stock Exchange.

**OPPRESSION** in a close corporation involves conduct by controlling shareholders that deprive a minority shareholder of legitimate expectations concerning roles in the corporation, including participation in management and earnings.

**OUTSIDE DIRECTOR** is a director of a publicly held corporation who does not hold an executive position with management. Outside directors, however, may include investment bankers, attorneys, or others who provide advice or services to incumbent management and therefore are not independent directors. *See* **INDEPENDENT DIRECTOR, INSIDE DIRECTOR**.

**PAR VALUE** or **STATED VALUE** of shares is a nominal value assigned to each share. At one time par value represented the selling or issuance price of shares, but in modern corporate practice, par value has little or no significance. Statutes of many states have eliminated the concept of par value.

**PARTICIPATING PREFERRED SHARES** are preferred shares that, in addition to paying a stipulated dividend, give the holder the right to participate with common shareholders in additional distributions of earnings under specified conditions. Participatory preferred shares may be called class A common or given a similar designation to reflect their open-ended rights.

**POISON PILL** is an issue of shares by a corporation designed to protect the corporation against an unwanted takeover. A poison pill creates rights in existing shareholders to acquire debt or stock of the target (or of the aggressor upon a subsequent merger) at bargain prices upon the occurrence of specified events, such as the announcement of a cash tender offer or the acquisition by an outsider of a specified percentage of the shares of the target. A poison pill is effective because it dilutes the interest being sought by the aggressor to a point where acquisition of control becomes impractical. The effect of a poison pill usually is to compel the aggressor to negotiate with the target in order to persuade it to withdraw the pill.

**POOLING AGREEMENT** is a contractual arrangement among shareholders relating to the voting of shares.

**PRE-EMPTIVE RIGHTS** give an existing shareholder the opportunity to purchase or subscribe for a proportionate part of a new issue of shares before it is offered to other persons. A preemptive right protects shareholders from dilution of value and control when new shares are issued. In modern practice, preemptive rights are often limited or denied by provisions in the governing corporate documents.

**PREFERRED SHARES** are shares that have preferential rights to dividends or to amounts distributable on liquidation, or to both, ahead of common shareholders.

**PROMOTERS** are persons who develop or take the initiative in founding or organizing a business venture. Where more than one promoter is involved in a venture, they are called co-promoters.

**PROSPECTUS** is a document furnished to a prospective purchaser of a security that describes the security being purchased, the issuer, and the investment or risk characteristics of that security.

**PROXY** is a person authorized to vote someone else's shares. Depending on the context, proxy may also refer to the grant of authority itself [the **PROXY APPOINTMENT**], or the document granting the authority [the **PROXY APPOINTMENT FORM**].

**PROXY STATEMENT** is the document that must accompany a solicitation of proxy appointments under SEC regulations. The purpose of the proxy statement is to provide shareholders with relevant information.

**PSLRA** is an acronym for the Private Securities Litigation Reform Act of 1995.

**PUBLIC OFFERING** is the sale of securities by an issuer or a person controlling the issuer to members of the public. Normally registration of a public offering under the Securities Act of 1933 is required though in some instances exemptions from registration may be available.

**PUBLICLY HELD CORPORATION** is a corporation that is required to register under the Securities Exchange Act of 1934.

**PUTS** are options to sell securities at a stated price for a stated period. *See also* **CALL**.

**QUO WARRANTO** is a common law writ designed to test whether a person exercising power is legally entitled to do so. Quo warranto may be used to test whether a corporation is validly organized or whether it has power to engage in the business in which it is involved.

**RAIDER** is a slang term for an aggressor (an individual or corporation) that attempts to take control of a target corporation by buying a controlling interest in its stock.

**RATIFICATION.** *See* **ADOPTION**.

**RECORD DATE** is the date on which the identity of shareholders entitled to vote, to receive dividends, or to receive notice is ascertained.

**RECORD OWNER** of shares is the person in whose name shares are registered on the records of the corporation. The corporation treats a record owner as the owner regardless of whether that person is the beneficial owner of the shares.

**REDEMPTION** means the reacquisition of a security by the issuer pursuant to a provision in the security that specifies the terms on which the reacquisition may take place. Typically, a holder of a security that has been called for redemption has a limited period thereafter to decide whether or not to exercise a conversion right, if one exists.

**REGISTERED CORPORATION** is a corporation that has registered a publicly held class of securities under the Securities Exchange Act of 1934. Registration under the 1934 Act should be contrasted with the registration of a public distribution of shares under the Securities Act of 1933.

**REGISTRATION** of an issue of securities under the Securities Act of 1933 permits the public sale of those securities in interstate commerce or through the mails. Registration under the 1933 Act should be distinguished from the registration of classes of publicly held securities under the Securities Exchange Act of 1934.

**REGISTRATION STATEMENT** is the document that must be filed to permit registration of an issue of securities under the Securities Act of 1933. A major component of the registration statement is the prospectus supplied to purchasers of the securities.

**RESCISSORY DAMAGES** are damages calculated on the basis of what an interest in a business would have been worth today if an invalid or voidable transaction that affected the value of that interest had not occurred.

**S CORPORATION** is a corporation that has elected to be taxed under Subchapter S. The taxable income of an S corporation is not subject to tax at the corporate level. Rather, it is allocated for tax purposes to the shareholders to be taxed as though all earnings were distributed. S corporation taxation is similar to but not identical with partnership taxation.

**SECONDARY MARKET** means the securities exchanges and over-the-counter markets where securities are bought and sold following their initial distribution. Secondary market transactions are between investors and do involve directly the corporation that originally issued the securities.

**SECURITIES** is a general term that includes not only traditional securities such as shares of stock, bonds, and debentures, but also a variety of interests that involve an investment with the return primarily or exclusively dependent on the efforts of a person other than the investor.

**SECURITY-FOR-EXPENSES** statutes enacted in some states require certain plaintiffs in derivative litigation to post a bond with sureties from which the corporation and the other defendants may be reimbursed for their expenses if the defendants prevail.

**SERIES OF PREFERRED SHARES** are subclasses of preferred shares with differing dividend rates, redemption prices, rights on dissolution, conversion rights, or the like.

**SHARE DIVIDEND** is a proportional distribution of additional shares to existing shareholders. A share dividend is often viewed as a substitute for a cash dividend, and shareholders may sell share dividends without realizing that they thereby dilute their ownership interest in the corporation.

**SHARE SPLIT** is a proportional change in the number of outstanding shares. In a 2-for-1 share split, for example, each shareholder receives one additional share for each share currently owned, thereby doubling the number of outstanding shares. A share split differs from a share dividend primarily in degree; there are, however, technical differences. For example, in a stock dividend no adjustment is typically made in the regular dividend rate per share while an adjustment in the dividend rate is usually made in a stock split. There are other technical differences in the handling of stock splits and stock dividends under the statutes of some states.

**SHORT FORM MERGER** is a merger of a largely or wholly owned subsidiary into a parent through a stream-lined procedure.

**SINKING FUND** is a sum of money to which periodic payments are made for the purpose of repaying a debt or replacing a depreciating asset.

**SQUEEZE-OUTS** are techniques to eliminate or reduce minority interests in a corporation. Squeeze-outs may occur in a variety of contexts.

For example, in a "going private" transaction minority shareholders may be compelled to accept cash for their shares, while controlling shareholders retain their shares. New shares may be offered for purchase to existing shareholders under terms that require minority shareholders either to accept a significant reduction in their proportional interest in the corporation or invest additional capital for which they will receive little or no return. Many squeeze-outs involve the use of cash mergers.

**STAGGERED BOARD** is a board of directors in which a fraction of the board is elected each year. In staggered boards, members serve two or three years, depending on whether the board is classified into two or three groups.

**STREET NAME** originally referred to the practice of registering publicly traded securities in the names of Wall Street brokerage firms to facilitate the closing of securities transactions occurring on various stock exchanges. This practice largely disappeared in the early 1960s with the creation of the modern central clearing corporation and book entry registration of securities ownership. Today, shares registered in book entry form are commonly referred to as "street name" shares.

**STRIKE SUITS** is a slang term for litigation instituted for its nuisance value or to improve changes of obtaining a favorable settlement.

**SUBSCRIBERS** are persons who agree to invest in the corporation by purchasing shares of stock.

Subscribers today usually commit themselves to invest by entering into contracts defining the extent and terms of their commitment; at an earlier time subscribers usually executed "subscriptions" or "subscription agreements."

**SUBSCRIPTION** is an offer to buy a specified number of unissued shares from a corporation. If the corporation is not yet in existence, a subscription is known as a "pre-incorporation subscription," that is enforceable by the corporation after it has been formed and is irrevocable despite the absence of consideration or the usual elements of a contract.

**SUBSIDIARY** is a corporation that is majority or wholly owned by another corporation.

**SURPLUS** is a general term in corporate practice that usually refers to the excess of assets over liabilities of a corporation. Surplus has a more definite meaning when combined with a descriptive adjective such as earned surplus, capital surplus, or reduction surplus.

**TAKEOVER ATTEMPT** or **TAKEOVER BID** are generic terms to describe an attempt by an outside corporation or group to wrest control away from incumbent management. A takeover attempt may involve a purchase of shares, a tender offer, a sale of assets, or a proposal that the target merge voluntarily into the aggressor.

**TARGET CORPORATION** is a corporation the control of which is sought by an aggressor corporation.

**TENDER OFFER** is a public invitation to shareholders of a corporation to tender their shares for purchase by the offeror at a stated price.

**TIP** is information not available to the general public passed by one person (the "tipper") to another (the "tippee") as a basis for a decision to buy or sell a security. Trading by tippees in many circumstances violates federal securities law.

**TREASURY SHARES** are shares that were once issued but have been reacquired by the corporation. Treasury shares are economically indistinguishable from authorized but unissued shares but historically have been treated as having an intermediate status. For example, treasury shares may usually be issued without regard to the par value rules applicable to the issuance of authorized shares. Statutes of several states eliminate the concept of treasury shares and treat reacquired shares as authorized but unissued shares.

**TRIANGULAR MERGER** is a method of amalgamation of two corporations in which the disappearing corporation is merged into a subsidiary of the parent corporation. Shareholders of the disappearing corporation receive shares of the parent corporation. In a reverse triangular merger the subsidiary is merged into the disappearing corporation so that the corporation being acquired becomes a wholly owned subsidiary of the parent corporation.

**ULTRA VIRES** is the common law doctrine relating to the effect of corporate acts that exceed the powers or stated purposes of a corporation.

**UNDERWRITERS** are persons who buy shares with a view toward their further distribution. Used almost exclusively in connection with the public distribution of securities, an underwriter may be either a commercial enterprise engaged in the distribution of securities (an investment banker), or a person who simply buys securities without an investment intent and with a "view" toward further distribution.

**UPSTREAM MERGER** is a merger of a subsidiary corporation into its parent.

**VENTURE CAPITAL FIRMS** provide financing for startups hoping to go public in exchange for a substantial fraction of the corporation's equity.

**VOTING TRUST** is a formal arrangement to separate share voting from share ownership. In a voting trust, record title to shares is transferred to trustees who are entitled to vote the shares. Usually, the beneficial owner of the shares retains all other rights of ownership, such as the right to receive dividends and to bring derivative suits.

**VOTING TRUST CERTIFICATES** are certificates issued by voting trustees to beneficial holders of shares held by the voting trust. Such certificates may be freely transferable and carry with them all the incidents of ownership of the underlying shares except the power to vote.

**WARRANTS** are options to purchase shares from a corporation. Warrants are typically long term options and are freely transferable. Warrants may be publicly traded.

**WATERED SHARES** are par value shares issued for property that has been overvalued and is not worth the aggregate par value of the issued shares. The phrases "watered shares" or "watered stock" are often used as generic terms to describe discount or bonus shares as well as watered shares. *See* **BONUS SHARES, DISCOUNT SHARES**.

**WHITE KNIGHT** is a friendly suitor who attempt to rescues a target corporation from an unfriendly takeover bid. The white knight typically makes its own bid in competition with the unfriendly aggressor.

# INDEX

## References are to Pages

---

**VOTING**
Shareholders, this index